Lecture Notes
in Business Information Processing 249

Series Editors

Wil van der Aalst
Eindhoven Technical University, Eindhoven, The Netherlands
John Mylopoulos
University of Trento, Povo, Italy
Michael Rosemann
Queensland University of Technology, Brisbane, QLD, Australia
Michael J. Shaw
University of Illinois, Urbana-Champaign, IL, USA
Clemens Szyperski
Microsoft Research, Redmond, WA, USA

More information about this series at http://www.springer.com/series/7911

John Krogstie · Haralambos Mouratidis
Jianwen Su (Eds.)

Advanced Information Systems Engineering Workshops

CAiSE 2016 International Workshops
Ljubljana, Slovenia, June 13–17, 2016
Proceedings

 Springer

Editors
John Krogstie
Department of Computer and Information
  Science
Norwegian University of Science and
  Technology
Trondheim
Norway

Jianwen Su
Department of Computer Science
University of California
Santa Barbara, CA
USA

Haralambos Mouratidis
University of Brighton
Brighton
UK

ISSN 1865-1348   ISSN 1865-1356   (electronic)
Lecture Notes in Business Information Processing
ISBN 978-3-319-39563-0   ISBN 978-3-319-39564-7   (eBook)
DOI 10.1007/978-3-319-39564-7

Library of Congress Control Number: 2016940335

Printed on acid-free paper

This Springer imprint is published by Springer Nature
The registered company is Springer International Publishing AG Switzerland

Preface

The Conference on Advanced Information Systems Engineering (CAiSE) has traditionally focused on aspects that intersect our field – technological and human, theoretical and applied, organizational and societal. The theme for CAiSE 2016 of "Information Systems for Connecting People" emphasized the wish to satisfy the needs and requirements of people, both as individuals and as parts of organizations, which are socio-technical systems. To further the research on these areas, it is important also to provide arenas where researchers can meet.

Each year CAiSE is accompanied by a significant number of high-quality workshops. Their aim is to address specific emerging challenges in the field, to facilitate interaction between stakeholders and researchers, to discuss innovative ideas, as well as to present new approaches and tools.

The 28th CAiSE was held in Ljubljana, Slovenia, June 13–17, 2016. This year, CAiSE had three associated working conferences (BPMDS, EMMSAD, and ICSOB) and seven workshops. The accepted workshops were chosen after careful consideration, based on maturity and compliance with our usual quality and consistency criteria providing a balanced set of events. This volume contains the proceedings of the following five workshops of CAiSE 2016 (in alphabetical order):

- The Third International Workshop on Advances in Services Design Based on the Notion of Capability (ASDENCA) co-arranged with the First International Workshop on Business Model Dynamics and Information Systems Engineering (BumDISE)
- The Fourth International Workshop on Cognitive Aspects of Information Systems Engineering (COGNISE)
- The First International Workshop on Energy Awareness and Big Data Management in Information Systems (EnBIS)
- The Second International Workshop on Enterprise Modeling (EM)
- The Sixth International Workshop on Information Systems Security Engineering (WISSE)

The 12th International Workshop on Enterprise and Organizational Modeling and Simulation (EOMAS) published proceedings in a separate LNBIP volume. The Second International Workshop on Socio-Technical Perspective in IS Development (STPIS) published their proceedings in the CEUR Workshop Proceedings series. Each workshop adhered to the CAiSE 2016 submission and acceptance guidelines. The paper acceptance rate for the workshops included in these proceedings was approximately 49 %.

As workshop chairs of CAiSE 2016, we would like to express our gratitude to all the workshop organizers and to all the corresponding scientific committees of the workshops for their invaluable contribution.

April 2016

John Krogstie
Haralambos Mouratidis
Jianwen Su

Third International Workshop on Advances in Services Design Based on the Notion of Capability – ASDENCA 2016

Preface

The notion of *capability* has been gaining much presence within the field of information systems engineering, owing to a number of factors: the notion directs the focus of business investment, it can be used as a baseline for business planning, and it leads directly to service specification and design. Historically, it has been examined in economics, sociology, and management science. More recently, it has been considered in the context of business-IT alignment, in the specification and design of services using business planning as the baseline.

Capability is commonly seen as an *ability* or *capacity* for a company to deliver value, either to customers or shareholders, under the business strategy. It consists of three major components: business processes, people, and physical assets.

Thus it is as an abstraction away from the specifics of how (process), who (agent), and why (goals), i.e., with a focus on results and benefits. At the same time, capability should allow fairly straightforward integrations with the established bodies of knowledge and practices, such as goals (through "goal fulfilment"), processes (through "modelling"), and services (through "servicing").

The idea for the ASDENCA workshop has come from the academic and industrial community gathered at the recently launched EU/FP7 project – CaaS. In its third year, ASDENCA is taking an interest in "capability" as a new modelling paradigm going beyond well-established processes and services and being a candidate to manage sustainability, adaptation, and flexibility of enterprise IS in the presence of often changing business conditions. At the same time, the workshop will try to gather and further enlarge scientific and practitioner communities interested in getting a chance to discuss and advance the theories and practices related to an emerging means for solving nontrivial challenges of managing enterprise IS.

The Program Committee selected five high-quality papers for presentation at the workshop, which are included in this proceedings volume. ASDENCA 2016 was run together with BUMDISE 2016. Divided into four sessions, the program of the workshop included three paper sessions and a discussion panel.

We owe special thanks to the workshop chairs of CAiSE 2016 for supporting the ASDENCA workshop, as well as for providing us with facilities to publicize it. We also thank the Program Committee, for providing valuable and timely reviews for the submitted papers.

April 2016

Jelena Zdravkovic
Oscar Pastor
Peri Loucopoulos

ASDENCA 2016 Organization

Organizing Committee

Jelena Zdravkovic	Stockholm University, Sweden
Pericles Loucopoulos	University of Manchester, UK
Oscar Pastor	University of Valencia, Spain

Program Committee

Mohhamad Danesh	Canada
Sergio España	The Netherlands
Janis Grabis	Latvia
Giancarlo Guizzardi	Brazil
Yoshinori Hara	Japan
Martin Henkel	Sweden
Dimitris Karagiannis	Austria
Marite Kirikova	Latvia
Evangelia Kavakli	Greece
John Krogstie	Norway
Raimundas Matulevicius	Estonia
Haris Mouratidis	UK
Andreas Opdahl	Norway
Ilias Petroounias	UK
Geert Poels	Belgium
Jolita Ralyte	Switzerland
Gil Regev	Switzerland
Iris Reinhartz-Berger	Israel
Kurt Sandkuhl	Germany
Janis Stirna	Sweden
Francisco Valverde	Spain
Gianluigi Viscusi	Switzerland
Hans Weigand	The Netherlands
Alain Wegmann	Switzerland
Carson Woo	USA
Eric Yu	Canada
Didar Zowghi	Australia

First International Workshop on Business Model Dynamics and Information Systems Engineering (BumDISE 2016)

Preface

Over the last two decades, the business model (BM) has received increasing attention and progressively established itself as a new dimension of innovation.

The study of BMs involves exploring and making sense of how firms do business at the system level. It encompasses new forms of organizing, of creating and of capturing value, often involving network plays facilitated by the development of information and communication technologies (ICT). The study of business model innovation (BMI) involves exploring and clarifying the nature of the mechanisms and dynamics underlying the emergence and evolution of BMs with an emphasis on both the design of new BMs and the reconfiguration or renewal of existing ones. Thus, BMI can be theoretically framed in terms of three broad task domains: discovering opportunities for new BMs (sensing), designing new BMs (seizing), and developing (transforming) a BM.

The Business Model Dynamics and Information System Engineering (BumDISE) workshop, powered by the Swiss National Science Foundation Sinergia project 147666, builds on these consideration to explore the potential of a cross-fertilization of insights from seemingly siloed disciplines such as strategy and organization theory on the one side and information systems engineering on the other side. While these domains clearly have a conceptual overlap, they have looked at the BM in isolation and from somewhat different angles. And yet, they seem to share a common ground in relationship to the BM, namely, the BM as a (complex) system orchestrated around information exchange (both formal, technology mediated and informal). Thus an opportunity exists to shed light on the phenomena underlying BMI by embracing a discussion encompassing these domains.

Gianni Lorenzoni's paper explores the dynamics of the BMs adopted by firms operating in the fast fashion business, which he defines as "offering fashionable products at a cheap or very cheap price [...] trying to capture trends rather than imposing them, [...] often over limited amounts of time." It is suggested that the strategic logic of the fast fashion segment, namely, introducing a complementary model to the one adopted by the traditional fashion industry and based on imposing trends by systematically introducing new seasonal products in advance, is, to some extent, trivial or more understood. What is less evident is the role of information processing capabilities in running such a model efficiently. Firms adopting the "fast fashion" BM are asset light, relying on and orchestrating a network of third-party manufacturers that have to respond very quickly to new requests. The study suggests that the key capability is information processing and the quick transformation of insights and signals relative to new trends into products and the ability to make this process an efficient routine. The generic configuration of the BM puts in evidence the restriction of the activity boundaries to some central components, while operating in a setting of distributed knowledge and competencies. Relational capabilities are key in that they improve information processing. Overall the paper suggests that to understand the functioning of BMs, the black box of the organization behind it should be opened and analyzed carefully.

Cattaneo and Hacklin suggest a similar perspective on the study of BM, namely, the importance of organizational-level dynamics for its study, but concentrate on the interplay of strategy and innovation in relationship to renewal. They study offers to focus on Bang & Olufsen, a Danish high-end producer of consumer electronics, which has experienced both success and failure in the process of strategic renewal, challenged by blurring industry boundaries and the rise of the digital technology paradigm. The authors conducted extensive ethnographic research (more than 40 days on site), which allowed them to study the company in the process of redefining its BM. The study suggests that the process of organizational renewal associated with discovering a new BM is carried out through actions of individuals and their inter-subjective relationships, influenced by both organizational context and their personal characteristics. It also suggests that such a process follows cycles between the domains of strategy and innovation. More specifically, the assessment against the external context triggers and informs subsequent organizational design challenges.

Finally, the paper by Achi, Salinesi, and Viscusi questions how to evaluate the level of maturity of an organization with respect to information systems-based innovation. In particular, the authors investigate the salient features of ICT-centered innovation maturity models. To this end, a comparative review is carried out on 16 innovation maturity models collected both from the professional and the academic literature.

We hope these papers will provide insights and ideas to both academics and practitioners suitable to support further investigation and experimentation for solutions bridging the academic silos between disciplines such as strategy and organization theory on the one side and information systems engineering on the other side. BUMDISE 2016 was arranged together with ASDENCA 2016.

April 2016

Lorenzo Massa
Christopher Tucci
Gianluigi Viscusi

BumDISE 2016 Organization

Organizing Committee

Lorenzo Massa	WU, Austria and EPFL, Switzerland
Christopher Tucci	EPFL, Switzerland
Gianluigi Viscusi	EPFL, Switzerland

Program Committee

Matteo Mura	University of Bologna, Italy
Fredrik Hacklin	ETH, Switzerland
Gianni Lorenzoni	University of Bologna, Italy
Alessandro Lomi	University of Svizzera Italiana, Switzerland
Simone Ferriani	University of Bologna, Italy

Fourth International Workshop on Cognitive Aspects of Information Systems Engineering (COGNISE 2016)

Preface

Cognitive aspects of information systems engineering is an area that is gaining interest and importance in industry and research. In recent years, human aspects and specifically cognitive aspects in software engineering and information systems engineering have received increasing attention in the literature and conferences, acknowledging that these aspects are as important as the technical ones, which have traditionally been at the center of attention. This workshop was planned to be a stage for new research and vivid discussions involving both academics and practitioners.

The goal of this workshop is to provide a better understanding and more appropriate support of the cognitive processes and challenges practitioners experience when performing information systems development activities. Understanding the challenges and needs, educational programs, as well as the development of supporting tools and notations may be enhanced for a better fit to our natural cognition, leading to a better performance of engineers and higher system quality. The workshop aimed to bring together researchers from different communities such as requirements engineering, software architecture, design and programming, and information systems education, who share an interest in cognitive aspects, for identifying the cognitive challenges in the diverse development-related activities.

The fourth edition of this workshop, held in Ljubljana on June 14, 2016, was organized in conjunction with the 28th International Conference on Advanced Information Systems Engineering (CAiSE 2016). This edition attracted 11 international submissions. Each paper was reviewed by three members of the Program Committee. Of these submissions, five papers were accepted for inclusion in the proceedings (45 %). The papers presented at the workshop provide a mix of novel research ideas, presenting full research, research in progress, or research plans.

We hope that the reader will find this selection of papers useful to be informed and inspired by new ideas in the area of cognitive aspects of information systems engineering. We look forward to future editions of the COGNISE workshop following the four editions we had so far.

June 2016

Irit Hadar
Barbara Weber

COGNISE 2016 Organization

Organizing Committee

Irit Hadar   University of Haifa, Israel
Barbara Weber   Technical University of Denmark/
                           University of Innsbruck, Austria

Program Committee

Daniel M. Berry   University of Waterloo, Canada
Kathrin Figl   WU Vienna, Austria
Stijn Hoppenbrouwers   HAN University of Applied Sciences, Arnhem/
                           Radboud University, Nijmegen, The Netherlands
Marta Indulska   University of Queensland, Australia
Joel Lanir   University of Haifa, Israel
Meira Levy   Shenkar College of Engineering and Design, Israel
Jonas Bulegon Gassen   WU Vienna, Austria
Jeffrey Parsons   Memorial University, Canada
Jakob Pinggera   University of Innsbruck, Austria
Hajo Reijers   VU University of Amsterdam, TU Eindhoven,
                           The Netherlands
Pnina Soffer   University of Haifa, Israel
Dirk van der Linden   University of Haifa, Israel
Irene Vanderfeesten   TU Eindhoven, The Netherland
Anna Zamansky   University of Haifa, Israel
Stefan Zugal   University of Innsbruck, Austria

First International Workshop on Energy-Awareness and Big Data Management in Information Systems – EnBIS 2016

Preface

Information systems are the basis for each organization. Recently, the amount of services has increased exponentially. To improve their efficiency and reduce costs, modern organizations are shifting their services to the cloud. Lower costs are increasing the demand for cloud services with a consequent increment in the size and kind of information to be stored, processed, and analyzed. A question is arising and is becoming a driver for innovation: "Is it sustainable?"

Energy demand is an important challenge that cannot be disregarded. Over the last decade, data center performance has increased tremendously without proportional energy efficiency. This issue is intensified by the increasing demand for cloud services, together with an inefficient usage of the resources. Also, the environment in which the information systems of modern organizations operate is characterized by a growing generation of data due to the pervasiveness of sensors and devices producing a wide range of information. These data can be of interest for the strategical decisions of the organization and need to be treated properly. Collecting, storing, and analyzing data, which have the features of big data (volume, velocity, variety), is highly expensive in terms of energy. Although this issue has been widely studied, there are still many open challenges. The attention to sustainability is motivated by several reasons. First of all, reducing energy consumption minimizes IS management costs, allowing organizations to save money and increase their competitiveness. Moreover, the environmental issue cannot be disregarded anymore, as the appeal of an organization is influenced by its behavior in terms of sustainability. In this context, it is clear that energy-awareness and energy-efficiency of ISs are important features for the organization that have to be enhanced while maintaining quality of service.

The goal of the EnBIS workshop, organized in conjunction with the 28th Conference on Advanced Information Systems Engineering (CAiSE 2016), was to tackle the energy-awareness of cloud-based business activities, from application to resource management, and to promote collaboration between scholars interested in the topic.

For the first year of the workshop, we received six submissions from researchers in different fields of information systems and business process management communities. Each paper was peer-reviewed by three members of the Program Committee. Out of these submissions, the Program Committee selected three high-quality papers for presentation during the workshop, which are included in this proceedings volume. The work by Pinarer et al. focuses on energy-aware dynamic sensor reconfiguration to minimize energy consumption in smart building systems. The second contribution, also in the smart buildings area, by Sora et al., introduces a platform able to micro-account the energy consumption of devices and presents two case studies for its usage.

Finally, the work by Cappiello et al. proposes a model to predict the CO_2 emissions of cloud data centers connected to the national grid. As can be seen, these contributions advance the state of the art in the area of energy efficiency in information systems.

The program of the workshop included one introduction talk held by the Program Committee chairs, one paper session reflecting important topics of Green IS management, and a discussion panel.

April 2016

Monica Vitali
Marina Zapater

EnBIS 2016 Organization

Organizing Committee

Monica Vitali   Politecnico di Milano, Italy
Marina Zapater   Universidad Complutense de Madrid, Spain

Program Committee

Ionut Anghel   Technical University of Cluj-Napoca, Romania
José Luis Ayala Rodrigo   Universidad Complutense de Madrid, Spain
Andreas Berl   Deggendorf Institute of Technology, Germany
Ivona Brandic   Vienna University of Technology, Austria
Cinzia Cappiello   Politecnico di Milano, Italy
Antonio Celesti   University of Messina, Italy
Georges Da Costa   Paul Sabatier University, France
Javier García Blas   Universidad Carlos III de Madrid, Spain
Carlo Mastroianni   ICAR-CNR, Italy
Alexandre Mello Ferreira   Universidade Estadual de Campinas, Brazil
Rodrigo Neves Calheiros   University of Melbourne, Australia
Barbara Pernici   Politecnico di Milano, Italy
Jean-Marc Pierson   Paul Sabatier University, France

Second International Workshop on Enterprise Modeling (EM 2016)

Preface

Enterprises today face many challenges including recent trends such as enterprise mobility, cloud computing, the Internet of Things, cyber-physical systems, and factories of the future. For the development of innovative solutions in this context, a number of aspects need to be taken into account. These range from the mastering of new technologies, the integration and interoperability of heterogeneous systems, to organizational aspects such as the adaptation of business processes or the acquisition of knowledge from decision makers and its transformation into products and services. Enterprise modeling offers concepts for coping with these challenges. By providing machine-processable languages for representing and analyzing complex business and technological scenarios, by engaging in knowledge management, and by supporting organizational engineering, enterprise modeling offers a wide range of options for designing, implementing, and evaluating new solutions. Thereby it spans from traditional fields such as business process management and business intelligence to more recent areas such as enterprise architecture and semantic information systems.

The aim of the Second International Workshop on Enterprise Modeling, which was again organized in conjunction with the International Conference on Advanced Information Systems Engineering (CAiSE 2016), was to bring together researchers working on innovative approaches for enterprise modeling. For this second issue of the workshop we received seven papers. From these papers three were selected based on at least two peer-reviews from an international Program Committee.

The papers take up current research topics in the area of enterprise modeling. The paper by Janssens et al. is positioned in the area of decision modeling and discusses the formalization of decisions in a business context as well as execution mechanisms for different input data. Hinkelmann et al. propose the concept of business processes as a service for aligning business processes with IT in cloud environments and discuss mechanisms for facilitating the alignment via modeling. Finally, Bettacchi et al. present an industry case study from the area of manufacturing where they compared and evaluated different algorithms for process mining.

The workshop organizers would like to thank the authors for their contributions and the members of the Program Committee and additional reviewers for their timely and thorough reviews. Furthermore, our thank goes to the workshop chairs and organizers of CAiSE 2016 for hosting the workshop.

March 2016

Hans-Georg Fill
Dimitris Karagiannis
Manfred Jeusfeld
Matti Rossi

Enterprise Modeling Workshop 2016 Organization

Organizing Committee

Hans-Georg Fill	University of Vienna, Austria
Dimitris Karagiannis	University of Vienna, Austria
Manfred Jeusfeld	University of Skövde, Sweden
Matti Rossi	Aalto University, Finland

Program Committee

Balbir Barn	Middlesex University, UK
Xavier Boucher	Ecole Nationale Supérieure des Mines de St. Etienne, France
Luis Camarinha-Matos	Universidade Nova De Lisboa, Portugal
Elisabetta Di Nitto	Politecnico di Milano, Italy
Nicola Guarino	Consiglio Nazionale delle Ricerche, Italy
Yoshinori Hara	Kyoto University, Japan
Igor Hawryszkiewycz	University of Sydney, Australia
Dimitris Kiritsis	EPFL Lausanne, Switzerland
Pericles Loucopoulos	Loughborough University, UK
Heinrich C. Mayr	University of Klagenfurt, Austria
Nikolay Mehandjiev	University of Manchester, UK
Andreas Oberweis	Karlsruhe Institute of Technology, Germany
Samuli Pekkola	Tampere University of Technology, Finland
Klaus Pohl	University of Duisburg-Essen, Germany
Claudia Pons	University of La Plata, Argentina
Kurt Sandkuhl	University of Rostock, Germany
Elmar J. Sinz	University of Bamberg, Germany
Kari Smolander	Lappeenranta University of Technology, Finland
Jan Vanthienen	Katholieke Universiteit Leuven, Belgium
Francois Vernadat	European Court of Auditors
Eric Yu	University of Toronto, Canada
Alfred Zimmermann	Reutlingen University, Germany

The Sixth International Workshop on Information Systems Security Engineering (WISSE 2016)

Preface

Information systems security problems are currently a widespread and growing concern that covers most areas of society, such as business, domestic, financial, government, health care, etc. The scientific community has realized the importance of aligning information systems engineering and security engineering in order to develop more secure information systems. Nevertheless, there is lack of an appropriate event that will promote information systems security within the context of information systems engineering. The proposed workshop fills this gap.

The International Workshop on Information System Security Engineering (WISSE) aims to provide a forum for researchers and practitioners to present, discuss, and debate, on one hand, the latest research work on methods, models, practices, and tools for secure information systems engineering, and, on the other hand, relevant industrial applications, recurring challenges, problems and industry-led solutions in the area of secure information systems engineering.

This sixth edition of the workshop, held in Ljubljana (Slovenia) on June 13, 2016, was organized in conjunction with the 28th International Conference on Advanced Information Systems Engineering (CAiSE 2016). In order to ensure a high-quality workshop, following an extensive review process, six submissions were accepted as full papers addressing a large variety of issues related to secure information systems engineering.

We wish to thank all the contributors to WISSE 2016, in particular the authors who submitted papers and the members of the Program Committee, who carefully reviewed them. We express our gratitude to the CAiSE 2016 workshop chairs, for their helpful support in preparing the workshop. Finally, we thank our colleagues from the Steering Committee, Jan Jürjens and Carlos Blanco, and our Publicity Chairs, Michalis Pavlidis, Luis Enrique Sánchez, and Akram Idani, for initiating the workshop and contributing to its organization.

April 2016

David G. Rosado
Nadira Lammari
Christos Kalloniatis

WISSE 2016 Organization

General Chair

David G. Rosado — University of Castilla-La Mancha, Spain

Program Chairs

Nadira Lammari — Conservatoire National des Arts et Métiers, France
Christos Kalloniatis — University of the Aegean, Greece

Steering Committee

Jan Jürjens — Technical University of Dortmund, Germany
Nadira Lammari — Conservatoire National des Arts et Métiers, France
David G. Rosado — University of Castilla-La Mancha, Spain
Carlos Blanco — University of Cantabria, Spain
Christos Kalloniatis — University of the Aegean, Greece

Publicity Chairs

Michalis Pavlidis — University of Brighton, UK
Luis Enrique Sánchez — University of Armed Forces, Ecuador
Akram Idani — University of Grenoble, France

Program Committee

Akram Idani — University of Grenoble, France
Antonio Maña — University of Malaga, Spain
Benjamin Nguyen — SMIS, Inria-Rocquencourt, France
Brajendra Panda — University of Arkansas, USA
Bruno Defude — Télécom SudParis, France
Carlos Blanco — University of Cantabria, Spain
Costas Lambrinoudakis — University of Piraeus, Greece
Csilla Farkas — University of South Carolina, USA
Daniel Mellado — Spanish Tax Agency, Spain
Djamel Benslimane — University of Lyon I, France
Eduardo B. Fernández — Florida Atlantic University, USA
El-Bay Bourennane — University of Bourgogne, Dijon, France
Eric Dubois — CRP Henri Tudor, Luxembourg
Ernesto Damiani — Università degli Studi di Milano, Italy
Frédéric Cuppens — Telecom Bretagne, France
Günther Pernul — University of Regensburg, Germany

Guttorm Sindre	NTNU, Norway
Isabelle Comyn-Wattiau	CNAM Paris, France
Jacky Akoka	CNAM Paris, France
Jan Jürjens	Technical University of Dortmund, Germany
Javier López	University of Málaga, Spain
Kashif Saleem	King Saud University, Saudi Arabia
Ludovic Apvrille	Telecom ParisTech, France
Luis Enrique Sánchez	University of Castilla-La Mancha, Spain
Marc Frappier	University of Sherbrooke, Québec. Canada
Michalis Pavlidis	University of Brighton, UK
Mohammad Zulkernine	Queen's University, Canada
Moussa Ouedraogo	Institute of Science and Technology, Luxembourg
Paolo Giorgini	University of Trento, Italy
Régine Laleau	LACL, Université Paris-Est Créteil, France
Sabrina De Capitani di Vimercati	Università degli Studi di Milano, Italy
Shareeful Islam	University of East London, UK
Stefanos Gritzalis	University of the Aegean, Greece
Tristan Allard	University of Montpellier 2, France
Vasilis Katos	Bournemouth University, UK
Yves Ledru	LIG, University of Grenoble, France

Additional Reviewer

Efstathios Stamatatos	University of the Aegean, Greece

Contents

ASDENCA/BUMDISE 2016 – Capability-Based Development Methods

Selection and Evolutionary Development of Software-Service Bundles:
A Capability Based Method 3
Jānis Grabis and Kurt Sandkuhl

LightCDD: A Lightweight Capability-Driven Development Method
for Start-Ups 15
Hasan Koç, Marcela Ruiz, and Sergio España

**ASDENCA/BUMDISE 2016 – Integration of Capability with Goals
and Context**

Comparison of Tool Support for Goal Modelling in Capability Management.... 29
Claas Fastnacht, Hasan Koç, Dimitrijs Nesterenko, and Kurt Sandkuhl

Extending Capabilities with Context Awareness 40
*Martin Henkel, Christina Stratigaki, Janis Stirna, Pericles Loucopoulos,
Yannis Zorgios, and Antonis Migiakis*

Design of Capability Delivery Adjustments 52
Jānis Grabis and Jānis Kampars

ASDENCA/BUMDISE 2016 – Business Modeling

The Fast Fashion Business Model............................. 65
Gianni Lorenzoni

Cycles of Organizational Renewal: The Interplay of Strategy
and Innovation at Bang & Olufsen 72
Giacomo Cattaneo and Fredrik Hacklin

Information Systems for Innovation: A Comparative Analysis of Maturity
Models' Characteristics 78
Abdelkader Achi, Camille Salinesi, and Gianluigi Viscusi

COGNISE 2016

Learning from Errors as a Pedagogic Approach for Reaching a Higher
Conceptual Level in Database Modeling 93
Adi Katz and Ronit Shmallo

'Mathematical' Does Not Mean 'Boring': Integrating Software
Assignments to Enhance Learning of Logico-Mathematical Concepts.   103
  Anna Zamansky and Yoni Zohar

User Involvement in Applications of the PoN.   109
  Dirk van der Linden and Irit Hadar

A Visual Logical Language for System Modelling in Combinatorial
Test Design   116
  Maria Spichkova, Anna Zamansky, and Eitan Farchi

Peel the Onion: Use of Collaborative and Gamified Tools to Enhance
Software Engineering Education   122
  Naomi Unkelos-Shpigel

ENBIS 2016

Energy Enhancement of Multi-application Monitoring Systems
for Smart Buildings.   131
  Ozgun Pinarer, Yann Gripay, Sylvie Servigne, and Atay Ozgovde

Micro-accounting for Optimizing and Saving Energy in Smart Buildings   143
  Daniele Sora, Massimo Mecella, Francesco Leotta, Leonardo Querzoni,
  Roberto Baldoni, Giuseppe Bracone, Daniele Buonanno, Mario Caruso,
  Adriano Cerocchi, and Mariano Leva

Modeling CO_2 Emissions to Reduce the Environmental Impact
of Cloud Applications   155
  Cinzia Cappiello, Paco Melià, and Pierluigi Plebani

EM 2016

Modeling and Enacting Enterprise Decisions   169
  Laurent Janssens, Johannes De Smedt, and Jan Vanthienen

A Modelling Environment for Business Process as a Service   181
  Knut Hinkelmann, Kyriakos Kritikos, Sabrina Kurjakovic,
  Benjamin Lammel, and Robert Woitsch

Understanding Production Chain Business Process Using Process Mining:
A Case Study in the Manufacturing Scenario   193
  Alessandro Bettacchi, Alberto Polzonetti, and Barbara Re

WISSE 2016

Software Vulnerability Life Cycles and the Age of Software Products:
An Empirical Assertion with Operating System Products   207
  Jukka Ruohonen, Sami Hyrynsalmi, and Ville Leppänen

APPARATUS: Reasoning About Security Requirements in the Internet
of Things... 219
Orestis Mavropoulos, Haralambos Mouratidis, Andrew Fish,
Emmanouil Panaousis, and Christos Kalloniatis

Associating the Severity of Vulnerabilities with their Description 231
Dimitrios Toloudis, Georgios Spanos, and Lefteris Angelis

Discovering Potential Interaction Violations among Requirements......... 243
Curtis Busby-Earle and Robert B. France

Extending HARM to make Test Cases for Penetration Testing 254
Aparna Vegendla, Thea Marie Søgaard, and Guttorm Sindre

File Type Identification for Digital Forensics 266
Konstantinos Karampidis and Giorgos Papadourakis

Erratum to: File Type Identification for Digital Forensics.............. E1
Konstantinos Karampidis and Giorgos Papadourakis

Author Index 275

ASDENCA/BUMDISE 2016 – Capability-Based Development Methods

Selection and Evolutionary Development of Software-Service Bundles: A Capability Based Method

Jānis Grabis[1(✉)] and Kurt Sandkuhl[2]

[1] Institute of Information Technology, Riga Technical University,
Kalku 1, Riga, Latvia
grabis@rtu.lv
[2] Chair of Business Information Systems, University of Rostock,
Albert-Einstein-Straße 22, Rostock, Germany
kurt.sandkuhl@uni-rostock.de

Abstract. Software-service bundles are combinations of software products and services offered by their vendors to clients. The clients select a combination of software product and associated service best suited to their specific circumstances. The paper proposes an information sharing based method helping clients to select the most appropriate combination or configuration and also supporting the continuous improvement of the solution in response to changing circumstances. The method utilizes principles of the Capability Driven Development to characterize performance objectives and contextual factors affecting delivery of a software-service bundle. Application of the method is demonstrated using an illustrative example of data processing.

Keywords: Software selection · Capability · Evolutionary development · Software-service bundle

1 Introduction

Software-service bundles are combinations of software products and services aimed at providing packaged offerings for specific applications. Software vendors provide these solutions to their clients. These services have different configurations with regards to functionality provided. Software product line engineering [1] investigates the problem of creating the solutions efficiently from the vendor perspective. Clients on the other hand are looking for the most feasible solution meeting their specific requirements. This problem is addressed in software selection research [2] though these investigations mainly take into account only information available to a client. However, vendors have a wealth of information about their software used by other clients [3]. That could include contextual information describing unique operating circumstances of the client as well as information about performance achieved by using specific configurations of the solutions. It is argued that vendors and clients can collaborate for finding the right configuration for every client on the basis of sharing historical context and performance data. This way every client would receive a configuration appropriate for its operating context as well as some estimates of expected performance of the solution. From a

© Springer International Publishing Switzerland 2016
J. Krogstie et al. (Eds.): CAiSE 2016, LNBIP 249, pp. 3–14, 2016.
DOI: 10.1007/978-3-319-39564-7_1

service science perspective, the colla-boration between vendor and client is considered as a precondition for successfully implementing the service part of software-service bundles (i.e. co-creation of value).

In order to enable aforementioned approach, a framework for defining contextual information and performance objectives is required. Recently, capability driven development (CDD) has been proposed as an approach for ensuring that solutions can be delivered in different contexts at the desired level of performance [4]. The approach presumes that rather than providing a simple business solution the vendor possesses certain capabilities and is able to provide such a capability to its clients facing different operating circumstances. It is a model based approach and encompasses three development phases: (1) capability design explicitly defines performance goals, context factors affecting capability delivery and context-dependent capability delivery solutions; (2) capability delivery phase concerns monitoring of context and performance data and adjusting the solution in response to changes in these data; and (3) feedback phase provides information for updating of the initial design.

The objective of this paper is to elaborate a CDD based method allowing colla-boration between vendor and client in selection of the right configuration of software- service bundles and continuous improvement of the selected configuration. It is assumed that a vendor has multiple clients. The clients share usage information about the software-service bundle. In case of preparing a bundle for a new client, this information is used to create a decision-making matrix for selecting an appropriate configuration for this new client. The new client usually starts with a minimum satisfactory configuration; performance of this configuration is continuously monitored and if necessary the client upgrades its configuration which here is referred to as evolutionary development in analogy to evolutionary software development [5].

The main contributions of the paper are: (1) combination of vendor and client perspectives in an information sharing based method for selection of software–service bundles; and (2) selection of software-service bundle as an interplay among contextual data and performance objectives (i.e., selection is made in a context-aware performance driven fashion). The rest of the paper is organized as follows. Section 2 provides overview of the method. Section 3 elaborates stages of the evolutionary development. The application example is provided in Sect. 4. Related work is reviewed in Sect. 5. Section 6 summarizes findings and future work.

2 Method Overview

The evolutionary development method for software-service bundles is based on the CDD approach and uses the capability model underlying the software-service bundle as a starting point for providing appropriate configurations to clients.

2.1 Problem Statement

The vendor offers its clients a software-service bundle S. The software-service bundle consists of a software product, know-how and supporting services ranging from helpdesk to business process outsourcing. S is designed in a way to deliver desired performance in different contextual situations, i.e., the vendor possesses the capability of providing the software-service bundle.

S is provided in one of N configurations $O_i,...,O_N$ and the configurations differ by their price (they are ordered ascendingly starting with the lowest costs configuration). Delivery of S depends on M context factors $C_1,...,C_M$ and its performance is measured by L key performance indicators $K_1,...,K_L$. Combinations of values of the context factors yield a context situation describing specific solution delivery circumstances. It is assumed that certain configurations provide better performance for specific context situations than other, i.e., they are better suited for these context situations. For instance, a configuration including an outsourcing service works better in the case of highly variable demand for troubleshooting services.

There are P clients using one of the configurations. It is assumed that existing clients have an incentive to share anonymized values of context factors and key performance indicators (KPI) during operations of the software-service bundle.

Two decision-making challenges are: (1) to select appropriate configuration for a new client; and (2) to upgrade configurations used by existing clients in the case of changing circumstance or unsatisfactory performance. In the former case, selection is performed by matching a context situation of the new client with context situations supported by the vendor of the software-service bundle. In the latter case, an existing client switches from one configuration to another to adapt to changing circumstances.

2.2 Evolutionary Development Process

The aforementioned challenges are addressed following an evolutionary development process (Fig. 1). A vendor uses the CDD approach [4] to develop a capability model. The model specifies capability delivery goals, delivery context and solutions (i.e. software-service bundles and their appropriate configuration) for capability delivery offered to clients (see Sect. 2.3 for further discussion). The capability model covers all configurations supported by the vendor. Relationships among context situations and configurations are described in a capability support matrix (CSM). The matrix indicates configurations suitable for a particular context situation. It is used by the vendor and clients to find appropriate solution for clients' needs. CSM is developed on the basis of historical data analysis or according to judgement of the vendor.

Upon engaging a new client, its typical context situation is assessed and the least expensive configuration supporting this context situation is selected. The selected configuration is provided to the client. It is used for capability delivery and delivery performance is monitored using the indicators defined in the capability model. If performance targets are not achieved or context values venture outside the defined context element range, the capability delivery solution is adjusted. Potential adjustments are: (1) selection of a more appropriate configuration; or (2) designing a new solution. The capability monitoring and adjustment are performed cyclically and the capability delivery solution evolves according to the business requirements of the client. The vendor accumulates capability delivery performance and context data from multiple clients and uses this information to update the capability delivery solution and validate CSM.

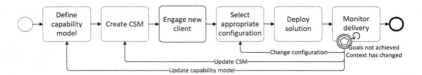

Fig. 1. The evolutionary capability development process

2.3   Capability Modeling

The capability model defines vendor's ability and capacity to provide a solution to clients facing specific circumstances. Figure 2 provides a simplified overview of the key elements used in capability modeling as well as their relation to the configuration concept used in this paper. Goals are business objectives the capability allows to achieve. They are measured by KPI. The capability is designed for delivery in a specific context as defined using context elements. The context elements name factors affecting the capability delivery while context situations refer to combinations of context element values. The process element specifies a capability delivery solution. Process variants describe the capability delivery process for a specific context situation while the associated configuration of the solution encompasses all technical, human and knowledge resources necessary to execute the process.

A configuration can include multiple process variants. The client can switch from one process variant to another or invoke them simultaneously during solution delivery depending on context situation.

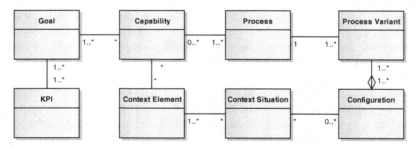

Fig. 2. Key concepts of capability modeling

From the evolutionary development perspective, the key aspects are that: (1) capability can be delivered in different context situations while each individual client faces just some of these context situations; (2) process variants specify a solution for dealing with one or several context situations. For software-service bundle these variants cover both, different process variants in the software product if this product has a process-oriented architecture and different variants for the service bundled with the software product as a part of configurations; and (3) relationships among context situations, performance and process variants are not necessarily know in advance and can be induced from the solution's usage data.

3 Evolutionary Development Stages

The evolutionary development process includes two distinctive phases: (1) design stage – when the initial configuration of the software-service bundle is selected and deployed for a new client; and (2) delivery stage – when the software-service bundle is used by the client and it is adjusted according to changing circumstances.

3.1 Design Stage

At the beginning of the design stage the vendor develops a capability model corresponding to the software-service bundle to be provided to clients. Every context factor used in selection of the configuration has a finite set of values or context range $CR_i = (cr_{i1}, \ldots, cr_{iT_i})$, where T_i represents a number of values for the ith context element. These values are obtained by categorizing actual values of context observations also referred as to measurable properties [6]. The categories enable for relative comparison of clients.

Combination of context element values form the context range yields a set of context situations $(CS_1, \ldots, CS_H) = CR_1 \times \ldots \times CR_N$ (H is the number of context situations). CSM is defined as a matrix with elements a_{ij}, $i = 1, \ldots, H$, $j = 1, \ldots, N$, where $a_{ij} \in \{0, 1\}$ relates context situations to suitable configurations. The matrix element $a_{ij} = 1$ indicates that configuration O_j is suitable in the case of context situation CS_i. The same configuration could be suitable for multiple context situations. One configuration could encompass multiple process variants.

Upon engaging a new client, its most plausible context situation is identified as CS_{new}. Appropriate solution is identified by

$$\min(j \mid a_{ij} = 1 \wedge CS^{new} \in CS_i) \tag{1}$$

Equation 1 selects the least cost configuration O_j appropriate for context situation faced by the new client. If no appropriate configuration is available, the client has a choice to select a configuration having the highest level of overlapping with support context situations. The client also sets target values for KPI $K_1^{new}, \ldots, K_L^{new}$, where the superscript refers to the new client and the subscript l refers to the KPI. The selected configuration is setup for the client and it is ready for operations. There could be a setup time for deploying the configuration.

3.2 Delivery Stage

During the delivery stage, actual context situations and delivery performance are monitored. The performance monitoring is carried out by gathering real-time values of KPI K_{it}^{new}, where superscript identifies the client, the subscript i refers to KPI being measured and t refers to the measurement time. The actual value is compared to the performance target. If $K_{it}^{new} < K_i^{new}$ then the ith performance objective is not met and a recommendation to revise the solution is issued. Obviously, one should evaluate to what extent the software solution is responsible for underperformance.

The context monitoring is performed by comparing the observed context situation CS_t^{new} for the new client at the tth time moment to the context situations supported by the current configuration, i.e., relationship $CS_t^{new} \in \mathbf{CS}_O$ where $\mathbf{CS}_O$ is a set of context situations supported by configuration O_j used by the client. If the relationship does not hold then a warning is issued notifying that the observed context situation is not explicitly supported by the current configuration. The context monitoring serves as an advanced warning system to potential performance deterioration since it is not known whether the current configuration is suitable for the observed context situation. That might lead to an unexpected behavior.

3.3   Evolution

Violations of performance objectives or observation of unsupported context situations triggers a warning suggesting an upgrade of the current configuration. In response, to this warning a client might decide on upgrading the current configuration by selecting a more suitable configuration from CSM. This is a suitable approach if the actual context situation is different from the one identified during the design stage or it has changed. However, if underperformance is observed for the supported context situation and it is attributed to the software product then the vendor might need to reevaluate CSM or a special software-service bundle needs to be developed for the particular client.

4   Application Example

Business processes in many industries require collaboration among two or more companies. Often this collaboration involves business information exchange in a form of data exchange messages [7]. Such messages can contain errors, which need to be corrected before further utilization of the information. The correction of errors might require manual interventions which will be referred to as "cleaning services". The example is motivated by a real-life case in the energy industry, where a software development company provides software for exchanging energy consumption data as well as associated business process outsourcing services for handling data errors [8].

4.1   Description

A vendor offers a business information processing service. The service consists of data processing software, data processing services and – if required – cleaning services by the back office staff of the vendor based on knowledge about the most common data exchange exceptions. The data processing services ensure business information processing on behalf of the client. Clients can choose between doing data processing and cleaning in-house or outsourcing it to the vendor. Figure 3 shows an overall data exchange process from the client's perspective. The client receives a message. Depending on a decision-making logic the messages are processed along one or several process branches. The first branch represents a manual processing (client's employees correct errors). The second branch represents an automated processing using the knowledge base on common exceptions provided by the vendor. However, some of the exceptions might require manual intervention ("cleaning"). A client uses the out-sourcing service provided by the vendor to deal with exceptions in the third branch. The client transfers the exceptions to the outsourcing service and receives back the remedied data. Multiple branches can be used simultaneously. For example, the client mainly uses in-house automated processing and invokes the outsourcing service only if internal resources are overloaded. This decision is made during the service delivery. Nevertheless, the solution should be configured in a way to support both automated in-house processing and usage of the outsourcing service.

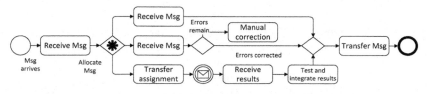

Fig. 3. The overall business information exchange process.

The process execution goals are timely processing of all messages and handling of all exceptions. The main context factors affecting the process execution are the number of data exchange messages received or processing load and load volatility. The load volatility characterizes variations in the processing load what might have adverse consequences on scheduling of resources assigned to the manual processing.

4.2 Model

The vendor possesses the data exchange capability provided to its clients by means of the software-service bundle. The data exchange capability model is created using the concepts defined in Sect. 2.3. Goals, context and process variants are the main ele-ments of the capability model important for the software solution selection method.

The main data exchange goals are timely data processing, correction of data exchange errors as well as cost minimization and efficient utilization of resources involved in the data exchange process. These goals are measured by the corresponding KPIs. For instance, the timely data processing goal is measured as the processing time KPI K_{PT}. The context elements affecting the capability are defined in Table 1. The processing load context element is measured by the number of messages received per day and it assumes values from the range of values. Not all context elements are used in configuration selection for the software-service bundle. Current backlog and schedule context elements are used for run-time decision-making.

The capability model also defines the overall data exchange process including three processing variants (Fig. 3). These process variants serve as the basis for defining configurations of the software solution. The Allocate messages gateway represents decision logics for run-time allocation of messages among process variants if several of them are included in the configuration.

Table 1. Context values and their context ranges

Context element	Context element range
Processing load (C_{PL})	Low, medium, high
Processing load volatility (C_{LV})	Low, medium, high
Backlog (number of messages waiting for processing)	0...1000
Calendar (scheduled hours for human resources)	0...100

Table 2. Capability support matrix for data exchange software-service bundle

Processing load level	Load volatility	O_1	O_2	O_3
Low	Low	1		
Low	Medium	1	1	
Low	High		1	
Medium	Low		1	
Medium	Medium		1	1
Medium	High			1
High	Low		1	
High	Medium			1
High	High			1

Three configurations are offered to clients: O_1 – manual processing of data exchange exceptions; O_2 – automated processing of data exchange exceptions; and O_3 – combination of automated processing of data exchange exceptions with availability of exceptions handling outsourcing services. The vendor also uses its expertise and historical data to prepare CSM (Table 2). The matrix lists context situations as combinations of values of C_{PL} and C_{LV} context elements. It shows that, for instance, configuration O_1 is suited for $CS_1 = \{low, low\}$. Advanced configurations could be used in simple context situations though that is not promoted to avoid inefficiencies.

4.3   Results

The aforementioned capability model provides foundation for delivering data exchange solutions to clients. A simulated experiment is conducted to illustrate the software-service bundle selection method. It simulates a flow of data exchange messages for a single client and the client attempts to process these messages using one of the solutions provided by the vendor. Execution of manual data processing activities in all configurations requires human resources drawn from a limited pool of resources and has a variable duration depending on complexity of exceptions.

The message flow D_t varies over time and is described as an autoregressive process $D_t = \rho + \alpha D_{t-1} + \varepsilon$, where ρ and α are coefficients defining process shape and $\varepsilon = N(0, \sigma)$ is normally distributed with the standard deviation σ. The average flow of messages $\mu = \rho/(1-\alpha)$ and affects the processing load context element. The relationship between D_t and value of the processing load context element C_{PL} is expressed as

$$C_{PL} = \begin{cases} \text{low, if } \mu < 100 \\ \text{medium, if } 100 \leq \mu < 1000 \\ \text{high, if } \mu \geq 1000 \end{cases} \tag{2}$$

The coefficients α and σ affect processing load volatility, i.e., larger values of these coefficients result in a more volatile message flow. In this experiment $\alpha = 0.8$ and $\sigma = \mu/5$. The value of ρ is varied to evaluate different context situations: (1) In the first experiment (EXP1) ρ is set to 10 to evaluate a low processing load situation; and (2) in the second experiment (EXP2) ρ is increased from 10 to 100 during the course of message processing simulation to evaluate the impact of changes in context. Numerical values used in the experiments are practically grounded though do not represent actual observations. A new client defines that its typical context situation $CS^{new} = \{$low, low$\}$. The least cost configuration appropriate for this context situation is O_1. This configuration is setup for the client. That implies client receiving data exchange software and using manual exceptions handling.

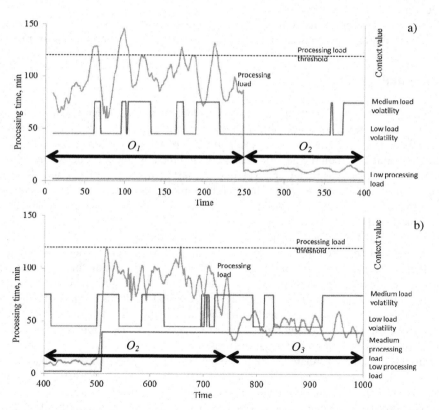

Fig. 4. Dynamics of simulated delivery results and configurations used: (a) EXP1 and (b) EXP2

Figure 4a shows monitoring results for EXP1. It includes values of $K_{PT,t}^{new}$ and the threshold value $K_{PT,t}^{new}$ = 120 min. The processing load context element C_{PL} is constant while load volatility C_{LV} exhibits slight variations and occasionally assumes Medium value not explicitly supported by the current configuration O_1. More importantly, $K_{PT,t}^{new}$ frequently exceeds the threshold value what triggers a recommendation to reconsider the configuration. CSM suggests that O_2 is appropriate for dealing with CS_2 = {low, medium}. The switch to O_2 takes place at time period 250. One can observe that performance is significantly improved.

EXP2 simulates a permanent change of the context situation and C_{PL} assumes Medium value. O_2 is suitable for both CS_4 = {medium, low} and CS_5 = {medium, medium}, and experimental results (Fig. 4b) show that O_2 delivers satisfactory performance after the change in context. However, $K_{PT,t}^{new}$ is close to its threshold. Assuming, that a similar behavior is observed also for other clients using O_2 in similar conditions, the vendor might decide on updating CSM and recommending to used exclusively O_3 in context situation CS_5 = {medium, medium}. The simulated switching takes place at time period 750, when O_3 is deployed. This change results into reduction of the processing time.

The experimental results demonstrate that context observations can be used to drive selection of appropriate configurations on the basis of the common capability model.

5   Related Work

Related work can be found in the areas of selection of packaged applications and version management. The multi-objective methods for selecting packaged applications approach allows for comprehensive evaluation of offerings by different vendors [2]. The selection is based on the generic set criteria and the alignment of these criteria with business needs is not ensured. Capilla et al. [9] describe methods for designing different versions of business software depending on the application context. These works focus on software architecture and design issues rather than the software management decisions. Evolutionary development in software engineering [5] concerns the operational level evolution of atomic development requirements.

The method proposed relies on several existing methods. Goal modeling techniques [10] help to identify the relevant objectives. Business activity monitoring techniques allow measuring the process performance according to the specified goals and to identify significant changes in performance [11]. Context model techniques [12] help to identify relevant context factors and to represent their impact on process design. The method extensively uses categorized context values. A similar approach is taken by [13] to model context-driven business processes.

Furthermore, there is related work in the field of service management from a service science perspective. In recent years, the perspective on what is characterizing a service has shifted from an intangible product to a more process-oriented focus [14]. A service process "[…] can be viewed as a chain or constellation of activities that allow the service to function effectively" [15, p. 68]. Existing work tries to understand service processes from three overall perspectives: input, transformation process and outcome

[16]. In contrast to manufacturing-based production processes, also customers provide significant input in service processes [17]. This is clearly visible in our product-service bundle. However, this input is not only limited to one customer, but also multiple customers which is also acknowledged service science [18]. The transformation process "entails the service delivery and consumption process, and involves customer participation in the service delivery/consumption process" [16, p. 1016]. For software-service bundles, we thus can divide this perspective into the continuum of service co-production [19] and consumption process flow. Latter is considered in existing work as a characteristic of services from a service operations management perspective. The final outcome of the service is determined by the service provider as well as by the service beneficiaries [20].

6   Summary and Future Work

The paper presented and discussed a method for evolutionary development and configuration of software-services bundles. The paper showed that the vendor-client collaboration for selecting the most suitable configuration of a given software-service bundle is feasible and represents value co-creation between vendor and client. The capability concept and the CDD approach have been useful for this method to provide the common basis for defining software solution and explicitly representing relationships among performance, context and solutions. The method so far is evaluated only using a simulation approach and experiences from real-world application cases are needed for further validation.

There are multiple directions of further research. Updating the capability support matrix according to monitoring results is an important part of the method what requires further elaboration. Classification and machine learning methods can be used for these purposes. The decision to upgrade the solution is not an automated decision and usually involves a number of considerations (e.g., business relations) not covered by the evolutionary development method. Switching to a new configuration incurs additional costs. This factor also could be incorporated into the decision-making process to evaluate cost-benefit aspects currently not considered in the paper.

From a service science perspective, the co-production of services has to be seen as a continuum which "[…] can vary from none at all to extensive co-production activities by the customer or user" [21, p. 8]. When specifying service processes, it thus needs to be highlighted which tasks are performed by which entity of the service system or service system network. For software-service bundles, modeling of the service process with explicit distribution of tasks between vendor and client could be a way to further optimize gathering of relevant data. This will be part of future work.

References

1. Pohl, K., Böckle, G., Van der Linden, F.: Software Product Line Engineering. Foundations, Principles, and Techniques. Springer, Heidelberg (2005)
2. Jadhav, A.S., Sonar, R.M.: Evaluating and selecting software packages: a review. Inf. Softw. Technol. **51**, 555–563 (2009)

3. Olsson, H.H., Bosch, J.: Towards continuous customer validation: a conceptual model for combining qualitative customer feedback with quantitative customer observation. In: Fernandes, J.M., Machado, R.J., Wnuk, K. (eds.). LNBIP, vol. 210, pp. 154–166. Springer, Heidelberg (2015)
4. Bērziša, S., Bravos, G., González, T., Czubayko, U., España, S., et al.: Capability driven development: an approach to designing digital enterprises. Bus. Inf. Syst. Eng. **57**, 15–25 (2015)
5. Sommerville, I.: Software Engineering. Pearson, Boston (2015)
6. Grabis, J., Stirna, J.: Advanced context processing for business process execution adjustment. In: Persson, A., Stirna, J. (eds.) CAiSE 2015 Workshops. LNBIP, vol. 215, pp. 15–26. Springer, Heidelberg (2015)
7. Schmidt, A., Otto, B., Österle, H.: Integrating information systems: case studies on current challenges. Electron. Markets **20**, 161–174 (2010)
8. Sandkuhl, K., Koc, H.: On the applicability of concepts from variability modelling in capability modelling: experiences from a case in business process outsourcing. In: Iliadis, L., Papazoglou, M., Pohl, K. (eds.) CAiSE Workshops 2014. LNBIP, vol. 178, pp. 65–76. Springer, Heidelberg (2014)
9. Capilla, R., Ortiz, O., Hinchey, M.: Context variability for context-aware systems. Computer **47**, 85–87 (2014)
10. Kavakli, E.: Modeling organizational goals: analysis of current methods. In: Proceedings of the ACM Symposium on Applied Computing, pp. 1339–1343 (2004)
11. Friedenstab, J., Janiesch, C., Matzner, M. Müller, O.: Extending BPMN for business activity monitoring. In: Proceedings of the Annual Hawaii International Conference on System Sciences, pp. 4158–4167 (2012)
12. Koç, H., Hennig, E., Jastram, S., Starke, C.: State of the art in context modelling – a systematic literature review. In: Iliadis, L., Papazoglou, M., Pohl, K. (eds.) CAiSE Workshops 2014. LNBIP, vol. 178, pp. 53–64. Springer, Heidelberg (2014)
13. Born, M., Kirchner, J., Muller, J.P.: Context-driven business process modeling. In: Camp, H. S.O. (eds.) Advanced Technologies and Techniques for Enterprise Information Systems, ICEIS 2009, pp. 17–26 (2009)
14. Sampson, S.E.: Visualizing service operations. J. Serv. Res. **15**, 182–198 (2012)
15. Bitner, M.J., Ostrom, A.L., Morgan, F.N.: Service blueprinting: a practical technique for service innovation. Calif. Manage. Rev. **50**, 66–94 (2008)
16. Yalley, A.A., Sekhon, H.S.: Service production process: implications for service productivity. Int. J. Prod. Perform. Manage. **63**, 1012–1030 (2014)
17. Sampson, S.E., Froehle, C.M.: Foundations and implications of a proposed unified services theory. Prod. Oper. Manage. **15**, 329–343 (2006)
18. Tax, S.S., McCutcheon, D., Wilkinson, I.F.: The service delivery network (SDN) a customer-centric perspective of the customer journey. J. Serv. Res. **16**, 454–470 (2013)
19. Hilton, T., Hughes, T.: Co-production and self-service: the application of service-dominant logic. J. Mark. Manage. **29**, 861–881 (2013)
20. Spohrer, J., Kwan, S.K.: Service science, management, engineering, and design (SSMED): an emerging discipline. Int. J. Inf. Syst. Serv. **1**, 1–31 (2009)
21. Vargo, S.L., Lusch, R.F.: Service-dominant logic: continuing the evolution. J. Acad. Mark. Sci. **36**, 1–10 (2007)

LightCDD: A Lightweight Capability-Driven Development Method for Start-Ups

Hasan Koç[1]([⊠]), Marcela Ruiz[2], and Sergio España[3]

[1] University of Rostock, Albert-Einstein-Str. 22, 18059 Rostock, Germany
hasan.koc@uni-rostock.de
[2] PROS Research Centre, Universitat Politècnica de València, Valencia, Spain
lruiz@pros.upv.es
[3] Utrecht University, Utrecht, The Netherlands
s.espana@uu.nl

Abstract. Novice innovators and entrepreneurs face the risk of designing naive business models. In fact, lack of realism and failing to envision contextual constraints is one of the main threats to start-up success. Both the literature and the responses we gathered from experts in incubation confirm this problem. Capability Driven Development (CDD) is an integrated approach consisting of a method, tools, and best practices. It has proved to be successful when applied to mature enterprises that intend to become context-aware and adaptive. In this paper we report on the application of CDD to two start-up projects and how, despite being useful in making the entrepreneurs aware of dynamic business environments and constraints, a trade-off analysis showed that a simpler version of the method was necessary. Therefore, we present LightCDD, a context-aware enterprise modelling method that is tailored for business model generation. It reduces the set of modelling constructs and guidelines to facilitate its adoption by entrepreneurs, yet keeping it expressive enough for their purposes and, at the same time, compatible with CDD methodology. We also discuss what implications this simplification has with regard to the CDD tool environment.

Keywords: Capability-driven development · Entrepreneurship · Context-aware business model · Start-up incubation · Business model generation

1 Introduction

By exploiting the niches and offering novel products and services, enterprising individuals with economic initiatives may create the resource for further employment. Hence the entrepreneurship and innovative activities is perceived to be a key factor in economic development [1]. However, the failure risks of start-ups are high and among the indicated reasons are the lack of realism in business ideas [2], i.e. not enough

This work has been supported by the Generalitat Valenciana project IDEO (PROMETEOII/2014/039); the FPI-UPV pre-doctoral grant; the European Commission Project CaaS (FP7 611351); and the ERDF structural funds. We acknowledge the participation of the DELITELABS startup school in the yes!PoEM 2015.

© Springer International Publishing Switzerland 2016
J. Krogstie et al. (Eds.): CAiSE 2016, LNBIP 249, pp. 15–26, 2016.
DOI: 10.1007/978-3-319-39564-7_2

examination of end user needs, which are prone to change rapidly and neglect of the real world context. The lack of realism when modelling business ideas needs to be tackled by the enterprise modelling community. One way to bridge this gap could be the application of a modelling method that allows an integral view and supports different business perspectives, such as the needs of the entrepreneurs and end users, the sequence of activities to be followed to fulfil the needs, as well as the contextual factors influencing the procedures.

Recently, modelling and management of capabilities have been proposed as a way to cope with the challenges in dynamic environments. In that respect, a EU-FP7 project Capability as a Service in Digital Enterprises (CaaS) addresses methods and approaches with which the organisations may adapt to the changes and secure a competitive advantage [3]. To enable digital enterprises to sense and take advantage of changes in business context, CaaS engineers the Capability Driven Development (CDD) method. The CDD has been applied in various case studies for the evolution of information systems that need to incorporate context aware capabilities. Osterwalder & Pigneur states that "a business model describes the rationale of how an organisation creates, delivers and captures value" [4]. By adopting this definition, organisations are start-ups. Concerning the value creation part, we focus on the specification of business processes, goals, business capabilities, and contextual constraints for venues. In this paper we present the application of CDD for helping entrepreneurs in the analysis, design and specification of start-ups. We explore CDD as a business tool that can complement current suites of business tools like the ones proposed in [4].

To shape our research, we conduct a design science project [5]. We perform the first iteration of a design cycle from the problem investigation to the design validation (see Fig. 1). The first step is the problem investigation, which investigates the lack of

T1. PROBLEM INVESTIGATION (Section 2)
- Investigate the lack of realism when modelling start-ups as a fact of failure on the creation of new ventures
- Investigate the need for integrated modelling methods for entrepreneurship
- Explore the literature, establish research questions and conduct interviews to gather knowledge on the problem
- Define the criteria to judge solution success

T2. TREATMENT DESIGN (Section 3)
- Explore available solutions by reviewing the SOTA
- Select modelling method to support business modelling for start-ups (selection of CDD)
- Perform an analysis of CDD and select adequate modelling methodologies for business modelling of start-ups

T3. TREATMENT VALIDATION (Section 3 & 4)
- Validate the feasibility to apply CDD for entrepreneurship
- Perform an exploratory application of CDD to two case studies of start-ups: UpLite and Let's Get Better
- Anlyse the perceptions of the entrepreneurs on the application of CDD

REPRISE OF TASK 2 (Section 5)
- Design LightCDD

DESIGN AN ENTERPRISE MODELLING METHOD FOR START-UPS

Fig. 1. Overview of the research methodology

modelling methods as a threat of start-ups shutdown. The second step corresponds to the treatment design, in which an exploratory exercise to apply CDD for entrepreneurship is performed. The third step corresponds to the treatment validation, which applies the CDD to two case studies of start-ups. Following the results, a reprise of the treatment design step is performed by creating LightCDD.

The paper explores of the suitability of the CDD for start-ups, i.e. whether it helps the entrepreneurs to reason on their business ideas and design. For this, we report on the application of the CDD in two exploratory case studies of start-ups, present the results of a survey regarding the method support for start-ups and then present the LightCDD, which is a simplified version of CDD aimed at the enterprise modelling activities of start-ups. The paper is structured as follows. Section 2 discusses the main threats on start-up failures, outlines the related work, and presents the performed survey. Section 3 begins with the background information on the CDD paradigm, details its application in two case studies, and reports from the experiences gained during the application of CDD in practice, which motivates the LightCDD. Section 4 introduces the LightCDD and Sect. 5 concludes the work.

2 Problem Investigation

The problem investigation is centred on the research about the lack of realism and the risks of not considering contextual and operative constraints for start-ups. We performed a literature review to investigate about the reasons of start-ups' failure. Also, we conducted a structured interview to investigate start-up failure reasons from the point of view of counsellors or managers of start-ups incubators.

Studies and analysis show that encouraging the entrepreneurship and innovative activities in small businesses is a key factor in economic development [6]. By exploiting the niches and offering novel products/services, enterprising individuals with economic initiatives sustain high level of profitability, which may create the resource for further employment [7]. Based on this fact, the legislative bodies support the entrepreneurs to set up their own companies and consequently, the number of start–ups raise rapidly worldwide. However, the high start-up birth rates go hand in hand with a great risk of failure, it's estimated that nine out of 10 start-ups fail [8]. As stated in [9] *"the failure often surrounds five key dimensions: customers, business model, product, financials and team"*. Chorev & Anderson identify 8 top key topics and reports that team commitment, team expertise, marketing, customer relationships, core team expertise and management, strategy, R&D and idea have high effect factors on start-ups success [10].

Among the various factors leading to the start-up failures, wrong estimations on the market need is one of the most important cause. Many start-ups focus too much on product, and not enough on examining the needs of the end user, which is prone to change rapidly. Another observed cause for failure is that the entrepreneurs underestimate the importance of planning, before entering the market [11]. Hence, due to the lack of realism in business ideas, many start–ups fail. To be more specific, different scenarios are neglected; the activities are captured in a single high-level process and the processes are not specified. Moreover, the objectives motivating the ideas and wishes are not captured, which should help to find a proper solution. Instead, the entrepreneurs rely on the subjective, and often biased, perceptions when creating a new business [12]. As such, business planning may help as a decisive factor for the success of the start-ups.

We have asked two experts in enterprise incubation to answer our questions on the reasons for start-up failure[1]. The respondents were the manager of a start-up school

Factors that influence start-ups' failure

Entrepreneurs' goals and characteristics.	Entrepreneurs' environment.
- Most of people that are part of start-ups creation are not entrepreneurs. People belonging to start-ups might be smart and have vision statement, but "entrepreneurship is a trait". - "Entrepreneurs are not addicted to cash", they do not envision how to profit from their business ideas. For entrepreneurs it is easy to preach their ideas, but later they are not eager to work on them.	- It is difficult to set-up a team to run a start-up; a poor team is a high risk for start-ups' failure. - There are to many jobs prospects in IT, most of the start-ups just shutdown due to teams get job offers that are more attractive than pursue the success of a venture. - Start-ups are set-up "at the wrong time in the wrong place".

The behaviour of young entrepreneurs and their lack of realism when modelling business ideas
By young entrepreneurs we refer to entrepreneurs without experience for designing start-ups. The interviewees somewhat agree on the idea that entrepreneurs tend to oversimplify the key activities when designing business processes. Nevertheless, they argue "no entrepreneurs would go through the creation of a new enterprise if they knew how hard it is".   On the other hand, the interviewees completely disagree with our hypothesis that "the younger the entrepreneur is, the more naive s/he tends to be while conceiving business ideas". It is clear that practice makes the master, but some entrepreneurs during her/his first attempt to set-up a company get successful.

Lack of realism of business ideas
The interviewees agree on the fact that entrepreneurs are more focused in the design than in the analysis during the development process of their ventures. This lack of proportion is a cause of failure. On the other hand, opinions of the interviewees are opposite regarding to how realistic are entrepreneurs' initial business ideas.

Methods and instruments to support entrepreneurship
Interviewees perceive that existing methods and instruments are appropriate to think about contextual constraints of the real world, and then entrepreneurs come up with realistic business plans.   Perceptions are divided when analysing current methods. One of the interviewees perceives that current methods do not allow the entrepreneurs have an integral view of their goals, activities, and, contextual constraints. For that reason, providing mechanisms to represent contextual constraints and to reason about goals and processes would help entrepreneurs to anticipate and mitigate risks. Both of the interviewees agree on methods that provide separate specifications of enterprise models could help entrepreneurs to understand their business context. In addition, one interviewee indicates that modelling methods for entrepreneurs should be "graphical, technical and lightweight. Different perspectives should be possible". Regarding to the needed perspectives for modelling business ideas, they mention that it is important to provide various like the ones supported in the CDD methodology, but they claim on the need to "keep it simple". Despite the fact modelling is important for entrepreneurs, one of the interviewees comment that "it is the art of entrepreneurship to not get trapped in analysis paralysis and still having sufficient insight to take the right decisions".

---

[1] The questions can be found at https://goo.gl/92IekF.

(pre-accelerator), and the manager of an incubator who is also lecturer of a course named ICT Entrepreneurship. Both managers have from 3–10 years of experience running incubators. We now elaborate on the findings.

To conclude, we found various evidences on the need to provide lightweight and integrative modelling supports for start-ups. In the following sections we explore the applicability of CDD for entrepreneurship support and start-up modelling.

3 First Experiences on Applying CDD for Enterprise Development

3.1 Capability as a Service in a Nutshell

CaaS project aims to create an integrated approach consisting of a method, tools, and best practices that enable digital enterprises to sense and take advantage of changes in business context. The CaaS methodology for capability- driven development (CDD) consists of various components addressing different modelling aspects, such as context modelling, business process modelling, pattern modelling, and adjustments modelling. The method is supported by the CDD environment, which comprises of a Capability Design Tool (CDT) incorporating a context modelling module, a Capability Context Platform (CCP) to monitor the contextual values at run-time as well as a Capability Delivery Navigation Application (CNA), which enables adjustments in line with the service delivery context and reusable best practices [3].

Three use cases in the sectors of e-government [3], energy [13] and insurance [14] prove that the methodology is successful when applied to full-fledged enterprises that intend to become more context-aware and adaptive. However, studies on the application of the CDD and its effects in innovative start-up projects in entrepreneurial settings are missing.

3.2 Two Practical Start-up Cases

Digital technology powered by the growth in the digital economy caused an increase in the number of young entrepreneurs and innovative ideas. This specifically can be observed between the two main sectors, namely telecommunications and IT [7]. We have launched the yes!PoEM[2] seminar for entrepreneurs, in which the DELITELABS[3] start-up school has participated. This section focuses on the two innovative start-ups in IT field for which we apply the CDD paradigm[4]:

---

[2] http://www.pros.upv.es/en/yespoem.

[3] http://delitelabs.com.

[4] The posters with the projects' descriptions can be found at https://goo.gl/92IekF.

Case 1: Let's Get Better

Let's Get Better is an online platform that provides users with a health coach in their pocket. The main motivation of the project is that an active and healthy life is the key to a well-balanced life but the people struggle adopting healthy habits, since they are busy with their work and social life. As a solution, the platform takes advantage of digital technology and offers 1:1 professional coaching through instant messaging and weekly video calls, progress tracking and peer-to-peer networks. To further support and

encourage users, a social media will allow people to share their story, gain further support, and build common-interest relationships.

Case 2: UpLite

UpLite is a start-up project, where the entrepreneurs propose new way of charging smartphones by improving social contacts. The motivation behind the project is that difficulties arise when one looses the online connectivity, i.e. people feel lost and unsecure when these devices run out of battery and they are limited in terms of their reaching their contacts and information supply. As a solution, the digital entrepreneurs produced a hardware, which connects two mobile devices, allowing them to exchange battery life. In addition to that, they developed a mobile application, which supports such exchange by showing the energy providers and their locations on a map.

3.3   Applying the CDD in Full

The CDD supports different entry points and offers three strategies for capability modelling, namely goal-based, process-based, and concept-based approaches [15]. The procedure that describes the application of CDD to the two cases (case 1: Let's Get Better and case 2: UpLite) is depicted in Fig. 2.

Before starting the modelling sessions, the authors explained the teams the CDD concepts in detail, i.e. the terms business processes, context, and capability were defined. After that, both the Let's Get Better team and the UpLite team were asked to provide us with the business processes (see Procedure 2 in Fig. 2). The results were generic and did not quite reflect the actual implementation of their business ideas.

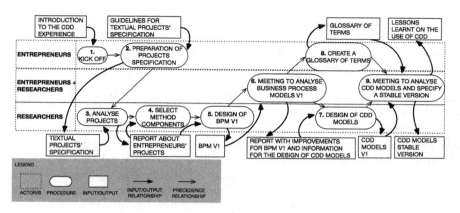

Fig. 2. CDD application procedure for the two start-up cases

CDD allows for different strategies when modelling capabilities [15]. To select the right strategy, we analysed the qualitative data provided by the entrepreneurs (see Procedure 3 in Fig. 2). The data included the descriptions of the use cases as well as the explanations of additional concepts, key activities, resources and stakeholders. Following that, we meet with the teams in an interactive group setting. Based on the gathered information, we identified that the goals were not reflected at all or only expressed ambiguously. Regarding the organizational structures, both teams had clearly defined roles and responsibilities. However, in terms of key concepts, the teams lacked a shared understanding, thus further work was needed to clarify such concepts. In this respect, the teams received an additional task to create *a glossary of terms* before starting with the capability modelling sessions. In contrast, we identified that in both use cases the teams possessed knowledge on the key activities. Consequently, the process-first capability design strategy seemed to be the most suitable one.

Using the CDD method, first the business process models were updated[5]. In the next step, we identified the core capabilities and together with the teams, we prioritized them and selected one capability per use case. Following that, the goals of the team alongside with the end user needs are analysed and modelled, these are related to the capability and to the business process models. Finally, based on the gathered information, the contextual factors that might effecting the service provision were explicated and modelled. In each iteration, additional context elements were identified and their effect on the business idea were discussed. The results were used as an input for a new interaction with the entrepreneurs, i.e. the steps regarding the modelling of the business processes and goals were revisited (see Procedure 9 in Fig. 2).

3.4 Lessons Learnt, Experiences

Looking back at the success factors as introduced in Sect. 2, the application of the CDD led to a more committed team with a shared understanding and clearly defined

---

[5] The respective models before and after CDD application can be found at https://goo.gl/92IekF.

objectives. In particular, the modelling activities enhanced the communication between the core team. The developed models contributed to an overview of the core product & service and how to offer it, the management had useful instruments to define their strategy. Moreover, goal models reflected not only the objectives of the start-ups, but also of the potential customers, which is expected to improve the customer relationships, probably opening new marketing channels. The whole CDD practice helped to enrich the business idea and minimize the risk of a false start.

Concerning the causes of the failure, the CDD improved the start-ups in the identification of the real world factors in the business. To exemplify, the UpLite team did not consider the context of the user in different scenarios, so their app did not incorporate the required functionalities, such as the user profiles, willingness to share, ratings from other users, distance to energy providers and battery status. For the Let´s Get Better Team, the capability model provided them with the information they needed to start developing an algorithm for the app, which was not considered before.

In line with the findings from the literature, another important failure factor was that the entrepreneurs tend to form simple processes. In both cases, the procedures were vaguely defined and many gateways were not considered explicitly. After applying the CDD, the core business process models are updated. Each meeting with the entrepreneurs resulted in a more matured process model and addressed additional discussion points for the teams in terms of a concrete implementation of the activities.

We interviewed the CEOs of the two cases that have applied CDD. Both of them did not have previous experience with enterprise modelling before the application of the CDD. Below we present the research questions that stand for the structure of the interview, and the insights providing answers to the research questions:

(RQ1) *What is the perceived usability and ease of use of CDD in start-ups projects?* - It was easy to apply and is useful to understand and design start-ups' projects. One CEO says, "CDD is a logical process, which helps to provide structure in a wildly abstract start-up". Nevertheless, the first impression that the entrepreneurs got from CDD was the uncertainty on how CDD could be applied to their projects. - Regarding the CDD's concepts: "The terminology used is still rather confusing though". The CDD's concepts need to be reviewed and tailored for end-users.
(RQ2) *What is the perceived impact after the use of CDD in start-ups projects?* - CDD would increase the chances that a start-up achieves its business goals in a changing environment. Although, one comment stands for the idea that CDD seems to be IT project-dependent. - CDD help to identify gaps in business plans. But, for future use of CDD, one CEO says that: "If I feel like there's a need to methodly define a process, then yes - definitely". - From the benefits point of view, the "CDD helped on structuring and clarifying the process" and "The business process model provided us with a clearer user journey. The capacity model provided us with the information we needed to start developing an algorithm for the app".

In general, CDD helped them to find out further configurations of their products and services by analysing their business ideas from the capability point of view. The entrepreneurs identified gaps in the distribution and revenue models, which were optimized (cf. RQ2). Nevertheless, applying the CDD in full had a few drawbacks.

First, the entrepreneurs were initially unsure on how to apply CDD to their projects, which is mainly related to the number of method components. The CDD focuses on the application scenarios of mature enterprises that intend to become context-aware and adaptive, which necessarily requires engineering of a comprehensive method with a number of components. For the two cases, the CDD was not applied in full and just some method components were selected for their application. Second, the method terminology was rather confusing for them and needed review. The teams were not able to apply the CDD by themselves, which created a complicated CDD application procedure, the intervention of the researchers to the modelling processes was required, and the created models are analysed with the entrepreneurs (cf. Fig. 2). To overcome these drawbacks, we propose the LightCDD, which balances the trade-off between the simplicity and expressiveness.

4   Light CDD for Enterprise Modelling of Start-Ups

As a result of the application of CDD in two start-up projects, we found that it is feasible to apply CDD for start-ups projects. As we presented in Sect. 2, all respondents of the questionnaire agree that the entrepreneurs are more focused in the design than in the analysis during the development process of their ventures; and this lack of proportion is a cause of failure. Thus, methods to analyse their idea should be provided to the entrepreneurs. Regarding the characteristics of such methods, they should support graphical representation of the business idea, be lightweight and simple. Moreover, it is required to provide mechanisms to represent contextual constraints that help entrepreneurs anticipate and mitigate risks of failure, and provide integrative view of goals, activities, and contextual constraints.

Taking into account the interview responses (cf. Sect. 3.4), we propose the LightCDD, which is a simplified version of CDD with a different purpose, i.e. not providing support in a full-fledged company, but rather in a start-up design. To meet the demands of the start-ups, the LightCDD incorporates the context modelling, goal modelling and business process modelling components. The important concepts that the LightCDD is based on are illustrated with a meta-model in Fig. 3. This is a simplification of the meta-model used in the CaaS project [3].

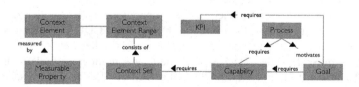

Fig. 3. The meta-model of the LightCDD

LightCDD consists of procedures that are classified into three phases, namely preparation, analysis and design phases, which are defined in the following (Fig. 4):

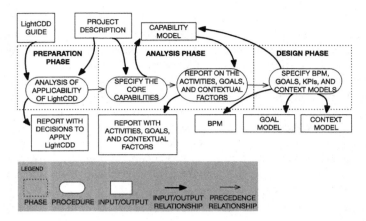

Fig. 4. LightCDD procedure

Preparation phase The entrepreneurs are provided with a LightCDD guide. The guide consists of the information, what enterprise modelling in general is, and how this could help to improve their case. Moreover, it includes the meta-model (cf. Fig. 2), the definitions of the CDD terms in a tabular form as well as a simple example, where the method is used.

Analysis phase The core proposition of the business idea is expressed as a capability. Then, key activities regarding the implementation of the capability are enumerated. Next, the goals are listed that needs to be fulfilled. Following that, the contextual factors influencing the objectives or the key activities are analysed. The gained information might require an update in the core proposition of the capability or result in additional capabilities, which is why the analysis phase may be iterated more than once.

Design phase The key activities are modelled as BPM and objectives are captured as goal models. The key performance indicators (KPI) are added to the goals. Based on the capabilities, the BPM and goal models are related to the context models, which represent the contextual constraints of the business environment.

The prerequisites for the method application are not taken into consideration. This should be fulfilled with the activities in the preparation phase. Likewise, the stakeholder types that participate to the different phases of the CDD were excluded in this version, due to the fact that the start-up teams include smaller number of individuals. As mentioned in Sect. 3, the CDD is supported by a number of tools including the CDT, CCP and CNA. For the LightCDD, the focus is on the enterprise modelling phase, hence the CDT is required for the method application, which is a graphical modelling tool for supporting the creation of models according to the simplified meta-model shown in Fig. 2.

5   Conclusions and Discussion

Studies and analysis show that the digital economy is growing worldwide and holds huge potential for European entrepreneurs. Encouraging the entrepreneurship and innovative activities in small businesses is a key factor in economic development [6]. However, the high start-up birth rates go hand in hand with a great risk of failure.

In this paper, we analysed the current problems of start-ups and focused on the lack of properly modelling methods as a threat for shutdowns. In other words, we investigated how methods and techniques for enterprise modelling could help on the development process of new ventures. We reviewed the literature and conducted a survey to know factors of failure when establishing start-ups. We have performed an exploratory application of CDD in two start-ups projects. As a result of this experience, we found that CDD is a feasible method for start-ups support. We interviewed the CEO of the two start-up projects to know their perceptions about CDD, and how it impacted their projects. Thanks to the evidences collected during the application of CDD, the survey, the interview to the CEOs, and literature related research; we found evidences on the need to design a lightweight method for start-ups. As a result, we proposed the LightCDD, a simplified version of CDD for entrepreneurship support, which is designed based on the following principles:

i. The users of LightCDD should be supplied with the information of what enterprise modelling in general is and how this could help to improve their case. Here, the specific terms regarding the capability modelling should be described. If possible, the description should be enriched with the examples from the cases.
ii. The LightCDD should focus on the goals, context and processes. The pattern modelling method component is excluded, since the business idea is somewhat unique and no best practices in the application field are expected. The adjustments modelling method component is also excluded due to its strong focus on the implementation of the business idea, which is the run-time aspect.
iii. From the CDD tool suite, CDT seems to be the only one that the entrepreneurs can use. This is advocated by the reason that for the business design, they only need CDD tools that support enterprise modelling.

We gained interesting feedback from the CEOs of the two projects in which CDD was applied, and the incubators' managers. Due to entrepreneurs' context sensitive approach, we predict that the respondents address the ability of CDD to overcome challenges in changing situations, i.e. if it is a relatively stable environment for the start-up, such as selling of a certain product with certain features, the method might be too complex to use.

LightCDD is going to be further developed and evaluated in new start-ups. In this respect, future work is going to focus on a few aspects. First, the guidelines and best practices for BPM are going to be improved and incorporated. This requirement stems from the feedback that the application of the (Light) CDD in further entrepreneurial projects depends on such support. Second, the CDD concepts are going to be refined and simplified. Third and last, important aspects such as the revenue models, channels, key resources, and team expertise is going to be addressed, which were mentioned during the interviews, but always remained out of the CDD boundaries.

References

1. Grossmann, V.: Entrepreneurial innovation and economic growth. J. Macroecon. **31**, 602–613 (2009)
2. Morris, M., Schindehutte, M., Allen, J.: The entrepreneur's business model: toward a unified perspective. J. Bus. Res. **58**, 726–735 (2005)
3. Berzisa, S., Bravos, G., et al.: Capability driven development: an approach to designing digital enterprises. Bus. Inf. Syst. Eng. **57**, 15–25 (2015)
4. Osterwalder, A., Pigneur, Y.: Business Model Generation: A Handbook for Visionaries, Game Changers, and Challengers. Wiley, New York (2010)
5. Wieringa, R.: Design Science Methodology for Information Systems and Software Engineering. Springer, Berlin (2014)
6. Summers, D.: The economic impact of entrepreneurship: setting realistic expectations. In: Allied Academies International Conference - Academy of Entrepreneurship (2015)
7. Ács, Z. J., Serb, L., Autio, E.: Global Entrepreneurship Index 2016 (2015). http://thegedi.org/2016-global-entrepreneurship-index/, Accessed on 21 Jan 2016
8. Griffith, E.: Why startups fail, according to their founders, Fortune.com (2014)
9. Fallon, N.: Beating the Odds: 4 Steps to Startup Success (2014). http://www.businessnewsdaily.com/6054-reduce-startup-failure-risk.html. Accessed on 01 Feb 2016
10. Chorev, S., Anderson, A.R.: Success in Israeli high-tech start-ups. Crit. Factors Process Technovation **26**, 162–174 (2006)
11. Chwolka, A., Raigh, M.G.: The value of business planning before start-up - a decision-theoretical perspective. JBV **27**, 385–399 (2012)
12. Koellinger, P., Minniti, M., et al.: "I think I can, I think I can": overconfidence and entrepreneurial behavior. J. Econ. Psychol. **28**, 502–527 (2007)
13. Koç, H., Sandkuhl, K.: A business process based method for capability modelling. In: Matulevičius, R., Dumas, M. (eds.) BIR 2015. LNBIP, vol. 229, pp. 257–264. Springer, Heidelberg (2015)
14. Bravos, G., González, T., Grabis, J., Henkel, M., Jokste, L., Koc, H., Stirna, J.: Capability modeling: initial experiences. In: Johansson, B., Andersson, B., Holmberg, N. (eds.) BIR 2014. LNBIP, vol. 194, pp. 1–14. Springer, Heidelberg (2014)
15. España, S., Grabis, J., Henkel, M., Koç, H., Sandkuhl, K., Stirna, J., Zdravkovic, J.: Strategies for capability modelling: analysis based on initial experiences. In: Persson, A., Stirna, J. (eds.) CAiSE 2015 Workshops. LNBIP, vol. 215, pp. 40–52. Springer, Heidelberg (2015)

ASDENCA/BUMDISE 2016 – Integration of Capability with Goals and Context

Comparison of Tool Support for Goal Modelling in Capability Management

Claas Fastnacht[1], Hasan Koç[1], Dimitrijs Nesterenko[1],
and Kurt Sandkuhl[1,2(✉)]

[1] University of Rostock, Albert-Einstein-Straße 22, 18059 Rostock, Germany
{claas.fastnacht,hasan.koc,dimitrijs.nesterenko,
kurt.sandkuhl}@uni-rostock.de
[2] School of Engineering, Jönköping University,
Box 1026, 55111 Jönköping, Sweden
kurt.sandkuh@ju.se

Abstract. Capability management is attracting more and more attention in different research and industry areas. A starting point for implementing capability management in an organization often is to identify desired and existing capabilities in relation to the organization's goals and to specify the capability. Due to the close relationship to organizational goals, tool support for capability modelling should also include capturing goal or even complete enterprise models. The aim of the paper is to contribute to an understanding what kind of tool support is suitable for capability management to capture enterprise goals. The focus in this paper is on goal modelling as part of capability modelling tools and aims at comparing modelling without computer support, modelling with tools enforcing a meta-model and modeling with support of a drawing tool. The comparison is based on experiments.

Keywords: Capability modelling · Goal modelling · Modelling tool · Experiment · Capability management

1 Introduction

Capability management is attracting more and more attention in different research and industry areas, such as enterprise architecture management [1], inter-organizational capabilities [3] or business capability optimization [2]. A starting point for implementing capability management in an organization often is to identify desired and existing capabilities in relation to the organization's goals and to specify the capability, for example by modelling the capability. Due to the close relationship to organizational goals, tool support for capability modelling should also include capturing goal models or even complete enterprise models. An example for such an integrated tool support is the capability design tool (CDT) that is developed in the CaaS project [14].

Capability management in many enterprises is involving different disciplines, including, e.g., the enterprise management, the responsible persons for business service delivery, controllers from accounting or IT people implementing the IT-support for delivery of capabilities. As a consequence, modelling tools should not only be suitable for people

© Springer International Publishing Switzerland 2016
J. Krogstie et al. (Eds.): CAiSE 2016, LNBIP 249, pp. 29–39, 2016.
DOI: 10.1007/978-3-319-39564-7_3

experienced in using modelling tools, but laymen in this area. Even though the actual modelling with the tool might be done by a tool expert, the models (while emerging or when finished) should be understood by the different disciplines and stakeholders involved.

The aim of the paper is to contribute to an understanding what kind of tool support is suitable for capability management to capture enterprise goals. More concrete, the focus in this paper is on goal modelling as part of capability modelling tools and we aim at comparing modelling without computer support, modelling with tools enforcing a meta-model and modelling with support of a drawing tool. The comparison is based on experiments; the participants in the experiments were on purpose recruited from groups without extensive IT-knowledge, modelling knowledge or knowledge about the concept of capability.

The rest of the paper is structured as follows: Sect. 2 summarizes the background for the work. Section 3 discusses the set-up of the experiments and presents the results. Section 4 summarizes the work and draws conclusions.

2   Background

As a background for the work presented in this paper, this section briefly summarizes work in the area of capability management and the capability design and delivery approach developed in the CaaS project[1].

2.1   Capability Management

The term capability is used in different areas of business information systems. In the literature although there seems to be an agreement about the characteristics of a capability, there still is no general acceptance of the term. The established definitions mainly put the focus on "combination of resources" [4], "capacity to execute an activity" [3], "perform better than competitors" [6] and "possessed ability [11]".

Capabilities are said to be enablers of competitive advantage; they should help companies to continuously deliver a certain business value in dynamically changing circumstances [7]. They can be perceived from different organizational levels and thus utilized for different purposes. According to [8], performance of an enterprise is the best, when the enterprise maps its capabilities to IT applications. Capabilities as such are directly related to business processes. Business processes often are affected from changes in their context, such as, new regulations, customer preference changes and modified system performance. As companies in rapidly changing environments need to anticipate variations and respond to them [5], the affected processes/services need to be adjusted quickly. In other words, adaptations to changes in context can be realized promptly if the required variations to the standard processes have been anticipated and defined in advance and can be instantiated.

In this paper capability is defined as the ability and capacity that enable an enterprise to achieve a business goal in a certain context [12]. Ability refers to the level

---

[1] http://caas-project.eu/.

of available competence, where competence is understood as talent, intelligence and disposition of a subject or enterprise to accomplish a goal. Capacity means availability of resources, e.g. money, time, personnel, tools. Capabilities are strongly related with enterprise strategies and stakeholder goals for a company to deliver value, they are used as fundamental abstraction instruments in business service design [19]. Our definition of capabilities supports this view, where capabilities are considered as specific business services delivered to the enterprises to reach a business goal in an application context.

2.2 Capability Modelling in CaaS

In digital enterprises, business services often are provided to the enterprise's customers using IT-based services. Business services usually serve specified business goals, they are specified in a model-based way and include service level definitions. The capability management approach developed in the CaaS project is based on the idea that a capability is tightly linked to the context of its delivery and the business service variants required for this. Thus, the CaaS approach includes explicit definition of (a) the potential delivery context of a business service (i.e. all contexts in which the business service potentially has to be delivered), (b) the potential variants of the business service for the delivery context and (c) what aspect of the delivery context would require what kind of variation or adaptation of the business service. As an enabler of the Business/IT alignment [2], the capability serves as a glue between the conceptualisation of the service, its context-dependent operationalisation as well as the extent to which the goals of the enterprise are fulfilled.

The potential delivery context basically consists of a set of parameters or variables, the so called context elements, which characterize the differences in delivery. The combination of all context elements and their possible ranges defines the context set, i.e. the problem space to cover. The potential variants of the business service, which form the solution space, are represented by process variants. Since in many delivery contexts it will be impractical to capture all possible variants, CaaS proposes to define patterns for the most frequent variants caused by context elements and to combine and instantiate these patterns to create actual solutions. If no suitable pattern is available, the conventional solution engineering process has to be used. The connection between context elements, patterns and business services has to be captured as transformation or adjustment rules. These rules are defined during design time and interpreted during runtime.

The above simplified summary of our approach has been further elaborated by defining meta-model and method components, by specifying a development and delivery environment which includes a tool support for capability design (CDT) and by performing feasibility studies. Detailed discussions of meta-model and method components is available in [9] and [13], respectively. Conceptually, the model of a capability consists of the following parts:

- strategic objectives or business goals related to the capability or motivating the creation of the capability. These objectives should be specified in a precise and measurable way accepted by the business stakeholders, for example by using Enterprise Modelling techniques and by elaborating a goal model.

- the business service(s) offered to customers within the capability. In CaaS, the business service(s) have to be specified using a model-based approach. More concrete, process-oriented approaches are used and it assumed that capabilities are context-aware business services.
- the specification of the potential application context where the business service is supposed to be deployed. The specification of the capability's potential deployment contexts is captured in a context model.
- an IT-based solution for delivering the capability in the defined context, i.e. executing the business service. For the initial methodology, it is assumed that all variations of the solution for different context instances are defined, e.g. as delivery pattern.
- patterns specifying reusable elements for reaching business goals under specific situational contexts. The CaaS methodology is providing a method component for identification, elicitation and representation of patterns.

For the purposes of this paper, we will be focusing on the first part by comparing the tools available for goal modelling. Detailed investigations on the remaining aspects can be found in [13, 14, 20].

2.3   4EM Enterprise Modelling Method

The goal modelling approach applied in the CaaS project and implemented in the CDT tool originates from the 4EM method [10]. 4EM uses six interrelated sub-models which complement each other and capture different views of the enterprise, i.e. each of the sub-models represents some aspect of the enterprise (see Fig. 1). These sub-models and issues they address are described in the following.

- Goals Model (GM) focuses on describing the goals of the enterprise. Here we describe what the enterprise and its employees want to achieve, or to avoid, and when. GM usually clarifies questions, such as: where the organisation should be moving, what the goals of the organisation are, what the importance, criticality, and priorities of these goals are, how these are related to each other and which problems are hindering achievement of goals.
- Business Rule Model (BRM) is used to define and maintain explicitly formulated business rules, consistent with the Goals Model. Business Rules may be seen as operationalization or limits of goals. BRM usually clarifies questions, such as: which rules affect the organisation's goals, how a business rule is related to a goal, how goals can be supported by rules.
- Concepts Model (CM) is used to strictly define the "things" and "phenomena" one is talking about in the other models. It represents enterprise concepts, attributes, and relationships. CM usually clarifies questions, such as: what concepts are recognised in the enterprise (including their relationships to goals, activities and processes, and actors), how they are defined, what business rules and constraints monitor these objects and concepts.
- Business Processes Model (BPM) is used to define enterprise processes, the way they interact and the way they handle information as well as material. A business

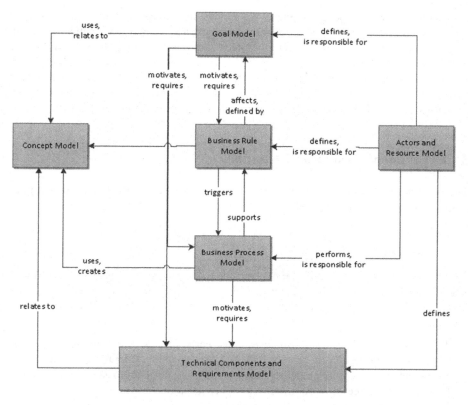

Fig. 1. Sub-Models of the 4EM approach and their relationships

process is assumed to consume input in terms of information and/or material and produce output of information and/or material. BPM usually clarifies questions, such as: which business activities and processes are recognised in the organisation, how the business processes, tasks, etc. should be performed (workflows, state transitions, or process models) and which information they need.

- Actors and Resources Model (ARM) is used to describe how different actors and resources are related to each other and how they are related to components of the Goals Model, and to components of the Business Processes Model. For instance, an actor may be the responsible for a particular process in the BPM or, the actor may pursue a particular goal in the GM. ARM usually clarifies questions, such as: who is/should be performing which processes and tasks, how the reporting and responsibility structure between actors are defined.

- Technical Components and Requirements Model (TCRM) becomes relevant when the purpose of enterprise modelling is to aid in defining requirements for the development of an information system. Attention is focused on the technical system that is needed to support the goals, processes, and actors of the enterprise. Initially one needs to develop a set of high level requirements or goals, for the information system as a whole. Based on these, we attempt to structure the information system in a number of subsystems, or technical components. TCRM is an initial attempt to define the overall structure and properties of the information system to support the business activities, as defined in the BPM. TCRM usually clarifies questions, such as: what the requirements are for the information system to be developed, which requirements are generated by the business processes, which potential the emerging information and communication technology for process improvement have.

3 Experiment Design and Results

The section describes the experiment performed in order to compare goal modeling as part of capability modeling tools.

3.1 Experiment Design

The modelling method used in the experiment is the goal modeling part of 4EM (see Sect. 2.3) which in the CaaS project is an important part of capability modeling (see Sect. 2.2). For the experiment, three different tools representing different categories are used:

- The "plastic wall" is a traditional tool for early phases of enterprise modelling, which uses large plastic sheets and coloured paper cards for documentation. Enforcement of the goal modeling notation basically does not exist. The participants have a high degree of freedom how to apply the tool,
- Microsoft Visio is a general purpose drawing tool. Equipped with a stencil set for 4EM, the goal modeling notation can be used. However, "modeling" here is a process of "drawing" the models, as enforcement of correct notation use is not implemented.
- The CDT tool developed in the CaaS project implements based on the CaaS meta-model the goal modeling notation of 4EM and ensures the correct use of the notation. Thus, CDT is no general drawing but a real modeling tool.

    With respect to the participants in the experiment, the principal decision had to be made whether to use people familiar with the goal modeling notation in 4EM or participants without specific method or modeling knowledge. In order to avoid any bias on the participant side for a modeling method or a modeling tool, we decided to use participants without modeling and tool knowledge. These participants all were Bachelor or Master students from Rostock University. Among the 12 participants were students from medicine, economics, law, biology and chemistry. The 12 participants were randomly grouped into 6 groups of 2. For each tool, two groups (independently of each other) were given an introduction to goal modeling with 4EM, to the task and to the tool within 15 min. All groups received a written introduction to goal modeling with 4EM prior to the modeling sessions. The modeling task was identical for all groups and taken from a textbook about the 4EM method. Each group decided on its own when they were finished, i.e. there was no time limitation.

As a means to compare the three modeling tools, we decided to consider two aspects: (1) the user experience, i.e. how the users perceive application of the tools and (2) the quality of the models developed by the participants. For both aspects we used rather simple metrics which are reflected in questionnaires.

User Experience questionnaire covers the following aspects:

- How did the participants perceive the introduction to goal modeling with 4EM?
- How satisfied are the participants regarding the clarity of the task to be performed?
- How did the participants perceive the tool?
- How satisfied are the participants with the results of the modelling?

For each aspect, several questions were included. For each question, the participants were asked to give a mark between 1 and 5, with 1 meaning "very bad" and 5 "very good". Furthermore, we took for every team the time needed to complete the modeling task.

Model quality is a much researched area with many different approaches. Examples for work in this area are quality frameworks, like SEQUAL [16], studies of user perception [17], cognitive complexity [15] and the impact of secondary notation [18]. As our participant groups had a rather small assignment, the resulting models also were comparatively small and not suitable for complex measurement approaches for model quality. Thus, we decided to only use the following parameters:

- size of the model with respect to number of goals and problems included,
- maximum number of refinement levels included,
- complexity measured in the average number of relation between model elements,
- layout of the models expressed in number of intersecting relationships.

3.2   Experiment Results

When performing the modelling sessions all groups were observed by the same two researchers, who took notes and jointly evaluated their observations after the modelling sessions. The following observations were made:

- Plastic wall: both groups said that they have no difficulties to use the tool. Interestingly, we noticed that the groups first put the model content (i.e. the colored paper slips) on a table, arranged them and then put them onto the plastic at the wall. Furthermore, we noticed a big difference regarding the time needed for modeling. One group finished after 30 min, the other one after 90 min.
- Visio: modelling with Visio took the groups between 30 and 40 min, which was the shortest period for the three tools. Both groups started by highlighting words or sentences in the written assignment description before putting them into Visio shapes. Smaller problems occurred regarding the direction of the relations and the way to enter or modify the labels of the model objects.
- CDT: the groups needed significantly more time as compared to Visio (approx. 60 min). They had some problems to use the tool, because of the mandatory

id-number for each model element and due to the high number of available model element types, such as context elements and capabilities. Furthermore, navigation in the model was considered difficult since the model grew quickly in size which required scrolling in the tool.

The questionnaires about model quality returned that in most aspects there were no significant differences between the three tools with only two exceptions (see Fig. 2):

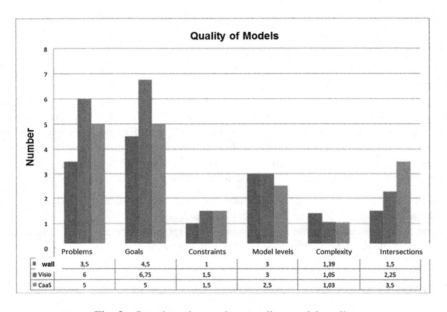

Fig. 2. Questionnaire results regarding model quality

- With respect to the number of model elements, the Visio models are the biggest and the plastic wall models the smallest.
- Regarding the layout, the CDT models had most intersecting relationships of all models. The reason for this might be that the participants had difficulties to move model elements and after some try and error were willing to accept the model layout without changes.

The questionnaires about user experiences resulted in the following: Visio and the plastic wall got the best marks. Visio was slightly better, probably because changes in labels or relations could be implemented a bit easier as compared to the plastic wall. The CDT result was not as good as the other two tools which can be explained by the larger functionality and the specialization of the tool (see Fig. 3).

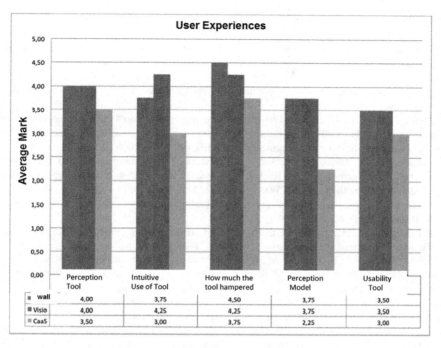

Fig. 3. Questionnaire results regarding user experience

4   Summary and Future Work

The paper focused on comparing three tools contributing to capability modelling from goal modelling point of view. The comparison was done using two groups for each tool who had to complete a predefined assignment. The evaluation focused on user experience and model quality.

As a result of the experiment performed and described in Sect. 3 we can conclude:

- CDT has some improvement potential regarding usability, e.g., when creating new model elements, navigating the model or regarding the layout of the models.
- General purpose drawing tools (like Visio) and non-IT based tools (like the plastic wall) contribute to capability modelling at least in early modelling phases. Like in enterprise modelling, the use of these tools should be considered when business stakeholders are involved.

Our study has a number of limitations which all require future work. One limitation is the low number of participants, which makes the results more anecdotes than statistically relevant. However, we got some indications of where potential problems and improvement or usage potentials are. Furthermore, the selection of tools to be evaluated was more directed by their availability than by systematic selection. In future work, we will also have to include more and different assignments addressing different aspects of capability management. The selection of participants for future work should move from students at universities to practitioners in enterprises.

References

1. Wißotzki, M., Koç, H., Weichert, T., Sandkuhl, K.: Development of an enterprise architecture management capability catalog. In: Kobyliński, A., Sobczak, A. (eds.) BIR 2013. LNBIP, vol. 158, pp. 112–126. Springer, Heidelberg (2013)
2. Cutter Consortium. https://www.cutter.com/article/business-capability-map-rosetta-stone-businessit-alignment-469506
3. Jiang, Y., Zhao, J.: An empirical research of the forming process of Firm inter-organizational e-business capability: Based on the supply chain processes. In: 2nd International Conference on Information Science and Engineering (ICISE), pp. 2603–2606. IEEE Press (2010)
4. Antunes, G., Barateiro, J., Becker, C., Borbinha, J.: Modeling contextual concerns in enterprise architecture. In: 15th IEEE International Enterprise Distributed Object Computing Conference Workshops (EDOCW), pp. 3–10. IEEE Press (2011)
5. Eriksson, T.: Processes, antecedents and outcomes of dynamic capabilities. Scandinavian J. Manage. **30**(1), 65–82 (2013)
6. Boonpattarakan, A.: Model of thai small and medium sized enterprises' organizational capabilities: review and verification. JMR **4**(3), 1–28 (2012)
7. Stirna, J., Grabis, J., Henkel, M., Zdravkovic, J.: Capability driven development – an approach to support evolving organizations. In: Stirna, J., Sandkuhl, K., Seigerroth, U. (eds.) PoEM 2012. LNBIP, vol. 134, pp. 117–131. Springer, Heidelberg (2012)
8. Chen, J., Tsou, H.: Performance effects of 5IT6 capability, service process innovation, and the mediating role of customer service. J. Eng. Tech. Manage. **29**(1), 71–94 (2012)
9. Zdravkovic, J., Stirna, J., Henkel, M., Grabis, J.: Modelling business capabilities and context dependent delivery by cloud service. In: Salinesi, C., Norrie, M.C., Pastor, O. (eds.) CAiSE 2013. LNCS, vol. 7908, pp. 369–383. Springer, Heidelberg (2013)
10. Sandkuhl, K., Stirna, J., Persson, A., Wißotzki, M.: Enterprise Modeling: Tackling Business Challenges with the 4EM Method. Springer, Heidelberg (2014)
11. Brézillon, P., Cavalcanti, M.: Modeling and using context. Knowl. Eng. Rev. **13**(2), 185–194 (1998)
12. Bērziša, S., Bravos, G., Gonzalez Cardona, T., Czubayko, U., España, S., Grabis, J., Henkel, M., Jokste, L., Kampars, J., Koc, H., Kuhr, J., Llorca, C., Loucopoulos, P., Juanes Pascual, R., Sandkuhl, K., Simic, H., Stirna, J., Zdravkovic, J.: Deliverable 1.4: Requirements specification for CDD, CaaS – Capability as a Service for Digital Enterprises, FP7 project no 611351, Riga Technical University, Latvia (2014)
13. Sandkuhl, K., Koç, H., Stirna, J.: Context-aware business services: technological support for business and IT-alignment. In: Abramowicz, W., Kokkinaki, A. (eds.) BIS 2014 Workshops. LNBIP, vol. 183, pp. 190–201. Springer, Heidelberg (2014)
14. Bērziša, S., Bravos, G., Gonzalez Cardona, T., Czubayko, U., España, S., Grabis, J., Henkel, M., Jokste, L., Kampars, J., Koç, H., Kuhr, J.-C., Llorca, C., Loucopoulos, P., Juanes Pascual, R., Pastor, O., Sandkuhl, K., Simic, H., Stirna, J., Zdravkovic, J.: Capability driven development: an approach to designing digital enterprises. Bus. Inf. Syst. Eng. **57**(1), 15–25 (2015)
15. Figl, K., Laue, R.: Cognitive complexity in business process modeling. In: Mouratidis, H., Rolland, C. (eds.) CAiSE 2011. LNCS, vol. 6741, pp. 452–466. Springer, Heidelberg (2011)
16. Krogstie, J.: Model-based Development and Evolution of Information Systems. A Quality Approach. Springer, London (2012)
17. Maes, A., Poels, G.: Evaluating quality of conceptual models based on user perceptions. In: Embley, D.W., Olivé, A., Ram, S. (eds.) ER 2006. LNCS, vol. 4215, pp. 54–67. Springer, Heidelberg (2006)

18. Schrepfer, M., Wolf, J., Mendling, J., Reijers, H.A.: The impact of secondary notation on process model understanding. In: Persson, A., Stirna, J. (eds.) PoEM 2009. LNBIP, vol. 39, pp. 161–175. Springer, Heidelberg (2009)
19. Togaf - enterprise architecture methodology, version 9.1 (2012)
20. Koç, H., Sandkuhl, K.: A business process based method for capability modelling. In: Matulevičius, R., Dumas, M. (eds.) BIR 2015. LNBIP, vol. 229, pp. 257–264. Springer, Heidelberg (2015)

Extending Capabilities with Context Awareness

Martin Henkel[1]([⊠]), Christina Stratigaki[2], Janis Stirna[1],
Pericles Loucopoulos[2], Yannis Zorgios[2], and Antonis Migiakis[2]

[1] Stockholm University, Stockholm, Sweden
{martinh, js}@dsv.su.se
[2] CLMS Ltd, London, UK
xristinastrathgakh@gmail.com,
{yz, a.migiakis}@clmsuk.com

Abstract. Organizations have the need to continuously adjust their capabilities to changes in the business context. If existing IT systems and associated development methods does not support this adjustment they need to be changed to do so. However, there exist specialized methods and tools that allow the design, and run-time monitoring of context information. In this paper an approach that allows existing systems to be extended with the management of context information is presented. The approach allows organizations to analyze the potential effect and effort of combing existing systems and tools with specialized tools that handle context information. The purpose of providing means for the integrated use of existing systems and specialized tools is to leverage the strength of both. The approach in grounded in and illustrated by a case of industrial symbiosis.

Keywords: Context analysis · Context monitoring · Capability modelling · Capability management

1 Introduction

Organizations work in changing environments, their capabilities need to be adjusted to meet the changes and in order to increase efficiency. Failure to adapt to changing environments can endeavour organizations profitability or even its existence [1]. The pace at which organizations need to adapt to changes is not slowing down. On the contrary, organizations that have a competitive advantage tend to keep that advantage for a shorter time [2]. Thus, organisations need to be aware of changes in their context and adapt accordingly. Central to being able to perform this adaptation is to know the context of the business, and to be able to measure and monitor it.

In this paper we present an approach that allows organisations to extend their existing IT systems and development tools with tools and methods that allow the analysis, design and monitoring of capabilities and their contexts. The approach makes use of the Capability Driven Development (CDD) [3] methods and associated design and run-time tools. The scope of this approach is (a) to make it possible to, on a case-by-case basis, outline the benefits and effects of extending existing systems and

© Springer International Publishing Switzerland 2016
J. Krogstie et al. (Eds.): CAiSE 2016, LNBIP 249, pp. 40–51, 2016.
DOI: 10.1007/978-3-319-39564-7_4

tools with the ability to design and monitor context information, (b) to make it possible to discern which method and software integrations that needs to be in place for such an extension, (c) to have a basis for the implementation of software components that are needed to perform changes to existing development tools and operational IT systems.

The approach is generic, but is specialized to make use of the CDD approach for capability and context analysis. A key component of CDD is the use of graphical models. The models used in CDD have a focus on describing organisational capabilities, their contexts and goals. CDD does not include specific methods and tools for the detailed creation of information systems. However it does provide tools that allow the analysis, design and run-time monitoring of context information. This can be put in contrast with traditional development tools that focus on components of software systems, such as, data objects, information management procedures, user interface components etc. Thus, combining the CDD approach with other development tools and systems gives the possibility to have support for capability analysis and monitoring (provided by CDD, or similar methods and tools) and the detailed implementation of information systems (provided by existing systems).

The generic approach presented is applied in an industrial symbiosis platform implemented by CLMS Limited. Industrial Symbiosis is an association between two or more industrial actors in which the wastes or by-products of one become the raw materials for another. This collaboration between two or more companies is called a *synergy*.

Traditionally, experts and consultants, involving highly complex, labour-intensive and error-prone tasks, performed the industrial symbiosis mediation process for the matching between producers and consumers manually. However, the company CLMS has implemented an *industrial symbiosis platform* that is improving industrial symbiosis by automating the process of mixing and matching the interests of different actors in the waste resource chain, and by providing knowledge-based support for managing resources and finding compatible ones. The platform suggests compatible matches to a company and facilitates the creation of synergies for these matches. The symbiosis platform is implemented using the state-of art model driven development tool zAppDev. As each step of the approach is described in subsequent section, we also describe its application in the symbiosis case.

In order to combine capability and context analysis with existing systems and development tools, both design-time and run-time options for integration need to be considered. We here outline four steps that can be followed to have a structured approach for selecting integration options, these are described in the following sections:

1. Perform capability and context analysis.
2. Select design time integration options.
3. Select run-time integration options.
4. Summarize tool support needed.

The rest of the paper is structured as follows. Section 2 is giving the theoretical background and the related work. Section 3 introduces the first step of the approach, capability and context analysis. Sections 3 and 4 describes subsequent steps in the approach, focusing on design and run-time options when combining existing systems with context aware design tools. Sections 6 and 7 contains summary and conclusions.

2 Related Work

In this paper we use the concepts of capabilities and context. These concepts have been described in the field of strategic management, enterprise modelling and in research on contextual systems.

In strategic management the notion of dynamic capability [4] can be used to describe the ability on an organisation to evolve and thrive in changing environments. The definition of the concept of capability has fluctuated somewhat in the area of strategic management; however there is a tendency to associate it with the organisation of resources and their allocation [5]. In this paper we use this interpretation of capability, that is, we view resources and their use as an integral part of capabilities. We define a capability as the ability and capacity that enable an enterprise to achieve a business goal in a certain context [3].

In the area of enterprise modelling and enterprise architecture, the concept of capability has been used as a mean to analyse organisations [6, 7]. It has also been used to describe an organizations ability to use enterprise architecture. This is most notable in the open groups TOGAF framework [8], where capability frequently refers the readiness of an organization to use enterprise architecture. Regarding strategic management and enterprise modelling, the contribution of this paper is to show how the notions of capability and context can be realised, rather than adding to the existing methods and conceptual foundation of capability analysis and architecture.

Examining the research in contextual systems, it can be said that a focus has been on both to provide extensive and formal descriptions of the context, as well as on development of context aware systems. Generally a context can be defined as information that can be used to characterize a situation of an entity [9], we elaborate this definition in Sect. 3. The relationships of an entity (such as an organisation, or an organisational capability) to its environment are a part of the context. Ontologies have been proposed by several authors as a mean to formally describe contextual information. For example, in [10, 11] the use of ontologies for context descriptions is central. There is also a class of systems referred to as context-aware systems that make context information an integral part of the IT systems. For example, [12] propose a system that in run-time replaces (software) services with adapted versions. Similarly, there have been proposals on how to design systems architectures for context aware systems, see for example [13, 14]. What these context aware systems have in common is that they replaces existing systems, or requires substantial modification of existing systems. In contrast to this, the approach presented in this paper provides a light-weight approach to extend existing systems with context awareness.

3 Capability and Context Analysis

This section provides a brief overview of how capability and context analysis was performed in the symbiosis case. This follows the CDD approach, as defined in [3].

For the purpose of improving the industrial symbiosis case an identification of the capabilities within the business was done. Capability identification is the process of finding the capabilities that the business relies on to function. Identification can be done in several ways. For example, an identification based on recursive capability refinement is described in our earlier paper [6]. Moreover the identification can be based on concept models, process models or goal models [15].

A small excerpt of the capability model is shown in Fig. 1. Central to the business was in this case the capability to enable web industrial symbiosis (Capability 1 in Fig. 1). This capability relies on that a relevance rating can be determined for each symbiosis (Capability 1.1), that the resources can be described properly (Capability 1.2) and that the symbiosis is compliant with regulations (Capability 1.3). One example of the need for compliance with regulations is that the transport of hazardous goods is regulated. Capability 1 is dependent on the other capabilities, this are shown by using rhombs in Fig. 1.

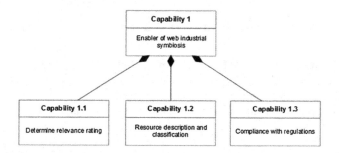

Fig. 1. Excerpt from the capability model for the symbiosis case

Given the identified capabilities their operational context could be analysed. We here start with the definition that context is any information that can be used to characterize the situation [9], in which the capability can be provided. Procedures for defining the context can be found in [15]. From an analysis perspective the identification of the context for a capability are based on questioning the assumptions under which the capability is working. More simply put, the context can be identified by asking questions such as "What external conditions affects the performance of the capability?". "External" in this case means that the organisation should not be able to control the capability context. Typical contexts that are clearly out of control for the organisation are legislation, weather and even to some extent the behaviour of customers or external (IT) systems. Moreover it is of interest to focus on external conditions that affect the capability as a whole, rather than a single instance of a capability. For example, the context in form of legislation may affect all ongoing work and future outcomes of a capability, while a change in how a single customer is sending their orders may only affect a limited part of ongoing work. Based on this discussion we specialize the definition in [9] so that the context of a capability is external information that affects the ability or capacity. This more specialized definition allows an analyst to focus on issues that may go undetected if only examining the regular flow of information that is used in a capability.

Figure 2 contains a small part of the context model for the capabilities in the symbiosis case. In the figure we apply the CDD context model syntax to describe the context. A *context element* denotes the context, while a *measurable property* denotes a specific way to measure the context. A *context set* is used to group potential ranges of context element values, these ranges are the expected values under which the capability can work. In Fig. 2, it is shown that the resource description capability is affected by the context in form of matching health (a context element), measured by the amount of relative matches in the system (a measurable property).

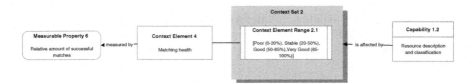

Fig. 2. Excerpt from the CDD model depicting context information

The context model shown in Fig. 2 can be extended by also introducing means to cope with changing contexts. For example, *variation aspects* could be described that each can define how to handle certain context values.

The CDD approach is supported by a set of tools, covering both design time and run-time needs:

- *Capability Design Tool* (CDT): This is the design time environment for creating capability and context models. For example, diagrams such as those shown in Figs. 1 and 2 can be drawn using the CDT.
- *Capability Navigation Application* (CNA). This is a run-time tool used to monitor the context of a capability. Essentially the current values of each context element are shown. The CNA can also signal if the capability needs to be adjusted to accommodate changes in the context.
- *Capability Context Platform* (CCP). This run-time tool work as a message broker that enable the monitoring of complex measurable properties from several context providers. The CCP continuously sends context information to the CNA.

The CDD approach also uses the concept of Capability Delivery Application (CDA) to denote the operational IT support system that a capability have. For example, the CDA can be in the form of an ERP system, or a more specialised system that are a part of a capability. In our case the symbiosis platform is the CDA.

Note that even though these tools are defined in the context of CDD, the concepts of context provider (CCP), context display/navigation (CNA) and operational IT system (CDA) are generic. Thus the approach is generic, even though it is described in terms of CDD.

4 Selecting Design Time Integration

The objective of this step is to decide how to integrate the design time tools of CDD and other tools that is currently in use. The design time tool of CDD is the CDT.

At design time, the components of the CDT environment and existing tools can be combined in several different ways. Likely, the CDT contains models, such as goal models, that may be on a higher level of abstraction compared to the tool currently in use. However, there may also be an overlap in the tools models, meaning that the concepts used during design are the same. In general, tools with this kind of overlap can be integrated in several ways. Depending on the overlap of the tools, and the desired design time functionality we have identified the following three options for performing design-time integration:

a. *Side-by-side*. Consider using the CDT as a side-by-side analysis tool that complements the existing tools. Essentially this means that the CDT and the existing tools are used in parallel, and no integration is performed. On a general level this option is useful if there is no overlap in the concepts used by the tools. This option is suitable when the CDD tools are just used for analysis purposes, and there is no need or desire to directly implement the CDD models in an IT system. The effect of choosing this option is that CDD is used as a side-by-side tool without any integration with the existing tools.
b. *CDT as a starting point* for using the existing tools. Using this option means that the models in CDT are used as input to create the initial solutions in the existing tools. A CDT model can be transformed into a model in an existing Model-driven Development (MDD) tool, or be used to generate code or configurations that can be further edited in existing tools. For example, the context models (Fig. 2) could be the base for creating an information model in a MDD tool, or an initial database schema in a DBMS. This option is useful if there is some form of overlap of the models, since some conceptual resemblance is needed to generate code or models from CDT. The effect of using this option is that initial models, code or configurations will be generated. However, the connection between CDD tools and the existing tools is one-way.
c. *Two-way integration* between CDD and existing tools. This is similar to the option of using the CDD as a starting point. However, here there is also a two-way integration, meaning that when changes are performed in the existing tool they should automatically be propagated to the CDD as well. The effect of using this option is that designers can work in an iterative fashion, performing updates in both the CDD and existing tools.

Table 1 can help in picking the desirable design time integration option. Note that the actual choice can be a combination of the above options, since each type of model in the CDT may use its own form of integration. An application of the options is described below.

4.1   Design Time Options in the Symbiosis Case

In the symbiosis case CLMS use an advanced model driven tool named zAppDev to develop the symbiosis platform. The model driven tool zAppDev contains several types of models, of which some have an overlap with the models used in CDT. For example,

Table 1. Design time integration options.

Option	When to use	Integration effort	Effect
Side-by-side	No or little conceptual overlap between CDD and existing tools	-	CDD is used side-by-side with the existing tools
CDD as starting point	Clear overlap between CDD and existing tools. CDD models commonly more abstract	A model transformation from CDD model to a models, code or configurations in the existing tool is needed	The use of the existing tools is guided by an initial input from the CDD design. The existing tool is used to refine the models
Two way integration	Clear overlap between CDD and existing tools. CDD models and existing tools on the same level of abstraction	Both existing tools and CDD tools need to be extended with synchronisation	The designer can use both CDD and existing tools, models are synchronized both ways

the zAppdev tool employs information models referred to as domain models, and also has the ability to express dynamic behaviour using IDEF0 process models. We here describe two cases of how the CDT and zAppDev tools can be integrated at design time using the *CDD as starting point for existing tools* option.

CDD Context model to zAppDev domain model. Comparing CDD and zAppDev a conceptual overlap can be found the CDD context models and zAppDevs domain models. A domain model in zAppDev depicts the information that the system is processing. By model transformations built into zAppDev the domain models becomes a relational database schema. The context models in CDD contain the concepts used for describing the context of a capability. If desired, the context model could be used as the basis for generating a domain model. By importing the CDD model into zAppDev, a solution engineer can get a draft of the context concepts needed in the domain model.

CDD variation aspect to zAppDev IDEF0 controls. A variation aspect in CDD describes a set of context elements that affect the execution of a capability. In essence, there can be variations of the execution of the capability that are affected by the variation aspect. If a capability is implemented as a process, the variation may be in the form of execution of different control flows in the process. zAppDev does not directly have the concept of variation aspect. However, the IDEF0 diagram in zAppDev has the notion of control flow. A control flow in this case works as a variable that is enabling/disabling a function in the IDEF0. Thus, the control flow could be generated from the CDD variation aspects. This would enable a change in context to enable a function as defined In the IDEF0.

5   Selecting Run-Time Integration

The purpose of this step is to decide how to integrate the run time tools of CDD and the IT system currently supporting the capability under study.

At run time the CDD tools, namely CNA and CCP, can provide a valuable addition to an existing IT system, or a system that is being designed. Using the CDD nomenclature such a system is denoted CDA - Capability Delivery Application. The CDA can be implemented using a model driven tool, or using a traditional development environment. While CDD can be used as a design-time aid, there are additional benefits using it in run time to extend the existing systems. We here distinguish between two options of run time use; as a *monitoring tool* and as an *adjustment tool*. The two options and sub-options are discussed below.

5.1   Monitoring Tool Extension

Using the CPP and CNA as monitoring tools entails making use of the CNA to monitor the context of capabilities. That is, existing system can be extended by allowing the users to monitor the context using the CNA. For this purpose two variants can be selected:

a. *Side-by-side monitoring*. In this option, the CDD is treated as an add-on to existing systems, and no run-time integration is performed. CDD is simply used to monitor how the context changes. For this option to be useful, the context must be defined so that it is not a part of the CDA. Otherwise an integration is needed to extract the context information from the CDA. Typically, side-by-side monitoring can be used for context elements that are affecting several instances of a capability, while context elements that are bound to a single instance are commonly an integral part of a CDA.

b. *Integrated monitoring*. This option can be used when the context information is held within the CDA. Typically the context information is local, that is describes the context of a single capability instance as it is executing. For this option, there is a need to implement a *data provider* in the CDA that sends information to the CCP. Since the CNA are designed for handling global context, there is also a need to perform data aggregation.

Table 2 provides an overview of the monitoring options, and the effect and integration effort they comes with.

5.2   Adjustment Tool Extension

The CDD environment has support for adjusting capabilities to match changes in the context. This is performed by the CNA, that based on current context values can propagate adjustments to the CDA. In an ideal case the adjustments can be designed and implemented, and then used at run time when the context changes. However, this fully automatic handling is not realistic in many cases. For example, some adjustments

Table 2. Summary of run time *monitoring* options

Option	When to use	Integration effort	Effect
Side-by-side monitoring	Context information is not a part of the CDA. Typically the context element is global	-	The CNA is used as a stand-alone tool for monitoring
Integrated monitoring	The CDA hold context information. Typically the context element is local	CNA and CDA need to be integrated, the CDA need to provide context data	CNA can be used to show context information from the CDA system

may need to be manually designed and applied when the context changes. An example of this kind of adjustment is changes needed to comply with new regulations - changed regulations may have a complex impact on the system, which may be impossible to foresee. For each context element there is thus a need to discern if a fully automatic adjustment can be made, or if a manual adjustment is a better option. To guide the adjustment selection, we below describe three options ranging from fully automatic to manual.

a. *Fully automatic*. This option allows the run-time discovery of context changes, and the triggering of adjustment running capabilities to cope with these changes. This requires that (1) the CNA has access to the context element, (2) that the CDA is able to receive information about needed changes and (3) that the CNA is able to notify the CDA when changes should occur. The effect of implementing this option is that the system can perform changes.

b. *Semi-automatic*. In this option, the system can detect changes in the context and suggest adaptations that are manually implemented. For example, this is a useful option if the changes needed are in the form of manual routines. This option requires that (1) the CNA has access to context elements, (2) that manual adaptations are defined. One options for defining manual adaptations is in the form of patterns. For example, in a help-desk there may be two different manual routines for answering questions under a high load compared a low load situation (in this example the current load is considered a part of the context). The effect of using this option is that the system can suggest changes.

c. *Manual*. Some context changes may be difficult to adapt to automatically, or even suggest how to address them. An example of this mentioned earlier is the adaptation to new legislation. However, in this case the context can be monitored with the help of CDD tools, and when a change occurs it can be handled manually. For example, a change in legislation may be monitored in order to start a manual analysis of the impact of the change when it occurs. This option requires no run-time integration with the CDA. The effect of using this option is that the system can discover changes.

Table 3 gives and overview of the effects, integration effort and recommendation of when to use each of the run time adaptations options.

Table 3. Summary of run time adaptation options

Option	When to use	Integration effort	Effect
Fully automatic	It is possible to implement fully automated adaptations that can be triggered at run-time based on context information	The CDA and CNA need to be integrated, the CNA need to be able to receive adaptation advice	The system (CDA + CNA) *detects* the need for, and perform changes
Semi-automatic	It is possible to design a set of adaptations, such as process variants, but these cannot be activated automatically	The adaptation need to be defined, for example as a pattern, but not implemented. CNA and CDA do not need to be integrated	The system suggests changes
Manual	The need for changes can be detected, but the change in itself is too complex to implement	The CNA only needs to monitor the context. No integration with the CDA needed	The system discovers change needs

5.3   Run Time Options in the Symbiosis Case

The i-Symbiosis platform is built using the zAppDev MDD tool and it can be integrated with the CDD runtime tools CCP and CNA. As an example, consider the context as shown in Fig. 2. The measurable property "Relative amount of successful matches" is a part of the CDA constructed by using zAppDev. By using the guidelines in Table 3, we select the monitoring option *integrated monitoring*. The reason for this selection is that the information is held within the CDA. This choice has the implication (see Table 3) that the CDA needs to relay the changes of the measurable property to the CCP, which in turn sends it to the CNA. This is done by implementing a CCP data provider. The CNA is then used to monitor the context element (this means that the CNA will display values from the context element range such as "Poor", "Stable" etc., see Fig. 2).

6   Summarize Tool Support Needed

In this step an overview of the integration need is created, to enable the planning of the integration implementation. Essentially the options selected in step 2 and 3 can be summarized in one large list. This list will include the types of integration options that are needed for a case. If there is a need to perform one single type of integration several times this may be the impetus to implement a generic and reusable solution. For example, there might be several context elements that have been selected for the option *integration monitoring at runtime*. In this case it is beneficial to implement a generic integration that allows the existing development tool to create the needed integrations for all these elements. On the other hand, if only one context element need *integration monitoring at runtime* it may be more cost-effective to perform the integration without having to change the existing development tool or implement generic integrations.

For a tool vendor the run time and design time options selected will have an impact on the type of integration that the tool need to support.

Table 4 summarizes the integration needs per option. Note that some options do not affect the existing tool at all. For a tool to have a full support of CDD most, or all, of the integration options should be supported.

Table 4. Summary of integration needs

Type	Option	Development tool support needed
Design time	Side-by-side	-
	CDD as starting point for existing tools	A model transformation from CDD model to a model in the tool is needed
	Two way integration	Both existing tools and CDD tools need to be extended with synchronisation
Run-time monitoring	Side-by-side monitoring	-
	Integrated monitoring	The existing tool needs to be able to create a CCP data provider so that the CDA can provide context data
Run-time adaptation	Fully automatic	The existing tool needs to be able to implement an interface such that the CDA can receive adaptation advice from the CDA The existing tool needs to enable the definition of adaptations, and map them into the created interface
	Semi-automatic	–
	Manual	–

7   Conclusions

In this paper we have presented an approach for the combined use of existing systems with tools for capability context design and run-time monitoring. The approach consist of four steps, the first being the analysis of capabilities and their context. Secondly the design-time options are selected such that a potential system analyst and/or developer can work with both context design and system design using existing development tools. The third step includes selecting run-time options, enabling the potential interconnection of context measurements with adaptation in existing systems. The last step involves making an overview of the potential changes that need to be made to existing development tools.

The approach has been used to analyse, and implement IT system support for the case of industrial symbiosis. The implementation shows that it is a viable approach. However possible future work entails applying the approach on more cases.

The approach has been described using the nomenclature of CDD, an approach for capability analysis and design. However, the approach is generic enough to be applied to other methods and tools as well.

Acknowledgments. This work has been performed as part of the EU-FP7 funded project no: 611351 CaaS - Capability as a Service in Digital Enterprises.

References

1. Audia, P.G., Locke, E.A., Smith, K.G.: The paradox of success: an archival and a laboratory study of strategic persistence following radical environmental change. Acad. Manag. J. **43**(5), 837–853 (2000)
2. Wiggins, R.R., Ruefli, T.W.: Schumpeter's ghost: is hypercompetition making the best of times shorter? Strateg. Manag. J. **26**(10), 887–911 (2005)
3. Bērziša, S., et al.: Capability driven development: an approach to designing digital enterprises. Bus. Inf. Syst. Eng. **57**(1), 15–25 (2015)
4. Teece, D.J.: Explicating dynamic capabilities: the nature and microfoundations of (sustainable) enterprise performance. Strateg. Manag. J. **28**(13), 1319–1350 (2007)
5. Schreyögg, G., Kliesch-Eberl, M.: How dynamic can organizational capabilities be? towards a dual-process model of capability dynamization. Strateg. Manag. J. **28**(9), 913–933 (2007)
6. Henkel, M., Bider, I., Perjons, E.: Capability-based business model transformation. In: Iliadis, L., Papazoglou, M., Pohl, K. (eds.) CAiSE Workshops 2014. LNBIP, vol. 178, pp. 88–99. Springer, Heidelberg (2014)
7. Stirna, J., Grabis, J., Henkel, M., Zdravkovic, J.: Capability driven development – an approach to support evolving organizations. In: Sandkuhl, K., Seigerroth, U., Stirna, J. (eds.) PoEM 2012. LNBIP, vol. 134, pp. 117–131. Springer, Heidelberg (2012)
8. Open Group Standard, TOGAF - Enterprise Architecture Methodology, Version 9.1 (2011). http://www.opengroup.org/togaf/. Accessed 07 Mar 2016
9. Dey, A.: Understanding and Using Context. J. Pers. Ubiquit. Comput. Springer **5**(1), 4–7 (2001)
10. Hervás, R., Bravo, J., Fontecha, J.A.: Context model based on ontological languages: a proposal for information visualization. J. Univ. Comput. Sci. **16**(12), 1539–1555 (2010)
11. Moore, P., Hu, B., Wan, J.: Smart-context: a context ontology for pervasive mobile computing. Comput. J. **53**(2), 191–207 (2010)
12. Chaari, T., Ejigu, D., Laforest, F., Scuturici, V.M.: A comprehensive approach to model and use context for adapting applications in pervasive environments. J. Syst. Softw. **80**(12), 1973–1992 (2007)
13. Baldauf, M., Dustdar, S., Rosenberg, F.: A survey on context-aware systems. Int. J. Ad Hoc Ubiquit. Comput. **2**(4), 263–277 (2007)
14. Vale, S., Hammoudi, S.: COMODE: a framework for the development of context-aware applications in the context of MDE. In: Proceedings of the 2009 4th International Conference on Internet and Web Applications and Services (ICIW 2009), pp. 261–266 (2009)
15. Sandkuhl, K., Koç, H., Stirna, J.: Context-aware business services: technological support for business and IT-alignment. In: Abramowicz, W., Kokkinaki, A. (eds.) BIS 2014 Workshops. LNBIP, vol. 183, pp. 190–201. Springer, Heidelberg (2014)

Design of Capability Delivery Adjustments

Jānis Grabis and Jānis Kampars[✉]

Institute of Information Technology,
Riga Technical University, Kalku 1, Riga, Latvia
{grabis, janis.kampars}@rtu.lv

Abstract. Capabilities are designed for ensuring that business services can be delivered to satisfy business performance objectives in different circumstances. Run-time adjustments are used to adapt capability delivery to these specific circumstances. The paper elaborates the concept of the capability delivery adjustments on the basis of capability meta-model proposed as a part of the Capability Driven Development approach. The types of adjustments are identified as their specifications are provided. An example of adjustments modeling is developed.

Keywords: Capability · Adaptation · Run-time · Context

1 Introduction

Capabilities specify an ability and capacity to deliver business services to meet specific business performance objectives in different circumstances [1]. They are delivered in ever-changing contextual situations. The purpose of capability delivery adjustments is to alter capability delivery in response to the changing context and delivery performance without the need for redesigning the capability and underlying information systems. The run-time delivery adjustments specified in this paper support this objective by: (1) enabling specification of complex contextual data processing logics; (2) providing reconfigurable data bindings; and (3) separating contextual dependencies from business logic.

The adjustments provide a uniform way of defining computations associated with the concepts defined in the capability model and primarily of those associated with context elements (represents any information that can be used to characterize the situation of an entity) and context indicators (a property of the context relevant to the capability design and used for monitoring capability delivery). These computations can be specified by a capability designer, and they are decoupled from the rest of capability delivery logics. That allows to make changes in context processing without changing the rest of the capability delivery application. Algorithms for context aware capability delivery adjustment are defined as capability adjustments and provide decision-making logics for capability delivery variations.

The reconfigurable data bindings are important to incorporate new context element in the capability design. The new context elements need to be incorporated because all context elements affecting capability delivery are not known in advance during the capability delivery. Adjustments use constants that can be changed during run-time,

© Springer International Publishing Switzerland 2016
J. Krogstie et al. (Eds.): CAiSE 2016, LNBIP 249, pp. 52–62, 2016.
DOI: 10.1007/978-3-319-39564-7_5

allowing to alter the way capability reacts to context without stopping the underlying systems and redeploying solution.

The paper elaborates technical aspects of designing adjustments. The adjustments are executed using a technical platform for capability design delivery as described in [2]. The platform consists of the (1) Capability Delivery Application (CDA), which is responsive for the execution of the business logic with no regard to contextual dependencies; (2) Capability Navigation Application, which processes the context information and provides context awareness to CDA as-a-service; (3) Capability Context Platform, which integrates the context information and notifies CNA of context information changes.

The rest of the paper is organized as follows. Section 2 introduces types of adjustments. These adjustments are further elaborated in Sect. 3. The adjustment modeling is illustrated in Sects. 4 and 5 concludes.

2   Capability Adjustment

Adjustments are developed as a technical addition to the capability meta-model to represent processing of context and indicator data as well as to adapt capability delivery.

2.1   Background

The methodological foundation of capability design and delivery is provided by the core capability meta-model (CMM) in Fig. 1 (more details in [1]). In brief, the meta-model has three main sections: (a) *Enterprise model,* representing organizational designs with Goals, KPIs, Processes (with concretizations as Process Variants) and Resources; (b) *Context,* represented with Context Set for which a Capability is designed and Context Situation at runtime that is monitored and according to which the deployed solutions should be adjusted. Context Indicators are used for high level overview of the contextual situation; and (c) *Patterns,* for delivering Capability by reusable solutions for reaching Goals under different Context Situations.

2.2   Types of Adjustments

Adjustments are used for adjusting the capability based on important factors like context or KPIs. They are also used for monitoring the capability in run-time, by interpreting raw context data (Measurable Properties) in a more comprehensible way and to calculate the KPI current and target values. Two adjustment groups can be distinguished (Fig. 2):

1. `Calculation`, used for calculating `KPI` and `ContextElement` values. Results from `Calculation` instances can be used as input data for `CapabilityAdjustment` instances.

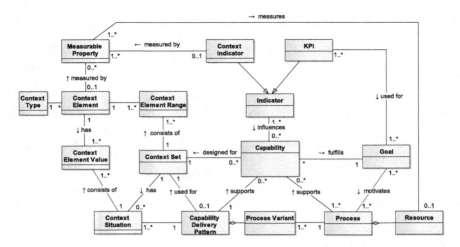

Fig. 1. A core meta-model for supporting capability driven development.

2. `CapabilityAdjustment`, that alter the capability based on context and other factors (e.g. if the average load time of a website is greater than 4 s, a new web server node is deployed in the cloud).

   `Calculation` is further divided into `ContextCalculation` and `KPICalculation`. `ContextCalculation` is used for interpreting measurable properties and calculating the value of a `ContextElement`. `KPICalculation` is responsible for calculating target and current values of KPI based on various input data. The KPI values can be visualized using a set of predefined widgets in CNA during run-time or used as an input data for other adjustments. `EventBasedAdjustment` is exposed as a REST web service from CNA and is used for enabling process-based capabilities. In cases when CDA requires to choose an exit for a business process gateway based on the current contextual situation, it can query the CNA web service for making the right decision. `ScheduledAdjustment` allows to implement schedule based, in-code adjustments. `ScheduledAdjustment` is execute periodically and can trigger a change in the CDA based on the current contextual situation by calling a web service exposed by the CDA. In most cases `CapabilityAdjustment` instances rely on results received from `Calculation` instances.

   Adjustment variables are used to implement the adjustment logic and they are accessible in the scope of the adjustment code. Optionally input parameters can be used for initializing the adjustment variable values. Adjustment variables are also initialized using Input Data Associations (IDA), which allow to bind adjustment constants or other global available data to local adjustment variables.

   There are multiple alternatives for implementing adjustments among which are Java (in-code adjustments) and MathML (implemented using a visual tool with no need to write code manually). The Adjustment engine is responsible for execution of the adjustment code.

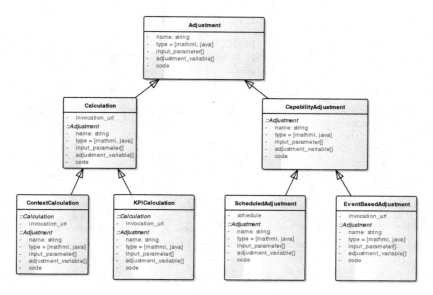

Fig. 2. Groups of adjustment

CapabilityAdjusment supports decision making for invoking an appropriate process variant for dealing with specific context situations It can use ContextElement value, KPI values and adjustment constants. Two subtypes of CapabilityAdjustment exist – EventBasedCalculation and ScheduledAdjustment. ScheduledAdjustment is executed based on a predefined schedule and it cannot be called through a web service. EventBasedAdjustment is deployed as a web service. It can be called whenever it is required to make a decision based on the current context.

3   Elaboration of Adjustments

This section briefly describes a procedure for adjustment modeling in the Capability Design Tool (an Eclipse based modeling tool which is part of the Capability Driven Development environment) consisting of three main activities (Fig. 3).

The Add ContextCalculation activity identifies all ContextElement class instances needed for adjusting the capability, creates a ContextCalculation instance for each of them and connects the ContextCalculation instance to the corresponding ContextElement instance (Fig. 4). Similarly, the Add KPICalculation specifies calculations for KPIs.

The Add EventBasedAdjustment activity specifies uses of adjustments for selecting the process execution variants. When using EventBasedAdjustment together with process gateways, their associations are used to specify what process instance specific values are passed to the EventBasedAdjustment and how the adjustment result is used to choose the desired process variant (Fig. 5).

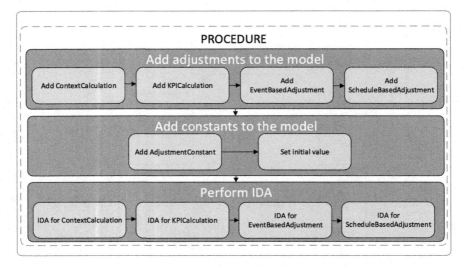

Fig. 3. Adjustment modelling procedure

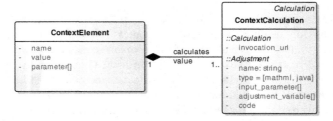

Fig. 4. Linking a `ContextElement` to a `ContextCalculation`

The IDA for ContextCalculation activity specifies data bindings for `ContextCalculation` instances. A `ContextCalculation` instance can be linked to instances of `AdjustmentConstant` and `MeasurableProperty`. The value of `AdjustmentConstant` can be changed during run-time by the designer, while the value of a `MeasurableProperty` is received from the CCP.

4   Example

An example illustrating usage of scheduled adjustments considers on-demand scaling of computational resources in the cloud. Different methods and computational platforms have been proposed to address this issue (e.g., [3, 4]). The methods differ by scaling algorithms used, performance measures used and contextual factors considered. The proposed application of capability modeling and run-time adjustments allows for

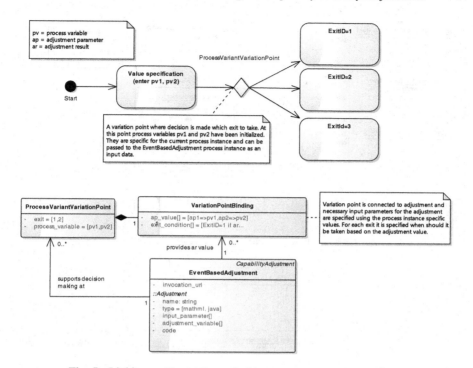

Fig. 5. Linking an `EventBasedAdjustment` to process variants

flexibility to use these different algorithms, performance measures and contextual factors within a single framework.

The adjustment model in Fig. 6 shows context elements affecting the scaling decisions and KPIs used to monitor the cloud performance. The scheduled adjustment continuously monitors the cloud platform and if necessary increases the number of computational nodes available.

Context elements `webServerLoad` (the current average load of webservers), `webServerResponseTime` (the current average response time of webservers) and `nodeCount` (the current web server node count in the cloud) are used to describe the contextual situation. A KPI of `avgResponseTime` is defined to use it as an overall quality measure of the cloud-based solution. Two `KPICalculation` instances are used to calculate the target and current values of the KPI. The scaling process is limited by adjustment constants `maxNodes` and `minNodes` which represent the maximum and minimum number of web server in the cloud. These constants can be changed during run-time for adding more resources to the web application and reaching KPI target value. In order to use the context element values, adjustments constants and KPI values in the `cloudScales` adjustment IDAs need to be established. For each `ContextCalculator` an instance a `MeasurablePropertyIDA` is created and linked to the corresponding `MeasurableProperty`. To set the server type `Mea-surablePropertyIDA` relies on the `serverType` adjustment constant.

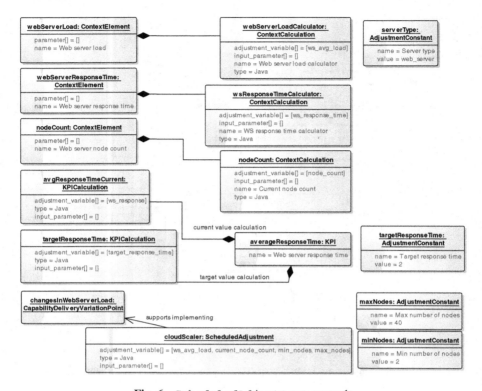

Fig. 6. ScheduledAdjustment example

Two ContextElementValueIDA instances are added to the model for using the contex element values. For using values of AdjustmenConstant instances, AdjustmentConstantIDA elements are created.

A simplified version of cloudScaler implementation is given in Fig. 7.

Based on the current load, current number of nodes and constants the cloudScaler can choose whether to scale up or down. cloudApi represents the cloud native API of the corresponding cloud computing platform.

5   Related Work

New business needs and requirements arise during service and software delivery and some of them might be introduced without interrupting the service and shutting down the software. These changes are variously described in literature as runtime adaptation, dynamic reconfiguration, autonomic computing, self-adaptation, dynamic evolution, runtime adjustment and others. The modern research on delivery and runtime modification originates from the vision of autonomic computing [5]. The vision was formulated in response to the software complexity, and it primarily focuses on technical aspects of running complex integrated software systems. The four main aspects of

```
//Implementation of execute method for cloudScaling
public String execute()
{
Integer minNodes =
Integer.parseInt(this.getVariableValue("min_nodes"));
  Integer maxNodes =
Integer.parseInt(this.getVariableValue("max_nodes"));
  Integer
currentNodes=Integer.parseInt(this.getVariableValue("current_node_co
unt"));
  String load= this.getVariableValue("ws_load");
  if ( load == "high")
  {
// CloudAPI is an external JAVA library packed inside the
resulting JAR file.
      if (currentNodes< maxNodes){
      cloudAPI.scaleUp();
      return "Scaling up, current nodes  "+ currentNodes;
```

Fig. 7. Adjustment implementation

self-management in autonomic computing are self-configuration, self-optimization, self-healing and self-protection.

There are different types of adaptive systems. The common features of the adaptive systems are monitoring of changes, goal driven adjustment of the system and a feedback loop measuring the success of the adjustment [6]. Self-adaptive systems recently have attracted the most attention in computer science. The self-adaptive systems are able to modify their behavior and/or structure in response to their perception of the environment and the system itself, and their goals [7].

Weyns et al. [8] elaborate a formal reference model of the self-adaptive systems. The model is represented using both UML diagrams and Z language what allows reasoning about behaviour of adaptive systems. Multiple case studies are provided. The literature review on self-adaptive systems [9] shows that researchers focus on software design issues of self-adaptive systems and single MAPE feedback loops.

Their self-adaptive software life-cycle model includes the offline and online activities [10]. Dynamic reconfiguration is a mechanism that allows the modification of a software system during the execution time without shutting it down or restarting it [11]. Methods used for dynamic reconfiguration make changes at the code level or at the component level. In the era of cloud computing, many aspects of dynamic reconfiguration are addressed by dynamic provisioning of cloud computing resources, where intelligent algorithms are used to make provisioning decisions during the service delivery (e.g., [12]). Mori [13] talks of software evolution as a software engineering process to design context-aware adaptive applications resilient to context and user needs variations. Oreizy et al. [14] claim that runtime adaption consists of two inter-linked cycles of evolution management and adaptation management. The evolution management deals with changing the application on the basis of interrelated models including code as a model.

The adjustment can be considered as a looser term compared to adaptation, which requires the adaptation goal and the feedback loop, and reconfiguration, which deals with structural properties of the system. Montani and Leonardi [15] use the term "run-time adjustment" in relation to agile workflow technologies. More importantly, the term is applied to modification of business processes rather than to modification of technical aspects of systems. User interface and underlying business logics also can be adapted using information provided in goal models [16]. Process adaption has been an active research area with initial emphasis on adaptive workflows, followed by QoS driven BPEL adaptation and lately on general business processes since BPMN has become executable. Change patterns are at the heart for the workflow adaptation [17]. The AGENTWORK [18] is one of the best know adaptive workflow management systems. The workflow can be automatically adapted either reactively or proactively. Alferez el al. [19] investigate dynamic adaption of service composition. They refer to dynamic adaption as opposite to static adaption, which requires shutting down the system for manual modification.

Business process variants currently is one of the most frequently used methods for supporting adjustment of business processes for specific conditions and requirements. These variants can be constructed either by configuration or adaptation [20]. That can be done in design time as well as in runtime. In the case of adaption, the variants are designed by applying business process change operations such as insertion, deletion of tasks or other process flow elements. Hallerbach et al. [21] elaborate a Provop approach to developing process variants. Their process variant life-cycle consists of four phases, namely, modelling, configuration, execution and optimization. The context-based configuration of the variants is supported. In the execution phase, switching between the process variants is possible to deal with dynamic context changes. A system is context-aware if it uses context to provide relevant information and/or services to the user, where relevancy depends on the user's task [22]. The context awareness does not necessarily involve adaption and reconfiguration. It is inherently dynamic since majority of context values are known only during the systems execution. Context awareness is also used in workflow adaptation. Smanchat et al. [23] show that majority of the surveyed context aware workflow solutions deal with workflow instance adaption.

6 Conclusion

The paper has described an approach for modeling capability delivery adjustments, which are used for context information processing and capability delivery adaptation in response to changing contextual situations during capability delivery. Capability delivery adjustment enable maintaining the desired level of delivery performance. The adjustments are specified as an extension of the capability meta-model.

The paper focused only on the adjustment modeling part. The adjustment deployment environment and adjustment execution activities are also essential for application of adjustments.

References

1. Bērziša, S., Bravos, G., González, T., Czubayko, U., España, S., Grabis, J., Henkel, M., Jokste, L., Kampars, J., Koç, H., Kuhr, J., Llorca, C., Loucopoulos, P., Pascual, R.J., Pastor, O., Sandkuhl, K., Simic, H., Stirna, J., Giromé, F.V., Zdravkovic, J.: Capability driven development: an approach to designing digital enterprises. Bus. Inf. Syst. Eng. **57**, 15–25 (2015)

2. Zdravkovic, J., Stirna, J., Henkel, M., Grabis, J.: Modeling business capabilities and context dependent delivery by cloud services. In: Salinesi, C., Norrie, M.C., Pastor, Ó. (eds.) CAiSE 2013. LNCS, vol. 7908, pp. 369–383. Springer, Heidelberg (2013)

3. Han, R., Guo, L., Ghanem, M.M., Guo, Y.: Lightweight resource scaling for cloud applications. In: 12th IEEE/ACM International Symposium on Cluster, Cloud and Grid Computing (CCGrid), pp. 644–651 (2012)

4. Lorido-Botran, T., Miguel-Alonso, J., Lozano, J.A.: A review of auto-scaling techniques for elastic applications in cloud environments. J. Grid Comput. **12**(4), 559–592 (2014)

5. Kephart, J.O., Chess, D.M.: The vision of autonomic computing. Computer **36**, 41–50 (2003)

6. Heylighen, F.: Web dictionary of cybernetics and systems; principia cybernetica web (2004). http://pespmc1.vub.ac.be. Accessed 27 Dec 2013

7. de Lemos, R., et al.: Software engineering for self-adaptive systems: a second research roadmap. In: de Lemos, R., Giese, H., Müller, H.A., Shaw, M. (eds.) Software Engineering for Self-Adaptive Systems. LNCS, vol. 7475, pp. 1–32. Springer, Heidelberg (2013)

8. Weyns, D., Malek, S., Andersson, J.: FORMS: unifying reference model for formal specification of distributed self-adaptive systems. ACM Trans. Auton. Adapt. Syst. **7**(1), 8–61 (2012)

9. Weyns, D., Ahmad, T.: Claims and evidence for architecture-based self-adaptation: a systematic literature review. In: Drira, K. (ed.) ECSA 2013. LNCS, vol. 7957, pp. 249–265. Springer, Heidelberg (2013)

10. Andersson, J., Baresi, L., Bencomo, N., de Lemos, R., Gorla, A., Inverardi, P., Vogel, T.: Software engineering processes for self-adaptive systems. In: de Lemos, R., Giese, H., Müller, H.A., Shaw, M. (eds.) Software Engineering for Self-Adaptive Systems. LNCS, vol. 7475, pp. 51–75. Springer, Heidelberg (2013)

11. Eddin, M.C.: Towards a taxonomy of dynamic reconfiguration approaches. J. Softw. **8**(9), 2202–2207 (2013)

12. Islam, S., Keung, J., Lee, K., Liu, A.: Empirical prediction models for adaptive resource provisioning in the cloud. Future Gener. Comput. Syst. **28**(1), 155–162 (2012)

13. Mori, M.: A software lifecycle process for context-aware adaptive systems. In: Proceedings of the 19th ACM SIGSOFT Symposium and the 13th European conference on Foundations of Software Engineering, pp. 412–415 (2011)

14. Oreizy, P., Medvidovic, N., Taylor, R.N.: Runtime software adaptation: framework, approaches, and styles. In: Proceedings of ICSE Companion 2008, Companion of the 30th International Conference on Software Engineering, pp. 899–910 (2008)

15. Montani, S., Leonardi, G.: Retrieval and clustering for supporting business process adjustment and analysis. Inf. Syst. **40**, 128–141 (2014)

16. Liaskos, S., Khan, S.M., Litoiu, M., Jungblut, M.D., Rogozhkin, V., Mylopoulos, J.: Behavioral adaptation of information systems through goal models. Inf. Syst. **37**, 767–783 (2012)

17. Weber, B., Reichert, M., Rinderle-Ma, S.: Change patterns and change support features - enhancing flexibility in process-aware information systems. Data Knowl. Eng. **66**, 438–466 (2008)
18. Muller, R., Greiner, U., Rahm, E.: AGENT WORK: a workflow system supporting rule-based workflow adaptation. Data Knowl. Eng. **51**, 223–256 (2004)
19. Alférez, G.H., Pelechano, V., Mazo, R., Salinesi, C., Diaz, D.: Dynamic adaptation of service compositions with variability models. J. Syst. Softw. **91**, 24–47 (2014)
20. Döhring, M., Reijers, H.A., Smirnov, S.: Configuration vs. adaptation for business process variant maintenance: an empirical study. Inf. Syst. **39**, 108–133 (2014)
21. Hallerbach, A., Bauer, T., Reichert, M.: Capturing variability in business process models: The Provop approach. J. Softw. Maint. Evol. **22**(6–7), 519–546 (2010)
22. Abowd, G.D., Dey, A.K.: Towards a better understanding of context and context-awareness. In: Gellersen, H.-W. (ed.) HUC 1999. LNCS, vol. 1707, pp. 304–307. Springer, Heidelberg (1999)
23. Smanchat, S., Ling, S., Indrawan, M.: A survey on context-aware workflow adaptations. In: Proceedings of MoMM 2008, pp. 414–417 (2008)

ASDENCA/BUMDISE 2016 – Business Modeling

The Fast Fashion Business Model

Gianni Lorenzoni[✉]

Department of Management, University of Bologna, Bologna, Italy
gianni.lorenzoni@unibo.it

Abstract. Fashion has a deep impact on the apparel industry and is used as a lever to gain a competitive advance position. The original idea of the fast fashion firm consists in offering fashionable products at cheap or very cheap prices. The fast fashion players try to capture the trends as opposed to imposing the trends, and simultaneously to reduce the risks of betting the future staying close to the "proof of the market" and be flexible to jump in as soon as signals become stronger and more reliable, therefore they are not incurring in the market risk of unmatched demand or, at least, strongly erase them.

Keywords: Fashion · Market risk · Business model · Cluster effect

1 The Apparel Industry

Fashion has a deep impact on the apparel industry and is used as a lever to gain a competitive advance position, for both larger and smaller companies. Some multi-national (MN) players emerged following an industry concentration process, grouping brands and scaling up revenues.

Fashion designers are acknowledged actors: they give a distinctive configuration to the industry by building new seasonal collections and creating new companies with their own brands. In the last few years an impressive amount of money was devoted to acquire the designers' firms and create MN holding companies spanning the global market.

An additional stone in the industry configuration is the systematic entry of new companies into the market through spin-off moves [1]. The incumbent firms influence the market demand in the higher layers and contribute to the creation of restyled or new performing products in order to attract a new flow of consumers pulled by creativity and innovation. In any case, the underlying magnitude of the innovation span is quite often classified as "architectural innovation" following the definition of Henderson and Clark [2] claiming that architectural innovation consists of resisting, reusing, recombining old and new components.

They systematically introduce new seasonal products in advance, to be bought in the following season. In this activity they disclose trends and collections several months before the sell out of the product to the final consumer. The practice represents, among others, a generic opportunity recognition for the fast fashion industry that conveys to the trends suggested by the big players but reverses the activity based system of the former through a new business model (BM) design and practices.

© Springer International Publishing Switzerland 2016
J. Krogstie et al. (Eds.): CAiSE 2016, LNBIP 249, pp. 65–71, 2016.
DOI: 10.1007/978-3-319-39564-7_6

The original idea of the fast fashion firm consists in offering fashionable products at cheap or very cheap prices. At first glance, this looks counterintuitive since fashion players try to charge premium prices. The basic idea of the fast fashion players is to capture the trends as opposed to imposing the trends, and simultaneously to reduce the risks of betting the future staying close to the "proof of the market" and be flexible to jump in as soon as signals become stronger and more reliable thus, not incurring on the market risk of unmatched demand or, at least, strongly erase them. Moreover, starting later inventory investments can drop substantially.

The clusters creation in fashion industry and the role of ties across individual firms has attracted the attention of various scholars [3]. The interplay of different actors contribute to sustain and give feasibility to a "creative field" [4] where Marshallian externalities and 3T factors [5] serve as a glue, with both weak and strong ties working out [6].

In the creation of a cluster an anchor firm plays a distinctive role in the genealogy of an emergent field [7], where mimicking and externalities offered by specialized actors act as generative rules over the years [8].

2 Research Design and Setting

We focused on the cluster of firms collocated in the CenterGross (CG) – a concentration of some 100 firms – in order to explore and try to get a better understanding of the fast fashion phenomenon. The cluster is significant for a collective movement of small and medium sized firms born in the last 30 years and scaling up in the fast fashion industry domain. At the same time, the CG cluster is at odds compared to the fast fashion big players such as Zara and H&M, working in the same segment of cheap prices, but faraway in terms of size and considering the number of shopping retail facilities owned or managed under their brand weapons.

The CG cluster firms had some previous experiences in the garment trade and transactions and recognized an opportunity within the industry where the fashion trends generated a fast rotation of add and drop products.

The study has been structured using an inductive multiple case research [9], with a recurrent liaison between literature suggestions, data collection and emerging field evidences. Cases are used as experiment, to confirm, reject or enrich inferences from other cases [10]. First, we focused on a single in depth historical case study following the perspective used by Burgelman [11] and Tripsas and Gavetti [12], centered on the recognized "anchor" (20 interviews) player that pioneered the cluster formation experimenting a new fast fashion business model.

The genealogy of the cluster formation suggested to start analyzing the first mover in 1985, that is the actor transforming an idea into a growing business model. The anchor played a role model for followers and laggards, influencing the spin off dynamic of the cluster emergence and amplification. Afterwards, we interviewed 12 additional firms in the same cluster and 6 complementary subcontractors, playing a crucial role in the fast garment manufacturing. The addition of competing firms in the same cluster overcome the limits of the single case study and offer more general evidences to the innovative shape of the fast fashion emerging process.

3 The Creative Machine

The value activity of the fashion players starts with a collection made mainly by external designers and generating a "first collection" that is evaluated and receives a "green light" by an internal jury. The jury is made by the owner, the front office connected with clients, and the sales employee, in different combination and articulation following the organization design. The outcome is a set of samples that are progressively transformed into products subcontracted in small batches in order to have a selection to show to the trader and test the market, thus gaining the reaction of the outlets' owners. Some outlets represent a sort of "second level jury", as they are closer to the consumers and able to quickly sense tendencies, putting the products on display, placing reorders, and therefore signaling a market tendency.

The fast fashion firm tries to grasp information and quickly respond involving the subcontractors and following their orders as quickly as possible. In the cluster jargon, fast fashion firms are supposed to fill "the holes" created by the demand selection and only partially to anticipate the demand that has some bizarre and unexpected feedbacks.

The third-party manufacturers receive orders and reorders when a central intelligence machine captures the trends responding to strong reordering information but often going beyond and using other weak signals to gain and exploit different sources of intelligence. Following this mechanism it is supposed that a signed order can be developed and delivered to the shop within a short span of time, sometime one week.

The key capability is the processing of the amount of information and the quick transformation of the intelligence into product, generating an innovative routine that needs to be replicated hundreds of times [13].

Therefore, the set of sample collection and the manufacturing plan are only partially pre-determined and are influenced by a discovery-driven process [14] that influences the operations through a rolling mechanism. The underlying business model [15, 16] can be classified as a light business model considering the limited investment in tangible assets, and the role played by external agents deliverable in both tangible and intangible assets.

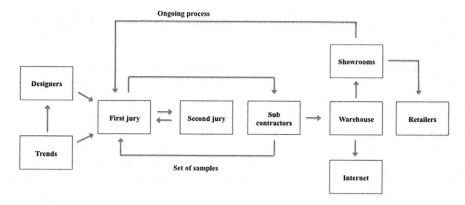

Fig. 1. The creative machine

Information generated in due time reduces the risk of demand, and the division of labor in operation schedules reduces the inventory and increases the flexibility and the product rotation at the focal firm's level. These conditions are rents generative (Fig. 1).

4 The Shop Connection

The companies operating in the wide fashion domain are often MN players, with strong brands and a huge number of labeled shop, and/or large selling space worldwide. This structural condition can afforded to pursue pushing demand initiatives through appropriate marketing clouts.

The companies in our setting can not afford the investments in shop openings at large scale, but try to supplement the lack of the underlying ties in several ways. First, some of them have "negozi civetta" in strategic locations and are able not only to sell, but also sniff or taste the market. Second, the smart guys of the creative machine progressively build a system of preferred clients that is not only a brand supporter, but contributes to sensing the market, send suggestion, are is ready to capture the holes in the collections and appropriate lateral tendencies.

The "product guys" are not only requested to push sales but to maintain the connection with clients' antennae, teaching and learning at the same time through a routinized track system. They are following simple rules in default of a specific shop chain but try to reach the same outcomes. At the micro-organizational level, due attention is given to the enrollment of these profiles, conducive to the creation of a positive atmosphere in the sale processes.

The fashion world has communities of "fans" eager to work in the sector and showing a special attitude to be involved in the fashion commons. One of our interviewee claims it clearly: "We are selecting fans, they can interpret the fashion world and be more easily connected with the various players involved, they speak the same jargon".

5 The Relay

The attention to fashion impacts on the product creation, however, fast fashion requires a matching between the design, the product selection, and the delivery in a short span of time.

The overwhelming majority of the firms in our sample have a tight, systematic connection with a cluster of subcontractors and, moreover, a consolidated routine energizing and committing to a quick response to impossible time reaction.

Several "laboratories" pre-existed the birth of new fast fashion firms, working for conventional garment companies but had to adapt to the new schedules of the fast program. Subcontractors are all located in the surrounding region and overtime learned the reciprocal jargon of velocity, that has a crucial cultural and linguistic backstage. Quick reactions need actors that squeeze the timing of transactions and use practices and routines accordingly.

It is an arm's length negotiation tempered by the main contractor's agenda of timing and deliverables' quality, complemented by the request of significant scale growth. Such an agenda implies investments and scalability and, also, the adaptability to tackle with some deviation from the product design following specific requests overtime. From the field analysis emerges a specific identity of the new subcontractors working in the fast fashion design.

The "creative machine" has a parallel problem with the fabrics' supply, that can not be fully ordered and stocked in advance, anticipating the demand incurring in risks of forecast and in inventory costs. How to solve the dilemma?

6 The Fast Fashion Business Model

The fast fashion business model relies on the exploitation of some central core capabilities and the leverage of a substantial amount of external contributions, yielding to a light business model format.

This generic configuration puts in due evidence the restriction of the activity boundaries to some central components, defining its own domain of action and the relationships within the economic environment [17]. Zott and Amit [16], in particular, define the BM as the relationship of an individual firm versus its external agents and their mutual relationships. For a research domain of new established firms entering in a new field, claiming a sharp business model is important for their identity, but organizational evolution matters as well. In fact, new innovative routines take place and they are supposed to evolve following daily practices' improvements, single routines and practices linked together over time [13] and, as we perceived, with significant experiments at the micro-organizational level [18].

Fast fashion needs to catch weak signals in the market tendencies at different stages of the process of the collection creation and transform information into products in order to quickly respond to market demands. The time brackets of the response in normally very tight and requires consistent organizational mechanisms.

The strategic side of the business model is focused on sucking and collecting information and feed-backs on fashion tendencies, arising from different sources, translating the funnel into a collection of products to be offered and sold. This activity is developed trying to involve limited resources to incur in variable costs as much as they can, using external capabilities to be orchestrated and limiting the fixed costs, with their impact on flexibility.

The same orientation is followed setting up a cluster of subcontracting firms charged of the total manufacturing activity, consistent with the search of an high flexibility of the product flow and aligned with demand waves requests. The same effect on the variability of the cost structure is achieved. The manufacturing is on demand, reducing the inventory and increasing the goods' rotation. The warehouse exists but serves as a showroom not as a deposit to buffer ongoing demand. The focal firms activities are concentrated on the sense making and enactment of external trends and the consequential organizational efficient delivery of the products to the final users. Therefore, the organizational side of the business model requires the orchestration of third parties outside the boundaries of the focal firms. The peculiarity of the BM is to serve the client with products made to order, as much as it can, manufacturing what is already sold in contrast to a more conventional practice to use the warehouse as a buffer.

Ultimately, the fast fashion business model is lean, discovery-driven, achieved with limited resources and focused capabilities centered on the creative machine and the simultaneous orchestration of third parties to finalize the operations. A business conceived, by necessity, to "do more with less".

In this routinized innovation, strategizing and organizing must move forward simultaneously considering the labor division of disintegrated activities that must be recombined.

7   Conclusion

The fast fashion firms investigated are operating in a setting of distributed knowledge resources and the first strategic decision influencing the business model configuration is the choice of a central position in a network value system [19].

The creative machine is a system of filtering various information sources enacted in a wide environment. The task requires a distinctive capability to deal with designers and trend-setters, and to be able to develop an absorptive capacity spread across the firms and impacting on the activity-based system [20].

At a different level in the value system, an important position is occupied by the capability to select the fabrics and create tight relationships with the fabric manufacturers considering that a consistent impact on innovation is reached through new fabric design, new materials, or both. An additional relational capability stands in the actions orchestrating the network of subcontracting firms, going beyond a conventional arm's length contract.

Why stress in the conclusion the relational architecture after mentioning the key resources and activities? The reason is to emphasize, contrary to most of the literature on the business model, that a lean business model strongly relying on the wide use of several partners is key since the outset of the model's journey. There is no value proposition or product offering without a robust interconnected system of partners at different stages of the decision process. Relational capabilities are a key competence in the fast fashion business model [21].

The creative machine metaphor used to stylize a creative collective weapon in action, is a central activity in the BM deployment that is strongly intertwined with an outside world to be enacted. Therefore, the partners' architectural organization in our setting has an important impact on the quality of the collection. At the same time, these partners' investments and discipline deeply impact the cost structure of the business model. To what extent can this model of routinized innovation and fast product made to order can work as much as the firms grow up and expand globally is a question left to future researches.

The feasibility and the effectiveness of the model are tested for smaller and medium sized organizations. However, we must remind that, especially in this sector, "dwarf starts small" [22] and the new entrants fashion design firms are the variance that keep the sector alive, breeding innovation and eventually being absorbed by incumbent firms.

References

1. Klepper, S.: Employee startups in high-tech industries. Ind. Corp. Change **10**(3), 639–674 (2001)
2. Henderson, R.M., Clark, K.B.: Architectural innovation: the reconfiguration of existing product technologies and the failure of established firms. Adm. Sci. Q. **35**, 9–30 (1990)
3. Uzzi, B.: The sources and consequences of embeddedness for the economic performance of organizations: the network effect. Am. Sociol. Rev. **61**, 674–698 (1996)
4. Scott, A.J.: Entrepreneurship, innovation and industrial development: geography and the creative field revisited. Small Bus. Econ. **26**(1), 1–24 (2006)
5. Florida, R.: The Rise of the Creative Class. Basic books, New York (2004)
6. Granovetter, M.S.: The strength of weak ties. Am. J. Sociol. **78**, 1360–1380 (1973)
7. Lazerson, M., Lorenzoni, G.: Anchoring new clusters: fleshing out the entrepreneurial role. In: Boari, C., Elfring, T., Molina-Morales, X.F. (eds.) Entrepreneurship and Cluster Dynamics. Routledge, London (2016)
8. Kogut, B.: The network as knowledge: generative rules and the emergence of structure. Strateg. Manag. J. **21**(3), 405–425 (2000)
9. Eisenhardt, K.M.: Building theories from case study research. Acad. Manag. Rev. **14**(4), 532–550 (1989)
10. Yin, R.K.: Case Study Research. Design and Methods. Sage, Thousand Oaks (1994)
11. Burgelman, R.A.: A process model of internal corporate venturing in the diversified major firm. Adm. Sci. Q. **28**, 223–244 (1983)
12. Tripsas, M., Gavetti, G.: Capabilities, cognition, and inertia: evidence from digital imaging. Strateg. Manag. J. **21**(10–11), 1147–1161 (2000)
13. Feldman, M.S.: Organizational routines as a source of continuous change. Organ. Sci. **11**(6), 611–629 (2000)
14. McGrath, R.G., MacMillan, I.C.: Discovery Driven Planning. Wharton School, Snider Entrepreneurial Center, Philadelphia (1995)
15. Baden-Fuller, C., Mangematin, V.: Business models: a challenging agenda. Strateg. Organ. **11**(4), 418–427 (2013)
16. Zott, C., Amit, R.: Business model design and the performance of entrepreneurial firms. Organ. Sci. **18**(2), 181–199 (2007)
17. Aldrich, H.E., Ruef, M.: Organizations Evolving. Sage, London (2006)
18. Pentland, B.T., Feldman, M.S., Becker, M.C., Liu, P.: Dynamics of organizational routines: a generative model. J. Manage. Stud. **49**(8), 1484–1508 (2012)
19. Lorenzoni, G., Baden-Fuller, C.: Creating a strategic center to manage a web of partners. Calif. Manag. Rev. **37**(3), 146–163 (1995)
20. Cohen, W.M., Levinthal, D.A.: Absorptive capacity: a new perspective on learning and innovation. Adm. Sci. Q. **35**, 128–152 (1990)
21. Lorenzoni, G., Lipparini, A.: The leveraging of interfirm relationships as a distinctive organizational capability: a longitudinal study. Strateg. Manag. J. **20**(4), 317–338 (1999)
22. Aldrich, H., Auster, E.R.: Even dwarfs started small: liabilities of age and size and their strategic implications. Res. Organ. Behav. **8**(1986), 165–186 (1986)

Cycles of Organizational Renewal: The Interplay of Strategy and Innovation at Bang & Olufsen

Giacomo Cattaneo[✉] and Fredrik Hacklin

Department of Management, Technology and Economics, ETH Zurich,
Chair of Entrepreneurship, Weinbergstrasse 56/58, 8092 Zurich, Switzerland
{gcattaneo,fhacklin}@ethz.ch

Abstract. Bang & Olufsen, a Danish high-end producer of consumer electronics, has experienced both failure and success in the process of strategic renewal, challenged by blurring industry boundaries and the rise of the digital technology paradigm. A study of the last decade shows how the company tried to renew itself by improving its new product development process from three angles: strategy, innovation and organizational design. Using ethnographic and grounded theory methods with a micro-foundational perspective we illustrate how the dynamics in the process of renewal can be accrued into a longitudinal perspective where the key drivers of change cycle between strategy and innovation.

Keywords: Innovation · Strategy · Renewal · Ethnography

1 Introduction

The concept of renewal is less about acknowledging new conditions than it is in linking environmental change to corporate strategy, and modifying such link over time [1]. By overcoming the inertial forces embodied in an established strategy, norms, and practice, a company needs to aim at closing the gap between the current core capabilities - the service of managers to successfully link core organizational resources - and the evolving basis of competitive advantage in the industry [2–4].

Studies in strategic renewal adopt a variety of theoretical perspectives, among others organizational learning [5], the resource-based view [6] or dynamic capabilities [7, 8] and share an understanding of renewal as a replacement of organizational attributes [9]. As [9] point out, the majority of such studies conceptualize renewal in terms of organizational *process*, rather than as content or outcome. Notably, [10], explicitly drawing on the work of [2, 4], put forward a definition of strategic renewal as "an evolutionary process associated with promoting, accommodating, and utilizing new knowledge and innovative behavior in order to bring about change in an organization's core competencies and/or a change in its product market domain" (p. 155). Environmental changes keep on rendering today's incumbents' existing capabilities obsolete, prompting them to be continuously renewed. Shorter product cycles and blurred industry boundaries are often recognized as the principal triggers [10, 11], together

© Springer International Publishing Switzerland 2016
J. Krogstie et al. (Eds.): CAiSE 2016, LNBIP 249, pp. 72–77, 2016.
DOI: 10.1007/978-3-319-39564-7_7

with non-technological market pressures, e.g. changes in competition [e.g. 12, 13], maturing or slowing customer demand [14–16] or deregulation [12]. Yet, several studies point to the challenges in accomplishing such renewal, among which the cases of Intel [3, 17], Polaroid [18], Hewlett-Packard [19], or Smith Corona [7]. Scholars have identified organizational dynamics hampering the process as with the success trap [20, 21], the myopia of learning [22], organizational inertia [18] or core rigidities [23]. Despite appearing in the literature since decades, strategic renewal it is oftentimes not necessarily recognized as a distinct phenomenon beyond organizational change [9] and is still poorly understood [24]. An attempt to give substance to the process is provided by a subset of studies that consider product innovation as a way to achieve renewal by creating and exploiting knowledge that links market and technology opportunities [25, 26]. Nevertheless, few studies build on the direct relationship between strategic renewal and innovation or provide clear explanations for it, rather rely on vaguely described capabilities [6]. A rising body of research is calling for organizational analysis to be fundamentally concerned with how individual-level factors aggregate to such collective level [27]. Unveiling such capabilities would help clarify the relationship between strategy and innovation in situations of renewal, which is so far only hinted at but rarely explored. We refer to [8] as a good example of a study focusing on the myriads of micro-activities in new product development that are central in shaping the development of capabilities and their dynamic adaptation.

Following the tradition of single company studies, we present the case of Bang & Olufsen (B&O), a Danish high-end consumer electronics producer that during the last decade has been facing remarkable challenges in the industry development. First, the blurring of industry boundaries has redefined the competitive landscape and brought along consumer electronics companies such as Apple or Google. Second, the rise of the digital technology paradigm has seriously impacted the value of B&O's expertise in analog audio technologies, upon which the company's success traditionally has been based. Third, a shift in the way people consume music has changed the whole concept behind a music system, as well as the inherent business model to reach a new generation of customers with valuable propositions. With the case of B&O we build on the relationship between strategy and innovation in situations of renewal. We illustrate how the interdependence between strategy, organizational design, and innovation is to be considered first at the individual level, in which day-to-day activities span the three domains contemporaneously, and from an organizational perspective, where the accrual of micro-activities follows cycles between the domains of strategy and innovation as drivers for the renewal process and adapts the organizational design.

2 Methods

Through an ongoing research collaboration with B&O, we had close access to senior managers throughout the organization, who consistently reported about the firm's challenging situation of continuously catching up with a converging industry. Early interviews made it clear that the causes for B&O's situation were rooted beyond the mere lack of systematic scouting activities, but rather seemed to reside in the complex interplay between strategy, innovation and organizational design. We opened up the topic of our research to a wider range of explanations and designed an exploratory study combining ethnographic and grounded theory methods as described by [28]. We set to uncover patterns and processes to make sense of the case [29] and to generate theories that could still speak to the everyday's reality of our informants. The principal researcher had extended stays at the company's headquarters in Struer, with a total of 40 full days on-site. In between periods of data collection, rounds of analysis have been undertaken. Data collection was carried out through internal referrals aiming at covering all the functions of the company potentially relevant for the study. Informants range from operative to top management, which exposes us to a variety of interpretations of the events under examination. The principal mean of collection was semi-structured interviews, guided by a list of topics flexible enough to provide the freedom of engaging in narratives of detail-rich stories. Currently, 56 interviews with 36 informants have been carried out, spanning from 45 min to five hours. Additional data was collected through participant observation of eight meetings in which people of different departments would confer about current projects and issues, as well as field notes for the 40 days. Additionally, we collected secondary data in the form of internal news, e-mail exchanges, PowerPoint presentations and employee manuals.

Following guidelines by [28] we relied on grounded theory methods to identify themes as they emerged during data collection and to guide data analysis. The first round of open coding of detailed interview reports allowed us to classify information into practices that span the relevant content the interviewees have considered necessary to share to make sense of the dynamics across the strategic renewal and innovation processes. Through the aggregation of such practices into periods of time, we were able to identify two distinct phases in the process of renewal, as presented below.

3 Preliminary Findings

The first cycle of analysis provided us with insights on the interplay between strategy, innovation and organizational design at the individual level, underlying forces driving and hampering change. Due to space constraints, we focus here on the dynamism at the organizational level emerged by studying the company longitudinally and by accruing the micro-activities emerged in the first part of the study. We find a fluctuation between the domain of strategy and innovation as key drivers for the renewal of the company capabilities, and organizational design adapted consequently at each turn. We propose two types of organizational renewal. The *strategy-driven renewal* begins with a new strategy rollout after a check with the external context. Such strategy leads to an organizational design adaptation, often in the form of merges or creation of new organizational units. The innovation efforts of the company are aimed at supporting such a strategy, leading to a new generation of products. The *innovation-driven renewal* begins with an assessment of the recent innovation efforts, both in terms of market success as well as process-wise within the company boundaries. This leads to the consequent adaptation of the organizational design and the processes, which inform and trigger a revision of the overall strategy. Figure 1 illustrates such a model, while Table 1 provides a sequence of events relative to the case of B&O.

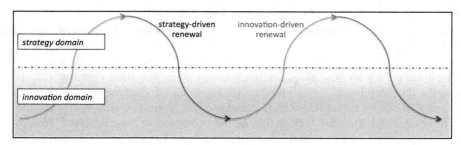

Fig. 1. Cycles of renewal

Table 1. Strategy vs. innovation-driven renewal at B&O

Strategy-driven renewal step	Example #1: 2008–2010	Example #2: 2011–2013
External context check, new strategy roll-out	Regain technology excellence	Re-establish the brand, become a business-driven company
Organizational design adaptation	New CEO, merge of two innovation subunits	New CEO, flatten hierarchical structure
New innovation guidelines and new generation of products	Platform-driven development and first product linking old and new technology paradigm	New innovation process framework, products championing selected core competences, exploration of new opportunities
Innovation-driven renewal step	Example #1: 2010–2011	Example #2: 2013–2014
External context check, assessment of innovation efforts	Products do not meet expectations, NPD undermined by current organizational design	Innovation process more collaborative but inefficient for radical products, products still fail to bring expected growth
Organizational design adaptation	Innovation unit moved under R&D, Innovation unit's head is replaced	Innovation process design adapted to solve inefficiencies, new COO position
Strategy revision	Platform development was good, Innovation process bad, need to expand the strategy beyond technology	Product development deserves more focus, sales need to be boosted, lack of resources hinders exploration

We encountered actions related to both concepts—both in the *strategy-driven* and in the *innovation-driven* renewal phases—yet at different levels of intensity. This suggests a claim of organizational renewal being neither a top-down (as in [30]) or a bottom-up approach [3, 17], rather a combination of both: the groups of people primarily driving the renewal efforts are indeed different (in terms of managerial level and area of expertise), but their influence is not limited to either one phase. The *strategy-driven process* includes elements of what [10] call "competence deployment" in which change in organizational structure, systems and people is driven by an accepted definition of strategic ends and means, as well as "competence definition" characterized by experimentation with new skills and exploration of new market opportunities. [10] describe the "definition" of sub-process as the result of challenging and contesting activities, while we rather found such attitudes in the *innovation-driven process*, albeit more represented by what they define as the "competence modification." Here, the newly established processes and behaviors are assessed towards the external context, and can either trigger their alteration or strengthening [4]. This could be specific for the case of B&O, where revolutionary efforts to change the strategic direction of the company as in [3] are not the case, but it also shows that the definition of new competences, when aligned with the renewed strategy, can be carried out through supportive and empowering actions. This prompts us to propose the following:

Proposition 1. The process of organizational renewal follows cycles between the domains of strategy and innovation. The assessment against the external context triggers and informs subsequent organizational design changes.

4 Conclusion

Research on strategic renewal points to the importance of innovation in driving such process, but has so far only partially provided clear explanations of how two such processes are linked, relying mostly on collective capabilities. We provide explanations for how the two processes are inextricably linked and a bridge for the two bodies of literature. We introduce a model of cycles between strategy and innovation as key drivers for the renewal of the organization, which are the result of the accrual of day-to-day actions. From a managerial perspective, we show how strategic renewal from three different angles hits the process at the heart of the company, the product development process, and the challenges in harmoniously orchestrating it.

References

1. Barr, P.S., Stimpert, J.L., Huff, A.S.: Cognitive change, strategic action, and organizational renewal. Strateg. Manag. J. **13**, 15–36 (1992)
2. Burgelman, R.A.: Intraorganizational ecology of strategy making and organizational adaptation: theory and field research. Organ. Sci. **2**(3), 239–262 (1991)
3. Burgelman, R.A.: Fading memories - a process theory of strategic business exit in dynamic environments. Adm. Sci. Q. **39**(1), 24–56 (1994)
4. Huff, J.O., Huff, A.S., Thomas, H.: Strategic renewal and the interaction of cumulative stress and inertia. Strateg. Manag. J. **13**, 55–75 (1992)
5. Crossan, M.M., Berdrow, I.: Organizational learning and strategic renewal. Strateg. Manag. J. **24**(11), 1087–1105 (2003)

6. Danneels, E.: The dynamics of product innovation and firm competences. Strateg. Manag. J. **23**(12), 1095–1121 (2002)
7. Danneels, E.: Trying to become a different type of company: dynamic capability at smith corona. Strateg. Manag. J. **32**(1), 1–31 (2011)
8. Salvato, C.: Capabilities unveiled: the role of ordinary activities in the evolution of product development processes. Organ. Sci. **20**(2), 384–409 (2009)
9. Agarwal, R., Helfat, C.E.: Strategic renewal of organizations. Organ. Sci. **20**(2), 281–293 (2009)
10. Floyd, S.W., Lane, P.J.: Strategizing throughout the organization: managing role conflict in strategic renewal. Acad. Manag. Rev. **25**(1), 154–177 (2000)
11. Hacklin, F., Battistini, B., von Krogh, G.: Strategic choices in converging industries. MIT Sloan Manag. Rev. **55**(1), 65–73 (2013)
12. Capron, L., Mitchell, W.: Selection capability: how capability gaps and internal social frictions affect internal and external strategic renewal. Organ. Sci. **20**(2), 294–312 (2009)
13. Knott, A.M., Posen, H.E.: Firm R&D behavior and evolving technology in established industries. Organ. Sci. **20**(2), 352–367 (2009)
14. Kim, H.E., Pennings, J.M.: Innovation and strategic renewal in mature markets: a study of the tennis racket industry. Organ. Sci. **20**(2), 368–383 (2009)
15. Gulati, R., Puranam, P.: Renewal through reorganization: the value of inconsistencies between formal and informal organization. Organ. Sci. **20**(2), 422–440 (2009)
16. Tripsas, M.: Technology, identity, and inertia through the lens of "the digital photography company". Organ. Sci. **20**(2), 441–460 (2009)
17. Burgelman, R.A.: A process model of internal corporate venturing in the diversified major firm. Adm. Sci. Q. **28**(2), 223–244 (1983)
18. Tripsas, M., Gavetti, G.: Capabilities, cognition, and inertia: evidence from digital imaging. Strateg. Manag. J. **21**(10–11), 1147–1161 (2000)
19. House, C.H., Price, R.L.: The HP Phenomenon: Innovation and Business Transformation. Stanford Business Books, Stanford (2009). xv, 638 p.
20. March, J.G.: Exploration and exploitation in organizational learning. Organ. Sci. **2**(1), 71–87 (1991)
21. Walrave, B., van Oorschot, K.E., Romme, A.G.L.: Getting trapped in the suppression of exploration: a simulation model. J. Manag. Stud. **48**(8), 1727–1751 (2011)
22. Levinthal, D.A., March, J.G.: The myopia of learning. Strateg. Manag. J. **14**, 95–112 (1993)
23. Leonardbarton, D.: Core capabilities and core rigidities - a paradox in managing new product development. Strateg. Manag. J. **13**, 111–125 (1992)
24. Corbett, A., et al.: Corporate entrepreneurship: state-of-the-art research and a future research agenda. J. Prod. Innov. Manag. **30**(5), 812–820 (2013)
25. Dougherty, D.: A practice-centered model of organizational renewal through product innovation. Strateg. Manag. J. **13**, 77–92 (1992)
26. Bowen, H.K., et al.: Regaining the lead in manufacturing - development-projects - the engine of renewal. Harvard Bus. Rev. **72**(5), 108–109 (1994)
27. Barney, J., Felin, T.: What are microfoundations? Acad. Manag. Perspect. **27**(2), 138–155 (2013)
28. Charmaz, K.: Constructing Grounded Theory. Sage Publications, London (2006). xiii, 208 p.
29. Langley, A.: Strategies for theorizing from process data. Acad. Manag. Rev. **24**(4), 691–710 (1999)
30. Hornsby, J.S., et al.: Managers' corporate entrepreneurial actions: examining perception and position. J. Bus. Ventur. **24**(3), 236–247 (2009)

Information Systems for Innovation: A Comparative Analysis of Maturity Models' Characteristics

Abdelkader Achi[1]([⊠]), Camille Salinesi[1], and Gianluigi Viscusi[2]

[1] Centre de Recherche en Informatique, Université Paris 1 Panthéon-Sorbonne,
Paris, France
abdelkader.achi@malix.univ-paris1.fr,
camille.salinesi@univ-paris1.fr
[2] College of Management of Technology (CDM), École Polytechnique Fédérale
de Lausanne (EPFL), Lausanne, Switzerland
gianluigi.viscusi@epfl.ch

Abstract. Nowadays, virtually all industries are impacted by the digitalization of business enabled by information and communication technologies. Consequently, it is a major challenge to any business to increase its ability to innovate through information systems. However the effort and the investments of companies are extremely varied, they do not have the same level of maturity with respect to their innovation strategy. While some highly mature use effective approaches, others still act as novices or use inadequate practices. The question raised in this paper is how to evaluate the level of maturity of an organization with respect to information systems based innovation. Also, the question concerns the identification of the salient features of ICT centred innovation maturity models. Taking these issues into account, the paper makes the following contributions: (i) a review of sixteen innovation maturity models collected from the research and the practitioners community, gathering facts about the models and about their effectiveness; (ii) a comparative analysis of these models.

Keywords: Innovation capacity · Innovation engineering · Capability Maturity · Maturity model · Innovation maturity models · Assessment maturity model

1 Introduction

There have never been as many disruptions as those observed the past 20 years with the increased diffusion and adoption of information and communication technologies (ICTs). New ICT based innovations emerge every day both in the public and the private sector, as well as in everyday life. All businesses are actually impacted by ICTs, and not just because of the new technologies themselves: indeed, ICTs are at the origin of new customer behaviours, new business models, and new markets. Even more: there are now new ways to achieve innovations that were not imagined before the invention of the Internet, open source development and open data, peer to peer, wikis, social networks, copyleft and the like. Thus, both the internal and external environments of

© Springer International Publishing Switzerland 2016
J. Krogstie et al. (Eds.): CAiSE 2016, LNBIP 249, pp. 78–90, 2016.
DOI: 10.1007/978-3-319-39564-7_8

organizations are impacted by information technologies [26, 38]. While each company defines its own strategy to cope with these changes, many companies have difficulty to define and implement a proper innovation strategy, use inadequate approaches, and are not mature in terms of innovation practices. In most cases, the competition requires the use of ICTs to enter on dominant markets. In order to cope with these problems, companies are increasingly trying to take a systematic and proactive approach to realizing innovation [44]. Many companies are turning to assess their innovation process and determine key improvement actions [8]; others start concrete actions through open innovation [6, 7, 46] or creativity techniques [2] to improve their innovation capacity.

Some works have already demonstrated the benefits of using maturity models [2]. However, there are still many open questions about innovation-specific features of maturity models. Taking these issues into account, the research presented in this article is part of an effort to identify effective innovation maturity models driven by ICTs, and support their use in organizations. We believe that understanding existing innovation maturity models is a key step towards this goal. Therefore, the core research question of the paper is *"what are the salient features of ICT centred innovation maturity models?"* Starting from a collection of innovation maturity models selected from scientific as well as practitioners oriented literature, we provide a classification of their main characteristics that we use as the key building block of a structured analysis framework. A comparative analysis is then presented, considering (a) general purpose maturity models, and (b) innovation maturity models proposed at industry level.

The article is structured as follows. Section 2 introduces maturity innovation by defining the main concepts of maturity models of innovation. Section 3 describes the innovation maturity models selected for the review for the comparative study, and proposes a systematic description of their salient features. Section 4 reports measures and validation instruments for the considered maturity models. Section 5 discusses the findings and its practical implications. Research perspectives for future work conclude the paper.

2 Related Work

As shown by [49], although innovation and especially the ability of organisations to innovate has raised the attention of many researchers, there is no consensus on its definition. While Link and Siegel [28] consider innovation as the implementation of a new idea leading to a change that creates value. Wang and Ahmed [47] have a more organisation centric view. They call *"innovativeness"* the ability of organizations to innovate, more precisely, innovativeness is *"the overall internal receptivity to new ideas and innovation that is demonstrated through individuals, teams and management, and that enables the formation of an innovative culture"* [47]. Carlson and Wilmot [5] have a slightly different definition. For them, innovativeness is founded on the concept of innovation, the process of creating and delivering new customer value in the marketplace [5]. For [43], innovation capacity refers to the continuous improvement of the ability to generate innovation in order to develop new products that meet customer needs. Considering business practices, many researchers made use of maturity models that focus on a set of constructs suitable to stimulate innovation capacity at firm level, thus provisionally overcoming the challenges associated to establishing a semantic definition of innovation. Yet, the various models available in the literature [33] represent a set of concepts of the state of the art related to best practices in an area of activity such as CMMI for software development [41]. Furthermore, it can be argued that most of them draw their origins in the work of Crosby [10, 20] and they are heavily inspired by the CMMI maturity model (Capability Maturity Model Integration) by SEI (Software Engineering Institute). Indeed, using a maturity model helps an organization to assess the current state of its processes and to plan for improving its practices [42, 48]. It serves for assessing organizational practices processes implemented and support their improvement. The use of the concept of maturity is thus adopted in various fields both in research and business practice such as, e.g., systems engineering, purchase, service [11], Research and Development processes [3], assessing innovation capability [13, 16]. According to [22], the maturity grids can be applied to all processes of all companies to get higher performance. Organizations evolve, change to achieve the most mature large as possible at a given time. Thus, we argue that the innovation capacity of a process or activity can be evaluated depending on different levels, which similarly to the CMMI can be classified, e.g., as *initial, managed, defined, quantitatively managed, optimizing* [17, 35]. Therefore, strengthening an organization's innovation capacity requires a combination of different measurements, in order to improve critical points and progress towards a higher maturity level [13].

Furthermore, the main objective of maturity models is to improve the quality of the processes by assessing processes and improving their weak spots. The maturity models account for a well balance between standardization and flexibility of innovation processes related in order to change the business environment and meet to requirements of stakeholders. However the relevance and diffusion of maturity models, the salient features and characteristics of innovation within these maturity models have been little investigated from a systemic perspective. Thus, in what follows we detail the results of a review of the literature, which leads to the selection of more than 50 maturity models and specific characteristics. Among those models, we then choose those that are specifically dedicated to innovation management.

3 Innovation Maturity Models in Research and Practice

The use of maturity models in companies has intensified and it has recently expanded in various fields. This expansion gave rise to several maturity models, both from the research and the practitioner community. In this article, we consider sixteen maturity models selected for discussion here that are particularly relevant to the assessment of innovation capacity proposed in the literature. To analyse these maturity models, they have been grouped into three categories on the basis of the community producing or else using them. Furthermore, the following characteristics with regards to the objective of the research were defined:

- Concept of maturity levels,
- Process areas or items,
- Focus on innovation in general, open innovation, or innovation and IS/IT.

The results of the analysis of the literature are presented in Table 1a (showing models from the research community), Table 1b (showing models from the community of practitioners), and Table 1c (showing hybrid models), where the selected models are described considering: *Model name, Process areas or dimensions, Type of innovation, References.*

The selection of the models from the research community (shown in Table 1a) usually is based on the presence of relevant literature that supports the model and the usability for innovation managers and practitioners. Whereas for the models coming from the community of practitioners (see Table 1b), the selection considers the use of the model by the company creator or the client companies to improve innovation capacity.

Yet, as for hybrid models in Table 1c, both the criteria for research and practitioners communities are considered.

Notwithstanding each model, either from the research or the practitioners community, has its own structure, most models are based on the original concept of maturity as already defined in the CMMI model [36], representing an assessment of maturity of the whole organization. In CMMI models [21] with a staged representation, there are five maturity levels (initial, managed, defined, quantitatively managed, optimizing) that consist of a predefined set of process areas; each of the five maturity levels captures performance expectations, practices or activities performed collectively to achieve the objective of that process area. Similarly, for every model considered at the state of the art there are certain process areas determined for each maturity level that an organization must implement in order to achieve a given maturity level. Thus, it can be argued that innovation maturity models have taken the same principles.

Taking these issues into account, Table 2 shows a relative similarity among the levels considered by state of the art maturity models. Indeed, the five maturity levels of the first CMMI model inspired most of the subsequent models. Furthermore, some models have taken the five maturity levels of CMMI. For others, they adopted their own terms to designate levels of maturity. The number of models studied levels of maturity varies from 3 to 6. Noting that the IMM model (B) does not have adopted maturity levels.

4 Models' Structures and Validation

As shown in Sect. 3, measuring the maturity of innovation capacity, its determinants or processes/practices may vary from one model to another. Different authors propose assessment models and representational capacity to innovate that we have summarized Tables 1a, 1b and 1c. Indeed, the areas as well as the dimensions of different models are very heterogeneous, thus resulting in various models' structures. Yet, all models agree on a set of key factors suitable to improving a company ability to innovate; in fact, it depends on firstly understanding the innovation capability of a given organization and what is needed to that organization to improve it, even if the constructs considered by the various models are different. According to the models considered in previous Section and shown in Tables 1a, 1b and 1c, thirteen main dimensions have been identified: *culture, risk perspective, collaboration/open innovation process,*

Table 1a. Analysis of innovation maturity models (research community)

Maturity models	Process areas or dimensions	Type of innovation			References
		IS/IT innovation	General	Open innovation	
A Innovation Capability Maturity Model (ICMM)	3 process areas: innovation process, knowledge and competency, and organizational support		•		[14]
B Innovation Maturity Model (IMM)	8 process areas: Culture, Risk Perspective, Resources, Customer Focus, Learning, Collaboration, Leadership, and Process score		•		[45]
C Service Innovation Capability Maturity Model (SICMM)	2 process models (The New Service Development process model consists of six main processes, and The Innovation process model, based on the concept of open service innovation)			•	[27]
D Open Innovation Maturity Framework (OIMF)	3 items : partnership capacity, climate for innovation and internal processes			•	[13]
E Open Innovation Maturity Management Framework (OIMMF)	3 dimensions: open innovation process, individual capabilities, competencies	•		•	[24]
F Knowledge Management Framework (KMF)	1 dimension: knowledge		•		[17]
G Model of An Adaptive Organization (MAO)	7 process areas: vision and strategy, culture and beliefs, senior leadership, processes, plans, people, and desired outcomes		•		[12, 39]

Table 1b. Analysis of innovation maturity models (*community of practitioners*).

Maturity models		Process areas or dimensions	Type of innovation			References
			IS/IT Innovation	General	Open innovation	
H	Continuous Delivery Maturity Model (Forrester Consulting)	The model help to evaluate continuous delivery capability of companies; the level of continuous deployment capability have a incidence for capacity to innovate through custom software	•			[19]
I	PRTM PRTM and Microsoft Corporation) Innovation Maturity Model (PRTM and Microsoft Corporation)	Each stage of the model is characterized by a set of representative management practices in four areas (vision and strategy, insights, management, organization)		•		[31]
J	Integrated Innovation Maturity Model (I²MM) (Pumacy Technologies AG)	The model is structured into four process areas : ideation and product development, innovation management, requirements engineering and quality management		•		[33]
K	Innovation Maturity Model (Berg Consulting Group)	The model addresses for each level of maturity for the organization the strategic focus and capability. It identifies the priority actions. It		•		[4]

(*Continued*)

Table 1b. (*Continued*)

Maturity models		Process areas or dimensions	Type of innovation			References
			IS/IT Innovation	General	Open innovation	
		is advises to place a preliminary focus on developing capability and culture				
L	Innovation Management Maturity Model™ (Planview)	The model is based on four dimensions: strategy, people, processes, and tools		•		[34]
M	Maturity Model for Innovation Management (Gartner)	The model is based on six dimensions: strategy and intent, processes and practices, culture and people, organization and infrastructure, partnerships and open innovation, innovation how we innovate	•			[18]

partnership capacity, climate for innovation, processes and practices/organization, individual capabilities, knowledge, learning and competencies/people, ideation and product development, innovation management, requirements engineering/customer focus/continuous delivery, quality management, leadership/strategy and intent/vision and strategy, infrastructure/tools/resources and organizational support.

Each factor promoting innovation is defined by sub factors or practices under represent the activities or business processes. For example, between ideation/generation concepts and individuals/organization/culture, there is a link because a culture of innovation facilitates the emergence of new ideas. We find the interactions between all dimensions/factors. It exists therefore a synergistic effect that enhances the company's innovation capacity. The analysis of the factors/areas and processes of the innovation assessment models thus shows a clear trend of the complexity for assessment the innovation capacity as multi-criteria that have relationships between them. It also demonstrated similarities in the form of a list of factors/process areas that allow assess innovation capacity and trigger an improvement plan.

Otherwise, for validation of maturity models, the Table 3 below shows methods of validation of each model. Most models have been validated by various methods. For

Table 1c. Analysis of innovation maturity models (hybrid models).

Maturity models		Process areas or dimensions	Type of innovation			References
			IS/IT innovation	General	Open innovation	
N	Breakthrough Innovation (Brinnovation™)	Brinnovation builds on employees' natural talents, and simplifies the innovation process. The methodology for developing innovative solutions is TEDOC (Target, Explore, Develop, Optimize and Commercialize)		•		[23]
O	Innovation Capability Maturity Model (ICMM)	The key to improving your ability to innovate depends on the first understanding the innovation capability of your organization and what you need to do to improve		•		[29, 30]
P	Innovation Capability dEtermination (ICE)	The model is based on innovation assessment and process capability. Five types of processes (idea to innovation, connected innovation driver, supporting, innovation objective analysis and decision, quantitate processes)		•		[37]

example the model IMM (B) was validated by three different methods: workshops, interviews and surveys collected from broad engineering-procurement and construction (EPC) organizations.

Taking these issues into account, we propose to select only the maturity models from research based on a robust validation (through intensive interviews, survey

Table 2. Maturity levels of models

Models		Number of levels	Maturity levels
A	ICMM	5	Ad hoc, defined, supported, aligned, synergised
B	IMM	0	Not available
C	SICMM	6	Incomplete, performed, disciplined, defined, managed, optimized
D	OIMF	5	Initial, repeatable, defined, managed, optimizing
E	OIMMF	4	Closed, defined, managed, aligned
F	KMF	3	Ad hoc and limited, formalization and predictability, integration, synergy and autonomy
G	MAO	5	Ad hoc, vision & strategy, processes, culture & beliefs, innovation
H	Model of Forrester	5	Initial, managed, defined, quantitatively managed, optimizing
I	Model of PRTM and Microsoft	4	Stages I, II, III, IV
J	I^{2}MM of Pumacy Technologies	5	Chaotic, organized, standardized, predictable, black belt
K	Model Of Berg Consulting	5	Entry level innovation practices, emerging innovation practices, co-ordinated innovation practices, innovation leadership, industry innovation leadership
L	Planview Model	5	Levels 1, 2, 3, 4, 5
M	Gartner Model	5	Reactive, active, defined, performing, pervasive
N	Brinnovation	5	Sporadic, idea, managed, nurtured, sustained
O	ICMM of Mann	5	Seeding, championing, managing, strategizing, venturing
P	ICE of Peisl and Johanson	5	Levels 1, 2, 3, 4, 5

methods, case studies or workshops) and implemented within companies (see Table 3). Yet, due to the relevance of information systems (IS) for innovation, two more frameworks are worth considering. These include the model CMMI-DEV for software [9], and COBIT V5 for governance and management of IT [25]. Indeed, CMMI-DEV is composed of 22 process areas. Among these areas, there is the area of "Organizational Innovation and Deployment", its purpose is to select and deploy incremental and innovative improvements that measurably improve the organization's processes and technologies. For COBIT V5, it is composed of 37 processes of governance and management, and each process describes its objectives, best practices, activities and deliverables. Furthermore, the process "Manage Innovation" is made up of six practices (creating an enabling environment for innovation, maintaining an understanding of the business environment, evaluating the potential of emerging technologies, evaluating the potential of emerging technologies, and monitoring implementation of innovations).

Table 3. Types of validation for the models.

Models		Validation					
		Interviews	Survey	Workshop	Case study	Number of companies	References
A	ICMM			•	•	5	[15]
B	IMM	•	•	•		46	
C	SICMM	•			•	1	
D	OIMF	•		•		15	[13]
E	OIMMF	•			•	1	[24]
F	KMF	•				5	
G	MAO	•			•	1	[11, 40]

5   Discussion of the Results

According to [11], *"The SW-CMM approach was based on principles of managing product quality that have existed for the past 60 years. A CMM follows the quality work of Crosby [Crosby 1979] where he observed progressing levels of maturity in an organization's ability to anticipate, resolve, and eventually nullify quality problems."* For innovation models, we found that most models are based on the principles of CMM models (SEI) and partly some quality research including works of Crosby (1979–1986), TQM (1995–1998), ITIL (1980–2007) and ISO15504 (2005). The development of academic and industrial models in the time allowed integrating a multitude of factors or processes areas of innovation process or business innovation systems to assess the maturity of the innovation capacity, comparing levels of business maturity and implement improvement plan. Indeed the OIMF model (2011) took into account the work on the ICMM model (2009) and in the MOA model (2013) took into account the work on the I^2MM model (2011). So there is a capitalization of knowledge anchored to the CMM original source as a "blueprint" actually evolving through different model instances as well as configurations for improving innovation practices and meeting the challenges of innovation imposed by a permanent change in competitive environment. Otherwise, we have also found that while maturity models are focusing more and more on open innovation, they still remain at a general level of description and to date there is no dedicated maturity model of innovation by technologies or IS except for a small part of the COBIT framework V5 devoted to innovation through technologies. Academic and industrial community seek to identify innovative levers adapted to the changing economic environment. However, the models proposed in the literature take more into account open innovation, to date, to our knowledge, there are no innovation models focused on the role of IS. Finding the right model of assessing the ability to innovate and thus able to analyze the management of mobilized resources for innovation in the current context where information and communication technologies plays a crucial role for innovation is an important challenge for research and businesses [1, 32].

6 Conclusion and Future Work

This research has presented a comparative study of maturity models for innovation based on an extensive review of both academic and practitioners oriented literature. Thus, this paper contributes to understand the key characteristics of state of the art maturity models, particularly with regard to the innovation they enable in a given company. As for the diverse levels suitable to improve innovation capacity, although some models adopt different levels of maturity, a common root has been identified in the five maturity levels of the first CMMI model. Furthermore, strengthening an organization's innovation capacity requires a combination of different measurements/factors, in order to improve critical points and to achieve a higher maturity level. The assessment of the maturity of the innovation process is the first step on a path of continuous improvement. In particular, the study also revealed four basic observations:

1. The principles of CMMI model are widely used in the design of innovative maturity models.
2. Heterogeneous constructs or process areas are nonetheless characterising the diverse models emerging from both research and practitioners literature.
3. Capitalization of knowledge is a key factor in innovation maturity models over time.
4. Various practices of assessment methods and constructs can be applied to the validation of maturity models targeting innovation.
5. The models proposed in the literature improve increasingly take more account of open innovation; yet, to our knowledge there a few or none innovation models by IS.

In summary, the analyses presented in this article provide the basis for the design and development of a framework for innovation capacity maturity driven by information systems. In future work the authors intend to take advantage of the analysed models, in particular areas or topics for each model and assessments methods, thereby potentially enabling an automated assessment of innovation capacity, which can be used by managers in order to adapt their processes of innovation.

References

1. Applegate, L.M., Elam, J.J.: New information systems leaders: a changing role in a changing world. MISQ Q. **16**(4), 469–490 (1992)
2. Banerjee, B., Gibbs, T.: Teaching the innovation methodology at the Stanford d.school. In: Banerjee, B., Ceri, S. (eds.) Creating Innovation Leaders, pp. 163–174. Springer, Heidelberg (2016)
3. Berg, P., et al.: Assessment of quality and maturity level of R&D. Int. J. Prod. Econ. **78**(1), 29–35 (2002)
4. Berg, R.: The Innovation Maturity Model. Berg Consulting Group Pty Ltd., Melbourne (2013)
5. Carlson, C.R., Wilmot, W.W.: Innovation: The Five Disciplines for Creating What Customers Want. Crown Business, New York (2006)

6. Chesbrough, H., et al.: Explicating open innovation: clarifying an emerging paradigm for understanding innovation. In: Chesbrough, H., et al. (eds.) New Frontiers in Open Innovation, pp. 3–28. Oxford University Press, Oxford (2014)
7. Chesbrough, H., Brunswicker, S.: Managing open innovation in large firms, survey report (2013)
8. Chiesa, V., et al.: Development of a technical innovation audit. J. Prod. Innov. Manag. **13** (2), 105–136 (1996)
9. Chrissis, M.B. et al.: CMMI pour le développement, Version 1.3. Pearson, Paris (2011)
10. Crosby, P.B.: Quality is Free. McGraw-Hill Companies, New York (1979)
11. Cross, S.E.: A Model to Guide Organizational Adaptation. Presented at the June (2013)
12. Cross, S.E.: A model to guide organizational adaptation. Presented at the Proceedings of the 2013 IEEE International Technology Management Conference & 19th ICE Conference, The Hague, The Netherlands, June 2013
13. Enkel, E., et al.: Open innovation maturity framework. Int. J. Innov. Manag. **15**(06), 1161–1189 (2011)
14. Essmann, H., Du Preez, N.: An innovation capability maturity model–development and initial application. World Acad. Sci. Eng. Technol. **53**, 435–446 (2009)
15. Essmann, H., Du Preez, N.: An innovation capability maturity model-development and initial application. World Acad. Sci. Eng. Technol. **53**, 435–446 (2009)
16. Essmann, H., Du Preez, N.: Practical cases of assessing innovation capability with a theoretical model: the process and findings (2009)
17. Esterhuizen, D., et al.: A knowledge management framework to grow innovation capability maturity. SA J. Inf. Manag. **14**, 1 (2012)
18. Fenn, J., Harris, K.: A Maturity Model for Innovation Management. Gartner
19. Forrester Research: Continuous Delivery: A Maturity Assessment Model, USA (2013)
20. Fraser, P., et al.: The use of maturity models/grids as a tool in assessing product development capability (2002)
21. Garceau, L.R., et al.: A proposed model of assessment maturity: a paradigm shift. J. Bus. Behav. Sci. **27**(1), 142 (2015)
22. Grant, K.P., Pennypacker, J.S.: Project management maturity: an assessment of project management capabilities among and between selected industries. IEEE Trans. Eng. Manag. **53**(1), 59–68 (2006)
23. Gupta, P.: Leading innovation change - the kotter way. Int. J. Innov. Sci. **3**(3), 141–150 (2011)
24. Habicht, H., et al.: Open innovation maturity. Int. J. Knowl.-Based Organ. **2**(1), 92–111 (2012)
25. Isaca: COBIT 5 A business framework for the ogvernance and management of enterprise IT. Isaca, Rolling Meadows, Illinois (2012)
26. Koehler, J., et al.: An impact-oriented maturity model for IT-based case management. Inf. Syst. **47**, 278–291 (2015)
27. Li, E.Y., et al.: A framework for the service innovation capability maturity model. Presented at the 4th International Conference on Operations and Supply Chain Management, Hongkong & Guangzhou, 25 July 2010
28. Link, A.N., Siegel, D.S.: Innovation, Entrepreneurship, and Technological Change. Oxford University Press, Oxford (2007)
29. Mann, D.L.: Automating innovation capability maturity measurement. E-Zine (156) (2015). http://systematic-innovation.com/past-e-zines-2011-2016.html
30. Mann, D.L.: Innovation Capability Maturity Model (ICMM) – An Introduction, IFR Press (2012)
31. Mohammad, M., Romeri, M.: The Road Map for Innovation Success. Whitepaper (2007)

32. Morabito, V., et al.: Understanding the changing role of CIOs in the big data and analytics era: an empirical investigation. In: WOA 2015 (XVI Workshop dei docenti e ricercatori di Organizzazione Aziendale), Padova, Italy (2015)
33. Müller-Prothmann, T., Stein, A.: I²MM – integrated innovation maturity model for lean assessment of innovation capability. In: XXII ISPIM Conference 2011: Sustainability in Innovation, Hamburg/Germany, 12–15 June 2011, p. 11 (2011)
34. Nauyalis, C.: A new framework for assessing your innovation program: introducing the innovation management maturity model™ by planview, white paper. http://www.planview.com/company/press-releases/introduces-innovation-management-maturity-model/
35. Paulk, M.C., Curtis, B., Chrissis, M.B., Weber, C.V.: Capability Maturity Model for Software, version 1.1, Software Engineering Institute, CMU/SEI-93-TR-24 February 1993
36. Paulk, M.C.: The Capability Maturity Model: Guidelines for Improving the Software Process. Addison-Wesley, Boston (1995)
37. Peisl, T., Johansen, J.: Innovation Maturity: Innovation competences depends on process capability (2012)
38. Peng, J., et al.: Impacts of essential elements of management on IT application maturity — a perspective from firms in China. Decis. Support Syst. 51(1), 88–98 (2011)
39. Rouse, W.B.: Necessary competencies for transforming an enterprise. J. Enterp. Transform. 1(1), 71–92 (2011)
40. Rouse, W.B.: Necessary competencies for transforming an enterprise. J. Enterp. Transform. 1(1), 71–92 (2011)
41. Rungratri, S., Usanavasin, S.: Project assets ontology (PAO) to support gap analysis for organization process improvement based on CMMI v.1.2. In: Wang, Q., Pfahl, D., Raffo, D.M. (eds.) ICSP 2008. LNCS, vol. 5007, pp. 76–87. Springer, Heidelberg (2008)
42. Saraph, J.V., et al.: An instrument for measuring the critical factors of quality management. Decis. Sci. 20(4), 810–829 (1989)
43. Szeto, E.: Innovation capacity: working towards a mechanism for improving innovation within an inter-organizational networknull. TQM Mag. 12(2), 149–158 (2000)
44. Tidd, J., Hull, F.M.: Managing service innovation: the need for selectivity rather than "best practice". New Technol. Work Employ. 21(2), 139–161 (2006)
45. Toole, T.M., et al.: A tool for improving construction organizations' innovation capabilities. In: Construction Research Congress 2010, pp. 727–836. American Society of Civil Engineers, Canada (2010)
46. Vanhaverbeke, W., Chesbrough, H.: A classification of open innovation and open business models. In: New Frontiers in Open Innovation, pp. 50–68. OUP Oxford, Oxford (2014)
47. Wang, C.L., Ahmed, P.K.: The development and validation of the organisational innovativeness construct using confirmatory factor analysis. Eur. J. Innov. Manag. 7(4), 303–313 (2004)
48. van de Weerd, I., Bekkers, W., Brinkkemper, S.: Developing a maturity matrix for software product management. In: Tyrväinen, P., Jansen, S., Cusumano, M.A. (eds.) ICSOB 2010. LNBIP, vol. 51, pp. 76–89. Springer, Heidelberg (2010)
49. Zawislak, P.A., et al.: Innovation capability: from technology development to transaction capability. J. Technol. Manag. Innov. 7(2), 14–27 (2012)

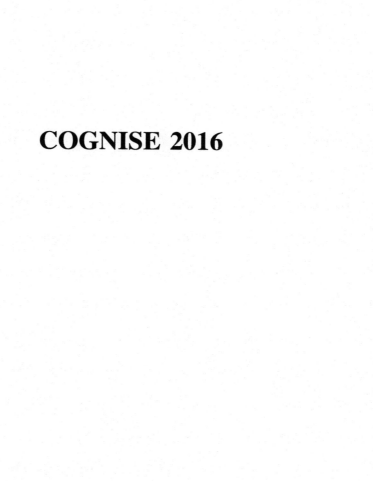

COGNISE 2016

Learning from Errors as a Pedagogic Approach for Reaching a Higher Conceptual Level in Database Modeling

Adi Katz[(✉)] and Ronit Shmallo

Sami Shamoon College of Engineering (SCE), Ashdod, Israel
{adis, ronitsl}@sce.ac.il

Abstract. We apply a pedagogic approach named learning from errors (LFE) to the area of relational database modeling. Database modeling is a complex cognitive process characterized by a high level of element interactivity. Finding an appropriate pedagogy to teach database modeling is a challenge for information systems educators. One of the challenges that practitioners meet is the need to help database students shift between different levels of abstraction. We metaphorically treat the LFE approach as a bridge over the gulf of abstraction levels. Errors have a powerful potential in education, to encourage students to move to a deeper processing level of the course material. We use Rasmussen's three levels of human performance model to explain and demonstrate the promising potential of the LFE approach in database modeling.

Keywords: Conceptual modelling · Databases · Learning from errors · Cognitive conflict · Levels of abstraction

1 Introduction

Teaching conceptual database modelling is a challenge to information systems (IS) educators. We apply a pedagogic approach named "learning from errors" (LFE) to the area of relational database design, to more effectively deliver and instruct the cognitively complex material of database modeling. The approach was already applied successfully in the areas of mathematics [1], physics [2] and computer science [3] education but not yet applied in the area of database design.

We recently examined the difficulties that students encounter in the activity of conceptual modelling by analyzing their solutions to a database course exercise, in the form of a textual scenario, and mapped their errors into categories [4]. Our plan is to design learning lessons, class and homework activities that utilize these errors for the learning process. We will then use our learning activities in an experiment, in which we intent to compare between the traditional database teaching approach and a combination of the traditional approach with the LFE approach to test the effectiveness of the latter.

In the current paper, our intention is to explain why the LFE approach that was already found to be beneficial in different educational areas is particularly powerful in the process of learning database conceptual modeling. We use Rasmussen's three levels

© Springer International Publishing Switzerland 2016
J. Krogstie et al. (Eds.): CAiSE 2016, LNBIP 249, pp. 93–102, 2016.
DOI: 10.1007/978-3-319-39564-7_9

of human performance model [5] as a theoretic framework, and we stress the importance of making transitions across abstraction levels in training database students. To demonstrate the promising potential of the LFE approach in database conceptual modeling activities, we present two examples; each is part of a different class exercise. The exercises we use for demonstration are of a type called "erroneous examples" [1, 6]. Of course, the literature describes other activities that utilize errors for the learning process such as "self-explanations" [7], "mistaken statements" and comparison of students' solutions to those of an expert [2].

2 Teaching Database Modelling as a Challenge to IS Educators

In database courses, students learn various activities that are related to defining, creating and manipulating databases. In each activity, database designers are required to observe data at three different levels of abstraction: internal (physical), conceptual (central/logical) and external (user view). For example, in database definition, data defining language (DDL) is divided into physical, central and view DDL. We focus on the conceptual level, in which a relational schema is created. A database schema includes a list of entities, attributes, relationships, user operations, database semantic constraints (business rules), and interrelation referential integrity constraints which are used to maintain consistency of reference among records from different relations [8]. Different levels of abstraction are also reflected in database course material, ranging from the theory level (e.g. learning the notion of a reference integrity constraint) to the practical level (e.g. writing a DDL code such as "on delete cascade" to ensure that a reference integrity constraint would not be violated). Educators have a twofold challenge in teaching relational database design concepts; they need to deliver the theory of relational databases and also provide students with practical skills to perform effectively in real life [9]. In our years of experience in teaching the database course, there is a gulf between theoretical concepts and their meaning at the concrete level of an organization's needs, demands and constraints.

In a typical database course, many elements are taught. Among them are: relational model principles, entity relationship (ER) model, key types, SQL, normalization rules, and optimization. Database modeling is a process characterized by a high level of element interactivity, since the different topics are understood and learned with reference to other topics, and cannot be considered independently. One of the challenges of database design instructors is dealing with the fact that the high-element interactivity material covers various activities that are related to the different levels of abstraction.

The contents of long term memory are sophisticated cognitive structures known as schemas that make up our knowledge base [10]. Complex schemas consist of huge arrays of interrelated elements [11]. High-element interactivity material is difficult to understand. Indeed, the elements can be learned individually, but they cannot be fully understood until all aspects and their interactions are processed simultaneously. Intrinsic cognitive load is affected by element interactivity and extraneous cognitive load is affected by instructional design [12]. This is why instructional approaches intended to reduce cognitive load are primarily effective when element interactivity is high. There is an additional type of cognitive load, referred to as germane or effective cognitive load, which is also influenced by the instructional designer, since he or she determines the learning activities and the way in which information is presented. Whereas extraneous cognitive load interferes with learning, germane cognitive load enhances learning, since cognitive resources are being devoted to schema acquisition and automation [12, 13]. A simultaneous processing of all essential elements must occur eventually despite the high-intrinsic cognitive load because it is only then that understanding takes place [13]. At the following sections, we explain and demonstrate how the LFE approach creates a germane or effective cognitive load that enhances simultaneous processing of all essential elements in database modeling.

3   Learning from Errors in Educating Database Modeling

There are previous pedagogic works in database modeling with attempts to deal with the challenge of effectively delivering theory and practice and bridging the gulf between different levels of abstraction. Such interesting attempts are the integrated spiral approach [14] and the cognitive apprenticeship based approach [9]. We offer an alternative approach called *learning from errors* (LFE) as an aid for tying elements that are highly integrated, but belong to different levels of abstraction. Empirical results have shown that LFE promotes the learning process [6, 7], and the approach was already applied successfully in mathematics [1], physics [2] and computer science [3]. Errors are often treated negatively, but our approach takes advantage of errors and utilizes them in educating relational database modeling as a bridge to transfer between different levels of abstraction. We claim that in the area of database design, the LFE approach may push students to a cognitive level in which connections between different elements are created to form viable mental models of database conceptualization.

Errors may trigger cognitive conflicts or dissonances, which, in turn, yield a process of reflection and critical thinking [1]. Learning activities should raise cognitive conflicts, since the point at which they arise, are the ones to yield the recognition of the source of the error [3]. A cognitive conflict driven learning approach encourages students to engage with the learning materials and motivate them to construct appropriate and viable mental models [15]. Erroneous situations fail to conform what needs to be, and therefore errors are subjectively experienced as conflicts between what the learner believes ought to be true, and what he or she perceives to be the case [16]). We claim that the LFE approach bolsters germane (effective) cognitive load, because it creates motivation to explore the learning material in more depth, in order to solve a cognitive conflict created by the deliberate errors presented. This exploratory process promotes new insights, and then knowledge in the long-term memory is updated to a schema with connections between the different elements that are related to database modeling and design.

The difference between a professional and a novice is that the latter hasn't acquired the schemas of an expert. Learning requires a change in the schematic structures of long term memory. During the learning process, as the learner becomes increasingly familiar with the material, performance progresses from clumsy, slow and difficult to smooth and effortless [10]. The transition between performance levels is in line with Rasmussen's model [5] of human performance, as we explain in the following section.

4   Rasmussen's Three Level Model of Human Performance

Rasmussen distinguishes three categories of human behavior: skill-, rule-, and knowledge-based [5]. We follow Rasmussen's three-level framework to explain the promising potential of the LFE approach in pushing students to a higher level of learning process of conceptual modeling. We do so by demonstrating the categories of human behavior on database conceptual modeling activities. All levels are expressed in learning database design; however, most interesting is the potential of the LFE approach to shift students from the rule-based to the higher knowledge-based level of learning, in which complex schemas of huge arrays of interrelated elements in the long-term memory are formed, transformed, reorganized and updated.

4.1   Skill-Based Behavior

The skill-based behavior represents sensory-motor actions. For example, when students listen to a teacher in a database course class, and during so they write in their note-books, they unconsciously and rapidly move the hand that holds the pen horizontally across the notebook lines and they move their hand vertically to the beginning of the next line each time they notice that the point of the pen is about to reach the edge of the page. This is a highly integrated pattern of behavior, done with almost no conscious attention or control. Also, translating the sounds of the teacher's utterances to a graphic textual display in the notebook is also a smooth, automated and coordinated behavior. In both examples, the students' senses are only directed towards the environmental aspects that are needed to update and orient their internal map and their activities are a sequence of skilled acts which are composed from a large repertoire of automated sub-routines.

4.2   Rule-Based Behavior

At the next level of rule-based behavior, students learn and store relational database related rules. For example, referring to Codd's normalization rules [17], they are instructed to follow a set of defined rules, in order to meet normal forms (NF). They learn how to apply these rules for decomposing existing relations (*design by analysis* approach, [8]) or for constructing relation schemas according to given textual scenarios (*design by synthesis* approach, [8]). Usually they are taught how to use these rules according to identified functional and multivariate dependencies between attributes. Then, existing relations or textual scenarios will release these stored know-how rules. In most exercises related to normalization, students are required to apply the rule that fits, according to similar situations or examples already taught. Figure 1 demonstrates an erroneous example of a "students" relation with arrows that express dependencies between attributes. The inclusion of all address attributes in the relation violates the 3rd normal form (3NF), because it allows a transitive dependency of zip code on the other address attributes. The arrows pattern serves as a *sign*, which is the perceived environmental information at the rule-based level [5], for identifying a transparent dependency that violates 3NF, and for activating predetermined actions of decomposing the relation according to the learned solution. Actually, even if the relation's attributes were totally meaningless or independent of a given scenario (e.g. A, B, C... G), the pattern of 3NF violation would still be apparent and easily identified. At this level of processing, the rule is recalled from memory after pattern recognition occurs.

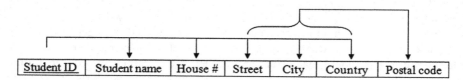

Fig. 1. Example for dependencies between attributes that violate 3NF

4.3   Knowledge-Based Behavior

At the highest level in terms of attention resources consumption, are knowledge-based behaviors, in which students are required to functionally understand and analyze the environmental information. Following the previous NF example, at this level students understand the importance of the rules, and the meaning or consequences of violating them.

As aforementioned, errors may trigger cognitive conflicts that force students to deeply understand concepts, and relations between concepts. Erroneous examples are a type of LFE activities that have a high potential for raising cognitive conflicts. In the case of teaching Normalization, there are usually various exercises for identification of NF rules. They usually present relations that violate these rules, and students are asked to repair the violations by adding and omitting attributes from the given relations, and by correcting erroneous keys. In most cases, erroneous examples indeed serve as situations with a potential to recall stored rules in order to repair accordingly. In many cases, the cognitive conflict accompanied by erroneous examples will motivate students to move to a higher conceptual level and then different plans are considered. For demonstration, we refer to the normalization example of the erroneous relation in Fig. 1. Presenting the "students" relation should raise the question of whether it is better to repair the relation or decide on de-normalization, an explicit violating of the 3NF rule. The student needs to predict the different effects that are related to the different possible solutions. In favor of violating the 3NF rule, considerations that are raised may be the user's perspective (it is more natural to see all address components together), and the system's performance (keeping all attributes in one relation spares JOIN actions, that would be required for queries). In favor of repairing the violation, is the consideration of saving storage space (violating 3NF wastes storage space because of data repetitions). The process of considering different consequences pushes the students to cognitively form connections between the elements, and to understand that in this case there is a tradeoff type of interaction between them. The conceptual level of abstraction, (a normalization rule) is tied to aspects related to internal abstraction level considerations (storage space and system performance) and to external level considerations (user view).

According to Rasmussen [5], there can be varying degrees of training for a person that is in a task depending on variations and disturbances. Constructively using errors in class and homework activities create more opportunities for cognitive conflict when learning initially and when practicing. The cognitive conflicts may motivate the students to move to a deeper learning process. In our view, Rasmussen's theoretical perspective is related to the conception of hierarchy of processing stages, which vary in depth. Greater depth implies a greater degree of semantic or cognitive analysis. Trace persistence in our memory is a function of depth of analysis, with deeper levels of analysis associated with more elaborate, longer lasting, and stronger traces [18]. Compared to the rule-based level, the knowledge-based is higher in processing depth. Educators can and should manipulate and influence the learning process to further elevate the students from simply rehearsing rules to a deeper analysis and a more elaborative level of semantics. Errors have a positive potential in education, being a source of critical and creative thinking, serving as a lever for a deeper learning process [1]. We believe that the powerful potential of errors exists in many topics and areas of learning, including database modeling. The LFE approach constructively uses errors and capitalizes on them as a departure point for an inquiry about the nature of database and about the various concepts and aspects related to database design.

5   Errors as means for Shifting Between Levels of Abstraction

In database modeling training, modeling aids are required to facilitate an easy transition from one level of abstraction to another, and to allow a view of multiple levels simultaneously [19]. We see how errors and therefore the various LFE activities can serve as such modeling aids.

Error or fault events are identified with reference to intended states, normal functions, or other variants of propose or meaning. *Causes* of improper functions depend upon changes in the physical world, and are explained "bottom-up" while *reasons* for proper function are derived "top-down" from the functional purpose. The difference between causes and reasons shows different levels of an abstraction hierarchy [5]. We claim that erroneous events will force the student to consider the functions of a database system at several levels, and that they will have to go through different information flow paths, top-down and bottom-up. Therefore, errors have a powerful potential in education, since they encourage students to get on a metaphorical bridge over the gulf of abstraction levels in database modeling and design, and to transition between levels.

In the following example appearing in Fig. 2, we demonstrate how an erroneous database schema (a partial schema, taken from an 'erroneous example' exercise type) can serve as a bridge over the gulf of abstraction levels, and how in particular it encourages students to think of the hierarchical nature of a database schema, and about the meaning of referential constraints. Figure 2 shows a partial solution for an online flower shop scenario with diagrammatic displays of foreign key-primary key (FK-PK) relations. We deliberately added two erroneous FK-PK relations and deliberately omitted a necessary FK-PK relation. In "Bouquet Order Details", the attributes ID, Catalog Num, and Date should be defined as a FK in reference to "Bouquet Orders", but instead, attribute ID is defined as a FK in reference to "Customers" and Catalog Num is separately defined as a FK in reference to "Bouquets". The omission of the FK-PK relations between "Bouquet Order Details" and "Bouquet Orders" enables abnormal data entries such as the two records appearing in "Bouquet Order Details"; the first showing a bouquet (456) along with a customer ID (111) who did not actually ordered it, and the second showing a bouquet order that did not occur at the inserted date (4/20/2015). In other words, records in "Bouquet Order Details" refer to none existing records in "Bouquet Orders". These inconsistent records presented at the physical world are expected to raise a cognitive conflict that will encourage an inspection, which with proper and effective teacher guidance would lead to thoughts about the meaning of imposing referential integrity constraints, and about the hierarchic nature of a database schema. In the process of finding a solution for the deviation from the valid state of system integrity, students will be encouraged to find the cause for the spurious records, a referential integrity constraint not specified between "Bouquet Order Details" and "Bouquet Orders", and the explanation at this level will be "bottom-up". A discussion about the hierarchical structure of a database schema for proper function will be derived "top-down", with thoughts about the meaning or semantics of the schema and about the gradient transition from parent to child levels of the hierarchy: starting from entities (things) in the real-world that are clear and straightforward and gradually going down towards relations that represent entities that are relatively more abstract and more complex to understand. Discussing relationships between entities may open another discussion about relationship cardinality ratios (1:1, 1: N, M: N), and tying these types to the gradient shift from clear and tangible entities to entities that are more abstract and complex. Referring to the example in Fig. 2, the entities are graduating from top to bottom: since customers and bouquets are in a M: N relationship, but cannot be directly connected in a relational database, "Customers" and "Bouquets" are both parents of "Bouquet Orders". "Bouquet Orders" in turn should be the parent of "Bouquet Order Details". "Customers" and "Bouquets" are tangible and more easily understood than "Bouquet Orders", and the same can be said respectively about "Bouquet Orders" and "Bouquet Order Details".

In another more practical level of abstraction is the discussion about writing the DDL to specify only valid constraints. First, there is a need to add the DDL expression to respectively enforce the missing constraint. This addition involves a decision about the option that would deal best with a violation caused by deleting or updating a bouquet order (reject, cascade, set default or set null). Then, a question should be raised whether to remove or to keep the constraints defining "Bouquet order details" as a referencing relation to both "Customers" and "Bouquets". The discussion regarding this question would lead to understanding of the system's actions (checks) that occur each time a record is inserted to the referencing (child) relation, "Bouquet Order Details", and each time a record is deleted from the referenced (father) relations, "Customers" or "Bouquets". A hierarchical structure should include 'father-child' relations, but 'grandfather-grandchild' relations are redundant since there is an implicit FK relationship from a child to his grandfather through the father. This redundancy adds unnecessarily system checks of compliance with the defined referential integrity constraints. Therefore, this is an opportunity to also understand the practical conse-quences of (system performance) of incorrect semantics (conceptual schema).

Using an erroneous example exercise, we demonstrated how constructively incorporating errors in class and homework assignments can trigger a simultaneous processing of interrelated elements that belong to different levels of abstraction This processing would eventually lead to the essential high level of understanding of conceptual database modeling.

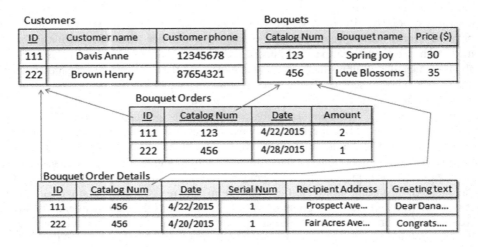

Fig. 2. A partial schema of a flower shop scenario to demonstrate erroneous example exercises

6   Conclusions: Future Directions and Instructional Implications

We introduced LFE as a new pedagogic approach to the area of database design. LFE has already been successfully applied in several areas, but not yet applied in the area of relational database conceptual modelling. We explained why a constructive use of errors is powerful in the process of training database conceptual modeling using Rasmussen's human performance model and focusing on the ability of errors to help database students make transitions across the different levels of abstraction.

We intend to empirically test whether the LFE approach is effective in educating conceptual modelling of relational databases. Our inquiry has three key phases:

1. Mapping errors of students, driven from solutions to scenario tasks. We already mapped students' errors using solutions to a scenario task in a form of a textual description (scenario) of an organization with certain needs and constraints. The students were required to identify relations, draw FK-PK relationships between relations and correctly apply database normalization rules. We analyzed the solutions and mapped the errors into categories and sub-categories [4].
2. Designing an educational program with learning activities that utilizes the errors found in the mapping phase. We are currently developing a number of class and homework assignments that focus on detecting errors, learning their consequences

and solving them. The assignments involve ideas from previous work such as "erroneous examples" [6] and "self-explanations" [7].

3. Conducting an experimental study that compares a group of students who will learn conceptual modelling through the traditional database teaching approach (a control group) to a group of students who will be exposed to a learning process that would have a combination of the traditional teaching approach with the LFE approach (an experimental group). The distinct groups belong to the same academic institution that has two separate campuses. The database course in both campuses is taught at the same semester, by the same lecturer, with the same background material, and so would be the exam questions. The results of the comparison will enable us to reach a conclusion regarding the effectiveness of the LFE approach in educating database modelling. We expect to find higher-quality solutions in the experimental group of students, and also a higher level of student satisfaction from the learning process.

If the LFE approach proves itself to be effective, it could be used as a guide for designing both database educational programs, as well as a guide for designing computerized learning supporting tools for an effective learning process that will lead to high performance in the task of database modeling.

References

1. Borasi, R.: Reconceiving Mathematics Instruction: A Focus on Errors. Ablex Pub, Norwood (1996)
2. Yerushalmi, E., Polingher, C.: Guiding students to learn from mistakes. Phys. Educ. **41**(6), 532–538 (2006)
3. Ginat, D., Shmallo, R.: Constructive use of errors in teaching CS1. In: Proceedings of the 44th ACM Technical Symposium on Computer Science Education, pp. 353–358 (2013)
4. Katz, A., Shmallo, R.: Improving relational data modeling through learning from errors. In: Proceedings of the IADIS Multi Conference of Computer Science and Information Systems MCCSIS, Theory and Practice in Modern Computing TPMC, pp. 198–202. IADIS Press, Las Palmas de Gran Canaria, Spain (2015)
5. Rasmussen, J.: Skills, rules, and knowledge; signals, signs, and symbols, and other distinctions in human performance models. IEEE Trans. Syst. Man Cybern. **3**, 257–266 (1983)
6. Grobe, C.S., Renkl, A.: Finding and fixing errors in worked examples: can this foster learning outcomes? Learn. Instr. **17**(6), 612–634 (2007)
7. Siegler, R., Chen, Z.: Differentiation and integration: guiding principles for analyzing cognitive change. Dev. Sci. **11**(4), 433–448 (2008)
8. Elmasri, R., Navathe, S.: Fundamentals of Database Systems, 6th edn. Addison-Wesley, Boston (2011)
9. Al-Dmour, A.: A cognitive apprenticeship based approach to teaching relational database analysis and design. J. Inf. Comput. Sci. **7**, 2495–2502 (2010)
10. Sweller, J.: Cognitive load during problem solving: effects on learning. Cogn. Sci. **12**, 257–285 (1988)
11. Artino Jr., A.R.: Cognitive load theory and the role of learner experience: an abbreviated review for educational practitioners. Aace J. **16**(4), 425–439 (2008)

12. Sweller, J., van Merriënboer, J.J.G., Paas, F.: Cognitive architecture and instructional design. Educ. Psychol. Rev. **10**, 251–296 (1998)
13. Paas, F., Renkl, A., Sweller, J.: Cognitive load theory and instructional design: recent developments. Educ. Psychol. **38**(1), 1–4 (2003)
14. Watson, R.T.: The essential skills of data modeling. J. Inf. Syst. Educ. **17**(1), 39–41 (2006)
15. Ma, L., Ferguson, J., Roper, M., Ross, I., Wood, M.: Improving the mental models held by novice programmers using cognitive conflict and Jeliot visualisations. ACM SIGCSE Bull. **41**(3), 166–170 (2009)
16. Ohlsson, S.: Learning from performance errors. Psychol. Rev. **103**(2), 241 (1996)
17. Codd, E.F.: Further normalization of the data base relational model. In: Rustin, R.J. (ed.) Data Base Systems: Courant Computer Science Symposia Series 6. Prentice-Hall, Englewood Cliffs (1972)
18. Craik, F.I., Lockhart, R.S.: Levels of processing: a framework for memory research. J. Verbal Learn. Verbal Behav. **11**(6), 671–684 (1972)
19. Srinivasan, A., Te'eni, D.: Modeling as constrained problem solving: an empirical study of the data modeling process. Manag. Sci. **41**(3), 419–434 (1995)

'Mathematical' Does Not Mean 'Boring': Integrating Software Assignments to Enhance Learning of Logico-Mathematical Concepts

Anna Zamansky[1(✉)] and Yoni Zohar[2]

[1] University of Haifa, Haifa, Israel
annazam@is.haifa.ac.il
[2] Tel Aviv University, Tel-Aviv, Israel
yoni.zohar@cs.tau.ac.il

Abstract. Insufficient mathematical skills of practitioners are hypothesized as one of the main hindering factors for the adoption of formal methods in industry. This problem is directly related to negative attitudes of future computing professionals to core mathematical disciplines, which are perceived as difficult, boring and not relevant to their future daily practices. This paper is a contribution to the ongoing debate on how to make courses in Logic and Formal Methods both relevant and engaging for future software practitioners. We propose to increase engagement and enhance learning by integrating 'hands-on' software engineering assignments based on cross-fertilization between software engineering and logic. As an example, we report on a pilot assignment given at a Logic and Formal Methods course for Information Systems students at the University of Haifa. We describe the design of the assignment, students' feedback and discuss some lessons learnt from the pilot.

Keywords: Education · Teaching · Automated reasoning · Software engineering · Logic · Testing · Engagement

1 Introduction

Core mathematical disciplines, such as discrete mathematics and logic, provide the foundations for application of formal methods (FM) in the software engineering domain. Deficient mathematical skills, and as a result, inability to cope with formal notations, are hypothesized as hindering factors for wider adoption of formal methods in industry ([4,12]). However, the question of how to teach core disciplines to future software engineering and information systems practitioners remains a subject of a fierce debate.

Recent voices [10,20,21] call for rethinking the traditional syllabi of mathematical courses, adapting them to the needs of practitioners and making them more tuned towards application of formal methods in the software domain. A notable study in this context is the Beseme project ([14]), which provides empirical evidence that studying discrete mathematics through examples focused on

© Springer International Publishing Switzerland 2016
J. Krogstie et al. (Eds.): CAiSE 2016, LNBIP 249, pp. 103–108, 2016.
DOI: 10.1007/978-3-319-39564-7_10

reasoning about software can improve students' programming skills. As pointed out by [17], software-related examples are also useful for increasing the motivation of students, who can see the applications of the studied material in the domain of their interest. And yet, although the importance of building bridges from logico-mathematical courses to software engineering seems to be widely acknowledged, discussions on practical ways of how this should be done are scarce in the literature.

Empirical studies have shown that students experience more difficulty with concepts from logic than with other computer science topics [1]. Together with a general tendency towards "softening" the teaching of engineering principles noted by [12], it leads to a vicious circle of students' lack of motivation, and perception of logico-mathematical courses as 'boring', 'difficult', 'detached and esoteric'.

In this paper we address the problem of increasing engagement and enhancing learning of logico-mathematical concepts by future software engineering practitioners in a *practical* way. More concretely, we propose to integrate in logic courses 'hands-on' software-related assignments. Such assignments could involve solving a given algorithmic problem with the help of a FM tool (e.g., SAT-solver or theorem prover). Alternatively, it could involve applying SE techniques already familiar to the students to FM systems and tools (e.g., designing a test plan or writing an SRS for a theorem prover). The rationale behind this idea is quite self-explanatory: logical concepts such as satisfiability, theorem, proof system, usually taught in a theoretical, 'paper and pencil'-like way, are transformed and "come to life" in the world of software, made into runnable, testable objects, which feel more real to most SE students. Specifying, validating, running and testing these objects can provide new insights into the nature of these concepts, as the students have a different angle of thinking about them. Having qualitative means to measure success in such assignments may also introduce an element of competitiveness and naturally increases engagement.

As simple as the above idea may sound, the devil is in the details, and the design and realization of such assignments calls for careful consideration with respect to both the educator and the student. Not all logic educators (especially those from math departments) are familiar with the intricacies of software tools. Moreover, many logic-related tools have heavy implementations, involve complex heuristics and may easily cause the "not seeing the forest for the trees" effect. The assignments, therefore, should be easy to replicate and not overflowing with technical details, while still being engaging and fun.

As a first step to implementing the above ideas, in what follows we report on an assignment we have designed and experimented with in two different Logic courses at the University of Haifa. The assignment is based on testing the generic theorem prover Gen2sat.[1] We describe the outcome and the feedback received from students and discuss lessons learnt from running this pilot.

---

[1] The tool, developed by the second author, is available at http://www.cs.tau.ac.il/research/yoni.zohar/gen2sat.html. The implementation is based on the algorithm in [9].

2   Previous Works

Mathematics anxiety is a well-studied phenomenon in education, described as involving feelings of tension and anxiety that interfere with the manipulation of numbers and the solving of mathematical problems (cf. [15]); This phenomenon may be particularly severe in the domain of mathematical logic: empirical studies show that students struggled more with questions related to logic than with those related to other computer science topics (cf. [1]). There have been attempts to develop more intuitive formalisms for teaching logic (e.g., Sowa's conceptual graphs [16]).

In the context of software engineering education, while numerous works discuss teaching of more advanced formal methods, basic logico-mathematical courses have received less attention in this context. Recently, however, more voices are calling for reconsideration of the traditional syllabi in these courses and its adaptation to the needs of future practitioners [10,11,19,21] . As noted by [11], "The current syllabus is often justified more by the traditional narrative than by the practitioners needs." [19] further notes: "...we still face the educational challenge of teaching mathematical foundations like logic and discrete mathematics to practicing or aspiring software engineers. We need to go beyond giving the traditional courses and think about who the target students are."

The Beseme project ([14]) provides an empirical validation to the common belief that studying logico-mathematical courses may improve software development skills. In a three-year study empirical data on the achievements of two student populations was collected: those who studied discrete mathematics (including logic) through examples focused on reasoning about software, and those who studied the same subject illustrated with more traditional examples. An analysis of the data revealed significant differences in the programming effectiveness of these two populations in favor of the former.

Tavolato and Friedrich [17] offers insights into integrating basic formal methods courses at universities of applied sciences, where there are usually limiting factors which are relevant to the IS context as well: (i) students have very limited theoretical background, and (ii) they are strongly focused on the direct applicability of what they are taught. In this context the authors stress the importance of making the practical applicability of the theory understandable to students, and making use of real software-related examples.

3   The Gen2sat Assignment

The first author has been teaching the Logic and Formal Methods course for Information Systems students at the University of Haifa for several years. The course covers introduction to logic and formal specification for the target audience of graduate students, many of whom already work in the industry, and a long time has passed since they took the basic mathematical courses (see [21] for further details on the challenges of logic course design for this target audience).

Looking for means to boost their motivation, we came up with the idea of an assignment that would have the "look and feel" of a software engineering assignment, so that its domain would be logic. We hoped that "tricking" the students into exercising their SE skills in the subject matter of logic would in fact encourage them to think of logical concepts in a way that would be both fun and beneficiary. Our main challenge was finding the right balance between requiring the students to dive into software technical details to keep the assignment interesting and related to SE, while still emphasizing enough the logical content as their main take-away message. In what follows we describe a concrete way we attempted to address this challenge.

3.1   Gen2sat

The choice of an appropriate software tool for 'hands-on' assignments in logic courses depends on what it is that we want to teach, and how we want to teach it. An interesting direction to consider in this context is the 'logic engineering' paradigm, ([2,13]) which aims to provide tools for automatic support of investigation of logics. In the spirit of this paradigm, various tools (e.g., MultLog ([3]), TINC ([5]), MetTeL ([18]) etc.) address large families of logics, thereby providing a "bird-view" of such logical concepts as semantics, proof system, axiom, theorem, etc. The tool Gen2sat is also a contribution to this paradigm, aiming to support the use of *sequent calculi* for the specification of logics. Sequent calculi are a prominent proof-theoretic framework, suitable for a wide variety of different logics, and quite a mainstream topic in logic and automated reasoning courses. Most efficient theorem provers based on sequent calculi utilize complex proof search algorithms which require a great deal of ingenuity and heuristic considerations (see, e.g., [6]). In contrast, Gen2sat uses a *uniform* method for deciding derivability using the polynomial reduction of [9] to SAT. Shifting the intricacies of implementation and heuristic considerations to the realm of off-the-shelf SAT solvers, the tool is lightweight and focuses solely on the logical content. For these reasons we chose Gen2sat as a tool for enhancing learning of the concept of sequent calculi. In addition, our deep familiarity with the code allowed us to introduce changes (e.g., planting bugs, changing the way the tool is called etc.) quickly and efficiently.

3.2   The Assignment

After teaching sequent calculi (in a two hour lecture), we introduced Gen2sat in class and explained its functionality and features. The students were then requested to play the role of *testers* of the tool. More concretely, they were requested to provide a test plan (as small as possible) which would cover all possible scenarios the tool could encounter. For a quantifiable measure for success we used a standard approach of measuring code coverage, instructing them to install the Eclemma plug-in for Eclipse ([7]) in order to determine the percentage of code activated for a given input. Thus, basically the students' assignment was producing a minimal test plan that would achieve maximal code coverage. While writing and analyzing different inputs to the tool, the students would potentially gain insights into the wide variety of non-classical logics defined in terms of sequent calculi.

In the second pilot we went one step further, introducing several easily detectable[2] bugs into Gen2sat code in the style of mutation testing ([8]), and encouraged the students to report as many bugs as they could find.

3.3 Results and Feedback

Eight students participated in the first pilot, all of them ended up submitting[3] test plans which achieved between 70 % – 85 % coverage, and included non-trivial sequent calculi for different languages. Five students participated in the second pilot, all of them got at least 70 % coverage, and two of them revealed two (out of three) bugs.

After submission they filled in an anonymous feedback questionnaire. Several students pointed out that the assignment was helpful in understanding logical concepts, e.g., *"it helped me see the variety of different connectives and rules"*, *"for me thinking of the extreme cases was really illuminating"*. The majority of students found the assignment engaging and fun: *"Really fun and challenging!"*, *"It's like a logical riddle, a game I enjoyed playing."*, *"I was sucked into this assignment and did not quit until I found a bug"*, etc. Notably, after receiving detailed instructions how to install Eclemma and use the code of the tool, no technical difficulties were reported by the students.

4   Summary and Future Research

In this paper we have described a practical way of enhancing the learning of concepts in formal logic using software-related assignments. Although drawing concrete conclusions is still premature, we believe that the pilot reported above is an indication of the potential of integrating hands-on assignments based on an interplay between software engineering and logic. It is our hope that this paper will initiate discourse on collecting and evaluating easy-to-use and shareable teaching resources which could be used in a 'plug-and-play' manner for teaching logico-mathematical concepts in ways relevant for modern software practitioners.

References

1. Almstrum, V.L.: Investigating student difficulties with mathematical logic. In: Dean, N., Hinchey, M.G. (eds.) Teaching and Learning Formal Methods, pp. 131–160. Academic Press, Cambridge (1996)

---

[2] The were two types of bugs: (i) those which caused unexpected messages to be printed, and (ii) those which produced unexpected results, e.g., refuting an axiom.

[3] Interestingly, seven students employed new connectives with arity greater than 2 and three employed also 0-ary connectives (which indeed increased coverage), although they have not seen any such example in class.

2. Areces, C.E.: Logic Engineering: The Case of Description and Hybrid Logics. Institute for Logic, Language and Computation (2000)
3. Baaz, M., Fermüller, C.G., Salzer, G., Zach, R.: Multlog 1.0: towards an expert system for many-valued logics. In: McRobbie, M.A., Slaney, J.K. (eds.) Automated Deduction–Cade-13. LNCS, vol. 1104, pp. 226–230. Springer, Heidelberg (1996)
4. Bjørner, D., Havelund, K.: 40 years of formal methods. In: Jones, C., Pihlajasaari, P., Sun, J. (eds.) FM 2014. LNCS, vol. 8442, pp. 42–61. Springer, Heidelberg (2014)
5. Ciabattoni, A., Spendier, L.: Tools for the investigation of substructural and paraconsistent logics. In: Fermé, E., Leite, J. (eds.) JELIA 2014. LNCS, vol. 8761, pp. 18–32. Springer, Heidelberg (2014)
6. Degtyarev, A., Voronkov, A.: The inverse method. In: Robinson, A., Voronkov, A. (eds.) Handbook of Automated Reasoning, vol. 1, pp. 179–272. MIT Press, Cambridge (2001)
7. Hoffmann, M., Iachelini, G.: Code coverage analysis for eclipse. Eclipse Summit Europe (2007)
8. Howden, W.E.: Weak mutation testing and completeness of test sets. IEEE Trans. Softw. Eng. **SE–8**(4), 371–379 (1982)
9. Lahav, O., Zohar, Y.: SAT-based decision procedure for analytic pure sequent calculi. In: Demri, S., Kapur, D., Weidenbach, C. (eds.) IJCAR 2014. LNCS, vol. 8562, pp. 76–90. Springer, Heidelberg (2014)
10. Makowsky, J.: Teaching logic for computer science: are we teaching the wrong narrative? In: Fourth International Conference on Tools for Teaching Logic, TTL (2015)
11. Johann, A.: Makowsky.: from Hilberts program to a logic tool box. Ann. Math. Artif. Intell. **53**(1–4), 225–250 (2008)
12. Mandrioli, D.: On the heroism of really pursuing formal methods. In: 2015 IEEE/ACM 3rd FME Workshop on Formal Methods in Software Engineering (Formalise), pp. 1–5. IEEE (2015)
13. Ohlbach, H.J.: Computer support for the development and investigation of logics. Logic J. IGPL **4**(1), 109–127 (1996)
14. Page, R.L.: Software is discrete mathematics. In: ACM SIGPLAN Notices, vol. 38, pp. 79–86. ACM (2003)
15. Sherman, B.F., Wither, D.P.: Mathematics anxiety and mathematics achievement. Math. Educ. Res. J. **15**(2), 138–150 (2003)
16. Sowa, J.F.: Conceptual graphs as a universal knowledge representation. Comput. Math. Appl. **23**(2), 75–93 (1992)
17. Tavolato, P., Vogt, F.: Integrating formal methods into computer science curricula at a university of applied sciences. In: TLA+ Workshop at the 18th International Symposium on Formal Methods, Paris, Frankreich (2012)
18. Tishkovsky, D., Schmidt, R.A., Khodadadi, M.: Mettel2: towards a tableau prover generation platform. In: PAAR@ IJCAR, pp. 149–162 (2012)
19. Wing, J.M.: Teaching mathematics to software engineers. In: Proceedings 4th International Conference Algebraic Methodology and Software Technology, AMAST 1995, Montreal, Canada, 3–7 July, 1995, pp. 18–40 (1995)
20. Wing, J.M.: Invited talk: weaving formal methods into the undergraduate computer science curriculum. In: Rus, T. (ed.) Algebraic Methodology and Software Technology. LNCS, vol. 1816, pp. 2–7. Springer, Heidelberg (2000)
21. Zamansky, A., Farchi, E.: Teaching logic to information systems students: challenges and opportunities. In: Fourth International Conference on Tools for Teaching Logic, TTL (2015)

User Involvement in Applications of the PoN

Dirk van der Linden[1,2](✉) and Irit Hadar[1]

[1] Department of Information Systems, University of Haifa, Haifa, Israel
{djtlinden,hadari}@is.haifa.ac.il
[2] EE-Network, Luxembourg, Luxembourg

Abstract. In a previous paper [12] we argued for more user-centric analysis of modeling languages' visual notation quality. Here we present initial findings from a systematic literature review on the use of the Physics of Notations (PoN) to further that argument. Concretely, we show that while the PoN is widely applied, these applications rarely actively involve intended users of a visual notation in setting the requirements for the notation, nor in evaluating its improvement or design according to the PoN's criteria. We discuss the potential reasons for this lack of user involvement, and what can be gained from increasing user involvement.

Keywords: Visual notation · Cognitive effectiveness · User involvement

1 Introduction

While many modeling languages, in particular their visual notation, used to be designed by committees of experts, recent years have seen an increasing number of cases where notational design has been grounded in frameworks and theories for ensuring their quality. A particularly prominent theory over the last years has been the Physics of Notations (PoN) [7], for which it has been noted that the number of citations thereof has steadily climbed, while at the same time citations to other works have declined [2].

Several concerns regarding both the PoN itself, as well as its applications have been noted in literature (cf. [3,10]). Given its popularity, and the tendency of its wielders in using the PoN's scientific grounding as a justification for their notation being well constructed, it is important to ensure that this strategy indeed leads to designs suited to the notation's users. Several principles of the PoN are concerned with cognitive factors that require tailoring to the specific group of users [14], such as for example whether a symbol suggests its meaning, or whether the representational medium is appropriate for its users and tasks. Because of this, involving users in applications of the PoN is important, as *in vitro* applications cannot provide such tailoring.

The seemingly obvious way to do so is to involve them in the design process of a notation and elicit any requirements they may hold, both directly and indirectly. In this ongoing research we investigate the thoroughness of applications

© Springer International Publishing Switzerland 2016
J. Krogstie et al. (Eds.): CAiSE 2016, LNBIP 249, pp. 109–115, 2016.
DOI: 10.1007/978-3-319-39564-7_11

of the PoN on several dimensions. To this end, we conduct a systematic literature review for analyzing all reported applications of the PoN. In this paper
we focus on analyzing the dimension of user involvement, showing that very few
applications of the PoN involve users in determining requirements for a visual
notation. Concretely, we ask: **RQ1.** *How many applications of the PoN involve
notation's users in determining requirements?* **RQ2.** *For what reasons do applications of the PoN not involve users?* To answer these questions we focused on
evaluating whether a paper's application of (parts of) the PoN involves users
in determining their requirements for the notation, i.e., if there is an explicit
requirements phase involving (intended) users of the visual notation before or
during iterations of the notation's design phase.

2   Reviewing Applications of the PoN

2.1   Literature Review Protocol

In an ongoing effort on analyzing the quality of applications of the PoN, we have
published a detailed research protocol and preliminary findings of a systematic
literature review (SLR) in [13]. The SLR includes peer-reviewed articles and
tech reports published by scientific institutions up to November 26th, 2015; the
articles were found to have used the PoN if they either: applied the PoN theory or
a part thereof to a visual notation, or discussed an application of the PoN theory
or a part thereof. Articles were excluded if they did not apply or discuss (any
part of) the PoN framework, were published in a language other than English,
were unpublished theses, or were overlapping versions of already including work.
Through the search criteria of papers citing the primary PoN publication [7] we
gathered a list of 502 articles. This list was analyzed by per-year queries in order
to select papers for inclusion in the SLR based on title, abstract and preliminary
reading. The initial selection resulted in 41 papers, of which 4 were excluded
after analysis of the full paper for lacking application of the PoN, which resulted
in a final list of 37 selected papers, in line with expected amounts for SLRs
focusing on technology evaluation papers [5].

2.2   Relevant Findings

Given the focus of this paper on user involvement, it is of note that the majority
of the selected papers (62 %) reported on novel (versions) of visual notations,
whereas the rest of the papers analyzed existing notations. With this number
of papers designing new notations, one would hope for a large user involvement
as well. Out of the thirty-seven analyzed papers, we found that only 5 of them
involved users in setting or determining the requirements for the visual notation.
Of those 5, only 2 reported any details, whereas the remaining 3 papers gave only
a cursory mention of users. This means that out of all the papers we investigated,
a mere 14 % involve and report on users for determining a visual notation's
requirements. If we look specifically at only those papers reporting on novel

or new versions of notations, only 3 papers reported to some degree on user involvement. Interestingly, papers that did not report on any involvement of users in requirements also often did not justify their use of the PoN: only in 24 % of the papers investigated in our SLR was any kind of justification (even if little more than re-iterating its prominence) given for using the PoN.

3 Potential Reasons for the Lack of User Involvement

In this section we will discuss the potential reasons for this significant lack of user involvement as can be inferred from further reading of the selected papers.

3.1 Notation Designers Considered as the Prototypical User

Many papers that propose new notations for conceptual modeling are based on the expertise and experience of the authors themselves. This manifests primarily in choices for the use of symbolic and iconic representation that the authors find most suiting (e.g., using skulls as an icon on misuse diagrams to stress a negative connotation [9]). Given that there are several papers in which the primary affiliation of at least one author is non-academic, this is not necessarily a bad reason, as the notation designers can be either currently active in industry and thus take on the role of (implicitly) providing requirements. This is especially evident in a paper selected in the SLR focused on the creation of an architecture description language, which explicitly noted: "although some ADLs have been put to industrial use in specific domains [...] the majority of ADL projects remain confined to laboratory-based case studies." [16]. The same authors criticized existing architecture languages such as ArchiMate for being "vertically optimized, limiting their attractiveness in many industrial projects." [16] Thus, authors originating (or currently active in) industry might simply bring the requirements with them and by doing so chose to forgo explicit user involvement.

3.2 Users are Involved, but Afterwards

Some of the papers selected in our SLR seem to agree on the need for eliciting requirements from users and empirically validating that a notation is suited for them, but tend to do so *a posteriori*. For some notations this has taken the shape of empirical experimentation comparing a newly designed or enhanced notation with an older one to examine whether a measurable improvement in cognitive factors, like reading speed, can be found. For example, an application of the PoN to feature diagrams was followed up by a paper setting out to empirically validate suggested changes to the notation, indeed noting that: "Despite the proposed new notation being based on Moodys nine evidence-based principles, the proposed improvements will remain as mere heuristics unless they are empirically proven. Empirical validation is performed via two user studies ..." [8].

However, a concern with this reason for not involving users directly in the design of a visual notation is that this *a posteriori* validation aims at checking whether specific requirements are satisfied, but not whether some requirements were missed and not taken into account.

3.3   Requirements are Derived from Theory

Some papers specifically argue *against* user involvement, favoring theoretical grounding, primarily reasoning that using existing frameworks to reach an acceptable overall level of quality is more cost-efficient. For example, Thomas stated that "analytic techniques such as Moody proposes can help steer designs in the right direction and provide some preliminary evaluation, particularly in cases where it is envisioned that the proposed representation will be used by a wide variety of users in various contexts to reach various goals." [11].

Many other papers selected in the SLR were not as explicit, but simply stated that the design of the visual notation was based on the PoN. This ranged from claiming to do so because of a proper grounding, e.g., "For the visual language proposed here, the PoN principles are applied because of their scientific and theoretical validity." [4], to simply stating that the PoN was used, e.g., "In designing the visual notation we followed Moodys nine principles." [6].

What seems critical here is that some of the principles of the PoN are inherently subjective due to their nature, and thus likely require user involvement. For example, the principle of semantic transparency states that shapes in the notation (i.e., symbols) suggest their meaning, which can be done by using iconic and pictorial representations. What meaning is suggested by symbols however, is strongly bound to personal and cultural factors, and thus cannot 'just' be given as a general rule. For this reason it is important to know how the (intended) users of the visual notation will think, and what connotations they will have to particular shapes and colors if one is to design for them without involving them.

3.4   Existing Theory is Assumed to Cover Requirements

In other cases it is also argued that the PoN covers requirements that can be expected to be elicited from users. A recent study investigated requirements posed by users of business process modeling notations, finding that "Interestingly a lot these non-functional requirements closely resemble the principles constructed by Moody. For example, the demand for descriptive, graphic elements corresponds to the 'Principle of Semantic Transparency'. Furthermore, demanding non-redundant symbolic corresponds to the 'Principle of Semiotic Clarity'." [15].

Indeed, one could be tempted to assume that the PoN and its principles cover most requirements that would be elicited. A paper selected in the SLR [1] explicitly detailed 8 additional requirements next to the 9 PoN principles, but has strong redundancy between the two sets of requirements. For example "R15 Self-descriptiveness (diagram and graphical symbols describe their meaning themselves)" [1] maps quite clearly to the PoN's principle of semantic transparency. An additional user-elicited requirement, "R16 Simplicity (graphical elements must be easy and fast to draw)" [1], while not directly mapped to an entire principle, is treated by the PoN's principle of Cognitive Fit, in particular its prescription for adapting to the representational medium, ensuring that symbols are not made up of complicated shapes when needed to be drawn by hand.

Nonetheless, it is dangerous to accept that the PoN, as-is, covers all potential requirements, especially as new requirements might arise over the years with changing business and technology environments.

3.5 Cognitive Effectiveness is an Afterthought

While it is difficult to show that cognitive effectiveness is truly an afterthought in the creation of some visual notations, we feel that it is a valid and evident conclusion that follows from the low level of detail reported regarding the treatment of the PoN in some papers, which dedicate not more than a single line to the effect the PoN has had on the presented notation by stating the design 'follows', 'was inspired by', or 'employs' the PoN, especially if no information is given on any individual principles and how they are satisfied by the notation.

4 A Benefit of Involving Users in Notations Design

So far we have shown that many applications of the PoN do not involve users in setting requirements for the visual notation, that when they do sometimes it leads to redundant requirements, and that in some cases authors even argue against user involvement. Nonetheless, we see a main lesson to be learned from this to the benefit of cognitive effectiveness efforts employing the PoN.

By eliciting requirements from (intended) users of the visual notation to be designed, even or especially when those requirements overlap with the Principles of the PoN, useful information about the relative importance of those principles is gained. One of the shortcomings of the PoN is that there is not a clear guideline or mechanism for attributing weights to the individual principles for an overall analysis, as particular principles may become more or less important for some tasks. In the context of the PoN it has explicitly been discussed how certain principles affect each other [7]. For example, attempting to increase the semiotic clarity of a notation can simultaneously reduce its graphic economy by leading to an increase of graphical symbols. Finding a balance between how 'satisfied' the principles are is a complicated task requiring information about what is more important. This can be achieved by eliciting requirements from users, seeing which are most often stated, and comparing them to the PoN's principles.

This co-incidentally also eases the difficulty of having to deal with creating a workable notation based on a multitude of requirements due to the notations use by many different people, in different contexts and for different tasks that Thomas [11] described. Instead, as many requirements as possible can be elicited, and compared to the PoN principles in order to personalize the PoN by changing the weighting of the different principles for the group of users and, where necessary, even giving rise to different dialects of a notation when particular requirements are favored for a particular task or modeling context. Thus, explicitly involving users and their requirements for the notation does not come in place of the PoN, but actually complements and strengthens its ability to lead to cognitively effective visual notations.

5   Concluding Outlook

In this position paper we have discussed some initial findings from a systematic literature review on the use of the PoN theory. We showed that very little papers applying the PoN to design or analyze of a visual notation explicitly involve users in setting the requirements for that notation, and discussed potential reasons why there is such a lack of user involvement. Finally, we made an argument that contrary to some arguments against user involvement, explicitly eliciting requirements from users does not have to be in place of the PoN, but can actually strengthen its use by allowing one to personalize relative importance and weighting of the PoN principles to the audience of the notation.

References

1. Breitenbücher, U., Binz, T., Kopp, O., Leymann, F., Schumm, D.: Vino4TOSCA: a visual notation for application topologies based on TOSCA. In: Meersman, R., et al. (eds.) OTM 2012, Part I. LNCS, vol. 7565, pp. 416–424. Springer, Heidelberg (2012)
2. Granada, D., Vara, J.M., Brambilla, M., Bollati, V., Marcos, E.: Analysing the cognitive effectiveness of the webml visual notation. SoSyM pp. 1–33 (2013)
3. Gulden, J., Reijers, H.A.: Toward advanced visualization techniques for conceptual modeling. In: Proceedings of the CAiSE Forum 2015, Stockholm, Sweden, 8–12 June 2015
4. Herter, J., Brown, R., Ovtcharova, J.: A visual language for the collaborative visualization of integrated conceptual models in product development scenarios. In: Abramovici, M., Stark, R. (eds.) Smart Product Engineering. LNPE, vol. 5, pp. 805–814. Springer, Heidelberg (2013)
5. Kitchenham, B., Brereton, O.P., Budgen, D., Turner, M., Bailey, J., Linkman, S.: Systematic literature reviews in software engineering-a systematic literature review. Inf. Softw. Technol. **51**(1), 7–15 (2009)
6. Laurent, P., Mader, P., Cleland-Huang, J., Steele, A.: A taxonomy and visual notation for modeling globally distributed requirements engineering projects. In: 5th IEEE International Conference on Global Software Engineering, pp. 35–44. IEEE (2010)
7. Moody, D.L.: The "physics" of notations: toward a scientific basis for constructing visual notations in software engineering. IEEE Trans. Softw. Eng. **35**(6), 756–779 (2009)
8. Saeed, M., Saleh, F., Al-Insaif, S., El-Attar, M.: Empirical validating the cognitive effectiveness of a new feature diagrams visual syntax. Inf. Softw. Technol. **71**, 1–26 (2016)
9. Saleh, F., El-Attar, M.: A scientific evaluation of the misuse case diagrams visual syntax. Inf. Softw. Technol. **66**, 73–96 (2015)
10. Störrle, H., Fish, A.: Towards an operationalization of the "Physics of Notations" for the analysis of visual languages. In: Moreira, A., Schätz, B., Gray, J., Vallecillo, A., Clarke, P. (eds.) MODELS 2013. LNCS, vol. 8107, pp. 104–120. Springer, Heidelberg (2013)
11. Thomas, J.C., Diament, J., Martino, J., Bellamy, R.K.: Using the "physics" of notations to analyze a visual representation of business decision modeling. In: 2012 IEEE Symposium on VL/HCC, pp. 41–44. IEEE (2012)

12. van der Linden, D.: An argument for more user-centric analysis of modeling languages' visual notation quality. In: Persson, A., Stirna, J. (eds.) CAiSE 2015 Workshops. LNBIP, vol. 215, pp. 114–120. Springer, Heidelberg (2015)
13. van der Linden, D., Hadar, I.: Evaluating the evaluators-an analysis of cognitive effectiveness efforts for visual notations. In: 11th International Conference on Evaluation of Novel Approaches to Software Engineering (ENASE). ScitePress (2016)
14. van der Linden, D., Zamansky, A., Hadar, I.: How cognitively effective is a visual notation? on the inherent difficulty of operationalizing the physics of notations. In: 21st International Conference on Exploring Modelling Methods for Systems Analysis and Design (EMMSAD). Springer (2016)
15. Wiebring, J., Sandkuhl, K.: Selecting the "right" notation for business process modeling: experiences from an industrial case. In: Matulevičius, R., Dumas, M. (eds.) BIR 2015. LNBIP, vol. 229, pp. 129–144. Springer, Heidelberg (2015)
16. Woods, E., Bashroush, R.: Modelling large-scale information systems using adls-an industrial experience report. J. Syst. Softw. **99**, 97–108 (2015)

A Visual Logical Language for System Modelling in Combinatorial Test Design

Maria Spichkova[1], Anna Zamansky[2(✉)], and Eitan Farchi[3]

[1] RMIT University, Melbourne, Australia
maria.spichkova@rmit.edu.au
[2] University of Haifa, Haifa, Israel
annazam@is.haifa.ac.il
[3] IBM Haifa Research Lab, Haifa, Israel

Abstract. This position paper addresses some weaknesses of the standard logical languages used for specification of system models in combinatorial test design. To overcome these weaknesses, we propose a new logical language which uses visual elements with the aim to lower the cognitive load of the modeller and thereby reduce the risk of modelling errors.

Keywords: Cognitive aspects of modelling · Combinatorial test design

1 Introduction

Combinatorial Test Design (CTD) is an effective methodology for test design of complex software systems, in which a system is modelled using a *combinatorial model* [6,16]. The CTD approach aims to systematically optimise the number of test cases, while ensuring the coverage of given conditions.

There is a large body of works on different aspects of CTD (see [6] for a comprehensive survey), and numerous tools have been developed (e.g., 40 tools are currently listed in [7]). However, according to [6], only 5 % of publications on CTD address the process of constructing combinatorial models. As noted in [13], *"An under-explored challenge for wide deployment of CTD in industry is the manual process for modelling and maintaining the test space"*. Indeed, the task of combinatorial model construction for complex systems heavily relies on tacit human knowledge, and therefore will always remain the task of a human tester. The complexity and error-prone nature of this task calls for more emphasis on human-centric approaches for supporting CTD.

In previous works we have considered two directions for more human-centric support of the manual process of combinatorial model construction: agile error correction [15] and support of modelling with multiple levels of abstraction [11, 12]. In this paper, we focus on the *logical language* for specifying the restrictions in combinatorial models and discuss how it can be modified to better serve the needs of the human modeller.

© Springer International Publishing Switzerland 2016
J. Krogstie et al. (Eds.): CAiSE 2016, LNBIP 249, pp. 116–121, 2016.
DOI: 10.1007/978-3-319-39564-7_12

The logical languages currently used in CTD tools are based on the standard Boolean semantics. This semantics has been criticised as inadequate for supporting model evolution in [13], where a more sophisticated lattice-based semantics was proposed. In this position paper we point out some implicit assumptions which are made when using Boolean semantics in the context of CTD. We propose simple visual constructs to make these assumptions more explicit, thereby reducing the cognitive load of the modeller when specifying the logical restrictions, as well as the chances for human errors. We show how these constructs can be used as an alternative solution to the problems pointed out in [13].

2   Logical Restrictions in CTD Models

A *combinatorial model*, consists of a set of parameters, their respective possible values and a set of logical restrictions on the value combinations [6,16]. Thus, in CTD a system is modelled using a finite set of system parameters $\mathbf{A} = \{\mathbf{A}_1, \ldots, \mathbf{A}_n\}$ together with their corresponding associated values $\mathbf{V} = \{\mathbf{V}(\mathbf{A}_1), \ldots, \mathbf{V}(\mathbf{A}_n)\}$. A *scenario* (or test) is an assignment of a value from $\mathbf{V}(\mathbf{A}_i)$ to each $\mathbf{A}_i$. A *combinatorial model* for $\mathbf{A}$ is defined as a set of scenarios (tests).

For an example, consider the standard toy combinatorial model often used in CTD literature, cf. [13]. Suppose our system is modelled using three parameters:

- ItemStatus (denoted by **IS**)
- OrderShipping (denoted by **OS**)
- DeliveryTimeframe (denoted by **DT**)

Thus, the set of parameters is specified by $\mathbf{A} = \{\mathbf{IS}, \mathbf{OS}, \mathbf{DT}\}$, where the corresponding values of the parameters are defined by

$$\mathbf{IS} = \{InStock, OutOfStock, NoSuchProduct\}$$
$$\mathbf{OS} = \{Air, Ground\}$$
$$\mathbf{DT} = \{Immediate, 3\,Days, 1\,Month\}$$

Assuming that there are only three parameters in this example, a combinatorial model of the system is a set of scenarios, (which are assignments of values to parameters), such as:

$$s_1 : (\mathbf{IS} = InStock, \mathbf{OS} = Air, \mathbf{DT} = Immediate)$$
$$s_2 : (\mathbf{IS} = InStock, \mathbf{OS} = Ground, \mathbf{DT} = Immediate)$$

There are overall 18 possible scenarios in this example. However, in practice not all the scenarios are executable: e.g., it is not possible to have an immediate delivery time when the item is sent via ground. Therefore, the most challenging manual task in combinatorial modelling is separating the valid (executable) scenarios, and ruling out the invalid ones.

Usually this is done by using some dialect of classical logic. Figure 1 presents logical restrictions from a model for the above example, constructed using IBM FoCuS tool (IBM Functional Coverage Unified Solution), cf. [10,14].

Type	Expression
Exclusion	OrderDeliveryTimeframe.equals("oneMonth") && OrderShipping.equals("air")
If-Then	[OrderDeliveryTimeframe == "immediate"] ==> [OrderShipping != "ground"]

Fig. 1. Logical restrictions in IBM FoCuS

The semantics of the logical languages used in the context of combinatorial modelling is (implicitly) assumed to be the standard Boolean semantics. As we explain below, this implicit assumption may cause ambiguity and confusion at the time of model construction. In [13] the Boolean semantics is also criticised as inadequate for supporting model evolution. One of the main criticisms is an inconsistent interpretation of test validity in case a new value is added. Considering, e.g., the following logical restriction which can used to specify a combinatorial model: $R_1 : \mathbf{DT} = Immediate \rightarrow \mathbf{OS} \neq Ground$.

If a new value, e.g., Sea, is added to $\mathbf{V}(\mathbf{OS})$, then the test (scenario) $s_3 = (\mathbf{IS} = InStock, \mathbf{OS} = Sea, \mathbf{DT} = Immediate)$ is valid, according to R_1. Now the following restriction is equivalent to R_1 in the sense that it induces the same set of valid tests: $R_2 : \mathbf{DT} = Immediate \rightarrow \mathbf{OS} = Air$. But using R_2 instead of R_1 renders s_3 invalid, leading to an inconsistent interpretation of tests including the new value Sea.

Tzoref-Brill and Maoz [13] propose an alternative, lattice-based semantics to deal with the above problem, as well as another problem related to splitting values of a parameter. Referring to alternative solutions, they note: *"One may suggest to remove the negation operator from the constraint language made available to the practitioner. While this will resolve the inconsistent interpretation, it will extremely limit the flexibility of the practitioner to specify constraints in a concise manner, and is thus infeasible in practice"*.

We believe that the problematic negation operator is a symptom of a much deeper problem: lack of explicit representation of extra assumptions made in the CTD domain. The logic of CTD is related to classical logic in roughly the same way as in database theory: quite similar, but the devil is in the details. More concretely, a standard approach in database theory assumes the closed world assumption (CWA), cf. [8], according to which whatever is not entailed by the database is assumed to be false. A formalisation of this assumption, therefore, consists in adding to the database the negations of all literals not entailed by it. Another important issue in database theory is that of *integrity constraints* [9]. The idea is that only certain database states are considered acceptable, and an integrity constraint is meant to enforce these legal states.

Assumptions close in spirit to the above are mirrored in the CTD domain. The first is that whatever tests are not excluded by the logical restrictions, are considered valid. The second is that each parameter $\mathbf{A}$ of the model may assume *exactly* one of its possible values $\mathbf{V}(\mathbf{A})$.

We can now note the following: the two logical restrictions R_1 and R_2 are *not* logically equivalent in first-order classical logic (with equality). They are equivalent under the explicit integrity constraint $IC_1 : \mathbf{OS} = Air \vee \mathbf{OS} = Ground$. Note also that after adding the new value Sea to $\mathbf{V}(\mathbf{OS})$, the integrity constraint IC_1

becomes invalid. Hence, the answer to the question whether the test s_3 is valid depends on the assumed integrity constraint. Under the constraint IC_1 above, it is invalid. Under the refined constraint $IC_2 : \mathbf{OS} = Air \vee \mathbf{OS} = Ground \vee \mathbf{OS} = Sea$. it is valid. Therefore, what is called in [13] inconsistent interpretation, can be viewed as merely a change in the assumed integrity constraints.

3   A New Visual Logical Language

In light of the problems discussed above, our aim is to make the logical language of CTD modelling less ambiguous by integrating *explicitly* the assumption that any parameter $\mathbf{A}$ assumes *exactly* one value from $\mathbf{V}(\mathbf{A})$. In other words, given $\mathbf{V}(\mathbf{A}) = \{v_1, \ldots, v_n\}$, it holds that $\mathbf{A} = v_1 \vee \mathbf{A} = v_2 \vee \ldots \mathbf{A} = v_n$. Thus, if $\mathbf{A} \neq v_i$, then the value of $\mathbf{A}$ belongs to the set $\{v_1, \ldots, v_{i-1}, v_{i+1}, \ldots, v_n\}$. Drawing inspiration from the syntax of labelled formulas in non-classical logics (cf. [1,2]), we think of the basic atomic formula in the proposed language as an expression of the form: $\mathbf{A} : L$, where $L \subseteq \mathbf{V}(\mathbf{A})$. This formula is supposed to be true (or to hold) iff the value of $\mathbf{A}$ is an element of the set L.

The visual element corresponding to $\mathbf{A} : L$ explicitly contains both L and $\mathbf{V}(\mathbf{A})\backslash L$. More concretely, any such element is represented a partition of $\mathbf{V}(\mathbf{A})$ into valid and invalid elements, to remind the tester *explicitly* about the assumptions discussed above, cf. Fig. 2.

Parameter: A	
VALID	INVALID
v_1	v_3
v_2	v_4

Fig. 2. Basic partition formula for a parameter $\mathbf{A}$ (Color figure online)

The above visual formula is equivalent to the Boolean formula $(\mathbf{A} = v_1 \vee \mathbf{A} = v_2 \vee \mathbf{A} = v_3 \vee \mathbf{A} = v_4) \wedge \mathbf{A} \neq v_3 \wedge \mathbf{A} \neq v_4$, and so also entails $\mathbf{A} = v_1 \vee \mathbf{A} = v_2$.

It is important to note that negation is built-in already, by using different colours to denote the valid and invalid values. This resolves the problematic issues with using negation discussed above. This is not accidental that we used light green colour to denote valid values, and grey to denote invalid values. This conforms to the common standards in interface design, cf. [4]: grey is often used to denote options that exist but are not accessible for some reasons. Moreover, we would like to avoid combinations like green/red, which are perceived as aggressive by many users, and, moreover, are not distinguishable by colour-blind users. We also aim to avoid having areas of strong colour and high contrast, as they can produce afterimages when the viewer looks away from the screen, which increases the cognitive load and visual stress from prolonged viewing [3]. On addition to the (implicit) negation, the basic elements (or partitions) such as the one demonstrated on Fig. 2 can be connected via the usual binary logical operators of implication, conjunction and disjunction, whose semantics remains standard (and self-explanatory). Figure 3 shows that, e.g., the logical restrictions R_1 and R_2 described above have the same representation in our visual language:

Fig. 3. Representation of the logical conditions R_1/R_2

Note that our visual language provides simple and intuitive support for handling the problems of refinement and splitting, discussed in [13]. For instance, adding a new value 'Sea' to the Order Shipping (**OS**) parameter values should enforce the modeller to make a decision where to place it in the formula: either in the valid or invalid zone, see Fig. 4:

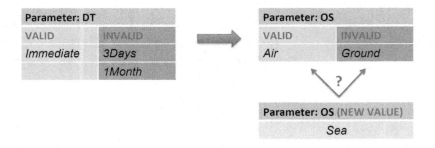

Fig. 4. Refining the logical condition when a new value is added

4   Summary and Future Research

The need for human-centric approaches in supporting the process of combinatorial test design is increasingly acknowledged [6,13]. This paper explores how standard logical languages used for the specification of model constraints can be better adapted to the needs of the human modeller. We propose a variation of a classical logic dialiect, in which implicit assumptions made in the context of CTD are explicitly represented using visual elements. Our next step will be implementing and evaluating a tool based on the principles proposed in this paper. We also plan to extend this work to support model evolution [13], update [10] and refinement [11]. Another interesting direction is investigating the ways in which human-centric approaches of combinatorial test design can benefit from the large body of research on cognitive effectiveness of visual notations, cf. [5].

References

1. Baaz, M., Fermüller, C., Salzer, G., Zach, R.: Labeled calculi and finite-valued logics. Stud. Logica. **61**(1), 7–33 (1998)
2. Baaz, M., Lahav, O., Zamansky, A.: Finite-valued semantics for canonical labelled calculi. J. Autom. Reasoning **51**(4), 401–430 (2013)
3. MacDonald, L.: Using color effectively in computer graphics. IEEE Comput. Graph. Appl. **19**(4), 20–35 (1999)
4. Marcus, A.: Siggraph'93 tutorial notes: graphic design for user interfaces (1993)
5. Moody, D.: The "physics" of notations: toward a scientific basis for constructing visual notations in software engineering. IEEE Trans. Softw. Eng. **35**(6), 756–779 (2009)
6. Nie, C., Leung, H.: A survey of combinatorial testing. ACM Comput. Surv. (CSUR) **43**(2), 11 (2011)
7. Pairwise Testing Website. http://www.pairwise.org/tools.asp
8. Reiter, R.: On closed world data bases. In: Gallaire, H., Minker, J. (eds.) Logic and Data Bases, pp. 55–76. Springer, Heidelberg (1978)
9. Reiter, R.: On integrity constraints. In: Proceedings of the 2nd Conference on Theoretical Aspects of Reasoning about Knowledge, pp. 97–111. Morgan Kaufmann Publishers Inc. (1988)
10. Segall, I., Tzoref-Brill, R.: Interactive refinement of combinatorial test plans. In: 2012 34th International Conference on Software Engineering (ICSE), pp. 1371–1374 (2012)
11. Spichkova, M., Zamansky, A.: A human-centred framework for combinatorial test design. In: Proceedings of ENASE (2016)
12. Spichkova, M., Zamansky, A., Farchi, E.: Towards a human-centred approach in modelling and testing of cyber-physical systems. In: Proceedings of the International Workshop on Automated Testing of Cyber-Physical Systems in the Cloud (2015)
13. Tzoref-Brill, R., Maoz, S.: Lattice-based semantics for combinatorial model evolution. In: Finkbeiner, B., et al. (eds.) ATVA 2015. LNCS, vol. 9364, pp. 276–292. Springer, Heidelberg (2015). doi:10.1007/978-3-319-24953-7_22
14. Wojciak, P., Tzoref-Brill, R.: System level combinatorial testing in practice-the concurrent maintenance case study. In: Proceedings of the 2014 IEEE International Conference on Software Testing, Verification, and Validation, pp. 103–112. IEEE Computer Society (2014)
15. Zamansky, A., Farchi, E.: Helping the tester get it right: towards supporting agile combinatorial test design. In: 2nd Human-Oriented Formal Methods workshop (HOFM 2015) (2015)
16. Zhang, J., Zhang, Z., Ma, F.: Introduction to combinatorial testing. In: Zhang, J., Zhang, Z., Ma, F. (eds.) Automatic Generation of Combinatorial Test Data. SpringerBriefs in Computer Science, pp. 1–16. Springer, Heidelberg (2014)

Peel the Onion: Use of Collaborative and Gamified Tools to Enhance Software Engineering Education

Naomi Unkelos-Shpigel[✉]

Information Systems Department, University of Haifa, Carmel Mountain,
31905 Haifa, Israel
naomiu@is.haifa.ac.il

Abstract. As software engineering and information systems projects become more and more of collaborative nature, project-based courses are an integral part of information system (IS) and system engineering (SE) curricula. Several challenges stem from the nature of these courses, the most significant are equal participation of all students, and creating projects of high quality and utility. Several mechanisms, such as gamification and collaborative tools, were helpful when dealing with these challenges. This paper present a teaching case, where several tools were used, based on the onion model for open source systems, and several motivation theories.

Keywords: Gamification · Collaboration · Education

1 Introduction

In recent years, the software and information industries has recognized the contribution of a collaborative projects, and projects are being developed according to agile manifesto [2], focusing on continuous review among practitioners, within the development team, and among teams. However, information system (IS) and software engineering (SE) students are not being trained during their studies to this type of collaborative work.

Project-based courses, where the students are required to develop a prototype as final assignment, are an integral part of IS and SE degrees curricula. The teachers of these courses face several challenges, such as ensuring equal participation of all students in the workload, and creating projects which will be both of high quality and utility, all in parallel to teaching a large amount of theoretical background. This paper describes the result of teaching several courses of this nature, mainly those requiring developing a prototype or a website, where several gamified and collaborative tools were used. The teaching method described in the paper can be used by other lecturers teaching similar courses. To actively receive feedback on their work, students were asked to test potential user's response to the prototype. To encourage interaction and collaboration among students, each group presented their project to other students in class. Each student was asked to share thoughts on other group projects, using an online form. This interactive method of experiencing other group's work, while

J. Krogstie et al. (Eds.): CAiSE 2016, LNBIP 249, pp. 122–128, 2016.
DOI: 10.1007/978-3-319-39564-7_13

presenting their own work, resulted in much positive feedbacks about the projects and the assessment method.

This paper presents the summary of a teaching case of a course in the discipline of software engineering. The teaching method drew inspiration from the onion model for OSS (Open Source Systems) [1], and motivation theories such as SDT – Self Determination Theory [7], and the flow theory [9]. These motivation theories discuss how to motivate employees to take active part in the work, and to encourage them to strive for more productive behavior, mainly by encouraging intrinsic and extrinsic motivation [7], and by achieving a state of flow, where the worker is immersed into the task [9]. The Kahoot! Application was used each lecture, to test students' knowledge from the previous lecture, and to present the results to all the class in a gamified manner. GoogleDocs were used to perform additional collaborative exploratory assignment during class. Google forms were used for a collaborative peer review.

Leveraging on the principles of collaborative and gamified tools for education, several questions: (1) How can we promote software engineering students productive behavior via using collaborative and gamified tools? (2) What are the benefits of embedding collaboration and gamification techniques in software development education?

The next section presents the background for the teaching case. Section 3 details the teaching method. Section 4 presents students' responses to the teaching method, and Sect. 5 discusses the conclusions and further evaluation.

2 Scientific Background

2.1 Collaborative Tools in Education

Collaborative tools have been used in high education for several decades [3], and in recent years, Web 2.0 tools are used in education, as part of an ongoing effort to enhance motivation among students. However, teachers' perception towards the use of these tools are still ambiguous, as many teachers do not believe these methods can help to raise student motivation.

Several attempts were made to use several tools [6], where students worked with various tools during the semester, and concluded that these days it is better to use experimental teaching, where students take an active role in class, rather than frontal teaching. However, additional research is in order in order to inspect collaborative work and its outcomes in SE and IS education.

2.2 Gamification in IS and SE Education

Persuasive technologies, and specifically Gamification, were acknowledged as changing employees' motivation and behavior. Gamification is defined as "the integration of Game Mechanics in non-game environments to increase audience engagement, loyalty and fun" [5, p. 2]. Gamification research from the last few years is targeted on using gamification mechanisms for changing behaviors of specific populations. In the context of IS and SE students [4, 6, 8]. In example, in order to engage software engineering students in development, documentation, bug reporting, and test coverage, using social rewords. The students who used these systems showed statistically proven improvement in their work results. A good example is [4], which identified three types of activities needed to be performed when engaging gamification into software engineering: analysis, integration, and evaluation, and found that students performing these activities had better results in software engineering.

These teaching cases and their outcomes are a strong motivation for using collaborative and gamified tools in SE education. The teaching method is described in the next section.

3   Collaborative and Gamified Teaching Method

3.1   The Method

This section describes the teaching method, used in an advanced software engineering course, intended for third year undergraduate students. The course consisted of 60 students, who were working in teams of four, developing a software product. All the teams received the same assignment – to build a plugin for Eclipse IDE, which provides a gamification tool for performing code review. The programming methodology was agile, so the students worked in three iterations. First, the students built a simple example of their project, and planned the iteration and their outcomes. The teams also implemented all the internal structure of their projects, mainly classes and APIs. At the next iteration, the teams completed the GUI of the system. At the last iteration, the teams performed final product integration, along with integration tests of the components.

The teaching method presented in this paper was inspired from the onion model for OSS projects [1]. This model aims to achieve quality of the open source software product by differentiating between contributors types - the core development team (core of the onion), contributing developers (first layer), bug reporters (second layer), and users (third layer). Each of these groups has its own contribution to the product, according to the definition of its role. In this teaching case, the onion model was an inspiration a model that reflecting the use of collaborative and gamified tools in education:

Student level – At the beginning of the lecture, after a brief recap of the previous lecture, students participated in a Kahoot! quiz. Each quiz included 5 questions regarding the material of the previous lecture. The students were asked to participate using their personal id number, and answered the quiz using their personal computers or smartphones. During the quiz, the students accumulated points, according to the correctness of their answers, and how fast they answered. Finally, a winner was chosen automatically by the application.

Team level – Toward the end of the semester, the students learned about cloud computing solution for software products. The students were given an assignment during class, where a case study was presented to them (based on a true story), and they were asked to provide a cloud computing solution, explaining why they chose this particular solution. They were instructed to work using Google Docs, where each student used their laptop or smartphone, while the document is written collaboratively by the team. They were told that the documents will be checked after the lesson is over.

Course level – In the middle of the semester, in order to encourage interaction and collaboration among students, each team presented their project to other students in class. Each student was asked to share thoughts on other group projects, using an online google form. As there were 15 teams in the class, each student was asked to review at least seven other teams, in order to receive credit for the assignment. In this interactive method of experiencing other group's work, each student experienced both the role of presenter of their team work, and a reviewer of other teams' work (Fig. 1).

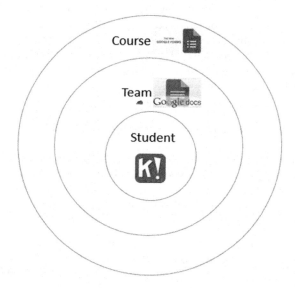

Fig. 1. The onion model for tools used by students

3.2   Analyzing the Teaching Model from a Motivational Perspective

Student level - According to the theory of flow, the use of Kahoot! supports the five elements of flow [9]: *Clarity* – The questions and game scoring are simple and clear; *Centering* – players feel they are in the center, gaining individual points as they answer the questions; *Choice* – As the game includes multiple-choice questions, choice is part of game participation; *Commitment* – each student wants to answer the question correctly as they perceive the success in answering correctly to be directly linked to succeeding in the course; *Challenge* - the game provides challenge to all the stakeholders in the process, when they are required to improve the quality of their work in order to earn additional individual and team points.

Team level - Using Google Docs in the context of team task supports the group flow elements [9]: *A compelling, shared goal* – all the players have the same goal of getting a high team score; *A sense of being in control* – since each player sends their work when they choose, each of them has full control on their progress in the game; *Blending egos* – since there is a team goal, along with the personal goal, all the players' egos are blended to achieved a higher team score; *Equal participation* – each of the players are allowed to participate in the writing the document equally; *Familiarity* – all the players in the same team are personally familiar; *Constant, spontaneous communication* – the Google Docs environment allows all the players to communicate with each other; *The potential for failure* – the players are aware of the fact that if the result of their work will not promote the overall product, it will considered as a team failure.

The course level – This method offers rules and regulation (in the form of a scheduled task), to encourage students to ask for review, and to share their knowledge with peers outside of their team, thus creating extrinsic motivation. Thus, the method supports the theory of SDT – Self Determination Theory, which can be used to encourage intrinsic motivation of employess engaged in SE tasks [7].

Additional factors in this task are in correlation with the principles of SDT: Team work was done under uncertainty; Having the students reviewing each other, expressing competence and autonomy; Students promoted their work to get review, thus expressing relatedness to their work.

4   Students' Responses to the Teaching Method

As mentioned before, at the end of the course, the students filled out a summary questionnaire, where they were asked about their opinions about the different tools used in the course, and whether they think the tools were helpful for them in understanding what is SE. Several comments for each level are presented below:

Student level

"I really liked the fact that it summarized an entire topic with a few questions"
"Helped to encourage student participation in the class"
"Nice and refreshing, very original, helped to understand the material"

Students were very enthusiastic about using the Kahoot! application. At the beginning of the lecture, after a brief recap, they were happy to pull out their smartphones and participate in the game. Interestingly enough, though the material was presented to them again a few minutes before, some of them still got the answers wrong. However, they still enjoyed the game and applauded the winner of each game. At the end of the semester, they asked for the questions, saying that reviewing the questions would help them during exam preparation.

Team level

"A collaborative tool that enhanced participation of the students"
"High usability for us as users"
"Great tool. This is the how we should learn nowadays"

Students had trouble at first to login to the joint document. When they started working, most of the teams fully participated. Some teams even stayed after the lecture to continue and work on the document. Students found the tool very helpful, completed the task quickly and successfully, and reported that they continued to use this tool later on, working on the project documentation and tasks in other courses.

Course level

"The interactive way of learning helped me in constructing the prototype"
"I learned that having a simple and easy to use application is highly important, so the users keep on using it"
"Reviewing other teams' prototypes helped us to come to improve our product"

Students responded very positively to the task, and spent more than an hour reviewing other teams. About 500 reviews were written, while teams were trying to draw other students to review them. Students reported they enjoyed the task, compared themselves to their peers and received many insightful ideas for improving their work. Each group got the reviews their work received, anonymously, so they could use them and improve the prototype. Students reported this experience was unprecedented in their studies. They said it was the first time they felt how is it like to be on both sides of the aisle –developers who need to defend their work, and reviewers who inspect other teams' work, and to write a critique.

5   Expected Contribution and Further Evaluation

In this teaching case, students used several collaborative and gamified tools, encouraged to participate in the student level, team level, and course level. According to their feedback, they felt the use of tools enhanced their learning experience, and assisted them in the development of the project. According to their responses, this experience of collaborative work, and reviewing the work of peers, was a good preparation for their future roles in industry, and to their overall performance in the course.

Future qualitative research is needed in order to explore the effect each tool has on the student, the collaboration within the team and between the teams. Quantitative research can be beneficial to understand if students' performance in the final exam was in correlation with their achievement in the various levels of the model.

References

1. Aberdour, M.: Achieving quality in open-source software. IEEE Softw. **24**(1), 58–64 (2007)
2. Beck, K., Beedle, M., Van Bennekum, A., Cockburn, A., Cunningham, W., Fowler, M., Kern, J.: Manifesto for Agile software development (2001). http://academic.brooklyn.cuny.edu/cis/sfleisher/Chapter_03_sim.pdf
3. Brown, S.A.: Seeing Web 2.0 in context: a study of academic perceptions. Internet High. Educ. **15**(1), 50–57 (2012)
4. Dubois, D.J., Tamburrelli, G.: Understanding gamification mechanisms for software development. In: Proceedings of the 2013 9th Joint Meeting on Foundations of Software Engineering, pp. 659–662. ACM (2013)
5. Deterding, S., Khaled, R., Nacke, L., Dixon, D.: Gamification: toward a definition. In: CHI 2011 Gamification Workshop Proceedings, pp. 12–15 (2011)

6. El-Masri, M., Tarhini, A., Hassouna, M., Elyas, T.: A design science approach to Gamify education: from games to platforms. In: Twenty-Third European Conference on Information Systems (ECIS), pp. 26–38 (2015)
7. Ryan, R.M., Deci, E.L.: Self-determination theory and the facilitation of intrinsic motivation, social development, well-being. Am. Psychol. **55**(1), 68 (2000)
8. Sheth, S.K., Bell, J.S., Kaiser, G.E.: Increasing student engagement in software engineering with gamification, pp. 43–47. ACM (2012)
9. Unkelos-Shpigel, N., Hadar, I.: Gamifying software development environments using cognitive principles. In: CAiSE Forum 2015 (2015)

ENBIS 2016

Energy Enhancement of Multi-application Monitoring Systems for Smart Buildings

Ozgun Pinarer[1,2(✉)], Yann Gripay[1], Sylvie Servigne[1], and Atay Ozgovde[2]

[1] Universite de Lyon, CNRS INSA-Lyon, LIRIS,
UMR CNRS 5205, 69621 Lyon, France
{ozgun.pinarer,yann.gripay,sylvie.servigne}@insa-lyon.fr
[2] Department of Computer Engineering, Galatasaray University,
Ciragan Cad. No: 36, 34349 Istanbul, Turkey
{opinarer,aozgovde}@gsu.edu.tr

Abstract. High energy consumption of sensor devices is a major problem in smart building systems, since it strongly impacts the system lifetime. However, existing approaches are often fitted to a single monitoring application and rely on static configurations for sensor devices: optimization of their acquisition and transmission frequencies to actual multiple application requirements is not tackled. In this paper, we focus on energy-aware dynamic sensor device re-configuration to lower energy consumption while fulfilling real-time application requirements. We introduce the Smart-Service Stream-oriented Sensor Management (3SoSM) that binds together sensor configuration and management of sensor data streams. We present a multi-application monitoring system architecture that optimizes application requirements for data streams into sensor device configurations, and we relate the experiments with our experimental platform.

Keywords: Sensor data management · Smart building · Wireless sensor network · Continuous query processing

1 Introduction

Nowadays it is well known that traditional buildings are primary consumers of a significant portion of energy resources, thus, most of the world's cities are concerned by the potential of smart buildings. The design of these buildings is based on sustainable construction standards to consume less energy than traditional buildings and to minimize their impacts on the natural environment. Smart building technology brings in some nice features such as security, comfort and accessibility, however with extra constraints to acquire and analyze "Big" and/or "Fast" Data generated by devices like sensors: providing useful services for occupants such as thermal comfort, air quality, physical security, etc., comes at the cost of managing/processing large and complex real-time datasets. Big Data, with its 5 Vs (Volume, Velocity, Variety, Veracity, Value), represents a new

This work is supported by INSA-Lyon, LIRIS Research Laboratory.

© Springer International Publishing Switzerland 2016
J. Krogstie et al. (Eds.): CAiSE 2016, LNBIP 249, pp. 131–142, 2016.
DOI: 10.1007/978-3-319-39564-7_14

era in data exploration and utilization, and tackles sensing, analysing, sharing, storing, querying, etc., very large amount of data [1].

Smart building technology can enhance the energy consumption of buildings, however its infrastructure often consists of a wireless sensor network with devices that have limited energy and battery lifetime [2]. These devices are autonomous in terms of energy: their energy consumption determines their lifespan. In general, sensor devices periodically sample physical quantity measures and transmit them with a defined frequency to fulfill requirements of smart building applications. Tougher requirements (more measures and/or faster frequencies) will inevitably lead to a greater energy consumption for these devices.

In this study, we focus on a sustainable architecture for multi-application monitoring systems that continuously adapt to application requirements, context and user configuration. We consider a monitoring system as a set of applications that exploit sensor measures in real-time, where these applications are declaratively expressed as (service-oriented) continuous queries over sensor data streams. This architecture supports multiple applications in parallel, with dynamic requirements: it can gracefully handle several different requests for a same device. However, when using a static configuration for acquisition and transmission frequencies of devices, energy consumption of the monitoring system can not be optimized with regards to actual application requirements.

In this paper, we propose a dynamic sensor configuration mechanism to avoid unnecessary data measurements and to promote less expensive data transmission for sensor devices. We present **S** *mart-* **S** *ervice* **S** *tream-o riented* **S** *ensor* **M** *anagement* (**3SoSM**), an approach to optimize interactions between application requirements and Wireless Sensor Network (*WSN*) environment in real-time at the gateway level, independently of inner application logic. Our *3SoSM* approach performs energy-aware dynamic sensor device re-configuration to lower energy consumption while fulfilling real-time application requirements.

The remainder of this paper is organised as follows: Related works are given in Sect. 2. Section 3 presents an overview of our multi-application monitoring system architecture. Optimization of application requirements into sensor device configurations is explained in Sect. 4. Section 5 gives a brief description of our experimental platform to implement our approach and Sect. 6 describes the experiments we conducted. Finally, conclusions are presented in Sect. 7.

2   Related Works

Smart buildings are an application domain for the more general notion of pervasive environments, that consist of physical devices, wireless sensors, actuators, middlewares, applications, etc. These components and platforms compose the infrastructure of a building management system. Along with *WSN*, other components are covered by different research domains: smart building design, sensor data management, energy management, etc.

In the literature, existing studies mainly focus on design and data management sides. [3] proposes a model for monitoring systems: a real-time decision unit that interacts with sensors for diagnosis of the building's state and with the building's controllers to select the appropriate interventions. [4] introduces a smart home energy control system and a smart interface to provide services to occupants. The authors focus on especially on lighting systems to reduce cost. [5] presents an occupant-centric design based on gathering/visualization of high density sensor network dataset to make the pervasive environment sustainable. [6] proposes a model for a better understanding of urban phenomena by exploring and exploiting heterogeneous data from various sources, such as physical sensors, surveys, social networks, etc.

Besides, energy consumption of building system is also discussed. For instance, [7] proposes an energy management technique to handle computational needs of ambient intelligence applications by using energy minimization workload assignment policies. [8] introduces the necessity of having a monitoring/control system for a building and proposes deploying digital smart meters that communicate wirelessly. The main idea is to search which equipments and system characteristics are responsible for the energy consumption of the smart meters.

[9,10] are the closest studies to ours. [9] presents intelligent building architecture based on self-adapting intelligent gateway. This gateway handles service decisions, device management, data aggregation, occupant-based pattern generation and provision of energy management services. A novel self-adapting intelligent system is introduced and proposed system can save approximately 16–24% energy. [10] presents self-adapting algorithms for context-aware systems. Proposed approach detects and analyses changes in the environment, decides how system should react respecting the given set of policies. In that approach, deployed sensor devices and actuators are capable to take adapted decisions. Approaches of [9,10] have some common characteristics: to propose a dynamic management system for smart building environment while processing user preferences. However, these studies are bounded by predefined building applications and application requirement-sensor configuration relation is not established. Besides, their approaches do not benefit from potential reconfiguration of acquisition and transmission frequencies: sensor configuration stays static during the system lifetime. Moreover, high energy consumption is not considered as a major issue. In our *3SoSM* approach, we introduce an energy-aware dynamic sensor reconfiguration process while fully fulfilling application requirements.

3   Overview of Multi-application Monitoring System

Smart building management systems are one of the main application area of pervasive environment research domain. Smart building systems are composed by wireless sensor devices, hence, high energy consumption and limited service lifetime are crucial problems. In this study, we focus on the energy consumption of monitoring architectures supporting multiple smart building applications.

▷ *Monitoring Architecture for Smart Building Applications:* In this study, we adopt a "declarative monitoring architecture", build upon a pervasive

environment management system (PEMS) using declarative (SQL-like) continuous queries that can interact with distributed devices like sensors. This architecture has 3 main layers, as illustrated in Fig. 1:

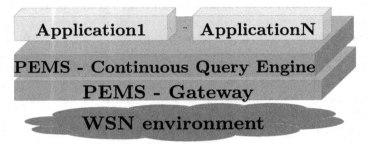

Fig. 1. Declarative monitoring architecture

- *Application layer*, where application requirements are defined, declaratively
  expressed as a set of continuous queries over distributed services [11];
- *PEMS* that integrates non-conventional, dynamic and heterogeneous data
  sources and manages query executions; it includes a continuous query engine
  that interacts with services provided by the lower layer through the logical
  gateway, and manages queries coming from application layer [11,12];
- *WSN environment*, where wireless sensor devices acquire physical quantity
  measures, and can communicate with other sensor devices and physical gateways.

▷ **Pervasive Environment Management Framework:** We adopt the *SoCQ*
(**S**ervice-oriented **C**ontinuous **Q**uery) framework [11] for the *PEMS* layer. It
takes a data-oriented perspective on pervasive environments such as smart buildings. It provides a unified view and access to various and heterogeneous data
resources, or services, available in the environment. *XD-relations* (eXtended
Dynamic Relations) can represent standard relations, that may be updated, or
data streams, that continuously produces data. Pervasive applications can then
be created in a declarative fashion using service-oriented continuous queries over
XD-relations. Queries may be one-shot queries (like standard SQL queries) or
continuous queries (with a dynamic result, like a stream). Queries can also interact with distributed services: service discovery, method invocation, stream subscription. Furthermore, invocations and subscriptions can be finely parametrized.

For instance, a service discovery query can search for sensor services that
provide a location, a method to get the current temperature, and a continuous
stream of temperatures. The result is a XD-relation with a ServiceID, a Location, and a virtual attribute for Temperature. Once relevant services are listed,
a continuous query can subscribe to the temperature stream of every discovered
services, to build a resulting data stream with Temperature values. If new services are discovered and/or some services become unavailable, the continuous
query automatically adapts the set of stream subscriptions.

▷ *Smart Service-Stream Oriented Sensor Management - 3SoSM:* *SoCQ* handles a multi-application mechanism and supports multiple parametrized subscriptions to the same service. Moreover, it supports real-time user configuration of applications and context-aware applications through queries that can dynamically combine data, streams and services. Interactions with services (discovery, invocations, subscriptions) are handled by a gateway positioned between the *PEMS* layer and the *WSN* environment. However, *SoCQ* does not tackle the issue of sensor configuration, and, thus, adopt a static configuration for sensor devices. Like for other approaches presented in the Related Works section, it is an issue for the energy enhancement of the system. Based on the existence of **dynamically configurable wireless sensor devices** [13], we propose a novel approach: a energy-aware dynamic sensor configuration based on real-time application requirements to improve energy consumption of the system.

From our perspective, application requirements are introduced by applications configured by users, as a set of continuous queries. For instance: *"Application A1 computes the average temperature over the last 10 min, with an update every 5 min, with an accuracy of 1 s and a maximum latency of 1 min"*. Those application requirements in terms of data management can be summarized by the following parameters:

- *temporal window size* introduces the time interval for calculating the result;
- *periodicity of result update* stands for the refreshing rate of the result;
- *data acquisition periodicity* represents the temporal accuracy of measure;
- *maximum latency* presents the maximum acceptable delay between the acquisition of data and its transmission to the PEMS layer for result calculation.

The first two parameters concern the computing of the result, whereas *data acquisition periodicity* and *maximum latency* parameters are related to sensor devices and acquisition/transmission of data. In this study, we propose *Smart Service-Stream Oriented Sensor Management (3SoSM)*: the main principle is to compute a data acquisition/transmission schedule for each device, called **sensor configuration oriented pattern** or SCO-pattern, based on application requirements at a given time instant. As application requirements change over time, *3SoSM* dynamically reconfigures sensor devices by updating their specific SCO-patterns, so as to avoid unnecessary data measurements and to enable aggregated data transmission (less and/or smaller network packets to be sent).

In summary, proposed approaches in the literature adopt static sensor configuration and are specialized for specific applications. However, existence of devices with a dynamic sensor configuration feature offers a different perspective. In this context, we propose the *3SoSM* approach that provides finer sensor configuration than duty-cycle and similar techniques. Our proposition of dynamic sensor management based on real-time application requirements is performed at the gateway layer, in order to optimize energy consumption of sensor devices independently from the application layer and/or the query engine.

4   Optimization of Application Requirements

In this section, we present the core of our *3SoSM* approach: an algorithm to compute data acquisition/transmission schedule for each sensor devices, based on real-time application requirements. We first present a formalization of application requirements (subscription requests) and of sensor configuration (SCO-patterns), and then the algorithm itself (called GeNoMe process).

4.1   Formalization of Application Requirements and Sensor Configuration

▷ **Query requirements:** A typical smart building is equipped with various wireless sensor devices $d_i \in D$, where D is the set of devices in the environment. Each sensor device may have multiple functionalities to acquire physical quantity measures $m_i \in M$, e.g., temperature, humidity. In our *3SoSM* approach, application requirements are defined within queries in terms of data source requirements (targeted sensors d and measures m) and of temporal requirements: temporal window size β, periodicity of result updates p^{upd}, measure acquisition periodicity p^{acq} and maximum latency of measure transmission *latency*. The unit for all these temporal parameters is the second (or millisecond, if required). Definition of these parameters have been introduced in the previous section.

We then represent application requirements on sensors at a given time instant by a set of parametrized subscription requests $\{s_1, s_2, \ldots, s_n\}$, where:
$s_i = (d_i, m_i, \beta_i, p_i^{upd}, p_i^{acq}, latency_i) \in D \times M \times \mathbb{N}^* \times \mathbb{N}^* \times \mathbb{N}^* \times \mathbb{N}$

▷ **SCO-Patterns:** We propose a **sensor configuration oriented pattern**, or SCO-pattern, to represent a data acquisition/transmission schedule used to configure a physical device. A SCO-pattern consists of a list of sensor events and the length ℓ of this pattern. A sensor event is a $< timestamp, action >$ couple. Here, we define two types of event actions: either a **data acquisition A** or a **data acquisition and transmission AT**. Event timestamps are enclosed by time interval $]0; \ell]$. The length of the pattern introduces the periodicity of the pattern: a sensor executes this pattern repetitively every ℓ seconds. Thus, a SCO-pattern P is denoted by:
P $= (\{(t_i, a_i)\}, \ell)$ with $\ell \in \mathbb{N}^+$, $t_i \in]0; \ell]$, $a_i \in \{A, AT\}$.

For instance, the SCO-pattern for a sensor device that should measure every second and transmit every 3 s is: P $= (\{(1, A), (2, A), (3, AT)\}, 3)$.

▷ **Algorithm and intermediate DOA-Patterns:** We design an algorithm to optimize a set of subscription requests for a sensor device into a SCO-pattern defining the configuration of this device. This algorithm, presented in the next section, relies on an intermediate **data-oriented acquisition pattern**, or DOA-pattern, that can represent a single subscription request and can also be merged.

In a similar way to SCO-patterns, a DOA-pattern consists of a list of acquistion-latency events and the length ℓ of this pattern. An acquistion-latency event is a triple $< timestamp, action, latency >$, where action is always an acquisition. A DOA-pattern ρ is denoted by:
$\rho = (\{(t_i, A, latency_i)\}, \ell)$, with $\ell \in \mathbb{N}^+$, $t_i \in]0; \ell]$.

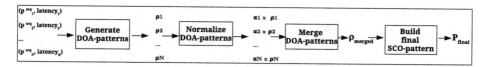

Fig. 2. Overview of the GeNoMe process

For instance, the DOA-pattern for a subscription request that requires a measure every second and a maximum latency of 3 s is: $\rho = (\{(1, A, 3)\}, 1)$. Here, a single acquisition-latency event is sufficient to describe this request.

4.2 Algorithm

The goal of this algorithm is to generate a sensor device configuration, or SCO-pattern, that fulfills all the application requirements expressed by a set of subscription requests targeting this device (with their specific acquisition period and latency). Even though a sensor device can have multiple functionalities such as measuring temperature and humidity, we here consider subscription requests only for a single physical measure (multi-modality patterns is a work in progress).

The generation process of the final SCO-pattern P_{final} is named *3SoSM GeNoMe* process (**Generate-Normalize-Merge**) and illustrated in Fig. 2. We now detail the 4 steps of this algorithm (due to space restrictions, we do not include the listings of pseudo-code for these steps):

1. **Generate DOA-Patterns:** we generate a DOA-pattern ρ_i for each subscription s_i with its parameters $(p^{acq}, latency)$: $\rho_i = (\{(p^{acq}, A, latency)\}, p^{acq})$.
2. **Normalize DOA-Patterns:** In order to merge DOA-patterns (next step), they should all have the same length, that will be the length of the final pattern. The lowest common multiple method is used on pattern lengths (in fact, acquisition periods): $\ell_{final} = LCM(\ell_i, \ell_j, \ldots) = LCM(p_i^{acq}, p_j^{acq}, \ldots)$. Then, a coefficient for each pattern is calculated: $\alpha_i = \ell_{final}/\ell_i \in \mathbb{N}$. This coefficient indicates how many times each pattern should be repeated in order to reach the length of the final pattern, i.e., to normalize this pattern. Thus, each pattern is extended with its specific coefficient: $\alpha_i \times \rho_i$.
3. **Merge DOA-Patterns:** We now merge the set of DOA-patterns to obtain the merged DOA-pattern ρ_{merged}, with the normalized length. The lists of events are merged into a single list. If two events occur at the same timestamp, those events are themselves merged into a single event with a "merged" latency (the minimum latency of those two events). Event actions are still always acquisition actions (no transmission action).
4. **Build final SCO-Pattern:** The DOA-pattern ρ_{merged} indicates data acquisition timestamps and latency, and the periodicity of that pattern. Data transmission is not indicated yet. As a final step, transmission actions are inserted on some events and latency values are then removed, in order to build a final SCO-pattern. Optimal transmission events are calculated based on latency

values of acquisition events, to fulfil maximum latency requirement for each acquisition event. As a first heuristic, starting from the first acquisition event, we search for the latest next event whose measure can be transmitted with all previous measures while respecting latency constraints. We then continue with the next acquisition event, until the end of the pattern.

Example: Suppose that there are two subscription requests to the same sensor device d_i for measuring temperature M_T. The first subscription requires data acquisition every *4* s with latency *7* s ($p^{acq} = 4$ s, $latency = 7$ s). The second subscription requires data acquisition every *5* s with latency *9* s ($p^{acq} = 5$ s, $latency = 9$ s). Regardless of window sizes β and result update periods p^{upd}, those subscriptions can be expressed as:
$s_1 = (d_i, M_T, \beta_i, p_i^{upd}, 4, 7)$ and $s_2 = (d_i, M_T, \beta_j, p_j^{upd}, 5, 9)$.

With our algorithm, we optimize this set of subscriptions into a SCO-pattern:

1. ***Generate DOA-Patterns:*** Subscription requests can be expressed as:
   $\rho_1 = (\{4, A, 7\}, 4)$ and $\rho_2 = (\{5, A, 9\}, 5)$
2. ***Normalize DOA-Patterns:*** Normalized length is LCM(4,5)=20. Coefficients are $\alpha_1 = 20/4 = 5$ for ρ_1 and $\alpha_2 = 20/5 = 4$ for ρ_2. Then, ρ_1 should be repeated five times and ρ_2 should be repeated four times:
   $\alpha_1 \times \rho_1 = 5 \times \rho_1 = (\{(4, A, 7), (8, A, 7), (12, A, 7), (16, A, 7), (20, A, 7)\}, 20)$
   $\alpha_2 \times \rho_2 = 4 \times \rho_2 = (\{(5, A, 9), (10, A, 9), (15, A, 9), (20, A, 9)\}, 20)$
3. ***Merge DOA-Patterns:*** The merged pattern has a length of 20, and only the last event (at 20) merges two events (with a latency of MIN(7,9)=7):
   $\rho_{merged} = (\{(4, A, 7), (5, A, 9), (8, A, 7), (10, A, 9), (12, A, 7), (15, A, 9),$
   $(16, A, 7), (20, A, 7)\}, 20)$
4. ***Build final SCO-Pattern:*** Transmission actions are added to relevant events at 10, 16 and 20 – all latency requirements are thus fulfilled:
   $P_f = (\{(4, A), (5, A), (8, A), (10, AT), (12, A), (15, A), (16, AT), (20, AT)\}, 20)$

We remark that the final pattern requires only 18 transmission actions per 2-min (3 AT per 20 s), whereas the two intial requests would require respectively 15 and 12, and a total of 24 AT considering a common AT every 40 s.

5   Experimental Platform

5.1   Continuous Query Engine: SoCQ Engine

In this study, we use the *SoCQ Engine* [11]. Benefits of the *SoCQ* framework as a pervasive environment management system was already introduced in Sect. 3. *SoCQ Engine* is a service-oriented continuous query engine implemented in Java. A Data Description Language (DDL) allows to define *XD-Relations*, and a SQL-like query language allows to specify one-shot and continuous queries over *XD-Relations* [12]. A user interface controls the query engine: users can visualize *XD-Relations* and their content, and launch one-shot/continuous queries.

5.2 WSN Simulator: Modified WSNet

In our platform, we integrated the *WSN* simulator *WSNet* [14]. *WSNet* is a modular event-driven simulator, more precisely a discrete event simulator (DES). *WSNet* adopts basic functionality of DES: in order to avoid simulating every time splice, the time line is split into events and no change is presumed to occur in the system between consecutive events; thus the simulation can directly jump in time from one event to the next. However, the *PEMS* works on real-time. To avoid time scheduling difference, **we modified the time scheduler** of the *WSNet* simulator: we introduced a time factor to run experiments in real-time or *n*-times faster ($\times 10$, $\times 20 \ldots$).

5.3 Gateway: 3SoSM Gateway

In the *3SoSM* architecture (Fig. 1), the *Gateway* is a technical bridge between two environments: it manages interactions and bidirectional communication between the *PEMS* and the *WSN*. We implemented the *3SoSM* principles in a **3SoSM Gateway**. It is implemented in Java, and interacts with the *SoCQ Engine* and *WSNet*. *3SoSM Gateway* has two primary modules: the **Service Manager**, that manages *SoCQ* services representing available sensor devices; and the **Subscription Manager**, that continuously analyzes application requirements to generate new SCO-patterns for sensor devices when required.

6 Experiments

6.1 Experiment Setup

The simulations are performed on the *modified WSNet*. We simulate one part of the topology of our physical platform *SoCQ4Home* deployed in our research laboratory [15]: 70 simulated sensor devices are located at specific positions over a floor of the building ($10\,\text{m} \times 60\,\text{m} \times 4\,\text{m}$). The deployed sensor devices have fixed positions during the simulation and we consider that they have enough energy until the end of the simulation. We adopt most known pervasive environment communication protocol *Zigbee IEEE 802.15.4*, simulated with a UDG propagation model and 35 m transmission range, and basic radio module states for devices. Calculation of energy consumption is based on CPU and radio components, adopted from [16,17].

6.2 Experimental Scenario

In a typical scenario, multiple applications launch continuous queries concerning sensors to the *PEMS*. The gateway manages required parametrized stream requests and, with *3SoSM*, generates optimal sensor configurations. To evaluate our approach, a scenario is performed with and without using *3SoSM* during one day (1440 min) to observe concrete performance of data stream management and evolution of energy consumptions. We designed two scenarios: "Comfort Temperature Range" and "Temperature of Occupied Rooms". In this paper, we present only one of the performed scenarios.

Scenario "Comfort Temperature Range": Smart buildings are responsible from thermal comfort of occupants. Based on the outdoor temperature, an indoor comfort temperature range is determined. During this scenario, there are two subscription requests to each sensor device. A first application requires temperature of each room with a data acquisition every 15 s and a latency of 60 s. A second application has a specific condition: it demands to track more frequently temperature of rooms that are out of the current comfort temperature range, with a data acquisition every 1 s and a latency of 4 s. A set of 3 *SoCQ* queries are implemented: 1 discovery query to determine available sensor devices, and 1 stream query for each application. The subscription requests to sensor services are generated by the *PEMS* and, based on these parametrized subscriptions, dynamic sensor configuration is realized by the *3SoSM Gateway*.

The first application receives a temperature data stream from each sensor device, however the second application receives data streams only from sensors in rooms where temperature is out of the current comfort range. Users want to track temperature of these rooms more frequently until temperature is in the comfort range again. Sensors are dynamically re-configured by our *3SoSM* Gateway when required. Since data transmission is the most expensive action on sensor side (in terms of energy consumption), we expect a higher energy consumption for sensor devices that are in a room where temperature is not in the comfort range. This functionality shows the context-aware feature of *3SoSM* approach. For the evaluation of our approach, we compare the results of dynamic re-configuration by *3SoSM* Gateway with the results of a static configuration of sensors that always fulfills requirements of both applications: $p^{acq} = 1$ s, *latency* $= 4$ s.

Experiment Result: Figure 3 shows the evolution of energy consumption of a single wireless temperature sensor in a room during the simulation with and without dynamic re-configuration. Upper graph presents indoor temperatures and dynamic comfort temperature ranges (dashed curves). Regions where indoor temperature is outside of comfort temperature range are visible. Lower graph shows the decrease of energy level, and thus lifetime, of that sensor device. Energy consumption increases while room temperature is outside of comfort temperature range: the second subscription is then requested, hence, data transmission frequency is increased from 60 s to 4 s.

Results show that the energy consumption of that sensor device is higher without dynamic re-configuration: as a consequence, the sensor device dies earlier. With a static configuration, it nearly dies at the end of the day, whereas it still has energy with dynamic re-configuration. Initial energy level of sensor device is here set on purpose to emphasize the lifetime difference between both cases. Based on the given scenario parameters, we achieve to reduce additional communication cost: For instance, while temperature is inside the given comfort range, without our approach, a single temperature sensor sends 900 data packets to base station during one hour. With the *3SoSM* Gateway, number of

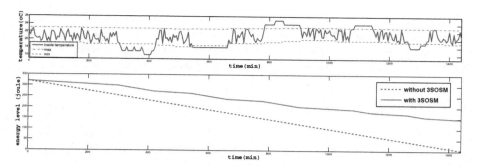

Fig. 3. Indoor temperature variations and energy level evolution of a sensor device with static configuration or dynamic re-configuration (1440 min, 1 day)

transmitted packet is only 60 for the same time period. Thus, at the end of the experiment, 83 % of energy level is saved by using the *3SoSM* approach.

Our approach can increase the lifetime of a sensor device. Let's consider a basic 9 V alkaline battery ($\simeq$ 18.8 kJ) connected to our sensor device. With given parameters, the sensor can survive only 59.5 days with a static configuration, however its lifetime can be extended up to 109.08 days with dynamic re-configuration. Here, *3SoSM* lengthens sensor lifetime by $\simeq$ 83 %. Obviously, service lifespan and the energy savings depend on the application requirements and context (here, actual temperature).

7   Conclusion

In this paper, we point at a major challenge of smart building technology: energy consumption of the monitoring architecture itself while dealing with data exploration/utilization. We expose that existing studies do not tackle neither energy consumption of deployed equipments nor lifetime of the whole system. Existing approaches commonly adopt static configurations for wireless devices. Here, we focus on the lifetime of a monitoring system and introduce new mechanisms for dynamic reconfiguration of sensor data acquisition/transmission schedules.

We present a sustainable declarative monitoring architecture to process massive raw data from sensors. We rely on declarative *PEMS* principles and tackle the energy optimisation of interactions between application real-time requirements and sensor devices. We introduce our approach *3SoSM* based on data-driven acquisition and transmission time patterns. We propose the *GeNoMe-X* process to optimize multiple parametrized subscriptions to a same device. We implemented a *3SoSM* Gateway that supports the *GeNoMe-X* process to fulfil dynamic application requirements. We conducted experiments using the *SoCQ* engine and a modified *WSNet* simulator. Impacts of our approach on energy consumption and on lifetime are presented and discussed.

As perspectives for *3SoSM* approach, we plan to extend time patterns to support multi-modality, and to benefit from real raw data measured by physical

SoCQ4Home platform. Besides, we also plan to integrate energy-aware dynamic sleep scheduling mechanism based on predictions, as a complementary of data driven scheduling. Furthermore, we are studying ways to decentralize parts of the optimization process into the *WSN*, on the smart devices themselves.

References

1. Zikopoulos, P., Eaton, C., et al.: Understanding Big Data: Analytics for Enterprise Class Hadoop and Streaming Data. McGraw-Hill Osborne Media, New York (2011)
2. Aloui, I., Kazar, O., Kahloul, L., Servigne, S.: A new itinerary planning approach among multiple mobile agents in wireless sensor networks (wsn) to reduce energy consumption. IJCNIS 7(2) (2015)
3. Doukas, H., Patlitzianas, K.D., Iatropoulos, K., Psarras, J.: Intelligent building energy management system using rule sets. J. Building Environ. **42**(10), 3562–3569 (2007)
4. Han, D.-M., Lim, J.-H.: Smart home energy management system using ieee 802.15.4 and zigbee. IEEE Trans. Consum. Electron. **56**(3), 1403–1410 (2010)
5. Khan, A., Hornbæk, K.A.S.: Big data from the built environment. In: Proceedings of the 2nd International Workshop LARGE 11, pp. 29–32. ACM (2011)
6. Sylvie, S., Gripay, Y., Jean-Michel, D., Céline, N., Jacques, J., Olivier, C., Radouane, M.: Data science approach for a cross-disciplinary understanding of urban phenomena: Application to energy efficiency of buildings. Procedia Eng. **115**, 45–52 (2015)
7. Zapater, M., Sanchez, C., Ayala, J.L., Moya, J.M., Risco-Martın, J.L.: Ubiquitous green computing techniques for high demand applications in smart environments. Sensors **12**, 10659–10677 (2012)
8. Preisel, M., Diaz, A., Wimmer, W.: Energy consumption of smart meters. J. Inf. Commun. Technol., 37 (2013)
9. Byun, J., Park, S.: Development of a self-adapting intelligent system for building energy saving and context-aware smart services. IEEE Trans. Consum. Electron. **57**(1), 90–98 (2011)
10. Cioara, T., Anghel, I., Salomie, I., Dinsoreanu, M., Copil, G., Moldovan, D.: A self-adapting algorithm for context aware systems. In: RoEduNet 2010, pp. 374–379. IEEE (2010)
11. Gripay, Y., Laforest, F., Petit, J.-M.: Socq: A framework for pervasive environments. In: ISPAN 2009, pp. 154–159. IEEE (2009)
12. Gripay, Y., Laforest, F., Petit, J.-M.: A simple (yet powerful) algebra for pervasive environments. In: EDBT 2010, pp. 359–370. ACM (2010)
13. Perera, C., Zaslavsky, A., Compton, M., Christen, P., Georgakopoulos, D.: Semantic-driven configuration of internet of things middleware. In: SKG 2013, pp. 66–73. IEEE (2013)
14. Wsnet/worldsens simulator. http://wsnet.gforge.inria.fr/. Accessed: 22 Feb 2016
15. Socq4home project. http://liris.cnrs.fr/socq4home/. Accessed: 04 Feb 2016
16. Pinarer, O., Ozgovde, A.: Improving the energy efficiency of wearable computing units using on sensor fifo memory. Int. J. e-Education, e-Business, e-Management e-Learning **5**(2), 105 (2015)
17. Pinarer, O., Ozgovde, A.: Application specific dynamic sleep scheduling. In: 23rd Signal Processing and Communications Applications Conference, SIU 2015, pp. 1765–1768. IEEE (2015)

Micro-accounting for Optimizing and Saving Energy in Smart Buildings

Daniele Sora[1]([✉]), Massimo Mecella[1], Francesco Leotta[1], Leonardo Querzoni[1], Roberto Baldoni[1], Giuseppe Bracone[2], Daniele Buonanno[2], Mario Caruso[2], Adriano Cerocchi[2], and Mariano Leva[2]

[1] Sapienza Università di Roma, Roma, Italy
{sora,mecella,leotta,querzoni,baldoni}@diag.uniroma1.it
[2] Over Technologies, Roma, Italy
{g.bracone,d.buonanno,m.caruso,a.cerocchi,m.leva}@overtechnologies.com

Abstract. Energy management, and in particular its optimization, is one of the hot trends in the current days, both at the enterprise level (optimization of whole corporate/government buildings) and single-citizens' homes. The current trend is to provide knowledge about the micro(scopic) energy consumption. This allows to save energy, but also to optimize the different energy sources (e.g., solar vs. traditional one) in case of a mixed architecture. In this work, after briefly introducing our specific platform for smart environments able to micro-account energy consumption of devices, we present two case studies of its utilization: energy saving in offices and smart switching among different energy sources.

Keywords: Micro-accounting · Energy switch · OPlatform · Saving

1 Introduction

Energy management, and in particular its optimization, is one of the hot trends in the current days, both at the enterprise level (optimization of whole corporate/government buildings) and single-citizens' homes. Energy efficiency is generally function of *out-door* techniques – renewable energy, smart energy production and distribution, etc. – and *in-door* techniques; in particular, very few energy managers – each of us can be an energy manager of his own home – can state "who, when and why is consuming", conversely this knowledge is fundamental in order to cut energy cost. As stated in [5], energy consumption feedback increases user's awareness, motivation and responsibility and can result in more than 12 % of energy saving when the feedback is real-time and at the granularity of the single electrical appliance.

Pervasive systems and Internet-of-Things (IoT) are gaining popularity due to their invisible integration into everyday life. In particular, among many other smart sensors and actuators, users are starting to introduce and integrate Home/Building Energy Management Systems (H/BEMSs) in their environments. Such systems allow users to monitor, control and optimize energy consumption [3].

© Springer International Publishing Switzerland 2016
J. Krogstie et al. (Eds.): CAiSE 2016, LNBIP 249, pp. 143–154, 2016.
DOI: 10.1007/978-3-319-39564-7_15

Energy saving can be achieved in many ways: by optimizing appliance usage, by shifting energy consumption to off-peak hours or by dimming light brightness based on the available natural light [12]. In [11], for example, authors present a system to save energy in PC networks by turning PCs on only when really needed thanks to the WoL (Wake on LAN) technology. An energy model to calculate achievable energy savings is proposed along with real world scenario evaluation resulting in remarkable savings in terms of both money and CO_2 emissions. The process of energy monitoring clearly involves, besides final users, also energy utility providers; with the term Advanced Metering Infrastructures (AMI), we refer to the bidirectional infrastructure and communication system at the base of smart grids [8,10]. Recent B/HEMS make use of social networks to motivate energy saving; in [7], for example, energy data are collected through a Zig-Bee network and are then published in a social network to let the users figure out how efficient its home appliance is, compared to others. The trend is therefore to provide knowledge about the micro(scopic) energy consumption.

In this work we briefly present in Sect. 2 our platform, named OPlatform[1], for smart environments able to micro-account energy consumption of devices, at the level of single power line, which allows at the same time the actuation of devices, thus being also an energy-aware smart space automation solution. Then in Sects. 3 and 4 we present two current applications of it: a case study of energy savings in offices and its usage for optimizing the smart switch-off among different energy sources. Finally, Sect. 5 concludes the paper.

2   The OPlatform

The OPlatform consists of two main devices: the OMeter and the OBox, which are responsible, respectively, for controlling electrical appliances and for accessing the whole space automation system through web based technologies. The typical deployment of the OPlatform consists of a single OBox and several OMeters, the number of which depends on the number of electrical devices to be controlled/monitored (Fig. 1).

OMeter. The role of an OMeter is to actuate electrical loads and to sense binary input commands. Each OMeter can handle up to 8 independent electrical circuits providing for their actuation by means of relays which bear a maximum current of 16 amperes. Each of these circuits can be, depending on the granularity that user wants to control, a power line to which many loads are connected to, or an individual electrical load. The OMeter, in addition, handles up to 16 dry contact inputs such as toggle switches, PIR (Passive InfraRed) sensors, magnetic contact sensors, etc. As each load can be switched on/off, the OMeter is able to monitor its power consumption in terms of voltage, current, power factor, apparent, active and reactive power.

---

[1] The "O" prefix assigned to the components (OMeter and OBox) and to the platform itself (OPlatform) comes from the name of the spin-off, Over, which has engineered the research.

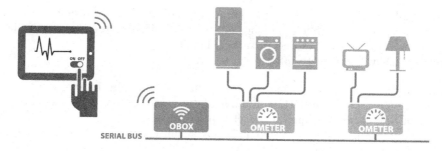

Fig. 1. The platform for energy micro-monitoring

As the system is designed to monitor power consumption and prevent its waste, in the design phase we payed special attention to the energy consumption of the OMeters themselves; a system that consumes more energy than it allows to save would be, in fact, useless. This is particularly critical considering that the system will be active 24/7. For this reason magnetic latching relays, have been adopted; this type of relay has the advantage that one coil consumes power only for an instant, while it is being switched, and the relay contacts retain this setting across a power outage. The base current drawn by the OMeter is 150 milliamps and the contribution due to the magnetization of the relay is negligible resulting in a total power absorption of less than 2 W.

As far as the electrical consumption monitoring, an OMeter is able to read the power drained by any load (up to 16 A) in a 230 V, 50 Hz electric network. For this, the OMeter is equipped with a microprocessor that samples, at very high frequency, instantaneous power data of each output, thus allowing to calculate TRMS (True Root Mean Square) values of the alternate current. This is particularly important for measuring non-linear loads (such as induction furnaces, PCs, displays), whose current waveform is not sinusoidal but typically distorted.

An OMeter explicitly provides information about apparent power, current and power factor, other measurements, such as voltage, active power and reactive power can be indirectly calculated by the OBox.

On the one hand, power consumption values can be inquired at any time through an explicit request, on the other one, they can be spontaneously notified by the meter itself according to different modes: (a) at regular (customizable) time intervals; (b) when the difference between the current value and the last sent value is greater than a customizable threshold; (c) when the difference between the current value and the last sent value is higher than a customizable percentage of the latter. The OMeter can be configured to work in one of the three above modes, the choice depends on the desired accuracy but should take in account also the bus load.

Whereas some applications, such as load monitoring or anomaly detection in electrical appliances, require instantaneous readings, other ones, e.g., electric bill analysis, may require more coarse grained values. For this purpose, the OMeter continuously calculates and stores average values of all the measurements; when average measures are explicitly requested, it replies with current average values and then resets such values and restarts calculating them.

In summary, the OMeter offers:

- three primitives for synchronously controlling outputs and inputs:
  - *controlOut*, given an output number and a value (on or off) it switches on or off the corresponding output channel;
  - *readOutState*, given an output number, it will reply with the current state of the output channel;
  - *readInState*, given an input number it will reply with the current state of the input channel;
- two primitives for asynchronously notifying informations about outputs and inputs:
  - *inVariation* is triggered when an input channel changes its state and informs about its new state;
  - *outVariation* is triggered when an output channel changes its state and informs about its new state;
- two primitives for synchronously retrieving power measurements:
  - *readMeasures*, given an output channel it will reply with current apparent power P, power factor (PF) and current (C);
  - *readAvgMeasures*, given an output channel it will reply with the average values of apparent power P, power factor (PF) and current (C);
- one primitive for asynchronously notify informations about power measurements:
  - *powerVariation*, triggered when one of P, PF, and C changes its values according to the rules explained above.

OMeters represent the nodes of a distributed system, and are interconnected via a serial bus, whose transfer rate is 9600 baud, that carries data and power (12 V) simultaneously. The low bandwidth allows longer deployments of the bus, as well as more reliable communication on noisy channels. The units are able to coordinate themselves autonomously, without the presence of a master unit, by exchanging appropriate messages defined in a specific communication protocol. A wired solution has been adopted, rather than a wireless one, to improve reliability in transferring data even though it requires a more expensive and intrusive installation. Wireless solutions can incur in interferences and connection problems when the number of installed appliances is high. Moreover, wireless solutions mainly rely on batteries, thus requiring a certain maintenance effort.

Each message sent on the bus, in addition to the payload, has an header identifying sender and recipient; once sent, the message is perceived and analyzed by all the units on the bus, but is processed only by the unit having the address specified in the recipient field of the message and discarded by the other units.

OBox. The OBox is an embedded PC that is physically connected to the bus via a RS232 serial port and to the building/home network, and it plays the role of bridge between the several OMeters deployed in the environment and the

Web clients of the system. It runs a lightweight web server and offers RESTful interfaces to configure, control and monitor the meters. The OBox is connected to the serial bus as well, it is then in effect a node of the system and operates in the same way of a OMeter, thereby generating messages that control the various units. It differs from the OMeters in the sense that it can not perform any electrical actuation or sensing. In addition, unlike others OMeters units, the OBox is interested in all messages passing on the bus and does not discard any, as it must be always up to date about the context of the devices deployed in the home. The average power absorption of an OBox is about 8 W.

The OBox plays both roles of controller and supervisor. Being a controller, it is able to send commands to devices, for example to turn on or off a light. At the same time it must be able to work as a supervisor, i.e., it is able to continuously monitor the states of all the actuators and the sensors deployed in the house in order to be always aware of the environmental context. On the one hand the OBox is able to communicate with the OMeters through the messages defined in the bus protocol and implemented in a specific driver, therefore it is able to operate home devices and to monitor their state and energy consumption both synchronously and asynchronously. On the other hand, it abstracts the bus protocol and offers high level functions to REST clients hiding all the technical details of the underlaying protocol. A Web browser-based user interface has been designed to make the system accessible from many different devices (PCs, smartphones, tablets) without installing any specific software. Despite the fact that the interaction with the system occurs via the browser, the OBox communicates with clients by sending raw data rather than formatted HTML and the client itself updates the UI by properly rendering such data. In this way it is still possible to develop ad hoc interfaces for Android or iOS platforms if needed.

By continuously monitoring the bus, the OBox is able to intercept power readings sent by the OMeters and consequently is able to provide real-time feedbacks (Fig. 2) to the clients and store them for future use. Collected measurements can be retrieved later in a raw textual form or can be visualized in a graphical panel summarizing all the relevant information (cf. Fig. 3(a)), or in other visual forms (e.g., the heat map shown in Fig. 3(b)).

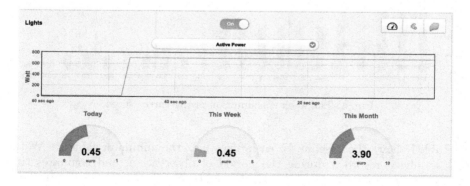

Fig. 2. Real-time power consumption

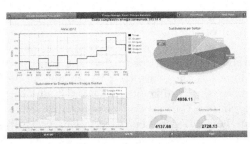

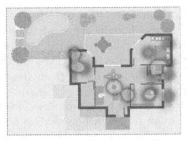

(a) Historical data screen   (b) Heat-map visualization

Fig. 3. Energy monitoring visualizations

3   Energy Savings in Offices

The offices of an institution have been clustered on the basis of their extension, in order to identify three typical classes: small-sized offices (less than 300 sq.m.), medium-sized offices (extension between 300 sq.m. and 1000 sq.m.) and big-sized offices (greater than 1000 sq.m.). Then an office for each class has been identified (all the three offices in the same town, in order to avoid distortion effects on the outcomes of the study), and such three offices have been equipped with the OPlatform and monitored during August–October 2015.

Figure 4 shows the average consumption of each office during a week, expressed in KWh and corresponding cost (assuming 0,20/Wh as energy unit cost). Notably, the consumption is quite high during week-ends, but the medium-sized office is more efficient than the others (its consumption during week-ends is 25 % of the working days, whereas for the other cases is about 75 %).

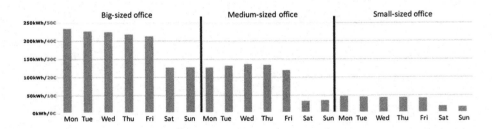

Fig. 4. The week consumption of the three offices

Table 1 shows the baseline for each office, i.e., the minimum value (in Watt) that has been recorded during the period of observation, and compares this with the average consumption during the nights. Notably, in an ideal case these two should be quite the same, and conversely they are quite different. Further

Table 1. Baselines

	Big-sized	Medium-sized	Small-sized
Measured minimal consumption	4341 W	905 W	620 W
Average hourly consumption during closing hours	5552 W	2710 W	1017 W

analyzing such data (by decomposing the consumption over the different lines, the OPlatform allows this) we can discover that in the case of the big-sized office the consumption during nights might be reduced to 1165 W, for the medium-sized office to 867 W and for the small-sized office to 650 W. This can be achieved by switching off lights and other environment-related equipment (air-conditioning, etc.) – which account for about 80 % of the consumption, and keeping on all the non-interruptible equipment (allarms, TV for security and control, etc.). The switching-off can be performed automatically through the same OPlatform, which can act as actuation platform as well and configured through appropriate user-friendly configuration (the OPlatform allows defining rules through a graphical language based on Blockly[2]).

4 Smart Energy Switch

Nowadays, renewable energies [1], and photovoltaic (PV) in particular, have been indicated as the best solution for a major independence from the hydrocarbons. The possibility of independently producing energy for covering the consumptions of private producers resulted in a strong growth of the number of private PV plants. However, the introduction of such energy into the public grid can represent a problem in terms of sustainability that strongly compromises the PV advantages [2]. In this sense, "self consumption" [6], intended as the capability of using the energy before it is reintroduced into the grid, can bring real benefits from the employment of PV, even for little private plants. In this section we illustrate the design and prototype implementation of a tool, called OEnergySwitch, which aims at maximizing the quantity of produced energy that is self-consumed in a domestic environment.

In general a solution that tries to maximize the self-consumption [2] indirectly reduces or avoids the grid-plant interactions. More in details, the exceeding energy produced by private PVs is sold to the provider, [4]; this technique is known as "*net metering*": it has been the main-stream solution of the former PV systems, but in general it is inefficient from the point of view and of the energy balance and, often, of the saving. Modern systems should try to use directly the energy, and to send to the grid just the exceeding one, thus the preferable approach is to maximize the immediate consumption of the energy produced by the plant. This technique is named "self-consumption". Clearly, the self-consumption is more convenient, but, at the state of the art, it is necessary

---

[2] https://developers.google.com/blockly/.

to dimension the plant for providing a peak energy higher than the real need due to the impossibility of dividing the loads. The aim is therefore to exploit the micro.-accounting capability of the OPlatform to design a tool that can split the total load into two sets $S1$ and $S2$ such that $S1$ contains the elements that maximize the quantity of self-consumed energy, while $S2$ is provided by the grid.

Our prototype operates in an house connected to the electric grid and to an off-grid photovoltaic small private plant[3]. The energy switch works at outlet granularity: each single outlet can be fed using either the renewable energy or the classical one. This implies an higher capability of optimization; when the energy consumption of the appliances exceeds the production due to few watts, this approach allows to turn off the minimum energy quantity that makes the total need satisfiable by the PV.

A working prototype implementing the energy switch has been built: a small real hybrid PV system has been set; the inverter is an Opti-Solar SP Efecto 1000, that provides until 800 W of energy. The inverter gives the priority usage to the solar power. Then if it is not sufficient, it takes energy from the battery. As last, if the battery is discharged, it uses the grid's power. So it can work in UPS mode [9]. Moreover it is equipped with a serial communication board based on RS232 protocol. The first characteristic provides a "free" protection system in case of wrong configuration, the second one provides an easy way for an informations exchange between the inverter and the micro-controller. The PV subsystem is completed by two panels, for a total maximum production of 220 W. This value is the DC power production, the effective AC outgoing from the inverter is lower, depending on the weather and the conversion lost. Since the inverter has a maximum applicable load and the environment is not fixed, a fuse should protect it from an excessive overload, in case of error.

The physical switching is implemented using relays. For the prototype we used 4 contact, 7 ampere, industrial relays. They are controlled through alternate current, so, if the prototype is composed by 3 relays, they are controlled by three OMeter outs. The other three outs are used for feeding the loads. Practically, half of the gates of the OMeter are delegated to loads feed, while the other half controls the relays, redirecting them to a source rather than another one. The micro-controller is an Olimex A-20 OLinuXino Micro, a dual core Cortex A7 1 GHz frequency board with 1 GB RAM. The prototype developed is a little system composed by three outlets connected both to the inverter and to the grid (Fig. 5).

The system computes the best outlet configuration and connect a subset of the total outlets to the domestic plant and lets the other to be fed by the grid energy. The fine granularity energy monitoring capability allows a precise control on the outlets configuration. In particular, combining the information about the produced energy from the inverter and the data about the monitoring activity of the outlets, the system computes the solution of a knapsack problem

---

[3] The dimension of the plant may range: if consumptions are high, the plant might produce up to 1 kW; otherwise, if the domestic consumption is lower, the total renewable production can be lower. We consider a range between 400 and 1000 W.

(a) Complete prototipe, external view

(b) Energy Switch core, internal view

Fig. 5. Two views of the prototype: (a) represents the external view, with the inverter on the left and the core on the right. (b) shows the different internal components: the Olimex, the OMeter and the relays block.

for maximizing the direct consumption of the energy produced. The knapsack problem is modeled as follows:

$$OP(i, w) = \begin{cases} 0 & \text{if } i = 0 \\ OP(i-1, w) & \text{if } (w_i > w_k) \\ max\{OP(i-1, w), v_i + OP(i-1, w - w_i)\} & \text{otherwise} \end{cases}$$

where $OP(i, w)$ is the maximum value subset of outlets $1, \ldots, i$ with consumption limit w (that is the capacity of the knapsack), i is the i-th item, w_i is its weight (apparent power absorbed) and v_i is its value. So the limit is represented by the PV instantaneous production, and the power absorption constitutes the value and the weight of each outlet. The naive solution of the knapsack problem has an exponential computational cost. The implementation is based on a dynamic programming algorithm that can resolve the knapsack in a pseudo polynomial time. More in details each value is rounded to the nearest integer value: the incoming energy is rounded down, while each single consumption is rounded up. So for the total energy amount we have that $W_c = \lfloor W \rfloor$ and $wa_i = \lceil w_i \rceil$ where W is the instantaneous total panels energy amount and w_i is the instantaneous consumption of the i-th outlet. This approach works fine if the values are read without any delay. In a real application, there is the need of considering the total information delay: from the inverter side, the delay can be considered negligible – indeed the production changes are quite slow, and in a second the change is not substantial. The delay for the monitoring system is quite significant. Indeed let's call this delay $L_{monitor}$. We have that $L_{monitor} = L_r + L_p + L_e$ where L_r is the delay related to the maximum reading frequency of the monitoring system, L_p the propagation delay of the information from the station to the computing unit and L_e is the elaboration time required by the computing unit. From an analysis of these elements, it appears that L_p is very small. Also L_e is quite short, since the hypothesis of low producing plant. L_r instead is around one second. A second is a quite high value in the electrical context, so the effective energy situation at the time of the actuation of the computed configuration can be different and an energy lack can happen. In order to avoid that, the approach proposed is based on the study of the previous behavior of each outlet and on the history of the consumptions. In particular, time is divided in time slots and for each time slot the mean and the variance of the consumptions are computed and considered for taking a decision. For choosing the best approach both the time slots size and the different logics for the system have been tested.

We took into account the following switching logics: *(i)* naive, *(ii)* threshold on variance, *(iii)* threshold on variance/mean ratio, *(iv)* adaptive on variance, and *(v)* adaptive on variance/mean ratio. All of them take into account a safety margin. A safety margin is a percentage of the incoming energy that is not considered as available for covering hypothetical errors and energy lacks. On the one hand, the bigger is the safety margin, the lower is the saving; on the other hand, the shorter is the margin, the higher is the error probability. The naive approach has been considered just as a comparison term. It does not add any information on the read data, so it is the most speculative approach and counts many errors. For the remaining approaches we can detect two groups: the first two approaches are static, while the others are dynamic.

A static approach implements a logic that excludes an outlet from the knapsack computation if the value of the considered metric overcomes a fixed threshold. Moreover, the percentage of the safety margin is fixed a priori. On the contrary, a dynamic (or adaptive) approach implements a logic that excludes an outlet from the knapsack computation if the value of the considered metric overcomes a dynamic threshold. The safety margin is defined dynamically as well: smaller is the value of the considered metric, lower is the percentage of the safety margin.

Starting from the analysis of the naive approach results, a clear trend has been detected: the bigger the safety margin is, the lower is the number of total errors, but the energy saving slowly decreases. Even the introduction of a little margin causes a big reduction of the errors. However without a supplementary consideration the system appears not feasible in practical terms. On the contrary, if the supplementary metric analysis is introduced, the performances are quite good with a small safety margin of the 20 % (see Fig. 6). The best results have been obtained with a time slot 30 min length: longer time slots give a less precise description of the consumption regularity, for shorter time slots can be difficult to catch the events and put the influence in the right time slot. However testing them in a real context the best performances have been reached with the adaptive approach using the variance. The saved energy has been the 17 % of the total, but the number of errors has been just two. This approach is very dynamic since it is not necessary to define the percentage of the safety margin as for the static approaches. Hence, the results obtained suggest that the most important metric for describing the electric consumption is the variance, computed on 48 daily time slots. If the environment is well known and there are few changes in the system settings, the static approach can be adopted. It allows a greater save but it is weak against the changes. Otherwise the solution adaptive is more general and does not require particular tuning. Its saving is a little bit lower, so it is a sound configuration also if the system setting is variable or not defined a priori.

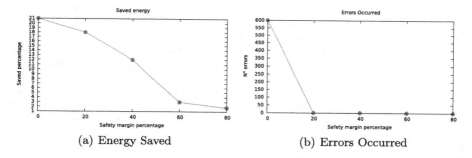

(a) Energy Saved   (b) Errors Occurred

Fig. 6. Threshold on *variance* approach simulation results. The number of time slots considered is 48. The approach tries to minimize the risks when the benefits would be few. The best results are obtained with a 20 % safety margin.

5   Conclusions and Future Works

This dissemination paper has presented the OPlatform and a couple of applications built on top of it, notably how micro-accounting of energy allows to optimize consumption of offices and a new approach to the renewable energy management for small production plants in a domestic environments. In both cases, we demonstrated that the OPlatform can warranty a saving in terms of energy and money (about 20 % in both cases).

The platform will be adopted in a recently funded H2020 project, namely GAIA, for accounting energy consumption and experiment new approaches to education of persons to save energy through gamification approaches. Initial proof-of-concepts about this concepts have been realized, notably a smart space simulator to be used for giving immediate feedbacks to users (cf. www.overtechnologies.com/casavirtuale) and an Android app with challenges to be conducted by students in order to change their habits (cf. https://play.google.com/store/apps/details?id=com. energyconsumption.diego_cecchini.noenergywaste). In future work we will report the outcome of such experimentations.

Acknowledgements. This work has been partly supported by the H2020 EU project GAIA (grant 696029). The authors would like to thanks the many persons involved in the developments described in this paper, namely Diego Cecchini, Vincenzo Forte, Rodolfo Pallotta, Silvia Ruggiero and all the other developers at Over Technologies.

References

1. Bull, S.R.: Renewable energy today and tomorrow. Proc. IEEE **89**(8), 1216–1226 (2001)
2. Carrasco, J.M., Franquelo, L.G., Bialasiewicz, J.T., Galván, E., Portillo Guisado, R.C., Prats, M., León, J.I., Moreno-Alfonso, N.: Power-electronic systems for the grid integration of renewable energy sources: A survey. IEEE Trans. Industr. Electron. **53**(4), 1002–1016 (2006)
3. Caruso, M.: Service Ecologies, Energy Management and Accessibility in Smart Homes. Ph.D. thesis, Dipartimento di Ingegneria Informatica, Automatica e Gestionale A. Ruberti, Sapienza, Universit di Roma (2015)
4. Castillo-Cagigal, M., Caamaño-Martín, E., Matallanas, E., Masa-Bote, D., Gutiérrez, A., Monasterio-Huelin, F., Jiménez-Leube, J.: PV self-consumption optimization with storage and active DSM for the residential sector. Sol. Energy **85**(9), 2338–2348 (2011)
5. Ehrhardt-Martinez, K., Donnelly, K.A., Laitner, S., et al.: Advanced metering initiatives and residential feedback programs: a meta-review for household electricity-saving opportunities. American Council for an Energy-Efficient Economy Washington, DC (2010)
6. EPIA the European Photovoltaic Industry Association. Self Consumption of PV electricity, July 2013
7. Han, J., Choi, C.S., Park, W.K., Lee, I.: Green home energy management system through comparison of energy usage between the same kinds of home appliances. In: 2011 IEEE 15th International Symposium on Consumer Electronics (ISCE), pp. 1–4. IEEE (2011)
8. Hart, D.G.: Using Am I to realize the smart grid. In: 2008 IEEE Power and Energy Society General Meeting-Conversion and Delivery of Electrical Energy in the 21st Century, pp. 1–2. IEEE (2008)
9. Karve, S.: Three of a kind [UPS topologies, IEC standard]. IEEE Rev. **46**(2), 27–31 (2000)
10. Masiello, R.: Demand response the other side of the curve [guest editorial]. IEEE Power Energ. Mag. **8**(3), 18 (2010)
11. Ricciardi, S., Santos-Boada, G., Careglio, D., Palmieri, F., Fiore, U.: Evaluating energy savings in WoL-enabled networks of PCs. In: Procedings of the 2013 IEEE International Symposium on Industrial Electronics (ISIE) (2013)
12. Rojchaya, S., Konghirun, M.: Development of energy management and warning system for resident: An energy saving solution. In: 6th International Conference on Electrical Engineering/Electronics, Computer, Telecommunications and Information Technology, 2009, ECTI-CON 2009, vol. 1, pp. 426–429. IEEE (2009)

Modeling CO$_2$ Emissions to Reduce the Environmental Impact of Cloud Applications

Cinzia Cappiello$^{(\boxtimes)}$, Paco Melià, and Pierluigi Plebani

Dipartimento di Elettronica, Informazione e Bioingegneria,
Politecnico di Milano, Milan, Italy
{cinzia.cappiello,paco.melia,pierluigi.plebani}@polimi.it

Abstract. Cloud computing has important impacts on the environment: data centers – that represent the physical infrastructure where the cloud resources run – are not always designed as green entities, as they consume large amounts of energy (in form of electric power or fuel) often producing significant amounts of CO$_2$ emissions. Such emissions depend on the energy sources used by the data centers and may vary over time with respect to the location in which the data center is operating. To decrease the carbon footprint of cloud computing, the selection of the site where to deploy an application, along with the decision of when to start the execution of the application, should be based not only on the satisfaction of the traditional QoS requirements but also on the energy-related constraints and their dynamics over time.

Goal of this paper is to propose a CO$_2$ emission model able to support emission forecasting, especially for data centers that are based on electricity from the national grid. The proposed emission model can be used to improve the decisions on where and when to deploy applications on data centers in order to minimize CO$_2$ emissions.

Keywords: CO$_2$ emissions · Cloud computing · Sustainability

1 Introduction

A substantial part of the energy demand of the IT sector is associated with the functioning of data centers: facilities responsible for the storage and processing of information which constitute the infrastructural basis of cloud computing. Due to the increasing adoption of cloud-based solutions, the role of data centers is becoming more and more crucial. Consequently, the energy required by data centers is now so high that it has been estimated to be comparable with the overall energy consumption of countries like Japan and India, and would rank 5th among world countries [6].

Several approaches have been proposed in the last years with the goal of reducing the energy consumption of data centers. As a significant fraction of the energy consumed in a data center is not consumed for running servers and network devices needed to execute the deployed application, but goes to supplementary elements (e.g., cooling system, lightning), most of the proposed approaches

© Springer International Publishing Switzerland 2016
J. Krogstie et al. (Eds.): CAiSE 2016, LNBIP 249, pp. 155–166, 2016.
DOI: 10.1007/978-3-319-39564-7_16

have focused on reducing this fraction of energy. Some other approaches have focused on optimizing the design, the deployment, and the execution of cloud applications [5] in order to minimize the waste of resources, find the servers with the lowest energy consumption, or distributing the workload looking at the amount of energy consumed by the different servers.

In this work we want to adopt a different perspective by looking at CO_2 emissions instead of at the pure energy consumption. Indeed, the actual environmental impact of energy usage very much depends on the specific energy mix used to generate electric power. In fact, as the ability of different power generation technologies to follow daily, weekly and seasonal fluctuations of power demand varies widely (with large nuclear or coal-fueled plants requiring hours, if not days, to change their power output, and natural gas turbines or hydro-electric plants being able to respond in minutes), the composition of the energy mix is subject to important variation over different time horizons. CO_2 emission factors hence change consequently, according to the different power generation sources running in different moments of the day and in different seasons. For this reason, the optimization of cloud applications requires appropriate tools to forecast the dynamics of the energy mix and the relevant emission factors over time, and to identify the best schedule to deploy cloud applications.

The goal of this paper is to propose a modeling framework to predict short and medium-term fluctuations of (i) electric energy consumption at the national scale, (ii) the composition of the energy production mix by energy source, and (iii) the consequent CO_2 emission factor. We demonstrate the framework by applying it to the assessment of a federated cloud infrastructure. We use data from two European countries, i.e., France and the United Kingdom, for which time series of energy production (disaggregated by generation source) and consumption are available in real time at high temporal resolution. We eventually show how the availability of accurate CO_2 emission forecasts can support IT systems managers in pursuing a greener deployment of cloud applications.

The paper is structured as follows. Section 2 reviews the state of the art of the literature on the topic to highlight the novelty of the proposed approach. Section 3 illustrates the modeling framework and demonstrates it through the application to the two case studies (France and the UK). Section 4 describes how the models developed in Sect. 3 can be used to select the most appropriate site for application deployment on the basis of predicted CO_2 emissions.

2   Related Work

Assessment, measurement and improvement of energy efficiency in data centers and clouds have been important mainstreams in research in recent years [16]. The work proposed in this paper also focuses on the improvement of the sustainability of data centers, but it aims to reduce the CO_2 emissions by adapting the applications running on federated cloud environments. The importance of CO_2 emissions has been already considered in the literature. Some contributions focus on how to use efficiently available renewable resources, while avoiding peak demand of energy from electricity providers. In [1], authors propose the usage of Geographical Load Balancing (GLB) to shift workloads and avoid peak power demands. This requires to predict both the incoming workload and the peak demand to the network. The algorithm is implemented as a network flow optimization problem. A similar approach is discussed in [11], which uses both workload shifting and local power generation for avoiding peak load demands on the energy network. The importance of considering the type of energy sources has been addressed also in [2], which proposes an integrated framework for sustainable clouds where information on data centers, communication networks and energy sources is considered. In [15], the authors focus on the optimization of power generation with respect to carbon emissions. Also [13] focuses on assessing the carbon footprint of cloud computing services. In this paper we aim to provide a tool to forecast carbon emissions and/or to suggest the most suitable deployment time to improve the sustainability of cloud applications. Mathematical models to forecast electric power demand over time horizons spanning from few minutes ahead (very short-term forecasts) up to a decade ahead (long-term forecasts) are key to support operations and planning of power systems, and have been the subject of research since the late 1960 [12]. In the early 2000s, Alfarez and Nazeeruddin [4] carried out an exhaustive review of the vast range of literature produced on the subject in the previous fifty years, and identified nine major categories of load forecasting techniques: multiple regression; exponential smoothing; iterative reweighted least-squares; adaptive load forecasting; stochastic time series; ARMAX models based on genetic algorithms; fuzzy logic; neural networks; and knowledge-based expert systems. In the last decade, other methods have been developed and tested (see, e.g., [9,10]), further improving forecasting reliability.

3   Energy Mix Analysis

Greener choices in the deployment of cloud applications should be performed by considering not only the typical quality aspects (e.g., response time, availability, security) but also green requirements which involve both energy consumption and CO_2 emissions. Focusing on the latter, evaluation of CO_2 emissions is based on emission factors (gCO_{2e}/kWh) provided by national grids. Emission factors largely vary from country to country. For example, if we consider France and the United Kingdom, technical reports describe that the country with the lowest carbon intensity is France, whose power generation is mainly based on nuclear plants. Estimated emission factors for France range between 62 [3] and 146 [8] gCO_{2e}/kWh. In contrast, United Kingdom energy is more carbon-intensive, with emission factors estimated to range between 567 [7] and 658 [8] gCO_{2e}/kWh.

As our goal is to deploy an application in a federated cloud environment, calculating and predicting emission factors for each of the sites included in the federation are crucial aspects in our approach. Indeed, knowing in advance which will be the emission factors of the countries in which the data centers belonging to the federation are established would allow us to calculate how CO_2 emissions may vary with respect to the location in which the application will be deployed and the time at which it will be executed. To this aim, we started from historical values about power generation disaggregated by energy source that some countries publish via public web sites. In particular, the French energy mix can be retrieved through the information service *éCO2mix* available on the RTE website[1]. Such service shows electricity demand, electricity generation classified by source and cross-border commercial exchanges (imports/exports). Data are automatically updated every 15 min. Similar information is available for the UK. Real-time and historic data about the energy generation in the UK are available through the BMRS (Balancing Mechanism Reporting System) website[2]. For this web site data are updated every 5 min.

Having the values from these two web sites, we constructed a model that reproduces in a simplified, but sufficiently precise way the analyzed systems, providing a tool to forecast CO_2 emissions and taking greneer decisions when deploying cloud-based applications.

To build the model, we adopted a traditional approach and went trough the following sequential phases:

- *Analysis of the problem*: it is necessary to observe the problem in order to understand the goals of the model and the data that have to be retrieved.
- *Conceptualization*: a model aims to provide a representation of a real world scenario. This phase focuses on guaranteeing the accuracy and completeness of the model. In fact, the model should be a simple, concise and correct view of the reality and should include all the elements that are considered as relevant. However, the model should not be too complex: complexity often implies a higher computational cost (i.e., longer execution time).
- *Calibration*: after gathering a sufficient amount of data, the calibration phase aims to estimate the parameters included in the model. For this reason, such phase is also called *parameterization* and can be performed by using several methods. We used the most common one: the Least Squares Method that minimizes the sum of the squares of the errors.
- *Validation*: the goal of the validation is to consider a new dataset and verify that the calibrated model is able to explain data trends and characteristics. If the results of the validation are not satisfactory, it is possible to enrich the dataset used for the calibration or go back to the conceptualization phase and change the model.

3.1   Analysis of the Problem

As already mentioned, the model to estimate CO_2 emissions has been designed by observing the available data on power production of France and the UK for two years: 2013 and 2014. As depicted in Fig. 1, the French energy mix is mainly composed of nuclear sources, while hydroelectric plants are the second most

---

[1] http://www.rte-france.com/fr/.

[2] http://www.bmreports.com/.

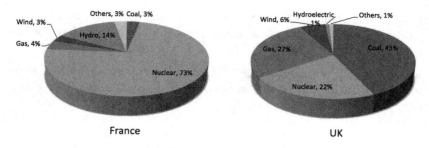

Fig. 1. Energy mix in France and the UK in 2013

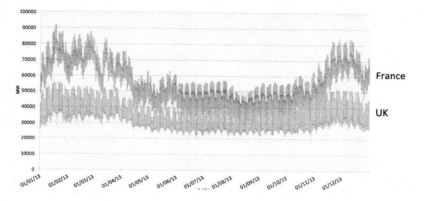

Fig. 2. Energy consumption in France and UK in 2013

important energy source, mainly used to dampen the fluctuations of nuclear production. The UK has a more diversified energy mix: 91 % of the energy production comes from coal, nuclear and gas. With respect to renewable sources, it is worth to notice that the UK relies on wind for 6 % of the whole energy production. This is due to the fact that the typical English weather is mainly windy especially in the cities close to the sea. Comparing the total production of the two countries (see Fig. 2), it is immediately apparent that, on average, the production of France is higher. This is not only due to the difference in population (nearly 67 millions in France against 60 millions in the UK), but also to the high production of thermonuclear energy in France, a considerable portion of which is exported to the neighboring countries.

3.2 Conceptualization

Based on the data gathered from the already mentioned web sites, Fig. 2 shows a comparison between energy consumption patterns in France and the UK during 2013. Regardless of the country, it is clear that some patterns occur periodically at different levels: from hour to hour, from day to day, from season to season.

To find a rationale behind this behavior, we analysed the data and we took into account the following time-variant elements that may be correlated with the energy consumption:

- *Temperature (T)*: considering the climate of the two countries, we assumed that higher consumption levels are related to lower temperatures (e.g., for heating).
- *Daylight Hours (DH)*: the electricity consumption raises in the periods characterized by a smaller number of hours of light.
- *Average seasonal Trends (Avg)*: we observed regular seasonal trends in weekdays data.
- *Power generation of close instants of time (P)*: we observed a clear autocorrelation between subsequent weekdays and among the same days of different weeks (e.g., every Monday or every Sunday).

On the basis of these considerations, we drafted a general model as:

$$P(t+1) = a \cdot f(P) + b \cdot f_1(T) + c \cdot f_2(DH) + d \cdot f_3(Avg) + e \cdot f_4(error) + error(t+1)$$

Analyzing such a model it is possible to notice that it can be formally represented by using a PARMAX model that is composed of the following parts:

- *The P (Periodic) part*: it is related to the time-variant parameters, that are parameters that have different values depending on the time in which they are considered. In the model this part includes the daily and seasonal parameters that vary on the basis of the day and season of the year.
- *The AR (Auto Regressive) part*: it links the estimated value with the previous values. In this case this part considers the emissions of the day and of one week before.
- *The MA (Moving Average) part*: is associated with the residual information that is the prediction error at previous time steps.
- *The X (eXogenous) part*: it is used to model the information contained in external variables (e.g., temperature and daylight hours)

For each energy source (e.g., nuclear, hydroelectric, coal) used by the two countries, a model has been defined. Due to space limitations, we do not list here all the models defined, but we present only the models of the most important sources for the two countries.

Model for Nuclear in France. French power production mainly relies on nuclear plants. Looking at the power production of this energy source over the year (i.e., 2013), it is possible to notice that there are recurrent seasonal and daily patterns: the production is higher in winter and lower in summer, and also during the day there is an oscillatory behaviour, which shows that the production is higher during the daytime while it decreases at nighttime. Note that the seasonal trend mainly depends on temperature, which is clearly correlated to power production as shown in Fig. 3.

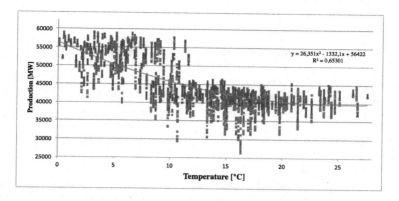

Fig. 3. Correlation between nuclear production and average daily temperature

Considering that time is expressed in hours, the formal model that we have defined to estimate the nuclear power consumption (N) of the next hour is:

$$N(t+1) = \alpha_1 \cdot N_{t+1}^* + \alpha_2 \cdot N_{t-5}^* + \alpha_3 \cdot N_{t-23} + \alpha_4 \cdot \zeta_{N_{t-23}^*} + \alpha_5 \varepsilon_{t-167} + \varepsilon_{t+1}$$

where:

N_{t-23} = nuclear power consumption one day before (same time)

ε_{t-167} = error of the model one week before (same day and same time)

$\alpha_{1...5}$ = coefficients to be estimated

$\zeta_{N_{t-23}^*}$ = error produced by N^* at the time instant $t-23$ (the same time of the day before)

N^* is the estimation of the value that has been formalized as:

$$N_t^* = (\tau_1 \cdot T_{t-24}^2 + \tau_2 \cdot T_{t-24} + \mu_1) + \Omega_t^h + \Omega_t^{h,s} + \Omega_t^{wd}$$

T_{t-24} = average temperature of the day before

$\tau_1 = 26.351, \tau_2 = -1332.1, \mu_1 = 56422$ = fixed coefficients that have been estimated through correlation

Ω_t^h = coefficient that is dependent on the time

$\Omega_t^{h,s}$ = coefficient that is dependent on the time and season

Ω_t^{wd} = coefficient that is dependent on the weekday

In our model the estimation N_t^* has to be calculated considered as parameters $t+1$ and $t-5$.

Model for Coal in the UK. Power production in the UK mainly relies on coal. Looking at the power production of such energy source over the year (i.e., 2013), it is possible to notice also in this case daily and seasonal trends and a correlation with temperature. The formal model obtained for this source is:

$$C(t+1) = \alpha_1 \cdot C_{t+1}^* + \alpha_2 \cdot C_{t-23} + \alpha_3 \cdot C_{t-167} + \alpha_4 \cdot \varepsilon_{t-23} + \varepsilon_{t+1}$$

where:

C_{t-23} = coal power consumption one day before (same time)

C_{t-167} = coal power consumption one week before (same day and same time)

ε_{t-23} = error of the model one day before (same time)

$\alpha_{1...4}$ = coefficients to be estimated

C^* is the estimation of the value that has been formalized as:

$$C_{t+1}^* = (\beta_1 \cdot D_t^2 + \beta_2 \cdot D_t + \mu_1) + (\tau \cdot T_{t-23} + \mu_T) + \Omega_t^{h,s} + \Omega_t^{wd}$$

D_t = number of days from the beginning of the year

T_{t-23} = average temperature of the day before

$\beta_1, \beta_2, \tau, \mu_1, \mu_T$ fixed coefficients that have been estimated through correlation

$\Omega_{t+1}^{h,s}$ = coefficient that is dependent on the time and season

Ω_{t+1}^{wd} = coefficient that is dependent on the weekday.

3.3 Calibration

The calibration of the defined models has been perfomed with the Least Squares Method. Figure 4 shows calibration results for the two models presented above. Considering the French model, it is possible to notice that the more relevant variable is the value of the power production recorded 24 h earlier. In the British scenario, three variables have a significant role in the model and, in particular, the values recorded 24 h and a week earlier and the estimation of coal production based on the season and temperature.

Parameters	Value
α_1	0.294
α_2	0.020
α_3	0.686
α_4	0.108
α_5	0.382

(a) Nuclear - France

Parameters	Value
α_1	0.296
α_2	0.339
α_3	0.369
α_4	0.332

(B) Coal- UK

Fig. 4. Calibration for the French nuclear and British coal models

3.4 Validation

The validation phase focuses on two steps: (i) the comparison between the estimated and real values for 2014, (ii) the aggregation of the different models for each country and (iii) the validation of the aggregated model on data for 2014.

Figure 5 shows the performances of the calibrated models of nuclear power production in reconstructing data from 2014. In fact, the correlation between observed data and model predictions is 0.945 (and thus R^2=0.893).

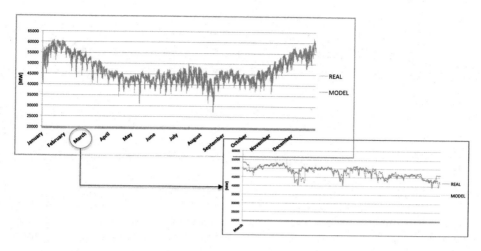

Fig. 5. Validation of the French nuclear model with 2014 data

Good results have been obtained also for the UK: the model for coal has a correlation with the real data R=0.944 and R^2=0.891.

In order to estimate CO_2 emissions coefficients for each country, it is necessary to aggregate the different models defined for the different energy sources. The aggregated model has been also validated. Results for France and the UK are reported in the following:

- *France*: Correlation model - real data= 0.971, R^2=0.942
- *UK*: Correlation model - real data= 0.940, R^2=0.884

4 CO_2-Driven Site Selection

To demonstrate how the approach presented in this paper can be applied to the estimation of CO_2 emissions, we refer to a scenario involving a federated cloud infrastructure. More in detail, we assume that several cloud platforms established in different countries around the world constitute a federation. This means that agreements between the owners of these platforms exist in order to optimize the usage of the installed resources (e.g., VMs, storage). As a result, migration of VMs among the sites, as well as the possibility to control the execution of the applications on top of them are all possible actions.

From the application perspective, we consider a real HPC application in the ecology domain [14] shown in Fig. 6 adopting BPMN notation. Without entering into details, the application starts with an initial setup (activity A1). The work is then split into several instances composed of two activities: data loading (A2) and computation (A3). Once all the instances are terminated, the partial results are aggregated (A4) to provide the result to the final user. We assume that one VM is required for A1 and A4, while for A2 and A3 the number of VMs may change according to the number of iterations required.

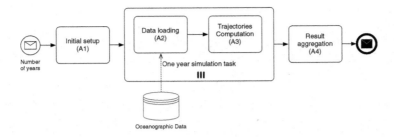

Fig. 6. Running example.

Along with the usual constraints about the VMs expressed in terms of number of cores, amount of memory, or storage, developers can also specify constraints on VM locations. Such constraints can be justified by legal issues (e.g., the data managed during A4 must not be moved to the USA) or to increase performances (e.g., A1 and A2 communicate very frequently and exchange a significant amount of data so it is better to put them at the same location).

Starting from this example, we want to show how the CO_2 emission model described in the previous sections can be exploited to decide when and where it is preferable – to minimize CO_2 emissions – to deploy and run the application. Since the only countries for which the CO_2 emission model has been produced in this paper are France and the UK, the following discussion refers to deployments that can occur on such locations. Similarly, as the data used to validate the CO_2 models refers to the year 2014, all the examples refer to this period.

As we are considering an HPC application, it is reasonable to assume that the same application has been already executed in the past. For this reason, we can also assume that some information about the energy consumed and the response time of the application when running in the UK or in France is already available. Based on our real experiments, we have the following situation [5]:

- UK: Response time = 17.07 h; Energy = 197.87 Wh.
- France: Response time = 13.50 h; Energy = 30.645 Wh.

These numbers refer to the scenario in which one VM is assigned to each of the activities and there is no concurrent iterations of activities A2 and A3. This assumption does not hamper the validity of our approach as having more instances of A2 and A3 simply reduces the response time regardless of the site in which the applications is running. The difference in response time and the energy consumed by the application depends on the characteristic of the physical machine installed on the two locations. More precisely, the British data center is equipped with less recent machines, so they are less performant and do not have low-power processors installed. Conversely, the French data center has been established more recently, with physical servers implementing several techniques to reduce power consumption.

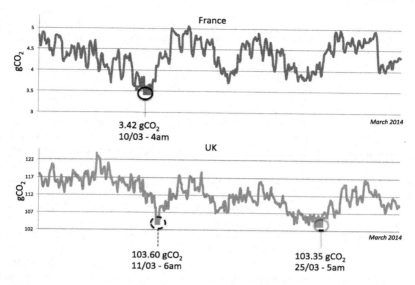

Fig. 7. Analysis of CO$_2$ emissions related to the considered application in the UK and France

Assuming that today is March 1st, 2014 and the application needs to run in 30 days, we use the proposed models to estimate the energy mix and, based on the energy consumed by the application, the related CO$_2$ emissions.

Figure 7 shows the result of this computation considering the two possible deployments: i.e., on the UK or on France. These CO$_2$ emission trends can be used to figure out if it is better to deploy the VMs on France or the UK, and when the application has to start, with the final goal of reducing the CO$_2$ emissions. Based on them, it is easy to understand that deploying the application in France is always the best choice: CO$_2$ emissions are always lower (about 4 gCO$_{2e}$) than in case the application run in the UK (about 110 gCO$_{2e}$). Stated this, the best time to run the application is on March 10th at 4 am, as the estimated CO$_2$ emissions are predicted to be 3.42 gCO$_{2e}$. In case, for some reason, the deployment must be done on the UK, then the lowest CO$_2$ emission is expected to occur on March 11th at 6 am or on March 25th at 5 am.

5   Concluding Remarks

This paper highlights the importance of CO$_2$ emissions in the deployment of applications. In particular, we show the way in which it is possible to build models to estimate future trends in emissions in order to suggest the most suitable deployment time able to improve the sustainability of the application. The validation scenario based on real data publicly available on the energy mix in France and UK shows how energy savings can be obtained by following a particular deployment strategy.

Acknowledgment. We would like to thank Valeria Crespi, Michele Del Vecchio, Alessandro Gentile and Marco Tangi for their valuable contribution in the definition of the different models.

References

1. Abbasi, Z., Pore, M., Gupta, S.K.S.: Impact of workload and renewable prediction on the value of geographical workload management. In: Klingert, S., Hesselbach-Serra, X., Ortega, M.P., Giuliani, G. (eds.) EDC 2013. LNCS, vol. 8343, pp. 1–15. Springer, Heidelberg (2014)
2. Addis, B., Ardagna, D., Capone, A., Carello, G.: Energy-aware joint management of networks and cloud infrastructures. Comput. Netw. **70**, 75–95 (2014)
3. ADEME: Guide des facteurs dmissions, Version 6.1. Chapitre 2, Facteurs associs la consommation directe dnergie. Technical report (2010)
4. Almeshaiei, E., Soltan, H.: A methodology for electric power load forecasting. Alexandria Eng. J. **50**(2), 137–144 (2011)
5. Cappiello, C., Ho, N., Pernici, B., Plebani, P., Vitali, M.: Co2-aware adaptation strategies for cloud applications. IEEE Trans. Cloud Comput. (2015), (pre-print)
6. Cook, G.: How Clean is Your Cloud? Technical report, Greenpeace, April 2012
7. Department for Environment, Food, Rural Affairs: Guidelines to Defra/DECC's GHG Conversion Factors for Company Reporting: Methodology Paper for Emission Factors. Technical report (2012)
8. European Commission: European Commission How to develop a Sustainable Energy Action Plan (SEAP). Technical report (2010)
9. Friedrich, L., Afshari, A.: Short-term forecasting of the Abu Dhabi electricity load using multiple weather variables. Energy Procedia **75**, 3014–3026 (2015)
10. Garca-Ascanio, C., Mat, C.: Electric power demand forecasting using interval time series: a comparison between VAR and iMLP. Energy Policy **38**(2), 715–725 (2010)
11. Liu, Z., Wierman, A., Chen, Y., Razon, B., Chen, N.: Data center demand response: avoiding the coincident peak via workload shifting and local generation. Perform. Eval. **70**(10), 770–791 (2013)
12. Matthewman, P.D., Nicholson, H.: Techniques for load prediction in the electricity-supply industry. Proc. Inst. Electr. Eng. **115**(10), 1451–1457 (1968)
13. Maurice, E., Dandres, T., Moghaddam, R.F., Nguyen, K.K., Lemieux, Y., Cheriet, M., Samson, R.: Modelling of electricity mix in temporal differentiated life-cycle-assessment to minimize carbon footprint of a cloud computing service. In: ICT for Sustainability 2014 (ICT4S-14), 25 August, 2014, Stockholm, Sweden (2014)
14. Melià, P., Schiavina, M., Gatto, M., Bonaventura, L., Masina, S., Casagrandi, R.: Integrating field data into individual-based models of the migration of European eel larvae. Mar. Ecol. Prog. Ser. **487**, 135–149 (2013)
15. Mirzaesmaeeli, H., Elkamel, A., Douglas, P., Croiset, E., Gupta, M.: A multi-period optimization model for energy planning with CO2 emission consideration. J. Environ. Manag. **91**(5), 1063–1070 (2010)
16. Vitali, M., Pernici, B.: A survey on energy efficiency in information systems. J. Coop. Inf. Sys. **23**(3), 1–38 (2014)

EM 2016

Modeling and Enacting Enterprise Decisions

Laurent Janssens[1,2]($\boxtimes$), Johannes De Smedt[1], and Jan Vanthienen[1]

[1] KU Leuven, Leuven Institute for Research on Information Systems,
Leuven, Belgium
{laurent.janssens,johannes.desmedt,jan.vanthienen}@kuleuven.be
[2] KU Leuven, Declarative Languages and Systems, Leuven, Belgium

Abstract. For years, the capturing of business decisions in enterprise models has not been treated as a separate concern. Rather, decisions were included in business process models or in knowledge models and ontologies. This leaves the overall view of a decision and its interplay with other decision and data requirements dispersed and hard to maintain.

The recently introduced OMG Decision Model and Notation (DMN) standard deals with decisions as a separate concern and presents decision modeling as a sovereign part of enterprise modeling. Decisions are modeled at the logical level, and the model is executable.

This work links the logical decision model to various execution strategies and processes by formalizing decisions within a business context, and by examining execution mechanisms for different availability of input data. These strategies can determine the preferred business process that handles the decision or allow to execute a decision model even when not all inputs are available up front.

Keywords: Decision modeling · Process modeling · Process enactment · Decision execution

1 Introduction and Related Work

Capturing the needs for making consistent, correct, and maintainable decisions is hard. Currently, many works focus on modeling decisions in processes (or as process steps). Most processes and business process models incorporate decisions of some kind, but they are often hidden in process flows, process activities or manual activities. It is not considered good practice to model the detailed decision paths in the business process model. Separating rules and decisions from the process simplifies the process model (separation of concerns).

Decisions are typically based upon a number of business decision rules that describe the premises and possible outcomes of a specific situation. Each decision may depend on a number of input data and on the outcome of one or more other decisions. Typical decisions are: creditworthiness of the customer in a financial process, claim acceptance in an insurance process, eligibility decisions in social security, etc. Since these decisions guide the activities and workflows of all process

© Springer International Publishing Switzerland 2016
J. Krogstie et al. (Eds.): CAiSE 2016, LNBIP 249, pp. 169–180, 2016.
DOI: 10.1007/978-3-319-39564-7_17

stakeholders (participants, owners), they should be regarded as first-class citizens in enterprise modeling.

Sometimes decisions can be included as an activity in a business process. The process then handles a number of steps, shows the appropriate decision points and represents the path to follow for each of the alternatives. In a large number of cases, however, a particular business process does not just contain decisions, but the entire process might be about a decision. The major purpose of a loan process e.g., or an insurance claim process, is to prepare and make a final decision. The process executes the decision by showing different steps, modeling the communication between parties, preparing required input data, recording the decision and returning the result. The purpose of this paper is to examine how such a model of a decision in the new OMG DMN standard can be brought to execution in a fixed process or in a flexible execution setting.

An alternative method, namely Product Based Workflow Design (PBWD) is presented in [1–3]. Similarities can be found between PBWD and case handling workflow management systems [4,5], as they focus on the data elements rather than on the control flow of the process. Our approach is related, but focuses on the decisions rather than on the data. The paper is organized as follows. First, related work including the DMN standard is discussed, as well as a formal definition of a DMN model. Next, the role of a decision model next to a process model is elaborated in Sect. 3 and illustrated in Sect. 4, supported by 3 new ways of executing a DMN model. Finally, a research agenda is formulated and a conclusion proposed.

2   Background

The term "decision modeling" refers to various ways to represent decision rules, constraints and conditional statements that describe the premises and outcomes of a specific situation and govern the actions that take place in applications and systems. Numerous decision models have been proposed to this end [6]. These are also used in many domains, e.g. business processes, credit risk [7,8], and medical diagnosis [9].

2.1   Decision Model and Notation (DMN)

Driven by an expanding need for decision support and automation, the OMG standards management group has developed a new standard: DMN, the Decision Model and Notation [10,11]. A first version of the standard has been made available in September 2015 and version 1.1 is awaiting publication. Many vendors (Oracle, IBM, Signavio, Decision Management Solutions, FICO, BlueRiq, OpenRules, among others) already offer tooling and industry users are starting to use the standard. An overview of some DMN concepts is provided in Fig. 1 where a decision model (right) is linked to a decision activity in a process model (left).

DMN consists of two levels: the decision requirements level (DRD, decision requirements diagram), indicating the requirements of a decision, and the decision logic level. The decision logic level provides a language for specifying decision logic (FEEL, the Friendly Enough Expression Language), and a corresponding notation (boxed expressions and decision tables) which allows such expressions to be linked to elements in the requirements level. Earlier research about decision modeling and management [12–14], decision tables and structures [15–17] is now becoming very important in the context of business processes and DMN.

DMN provides a common decision model notation that is readily understandable by users/modelers in all the development phases: modeling, execution, management and monitoring of those decisions. In DMN, decisions are based on criteria, conclude one or more results, require one or more subdecisions, and refer to a decision logic which is represented using a simple (e.g., decision tables) or a complex technique (e.g. analytics).

In Fig. 1 a simple car rental example is shown as executed next to a Business Process Model and Notation (BPMN) diagram [18]. DMN uses decision blocks (rectangles), business knowledge (cut-corner rectangles), and decision inputs (ovals). In this case, a decision table is used to capture the eligibility rules for assigning a customer a car, based on his/her employment status, country, and age. This eligibility is a decision that can be used as an input for another one, in this case the routing of the customer through the process. For this decision, the application risk is also evaluated and makes up the final decision for offering a product in the workflow.

2.2 Formalization

In DMN, decisions and their inputs are structured using decision requirement diagrams (DRD). These diagrams denote the information requirements of each decision, by connecting them with their subdecisions and inputs. This is represented by a directed acyclic graph. The DMN spececation allows a DRD to be an incomplete or partial representation of the decision requirements in a decision model. Thus, the complete set of requirements must be derived from the set of all DRDs in the decision model.

Definition 1. *The decision requirements level R_{DM} of a decision model DM is a single decision requirement graph depicted as a set of decisions requirement diagrams.*

We use R_{DM} to denote this set of DRDs. The DMN standard describes the requirement level of a decision model to consist of a decision requirement graph (DRG). This DRG is represented by a DRD which is self-contained, i.e. for every decision in the diagram all its requirements are also represented in the diagram.

Definition 2. *A decision requirement diagram $DRD \in R_{DM}$ is a decision requirement graph DRG if and only if for every decision in the diagram all its modeled requirements, present in at least one diagram in R_{DM}, are also represented in the diagram.*

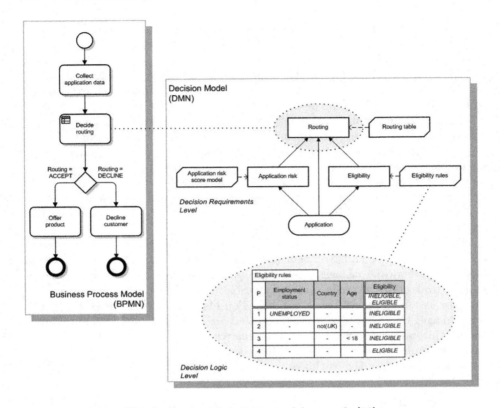

Fig. 1. Car rental decision model example [10].

According to the DMN standard [10] a decision can be dened as in Definition 3. In processes a decision is usually an activity, i.e. the act of using the decision logic. Another common meaning is that a decision is the actual result, which we call the output of a decision.

Definition 3. *A decision is the description of the decision logic used to determine an output from a number of inputs.*

In DRDs these decisions D are represented by the decision nodes $D \in R_{DM}$. We will use D to refer to both the decision and its representing node in a DRD. From the definition of DRGs we can derive an important property of decisions in the decision model.

Property 1. Given a decision model every decision D in that model has a unique decision requirement graph DRG_D with D as its single top-level decision.

From Definition 2 we know a DRG contains exactly all information requirements of its decisions. Thus there can only exist one DRG with D as its single top-level decision. We use DRG_D to denote this DRG. Decisions are often structured to use the results of other intermediate decisions, called subdecisions.

Definition 4. *A decision Ds is a subdecision of decision D if and only if it is part of DRG_D.*

An order can be defined on decisions in a decision model by using the property that DRDs are directed acyclic graphs. From this property we know each DRD has a topological order. The concept of topological orders is closely related to partial orders bringing us to Property 2.

Property 2. The topological order of a DRD induces a partial order $\leq$ on the decisions contained in the DRD.

For two decisions D_1 and D_2 we say $D_2 \leq D_1$ if and only if there is a directed path from D_2 to D_1, i.e. D_2 is a subdecision of D_1. Since decisions are declarative, this partial order does not dictate an execution order, but rather a requirement order.

3   The Role of Decision Models

The role of decision models must be framed within the context of business processes as well. Currently, many approaches have hidden the way in which the decision or chain of decisions contribute to the process to achieve the end result in a holistic way. This section relates the different ways in which a decision (model) can contribute to the overall achievement of integration of the dynamic execution of activities and the requirements that are imposed by a decision model and its inputs as described in [19].

3.1   A Decision Model Corresponding to a Single Decision Activity in a Process Model

Within a business process context, activities dominate the way in which the assignment of resources, data, etc. is done. Mainly due to this atomic division of the workflow, it is often assumed to have data only connected to one activity or one splitting node connected to many activities to avoid any faulty interactions over the global process model. In many cases in which there is no interleaving of data throughout the model, decisions can be used in this form of single branches that use the output of an activity that has implemented and evaluated the criteria for making the decision.

3.2   A Decision Model Spanning over Multiple Decision Activities in an Existing Process Model

Multiple activities in a process model may refer to different decisions that are all part of the same decision model. An important remark is whether the data needed as input for a decision is available before the decision is invoked. Activities producing the input required by decisions should occur before invoking those decisions. Otherwise, situations appear in which decisions cannot be made consistently due to incomplete or incorrect input. Next to the process, the decision model has as big an impact on how the system evaluates and uses data inputs as the process model. When decisions are dependent of intermediary results that are spawned earlier in the process, the decision model also puts constraints on the sequence ordering of the workflow, although they might not be defined explicitly in the process model itself. These issues have been addressed in [20].

3.3   A Decision Model that can Be Translated to a Straightforward Process for Execution

Sometimes the business process is really about a big decision. Some approaches were proposed [21] to model this in business process models, hence forgoing the purpose of decision models that were designed specifically for this task. Other approaches [22] rather seek to find the balance between data-driven models and business processes, however, the process part still remains a subordinate to the decision model. In this paper we assume that when the process is really about a big decision, the process model can be considered as the chosen execution flow to make the decision.

3.4   Executing a Decision Model Beyond One Fixed Decision: Flexibility

Once a decision model is built, it could be used for multiple purposes, not just the obvious decision that is present in the context of a current business question. The decision model could be designed for the current process, but also for other or future processes.

4   Three Scenarios for the Execution of Decision Models

Three types of scenarios for the execution of decision models can be identified. In this section we describe each of these scenarios in detail, and illustrate them using the example in Figs. 1 and 2. This table is an example instantiation of the Routing decision shown in Fig. 1.

Routing				
U	Eligibility	Application Risk	Age	Routing
1	INELIGIBLE	-	-	DECLINE
2	ELIGIBLE	HIGH	-	DECLINE
3		MODERATE	< 25	DECLINE
4			>= 25	ACCEPT
5		LOW	-	ACCEPT

Fig. 2. Routing decision table.

The identified scenarios can be seen as executing decisions in cases where all input is available, where enough input is available, and where only some input is available. Subsection 4.1 deals with the case of complete input, discussing this situation, and introducing additional formalisms to discuss these execution scenarios. In Subsection 4.2 scenarios where, although incomplete, enough input is available to make a decision. In these scenarios it becomes possible to optimize the decision process, either statically or dynamically. Subsection 4.3 ultimately details scenarios where insufficient input is available to make a decision, but it shows that even in these cases it is often possible to still execute a decision, e.g. to exclude some possible outcomes.

4.1   Standard Forward Decision Execution

Often the decision's input is available up front. The decision logic is captured in a straightforward decision model and the decision is to find the correct outcome for a specific set of input values. These are typical current DMN applications, e.g., determine the discount for specific clients, based on discount policy, client data, history, etc. or determine eligibility for insurance given the company policy. The reasoning mechanism does not need high flexibility, but it is important that company rules and policies can easily be adapted and brought to implementation.

To illustrate this and the following scenarios we extend our earlier formalization, to further describe a decision's inputs and outputs, and define what it means to execute a decision.

Definition 5. *The decision vocabulary Σ_D of a decision D is the set of the union of the decision input symbols Σ_I and the decision output symbols Σ_O.*

In other words, the decision vocabulary contains a symbol for each input and each output attribute. We will identify an attribute σ by its associated vocabulary symbol and say $\sigma \in \Sigma$. With each such symbol we associate an attribute domain.

Definition 6. *Each attribute $\sigma \in \Sigma_D$ has an associated domain D_σ, the set of all its possible values.*

Definition 7. *An attribute structure S of a vocabulary Σ contains for each attribute symbol $\sigma \in \Sigma$ a value $\sigma_S \in D_\sigma$.*

The set of symbols interpreted by S is denoted Σ_S.

Definition 8. *An attribute structure S' of a vocabulary Σ' is called a partial attribute structure of Σ iff $\Sigma' \subseteq \Sigma$. S is called an input structure or output structure of Σ_D if $\Sigma_S = \Sigma_I$ or $\Sigma_S = \Sigma_O$, respectively.*

Definition 9. *A total structure $S = S_I \cup S_O$, where S_I and S_O are input, respectively, output structures of D is an instance of D iff D maps input S_I to output S_O.*

In the case of a decision represented by a single-hit decision table a structure is an instance if a row maps its input to its output.

Definition 10. *A decision D is completely invokable for a partial attribute structure S if S is an input structure for Σ_D.*

The routing decision with the associated decision table shown in Fig. 2 is completely invokable when all its input is available, i.e. when the application is filled in completely, and the Eligibility and Application risk decisions have been made. Clearly this is a very strong restriction which is not always needed, this restriction is relaxed in the next subsection.

4.2 Optimized Forward Decision Execution

Often the decisions inputs are not available up front, but can be obtained at a certain cost (database lookup, user question). The decision logic is captured in a straightforward decision model and the decision is still to **find the correct outcome for a specific set of input values**. But the order of looking up input data and answers to user questions can have cost implications. If a decision can be made with only a partial set of inputs, it is more cost effective. The decision model is the same, but the execution of the specific decision might be optimized. So the question here is: what is the optimal process of executing the specific decision, given the cost of obtaining data and the frequency of cases? Since the optimal process of a decisions execution can be case dependent it becomes necessary to know when a decision can safely be made, i.e. when the outcome of a decision made with only partial input will not change if more data becomes available, this is formalized in the following definitions.

Definition 11. *Given a partial input structure S of vocabulary Σ for a decision D an input extension S' of S is a total input structure of Σ where $\sigma'_S = \sigma_S$ if $\sigma \in \Sigma_S$ and $\sigma'_S = v$ for some $v \in D_\sigma$ otherwise, for all $\sigma \in \Sigma_I$.*

Definition 12. *A decision D is safely invokable for a partial input structure S if there exists exactly one output structure SO such that $S' \cup S_O$ is an instance of D, for every input extension S' of S.*

This definition only applies when the definition is represented as a single hit table, and thus highlights an important benefit of using single hit tables, they allow safe invocation when sufficient input is available. This is not the case for multi-hit tables, as all applicable and non-applicable rules must be identified. As various process models can result from a decision model, the choice between different process models becomes an important issue. There is a need for criteria to rate the process models such that models can be compared to each other and the process model that best matches the business strategy can be chosen. Possible process modeling criteria are indicated in [23,24]. Applying these criteria shows some important strategies:

- Customer perspective: minimal points of contact.
- Business process behavioral perspective: starting with a labor-intensive activity is not optimal since the decision could be easily taken otherwise.
- Organizational perspective: the number of handovers can be minimized.
- Informational perspective: all necessary information could be easily acquired at one point in time.
- External environmental perspective: assessing external information should be limited.

With various decision process models to choose from, the decision process model that fits best with the business requirements can be chosen.

These criteria allow for two types of optimization, one static, the other dynamic. The approaches depend on the assumption made about input availability, offering optimization capabilities for both situations where all input is available as well as if only some input is available.

Static Optimization of Forward Decision Execution. In the static approach the assumption is that all input is available, the decisions execution can then be optimized by ordering the different subdecisions using the before mentioned criteria, or the cost, or frequency of these decisions. If we assume that for the example in Figs. 1 and 2 the Application Risk decision is very labor-intensive, then we can optimize the execution process by always invoking the Eligibility decision first, and having the Routing decision result in DECLINE, if the customer is ineligible. This constitutes an optimal process for the execution of the Routing decision when all input is available.

This is similar to the conversion of decision tables into program code, meaning that an efficient execution tree has to be generated for all the combinations of the condition values. Different paths in the execution tree can test the conditions in a different order, therefore the number of possible trees is enormous (and grows fast with a larger number of conditions). Additional information used in the conversion algorithm can be: the test time for each condition (if not available, all test times are considered equal) and case frequencies. In that way, the average execution time for the decision can be minimized. In the era between 1965 and 1980, much effort was devoted to research on this conversion of decision tables into efficient test sequences, leading to a growing list of conversion algorithms. A discussion of the evolution and results of the most important algorithms can be found in [25].

Dynamic Optimization of Forward Decision Execution. Apart from the previous static approach a dynamic approach can be taken if the assumption that not all input is available up front is not valid. Using the above criteria and the requirement order of the decision model, as described in Property 2, an optimal process for the execution of the decision can be generated dynamically on a case-by-case basis. By taking into account available input, Definition 12 can be used to guide the optimization, by invoking a high priority, or low cost decision as soon as it is safe to do so. In doing so, multiple unnecessary subdecisions may be excluded from the process, increasing its efficiency.

4.3 Flexible Decision Execution Scenarios

The specific **decision to be answered is not always fixed**. When dealing with a credit application, for example, sometimes the decision is not: Does this specific customer (with all input data available) get a loan?, but: What can we already derive from the available data? Another question could be: Which changes should be recommended to the customer to obtain a higher loan? DMN decisions do not specify whether the required input data is needed up front to be able to determine the outcome and assume a given decision path. This both has its advantages and disadvantages. A disadvantage is that an enactment of an ill-constructed DMN model might not be able to derive the results needed, due to missing input. If the user had not intended this, he might be unaware until runtime. On the other hand, it gives DMN a greater flexibility. Furthermore, it might not always be an impediment as there is a way to circumvent partial input. Given enough information it is often possible to exclude certain outcomes, as defined in Definition 13.

Definition 13. *A decision D is partially invokable for a partial input structure S_I if their exists an output structure S_O and there exists no input extension S'_I of S_I such that $S'_I \cup S_O$ is an instance of D.*

When resuming the example of the last subsection, partial invocation offers additional possibilities. Assume a customer who is eligible and of age 25 submits an application. If the outcome High can be excluded by partial invocation of the Application Risk decision, then the Routing decision can be safely invoked to result in the Accept outcome, since only the Moderate and Low outcomes remain for application risk.

5   Conclusions and Future Work

Business decisions are important, but are often not made explicit, hidden in processes or in the manual activities. In fast changing environments, decision models and better decision management will allow to create maintainable and flexible decision execution. This paper has shown how decision models differ, resemble, and complement business process models in enterprise modeling.

For future work, a plethora of opportunities exist in defining and optimizing the execution of decision models. First of all, many inference techniques can provide the enhancement of decision inputs, both in terms of completing partial input, as extending decision outcomes with examples, and so on. Secondly, it is the task of decision models to allow for the interplay of these different mechanisms that are each better tailored towards solving and extending certain decision domains as used in the models. Finally, it is yet to be proven how well decision models can truly relieve business process models in terms of flexibility, resulting in comprehensible though expressive declarative specifications.

References

1. Reijers, H.A., Limam, S., Van Der Aalst, W.M.: Product-based workflow design. J. Manage. Inf. Syst. **20**(1), 229–262 (2003)
2. Vanderfeesten, I., Reijers, H.A., van der Aalst, W.M.: Case handling systems as product based workflow design support. In: Filipe, J., Cordeiro, J., Cardoso, J. (eds.) Enterprise Information Systems. LNBIP, vol. 12, pp. 187–198. Springer, Heidelberg (2007)
3. Vanderfeesten, I.T., Reijers, H.A., van der Aalst, W.M.: An evaluation of case handling systems for product based workflow design. In: ICEIS, vol. 3, pp. 39–46 (2007)
4. Van der Aalst, W.: On the automatic generation of workflow processes based on product structures. Comput. Ind. **39**(2), 97–111 (1999)
5. Traganos, K., Grefen, P.: Hybrid service compositions: when BPM meets dynamic case management. In: Dustdar, S., Leymann, F., Villari, M. (eds.) Service Oriented and Cloud Computing. Lecture Notes in Computer Science, vol. 9306, pp. 226–239. Springer, Heidelberg (2015)
6. Koutsoukis, N.S., Mitra, G.: Decision Modelling and Information Systems: The Information Value Chain, vol. 26. Springer, Heidelberg (2003)
7. Kim, D.J., Ferrin, D.L., Rao, H.R.: A trust-based consumer decision-making model in electronic commerce: the role of trust, perceived risk, and their antecedents. Decis. Support Syst. **44**(2), 544–564 (2008)
8. Li, H., Zhou, X.: Risk decision making based on decision-theoretic rough set: a three-way view decision model. Int. J. Comput. Intell. Syst. **4**(1), 1–11 (2011)
9. Sun, X., Faunce, T.: Decision-analytical modelling in health-care economic evaluations. Eur. J. Health Econ. **9**(4), 313–323 (2008)
10. OMG: Decision Model and Notation (2015)
11. Taylor, J., Fish, A., Vanthienen, J., Vincent, P.: Emerging standards in decision modeling-an introduction to decision model & notation. In: Fischer, L. (ed.) iBPMS (2013)
12. Taylor, J., Raden, N.: Smart Enough Systems: How to Deliver Competitive Advantage by Automating Hidden Decisions. Pearson Education, Upper Saddle River (2007)
13. Taylor, J.: Decision Management Systems: A Practical Guide to Using Business Rules and Predictive Analytics. Pearson Education, Boston (2011)
14. Fish, A.N.: Knowledge Automation: How to Implement Decision Management in Business Processes, vol. 595. Wiley, Hoboken (2012)
15. Vanthienen, J.: What business rules and tables can do for regulations. Bus. Rules J. **8**(7), 2 p. (2007)
16. Ligeza, A., Nalepa, G.J.: A study of methodological issues in design and development of rule-based systems: proposal of a new approach. Wiley Interdisc. Rev. Data Min. Knowl. Discov. **1**(2), 117–137 (2011)
17. Nalepa, G.J., Ligeza, A., Kaczor, K.: Formalization and modeling of rules using the XTT2 method. Int. J. Artif. Intell. Tools **20**(06), 1107–1125 (2011)
18. White, S.A.: BPMN Modeling and Reference Guide: Understanding and Using BPMN. Future Strategies Inc., Lighthouse Point (2008)
19. Vanthienen, J., Caron, F., De Smedt, J.: Business rules, decisions and processes: five reflections upon living apart together. In: Proceedings SIGBPS Workshop on Business Processes and Services (BPS 2013), pp. 76–81 (2013)

20. Janssens, L., Bazhenova, E., De Smedt, J., Vanthienen, J., Denecker, M.: Consistent integration of decision (DMN) and process (BPMN) models. In: CaiSE Forum (Springer Accepted)
21. Kluza, K., Kaczor, K., Nalepa, G.J.: Enriching business processes with rules using the Oryx BPMN editor. In: Rutkowski, L., Korytkowski, M., Scherer, R., Tadeusiewicz, R., Zadeh, L.A., Zurada, J.M. (eds.) ICAISC 2012, Part II. LNCS, vol. 7268, pp. 573–581. Springer, Heidelberg (2012)
22. van der Aa, H., Reijers, H.A., Vanderfeesten, I.: Composing workflow activities on the basis of data-flow structures. In: Daniel, F., Wang, J., Weber, B. (eds.) BPM 2013. LNCS, vol. 8094, pp. 275–282. Springer, Heidelberg (2013)
23. Reijers, H.A., Mansar, S.L.: Best practices in business process redesign: an overview and qualitative evaluation of successful redesign heuristics. Omega **33**(4), 283–306 (2005)
24. Ferme, V., Ivanchikj, A., Pautasso, C.: A framework for benchmarking BPMN 2.0 workflow management systems. In: Motahari-Nezhad, H.R., Recker, J., Weidlich, M. (eds.) Business Process Management. LNCS, vol. 9253, pp. 251–259. Springer, Heidelberg (2015)
25. Henry Beitz, E., et al.: A Modern Appraisal of Decision Tables, a CODASYL Report. ACM, New York (1982)

A Modelling Environment for Business Process as a Service

Knut Hinkelmann[1,2(✉)], Kyriakos Kritikos[3], Sabrina Kurjakovic[1],
Benjamin Lammel[1], and Robert Woitsch[4]

[1] FHNW University of Applied Sciences and Arts Northwestern Switzerland,
Windisch, Switzerland
{knut.hinkelmann, sabrina.kurjakovic,
benjamin.lammel}@fhnw.ch
[2] Department of Informatics, University of Pretoria, Pretoria, South Africa
[3] FORTH Institute of Computer Science, Heraklion, Crete, Greece
kritikos@ics.forth.gr
[4] BOC Asset Management, Vienna, Austria
robert.woitsch@boc-eu.com

Abstract. Business processes can benefit from cloud offerings, but bridging the gap between business requirements and technical solutions is still a big challenge. We propose Business Process as a Service (BPaaS) as a main concept for the alignment of business process with IT in the cloud. The mechanisms described in this paper provide modelling facilities for both business and IT levels: (a) a graphical modelling environment for processes, workflows and service requirements, (b) an extension of an enterprise ontology with cloud-specific concepts, (c) semantic lifting of graphical models and (d) SPARQL querying and inferencing for semantic alignment of business and cloud IT.

1 Introduction

Currently cloud components are offered in a way that is well understood by IT-specialists. Many small and medium enterprises (SMEs) are currently excluded from using the Cloud due to high entry barriers, related to missing technical expertise to evaluate cloud services and to prepare the enterprise for the cloud usage. There is a big gap between pragmatic, legally influenced business processes and a huge cloud market with numerous offerings that rarely consider business situations but focus on technical details.

The EU-funded project CloudSocket aims to support the wide usage of cloud computing to SMEs such that they can easily benefit from cost reduction, as well as, from the dynamic and adaptive IT infrastructure in order to reduce their administrative burden and enable agility as well as new business opportunities.

This is achieved by the concept of Business Process as a Service (BPaaS), which maps to the ability to autonomously run whole business processes in the cloud. It is the objective of our approach that business users do not have to care for technical details, but specify their requirements in a business language. Then, through the environment proposed, support for the alignment between the business and IT level can be achieved

© Springer International Publishing Switzerland 2016
J. Krogstie et al. (Eds.): CAiSE 2016, LNBIP 249, pp. 181–192, 2016.
DOI: 10.1007/978-3-319-39564-7_18

mapping business-oriented models to technical ones that can drive the allocation and execution of business processes in the cloud.

The BPaaS Design Environment provides conceptual modelling tools for (a) designing domain specific business processes, (b) executable workflows, (c) additional description and rules for deployment as well as (d) key performance indicators. It not only allows the business user to model the requirements in a business language but also supports the smart alignment of business and IT in the cloud. This involves the identification of executable workflows for specific business process models through applying service discovery and composition techniques. This requires that the information about the business process, the service requirements and the workflows are represented in machine-interpretable format [16].

The BPaaS Design Environment (see Fig. 1) supports both *machine interpretation* and *human interpretation* of the enterprise model. The *human-interpretable, graphical* modelling is supported by the model stack as presented in Sect. 5. The machine-interpretation is supported by the BPaaS Ontology and used for alignment as described in Sects. 6 and 7. The integration of these two interpretation types is achieved by the semantical lifting of the graphical models (see Sect. 8).

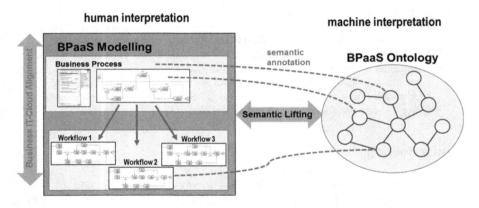

Fig. 1. General structure of the BPaaS Design Environment

2   Literature Review

Modelling the business processes, workflows and services in CloudSocket is part of enterprise modelling - the description and definition of the processes, structure, information and resources of an enterprise. According to Fox and Gruninger [11] an enterprise model must supply the information and knowledge necessary to support the operations of the enterprise. Enterprise modelling techniques are developed in several fields such as business process modelling, information modelling, systems modelling, and enterprise architecture.

Enterprise architecture (EA) models describe all relevant business structures, IT structures, and their relationships. The Zachman Framework is a two dimensional matrix, in which the cells contain models [32]. Another well-known EA framework is TOGAF [26]. The overall enterprise architecture comprises a set of closely inter-related architectures: Business Architecture, Information Systems Architecture, and Technology Architecture. The ArchiMate Standard [28] introduces an integrated language for describing enterprise architectures.

OMG has developed several specialized modelling languages for enterprise modelling, for example Business Process Model and Notation (BPMN) [24], Case Management Model and Notation (CMMN) [25], the Decision Model and Notation (DMN) [26] and the Business Motivation Model (BMM) [21]. The primary purpose of these graphical modelling languages is to support communication between human stakeholders, although there do exist execution engines for BPMN and decision tables.

The purpose of ontologies in enterprise modelling is to formalize and establish the shareability, re-usability, assimilation and dissemination of information across all organizations and departments within an enterprise. Describing enterprise architecture as an ontology started in the 1990s with TOVE [9], The Edinburgh Enterprise Ontology [30] and the organizational memory [1]. More recent work is the Context Based Enterprise Ontology [19]. Den Haan [8] has used an enterprise ontology to realize a Model-Driven Enterprise Engineering.

In the context of enterprise ontologies, the semantic business process management approach aims to achieve a new dimension of business IT alignment. Adding semantics to business processes enables machine reasoning and allows exploiting the full potential of process automation [15].

Conventional cloud services offerings include software as a service (SaaS), platform as a service (PaaS), and infrastructure as a service (IaaS). These offerings impose vendor lock-in and challenge the "developers to mix and match freely from diverse cloud services tiers" [22]. The concept of business process as a service (BPaaS) provides the flexibility of mixing different delivery models and focusing on the end-to-end business processes instead of single applications [22]. Flexibility is also archived by the atomized and dynamic configuration possibilities supported through the monitoring of threshold values on business and technical metrics. New resources can be added or removed to/from the BPaaS according to the individual needs.

BPaaS represents an initial field of research. Most of the research work proposed focuses on how to define BPaaS and the respective candidate architectures to realise it [2]. Some work has concentrated on dealing with security aspects (e.g., anonymisation-based protocols for BPaaS fragments [3]). Finally, initial work has been conducted on how elasticity can be realised for BPaaS through a specific formal model and a respective elasticity framework [20].

3   Overview of the BPaaS Design Environment

The BPaaS Design Environment comprises two modelling components - the BPaaS Modelling Environment and the BPaaS Ontology, including the inference engine for the smart alignment (see Fig. 2). The BPaaS Modelling Environment encompasses the meta-model for the human-interpretable, graphical modelling languages, i.e. Business Process Model and Notation (BPMN) [24].

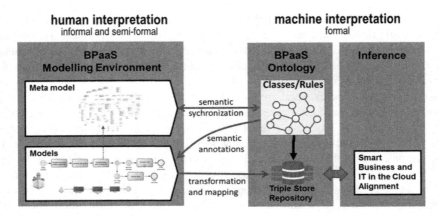

Fig. 2. Elements of the BPaaS Design Environment

The graphical models can then be semantically annotated with the ontological concepts, which are defined in the BPaaS Ontology. This means, that both ontology and meta-model development have to be synchronized in the sense that the ontology contains class definitions describing the intended semantics of the elements of the graphical modelling language. For the design environment user, this approach provides the possibility of modelling the business process and annotating the elements modelled with corresponding functional and non-functional service specifications, such as business, technical and compliance requirements.

4   Methodology

The development of the BPaaS Design Environment was supported by the OMiLAB LifeCycle, which is the basis of Agile Model Method Engineering [17] and has been developed and successfully used in the Open Models Initiative (http://www.openmodels.at).

Figure 3 depicts in the upper part the abstract developing methodology proposed by OMiLAB and in the lower part the concrete instantiation in the context of the BPaaS Design Environment. The research presented in this paper focuses on the first three methodology phases.

- *Create phase*: In this phase the domain and scope of the modelling framework were determined and the class hierarchy was defined. This phase is comparable to steps 1 to 5 of the approach for ontology development [21]. We analysed real situations of small and medium enterprises and identified a list of so called competency questions, which served as a basis to determine the scope of the ontology [29]
- *Design and formalize phase*: Those two phases are combined using a rapid prototyping approach. In ADOxx.org rapid prototypes of the BPaaS Modeling Environment were implemented. In parallel, a first prototype of the BPaaS Ontology was realized as an extension of the already existing ArchiMEO ontology.

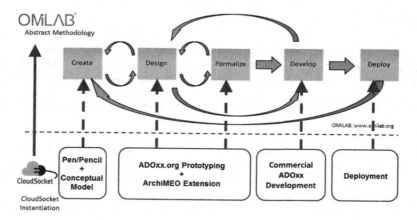

Fig. 3. Adapted OMiLAB methodology

For the development of the BPaaS Design Environment we analysed several real-world business scenarios. This was done in workshops with use case partners of the CloudSocket project. The business scenarios served as a starting point, since they represent real situations as they occur in enterprises. We implemented a cloud realization of a simple scenario - the sending of Christmas cards. This process is based on three main services (a) card designer, (b) customer relationship management, and (c) email service. Although this process seems to be simple, the underlying complexity increases by configuring the process such that particular requirements are met (e.g., industry compliance, data privacy, scheduling).

To determine the scope of the modelling framework we sketched a list of questions that the system should be able to answer. These questions are called competency questions. They have been introduced by Gruninger and Fox [13] as a method for enterprise engineering and ontology scope determination [29]. This approach is widely known and was amongst others adopted by De Leenheer and Mens [7], De Brujin [6] and Cardoso [4].

In order to develop the competency questions we analysed the individual components of the CloudSocket ecosystem. Who are the involved actors? What kind of value objects are exchanged? What are the value activities? Who are the composite actors? Four areas of competency questions have been identified that can be raised:

- General alignment: Questions regarding the mapping of business processes to workflows, e.g., which workflows are available for a given business process.
- Business perspective: Questions with respect to payment, contract, monitoring and support of the BPaaS and questions prospective customers might ask in order to assess the trustworthiness of the cloud service provider
- Security/legal perspective: Questions that are important with respect to security/risks/functionality or for SMEs in general or for SMEs operating in highly regulated industries.
- Technical perspective: Questions with respect to data formats, platforms or implementation.

5   BPaaS Modelling Method

Models are representing part of reality or a vision in an agreed modelling language. The BPaaS meta model defines the (a) domain specific business layer and (b) the IT-Cloud relevant technical layer, as well as the interaction between them (see Fig. 4).

- The business process layer includes business process, organisation and design models.
  - A *process map* model gives an overview of the organisation's processes. The modelling language of the BPaaS *business processes* is a subset of BPMN 2.0 that can be linked to: (a) service description (b) decision, and to (c) key performance indicator models. This subset is selected based on the authors' practical experience and the analysis of the use cases.
  - An *organization model* can be built to illustrate a detailed structure of a working environment for the business process.
  - *Document models* represent documents (templates), which are utilized in the processes as input and output to activities.
- The IT layer consists of *workflow models*. Workflows are described with BPMN 2.0 [24] extended by execution-specific technical details and IT-related KPIs.
- The interaction between the domain-specific business layer and the IT layer is done by semantically lifting business process and workflow models with the *Service Description Model*. Within this model type process tasks can be semantically enriched by describing the requirements derived from the business process for Cloud Services. We categorized service requirements in (a) functional-, (b) input- (c) output- (d) non-functional- (e) business-, and (f) regulatory dimensions.

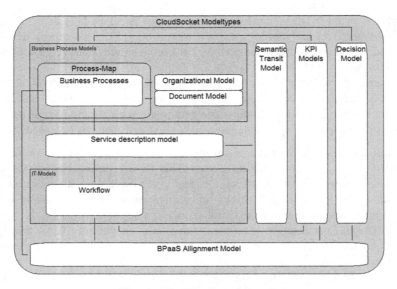

Fig. 4. The BPaaS model stack

- For both business and IT layers, there are links to the KPI and the decision models. The KPI cause effect model allows to model operational and strategic goals of cloud realizations. Such goals can be quantified by performance indicators. The aim of the decision model type, which corresponds to DMN, is to enable business users (e.g. analysts, technical developers) to comprehend the decisions and relate them to the data that might be held in the cloud.
- The Semantic Transit Model is used for semantic lifting of graphical models (see Sect. 8)

6 BPaaS Ontology

The BPaaS Ontology is implemented as an extension of the ArchiMEO enterprise ontology (http://ikm-group.ch/archimeo) with cloud-specific concepts, which are needed for smart alignment of the business and IT levels in the cloud. The cloud-specific extensions were determined from the analysis of the business scenarios and competency questions as described in Sect. 3. To enable a suitable and correct semantic lifting process, it is taken care that the BPaaS Ontology is consistent with the modelling method as described in Sect. 4.

ArchiMEO includes a top-level ontology, which contains general concepts, e.g. for location or time. Additionally it contains an Enterprise Upper Ontology with the concepts of the ArchiMate modelling language [28] as well as classes which represent the modelling elements of standard modelling languages like BPMN 2.0. The elements of these modelling languages are related to in the concepts coming from ArchiMate. For example, a BPMN activity is represented as a subclass of a Business Activity, which itself is a subclass of a Behaviour element in ArchiMate.

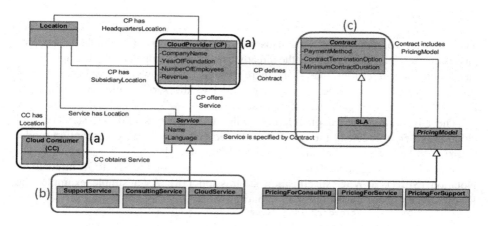

Fig. 5. Conceptual model of the business perspective

The BPaaS Ontology extends the ArchiMEO ontology according to the BPaaS requirements. Figure 5 depicts the class diagram of the overall conceptual model for the business perspective. The classes are integrated in the class hierarchy of ArchiMEO.

The class diagram highlights in red and labelled with (a) the classes of Cloud Provider (CP) and Cloud Consumer (CC). The ontology hierarchy in left part of Fig. 6 shows that these classes are modelled as sub-classes of the ArchiMate concept BusinessRole.

The right part of Fig. 6 shows the different kinds of services labelled with (b). Support and consulting services are classified as business services while cloud services represent a specialization of application services. A third part of the conceptual model (c) shows the (Cloud) Service Level Agreement (SLA), which is defined as sub-concept of Contract, which itself is a Business Object in ArchiMate.

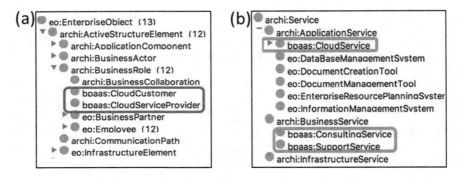

Fig. 6. Embedding cloud concepts into ArchiMEO

7   Alignment Support

The inference component for Smart Business and IT Alignment in the Cloud encompasses queries and rules to answer the already determined competency questions. These can be complex questions like: "Are there existing workflows for my business process?" or simpler like "Does the pricing model of the service allow payments per month?" or "Does the provider offer consulting services?"

The alignment is based on inference rules to propose workflows, services, and cloud providers that satisfy the requirements specified in the service description model referring to business process models and workflow models.

The inference engine applies the inference rules based on the SPARQL Inferencing Notation (SPIN), a W3C specification submission [18]. As a simple example, the following is a query that collects all Cloud providers offering consulting services:

```
SELECT DISTINCT ?cloudprovider ?service
WHERE {
    ?cloudprovider rdf:type bpaas:CloudProvider.
    ?cloudprovider bpaas:CPoffersService ?service.
    ?service rdf:type bpaas:Consultingservice .
}
```

SPIN allows to link class definitions with SPARQL [31] queries to capture constraints and rules and to formalize the expected behaviour of those classes. This is used in the BPaaS Design Environment to specify mapping rules between elements. For example, it can be used to derive requirements for the location of data depending on the type of data:

IF data contains personal data
THEN location of data is EU.

This rule uses the classes *personal data* and *location*, which are defined in the ArchiMEO and BPaaS Ontology. *Personal data* refers to instances of concrete process models.

8   Semantic Lifting

In order to apply the inference rules and queries for smart alignment, the content of the graphical models has to be translated into on ontology representation. This semantic enrichment of models and meta models corresponds to two approaches (Fig. 7).

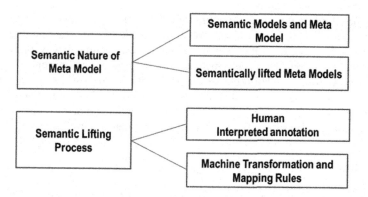

Fig. 7. Realization types of semantic lifting

- *Semantic nature of the meta model*: The concepts of the graphical meta models have corresponding classes in the ontology. Some meta-models already include semantics, while for others their content has to be semantically-lifted or enriched. This approach is called semantic synchronization in Fig. 2.
- *Semantic Lifting Process*: Elements of the graphical models are annotated with knowledge from an ontology. This can be can be performed by humans via manual annotations, or by machines that follow pre-defined mapping rules. The semantic annotation, transformation and mapping of Fig. 2 belong to this approach.

In order to enable smart business and IT-Cloud alignment, a transformation is implemented, which creates a formal representation of the graphical models. The basic mechanism is based on the transformation approach of the LearnPAd project [9].

Semantic annotations allow for the human modeller to add semantics to the modelling element while creating the graphical models [16]. There are seven different ways of implementing semantic annotation.

- *Non-Supported direct linkage* provides the possibility to annotate by using freely chosen keywords that correspond to ontology classes.
- *Supported pre-defined direct linkage* is the mechanism of providing a list of possible semantic annotations. The content of the lists is taken from the ontology, thus the selection can be interpreted.
- *Supported Direct Linkage* is the scenario where tool support enables the possibility to select semantic concepts from the ontology model. The linkage is established via a so-called "semantic tunnel", which can be implemented as Web-Services, which query the ontology tool to list all relevant semantic elements.
- *Indirect Linkage* describes the scenario where relevant concepts of the semantic target model are copied in a so-called "Semantic Transit Model", in order to simplify the selection of a semantic concept within the source model environment.
- *Direct and Indirect Linkage.* This scenario combines the direct linkage as well as the indirect linkage. High level and preferable stable concepts are copied into the Semantic Transit Model, whereas the flexible direct linkage is provided for lower and probably more agile concepts.
- *Loose Coupling.* In this scenario an intermediate ontological layer is introduced that enables the loose linkage of concepts in contrast to the aforementioned direct linkage. Loose coupling does not introduce a new technical way of introducing semantics but introduces an intermediate ontology acting as reference.
- *Graphical Annotation.* This scenario uses the graphical position of objects for its annotation. It is hence the realization of a semantic whiteboard, where the background image is the model which is to be annotated. Semantic tags – similar to post-its – are placed close to a model object and hence annotate it.

9   Conclusion

The design environment of the smart Business and IT-Cloud Alignment uses informal (text), semi-formal (graphic) and formal (ontology, rules) knowledge representation languages to support the modelling and provisioning of BPaaS.

Business scenarios were analysed and competency questions were derived in order to determine the scope of the modelling framework. The BPaaS modelling method was implemented in the ADOxx meta-modelling platform. The model types were extended with algorithms and mechanisms for semantic lifting to connect the graphical models with the BPaaS ontology. The BPaaS Ontology contains the relevant classes for the smart Business and IT-Cloud alignment. A first version of the prototype is available free for download from the project website (http://www.cloudsocket.eu).

The specification of the queries and alignment rules requires competence in ontology engineering. In a future version we plan to use the Decision Model Notation also for specification of the rules for service discovery, composition and alignment. They shall be translated into executable rules for better supporting the smart alignment of business and IT in the cloud.

Acknowledgement. The research leading to these results has received funding from the European Community's Framework Programme for Research and Innovation HORIZON 2020 (ICT-07-2014) under grant agreement number 644690 (CloudSocket).

Reference

1. Abecker, A., Bernardi, A., Hinkelmann, K., Kühn, O., Sintek, M.: Toward a technology for organizational memories. IEEE Intell. Syst. Appl. **13**(3), 40–48 (1998)
2. Amziani, M., Melliti, T., Tata, S.: A generic framework for service-based business process elasticity in the cloud. In: Barros, A., Gal, A., Kindler, E. (eds.) BPM 2012. LNCS, vol. 7481, pp. 194–199. Springer, Heidelberg (2012)
3. Bentounsi, M., Benbernou, S., Atallah, M.J.: Security-aware business process as a service by hiding provenance. Comput. Stand. Interfaces **44**(C), 220–233 (2016)
4. Cardoso, Y.C.: Creation and Extension of Ontologies for Describing Communications in the Context of Organizations. Universidade Nova de Lisboa (2010)
5. Cloud Service Level Agreement Standardization Guidelines. EC Cloud Select Industry Group (C-SIG), European Commission (2014)
6. De Bruijn, J.: Using Ontologies - Enabling Knowledge Sharing and Reuse on the Semantic Web. Technical report, DERI-2003-10-29, Digital Enterprise Research Institute (DERI), Galway, Ireland (2003)
7. De Leenheer, P., Mens, T.: Ontology evolution. In: Hepp, M., et al. (eds.) Ontology Management - Semantic Web, Semantic Web Services, and Business Applications, pp. 131–176. Springer Science + Business Media Inc., Berlin (2008)
8. Den Haan, J.: An Enterprise Ontology based approach to Model-Driven Engineering. TU Delft, Delft University of Technology, 15 October 2009. http://repository.tudelft.nl/view/ir/uuid:e2093132-9db7-4cba-bc68-9355f93cb9e3/
9. Emmenegger, S., Hinkelmann, K., Laurenzi, E., Thönssen, B., Witschel, H.F., Zhang, C.: Workplace learning - providing recommendations of experts and learning resources in a context-sensitive and personalized manner. In: MODELSWARD 2016, Special Session on Learning Modeling in Complex Organizations, Rome (2016)
10. Fox, M.S., Barbuceanu, M., Grüninger, M.: An organisation ontology for enterprise modelling: preliminary concepts for linking structure and behaviour. Comput. Ind. **29**(1–2), 123–134 (1996). doi:10.1016/0166-3615(95)00079-8
11. Fox, M.S., Gruninger, M.: Enterprise modeling. AI Mag. **19**(3), 109 (1998)
12. Gordijn, J., Akkermans, H.: Designing and Evaluating E-business Models. IEEE, 11–17 July/August (2001). http://doi.org/10.1109/5254.941353
13. Gruninger, M., Fox, M.S.: Methodology for the design and evaluation of ontologies. In: Industrial Engineering (1995)
14. Hepp, M.: A methodology for deriving OWL ontologies from products and service categorization standards. In: ECIS (2005)
15. Hepp, M., Leymann, F., Domingue, J., Wahler, A., Fensel, D.: Semantic business process management: a vision towards using semantic web services for business process management. In: ICEBE 2005: IEEE International Conference on E-Business Engineering, pp. 535–540 (2005)
16. Hinkelmann, K., Gerber, A., Karagiannis, D., Thoenssen, B., van der Merwe, A., Woitsch, R.: A new paradigm for the continuous alignment of business and IT: combining enterprise architecture modelling and enterprise ontology. In: Computers in Industry, vol. 80 (2015). http://doi.org/10.1016/j.compind.2015.07.009

17. Karagiannis, D.: Agile modeling method engineering. In: Proceedings of the 19th Panhellenic Conference on Informatics, pp. 5–10 (2015)
18. Knublauch, H., Hendler, J.A., Idehen, K.: SPIN - Overview and Motivation. W3C Member Submission. http://www.w3.org/Submission/spin-overview/ (2011). Accessed 23 December 2015
19. Leppänen, M.: A context-based enterprise ontology. In: Guizzardi, G., Wagner, G. (eds.) Proceedings of the EDOC International Workshop on Vocabularies, Ontologies and Rules for the Enterprise (VORTE 2005), pp. 17–24. Enschede, Netherlands (2005)
20. Lynn, T., O'Carroll, N., Mooney, J., Helfert, M., Corcoran, D., Hunt, G., Van Der Werff, L., Morrison, J., Healy, P.: Towards a framework for defining and categorising business process-as-a-service (BPaaS). In: 21st International Product Development Management Conference (2014)
21. Noy, N.F., McGuinness, D.L.: Ontology development 101: a guide to creating your first ontology. Stanford Knowledge Systems Laboratory Technical Report KSL-01-05, Palo Alto (2001)
22. Papazoglou, M.P., van den Heuvel, W.J.: Blueprinting the cloud. IEEE Internet Comput. **15** (6), 74 (2011)
23. OMG. Business Motivation Model, Version 1.1. Object Management Group OMG (2010). http://www.omg.org/spec/BMM/1.1/PDF/
24. OMG. Business Process Model and Notation (BPMN) Version 2.0. Object Management Group OMG, Needham, MA (2011). http://www.omg.org/spec/BPMN/2.0/PDF/
25. OMG. Case Management Model and Notation (CMMN), Version 1.0. Object Management Group OMG, Needham, MA (2013). http://www.omg.org/spec/CMMN/1.0/PDF
26. OMG. Decision Model and Notation Version 1.0. Object Management Group OMG, Needham, MA (2015). http://www.omg.org/spec/DMN/1.0/PDF
27. The Open Group. TOGAF® Version 9.1. Van Haren Publishing (2011)
28. The Open Group. ArchiMate 2.1 Specification. The Open Group. http://pubs.opengroup.org/architecture/archimate2-doc/ (2012). Accessed 3 November 2015
29. Uschold, M., Gruninger, M.: Ontologies: Principles, Methods and Applications. Technical report, University of Edinburgh Artificial Intelligence Institute AIAI, p. 191 (1996)
30. Uschold, M., King, M., Moralee, S., Zorgios, Y.: The enterprise ontology. Knowl. Eng. Rev. **13**(1), 31–89 (1997)
31. W3C. SPARQL 1.1 Overview. W3C Recommendation. http://www.w3.org/TR/sparql11-overview/ (2013). Accessed 30 December 2015
32. Zachman, J.A.: John Zachman's Concise Definition of The Zachman Framework. Zachman International (2008). http://zachmaninternational.com/

Understanding Production Chain Business Process Using Process Mining: A Case Study in the Manufacturing Scenario

Alessandro Bettacchi[✉], Alberto Polzonetti, and Barbara Re

Computer Science Division, University of Camerino, Camerino, Italy
{alessandro.bettacchi,alberto.polzonetti,barbara.re}@unicam.it

Abstract. Due to the continuous market change the enterprises need to react fast. To do that a better understanding of the way to work is needed. Indeed this was a real need of a manufacturing enterprise working in the production of coffee machines and selling them all over the world. In this paper, we present the experience made in the application of process mining techniques on a rich set of data that such enterprise collected during the last six years. We compare five mining algorithms, such as: α-algorithm, Heuristics Miner, Integer Linear Programming Miner, Inductive Miner, Evolutionary Tree Miner. We evaluated algorithms according to specific quality criteria: fitness, precision, generalization and simplicity. Even if comparison studies are already available in the literature we check them according to our working context. We conclude that the Inductive Miner algorithm is especially suited for discovering production chain processes in the context under study. The application of process mining gives the enterprise a comprehensive picture of the internal process organization. Resulting models were used by the company with successful results to motivate the discussion on the need of developing a flexible production chain.

Keywords: Process mining · Process discovery · Business process · ProM Framework · Mining algorithm · Production chain

1 Introduction

Manufacturing companies need to survive in a global market that asks for continuous align of the production and the internal organization, to the needs coming from the market. To do that a better understanding of the enterprise on the way to work is needed. This gives also the possibility to continuously improve production, avoid bottleneck and unwanted behaviors, or even workarounds enforced by the workers. This was the need of the manufacturing company working in the production of Coffee Machines motivated our work. After several meetings with the management board of such company we concluded that "a depth investigation of the production process is mandatory to learn from the past and to continuously improve the way to work". The company wanted to check the

© Springer International Publishing Switzerland 2016
J. Krogstie et al. (Eds.): CAiSE 2016, LNBIP 249, pp. 193–203, 2016.
DOI: 10.1007/978-3-319-39564-7_19

validity of the production processes, especially in exceptional events, for understanding optimizations to be done in order to save time and money and to have a more effective organization of work.

We based our study on such a real case study. The enterprise already have an internal traceability systems as part of its technology infrastructure. Based on the rich set of collected information (called log) via such system we run process mining techniques. Process mining aim is to extract non-trivial and useful information from event logs available in current information systems for discovering, monitoring and improving real processes [5]. Process mining is "evidence-based", it ensures a close correspondence between modeled and observed behavior because the evaluation and definition of the model is based on the real performance of the process. Moreover Process mining is based on facts, the event data, and it is addressed to discover the current "as-is" processes [15]. We use 450.000 events concerning six years production of 32 different products. At the end of the study we give to the company a more comprehensive picture of the internal process organization. The use of mining techniques allows to evaluate which is the historical course of the manufacturing process. Such awareness support the manager to enhance the entire production process.

This paper reports the results of the application of process mining in the production chain. We assess and compare five mining algorithms such as α-algorithm, Heuristics Miner, Integer Linear Programming Miner, Inductive Miner, and Evolutionary Tree Miner. In particular, we compared the algorithms performances according to specific quality criteria: fitness, precision, generalization and simplicity. Even if this is not the first study aiming to compare such algorithms [3,7], we run such analysis on our context to check general results on a specific application scenario.

The paper is organized as follow. Section 2 describes the case study, while Sect. 3 reports some background material. Section 4 gives an overview of the results coming from the application of the process mining algorithms on the case study. Finally, Sect. 5 reports conclusions and opportunities for further research.

2   Working Scenario

The case study refers to a manufacturing company producing and selling worldwide coffee machines since more than seventy years. The production chain relies on assembling components provided by several suppliers or internally produced. The production process is spread over six production lines enumerated from 1 to 6. Each production line, then, is organized into stations with specific objectives. The stations are identified by the letters A to F. According to the different types of coffee machines the organization of the stations in production lines can change. For production lines 5 and 6 there are only 5 stations: the station C is not present and all its activities are executed in station B.
The following are details of the stations.

– Station A starts with the activation of an RFID, which is used to uniquely identify a coffee machine. The second step is assembling the body and the frame of a new coffee machine. The activated RFID is then associated to the new coffee machine.

- Station B handles the hydraulic system: boiler installation, pipes assembly, etc. Considering the production lines from 1 to 4 in Station B only a portion of the hydraulic system is assembled, while in production lines 5 and 6 the entire hydraulic system is assembled.
- Station C in the production lines from 1 to 4 completes the assembly of the hydraulic system. In addition, when required by a particular quality certification, a test of hydraulic circuit is also performed. In production lines 5 and 6 this station is not considered.
- Station D deals with electrical circuit: control unit, wiring, electrical connections between control unit and components are installed.
- Station E performs the testing. It is executed simultaneously for multiple coffee machines.
- Station F completes the coffee machine including in the packaging manuals, accessories and identification tag.

Production lines activities are also supported by two areas of pre-assembly in which some electrical components (i.e. push button panels and electric cards) are set up and some types of boiler are built.

From IT infrastructure point of view the enterprise uses several information systems. In particular, the production lines, and related stations, are managed by a customized Process-Aware Information System named Automatic System for Chain COntrol (ASCCO). ASCCO traces all the information related to the production line (assembly steps, assembly times, faults, repairs, ...). ASCCO also integrates warehouse management providing real-time localization of components and assembled coffee machines.

3   Process Mining Techniques

Process mining techniques are grouped into four classes: *Discovery, Conformance, Enhancement* and *Operational Support* [15]. We concentrate on *Discovery* and already defined mining algorithms [14]. This section provides an overview of mining algorithms and a presentation of the tool and methods we use to run our research.

During the past 15 years, various process discovery techniques have been proposed based on different approaches. In this work we focus on five of the most common algorithms: α-algorithm [17]; HeuristicsMiner (HM) [20]; Integer Linear Programming (ILP) Miner [18]; Inductive Miner (IM) [6,7]; Evolutionary Tree Miner (ETM) [1]. These five algorithms were selected for two main reasons: their availability in ProM 6.5[1] [19], the tool used for process mining, and the format of the results that must be transformable to BPMN [11] for allowing the evaluation of the discovered models. Moreover, the results in [3] showed that ILP, HM and Genetic Miner [2] have good performance especially with real-life

---

[1] http://www.promtools.org/.

logs. Thus ETM was selected as evolution of the Genetic miner, while IM, which is presented after the considered study, was selected because it outperforms the other three algorithms according to its authors [7]. Finally the α-algorithm has been considered as the reference for the minimum level of performance.

The α-**algorithm** main aim is to investigate the relationship between transitions for reconstructing causality from a set of sequences of events [17]. Even if the application of the algorithm is quite simple it has a relevant problem to deal with noise, i.e. rare and infrequent behavior (outliers), and incompleteness, i.e. event logs containing only a fragment of all possible behaviors, namely too few events [14]. Moreover, the α-algorithm cannot deal with short loops, i.e. loops of length one or two, non-free-choice constructs and invisible and duplicated tasks.

The **HeuristicsMiner** can be considered an extension of the α-algorithm which takes into account frequencies of events and sequences in the log [20]. To do so, the algorithm only considers the order of the events within a case, while the order of events among cases is not contemplated. The ordering is determined by the timestamp of the activities in the log. The algorithm starts finding the dependency relations between activities and the construction of the dependency graph; then, for each activity, input and output expressions (group of connected activities that precede or follow the concerned activity) are defined, and, finally, long distance dependency are searched. The heuristic approach of the algorithm abstracts from exceptional behaviors and noise (removing edges) making such algorithm more suitable for many real-life logs.

The **ILP Miner** relies on concepts from the language-based theory of regions [8,18]. Such theory allows to derive a Petri net starting from different classes of languages. However, it seems to be not appropriate when it is directly applied to the field of process discovery. One of the main issues is the size of the resulting Petri net that is strictly (exponentially) dependent on the size of the log. To overcome this issue, the authors combined the ideas from theory of regions with Integer Linear Programming and used the causality relation introduced in the α-algorithm.

The **Inductive Miner** is an algorithm based on a divide-and-conquer approach [6,7]. Such approach is applied to the log splitting it in sub-logs and then recursively applied to these sub-logs until they contain only a single activity. In this way the problem of discovering a process model for a log is broken down in discovering several sub-processes, one for each sub-log. The algorithm ensures to return a sound, fitting and block-structured process model in finite time. Additionally the authors identified the conditions required to return a model that is language-equivalent to the model of the original process that generated the log.

The **Evolutionary Tree Miner** is a genetic process mining algorithm which allows the user to influence the discovery process based on preferences respect to the four quality dimensions described above [1]. This algorithm uses process trees as model representation which guarantees that all discovered models are sound, i.e. models without deadlocks, livelocks or other anomalies [16]. Like most of the genetic algorithms, ETM randomly creates an initial population then, according to a fitness function, it selects the best individuals on which random mutation and crossover operations are applied for evolution. Such steps are repeated till the model reaches one of the stop criteria. The algorithm, however, does not ensure the reproducibility of the model: if it is applied multiple times to the same log, the discovered model will most likely be different.

4   Process Mining into Practice

The complexity of the scenario is mainly given by the wide range of coffee machines, which are all assembled on interchangeable production lines. The use of process mining allows an in-depth analysis and representation of the production. It is possible to find out the deviation compared with the expected process model. In this work we considered 450.000 event logs related to six years of production of 32 different coffee machines types. Logs were converted from relational format to eXtensible Event Stream (XES) [4], an XML-based data format for processing event logs and natively supported by ProM. For each type of coffee machine was created a .xes file that is used as input for the five discovery algorithms: α-algorithm, Heuristics Miner, Integer Linear Programming Miner, Inductive Miner, Evolutionary Tree Miner.

This section provides criteria to evaluate the quality of process models discovered by mining algorithms.

4.1   Evaluation Criteria

In order to generate a process model in line with reality, mining algorithms should maintain a proper balance between overfitting and underfitting [14]. Overfitting means that the generated model is too specific and it only admits a behavior similar to the one observed. Underfitting means that the generated model is too general and it also accepts behaviors unrelated to the observed one. A "good" discovered process model needs a proper balance between underfitting and overfitting properties. To asses them we refer to four quality dimensions: *replay fitness, precision, generalization* and *simplicity* [14]. More in detail, *replay fitness* expresses the portion of the log behavior that can be replayed by the process model, *precision* is the measure of the level of underfitting, i.e. a poor precision means that a model admits unusual behaviors than those shown in the logs, conversely *generalization* is the measure of overfitting, i.e. an high generalization allows also behaviors not seen in the log (maybe not yet observed), while *simplicity* evaluates how easily a human interprets the process model. *Simplicity* could be subject to different interpretation, therefore we considered some complexity metrics [9] to perform an objective assessment. They are following reported.

- *Size* represents the number of nodes (activities and connectors) of the model.
- *Density* (Δ) represents the ratio between the total number of arcs and the maximum possible number of arcs for the same number of nodes.
- *Coefficient of Network Connectivity (CNC)* represents the ratio between arcs and nodes.

- *Average Connector Degree (ACD)* represents the number of nodes a connector is in average connected to.
- *Connector Mismatch (MM)* represents the sum of mismatches for each connector type, where a mismatch is the difference between the total number of outgoing edges from split connectors and the total number of incoming edges at join connectors.
- Control-Flow Complexity (CFC) represents the sum over all connectors weighted by their potential combinations of states after a split.

Generally, process models with higher values for such metrics are less understandable and more error-prone as empirical studies have shown [10, 12, 13].

4.2 Preliminary Results

For reasons of simplicity the logs are grouped for different types of coffee machines and they are enumerated from 1 to 32. For each log set we run the mining using the five algorithms and then we compare quality criteria on the resulting models. Figure 1 shows 5 charts, one for each process mining algorithm, in which values of *fitness*, *precision* and *generalization*, and the corresponding averages are shown. We can observe that independently from the used algorithm, the log sets related to coffee machine types from 1 to 5 and from 20 to 25 show high values for *fitness* and *precision*, but no *generalization*. Some log sets, such as 16 and 29 for example, show in particular the inefficiency of α-algorithm and ILP, while IM, HM and ETM have high performance. The log set related to coffee machine 7 shows a different behavior: not only α-algorithm and ILP have poor results, but also HM underperforms returning values even worse than α-algorithm.

A more detailed analysis of the results is achieved by taking into account the complexity measures. Table 1 shows all the quality values considering log sets with high variability. In Table 1 the first column contains the name of the log set, the second shows the used mining algorithm and the following columns present calculated measures of quality and complexity as indicated in the table header. Bold text highlights best values for each quality dimension. The evaluation of the best discovered model is not simple. Considering the log set 7 we conclude that ETM presents the best score compared to the other algorithms, it has high values of *fitness*, *precision* and *generalization* and low complexity measures. The choice for mining log set 19 is a bit more difficult. In this case HM has the highest *generalization*, while *fitness* and *precision* are very close to best values, but the complexity level is higher than the model resulting from the use of other algorithms. Considering that ILP, IM and ETM have the same level of *fitness*, *precision* and *generalization*, if we penalize models with bigger size, such as in our case, the best algorithm is between ILP and IM. They differ in the ACD and MM measures. Avoiding inconsistencies in the model we prefer to consider readable model, therefore, IM is the most suitable algorithm for log set 19.

More general, we determined the maximum, minimum, average and standard deviation of *fitness*, *precision* and *generalization* in order to obtain the

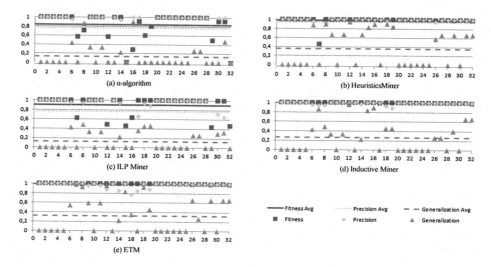

Fig. 1. Process mining results

overall trend of the five mining algorithms. Such values are reported in Table 2. All algorithms show very high maximum values. The only one exception is the *generalization* for ILP. It means that the algorithms have good performance for some logs. Considering the minimum value, good performance for *fitness* and *precision* are confirmed only by IM and ETM. These two algorithms also have high average values and SD very low for *fitness* and *precision* quality dimensions, which shows singular values very close. HM also has a very high average, but the SD indicates a higher variability compared to IM and ETM. Regarding *generalization*, the average level is rather low.

In conclusion, considering quality dimensions we observe that log sets without or with low noise show, in many cases, higher values, albeit slightly, of *fitness* and *precision* in model discovered with α-algorithm than those mined with ETM or HM, whereas the *generalization* is clearly in favor of the latter techniques.

4.3   Discussion and Comparison

A first remark is that no algorithm provides a single log set with the highest values for all the three quality dimensions. Another general remark is about the execution time. ETM is the only algorithm that requires several minutes to discover a model, all the others are significantly faster and they complete in a few seconds.

Complexity measures are not very relevant when considered individually [9]. In order to obtain a better assessment, we estimated all values at once. Furthermore, since the maximum number of activities in our models are 6, complexity measures rarely have very high values, therefore even small differences between two models may be considered relevant. In addition, we point out that the smaller

Table 1. Quality and complexity measures of some discovered models

		Fitness	Precision	Generalization	Size	Δ	CNC	ACD	MM	CFC
7	α	0.564187531	0	0	10	0.18889	1.7	4.5	7	4
	HM	0.454466469	0	0	9	0.13889	1.11111	3	2	2
	ILP	0.627994965	0	0	11	0.15455	1.54545	4.333	6	4
	IM	**0.999820965**	0.94658	0.86624	10	0.12222	1.1	4	0	1
	ETM	0.998522961	1	**0.98718**	8	0.125	0.875	0	0	0
8	α	0.714285714	0.875	0.85417	11	0.10909	1.09091	3	2	2
	HM	0.998500664	0.92188	0.90093	10	0.12222	1.1	3	4	4
	ILP	**1**	0.94444	0.49259	11	0.10909	1.09091	3	2	1
	IM	**1**	0.94444	0.49259	11	0.10909	1.09091	3	2	1
	ETM	0.997286013	1	**0.93333**	8	0.125	0.875	0	0	0
12	α	0.564394626	0	0	9	0.22222	1.77778	5	4	1
	HM	**0.998831267**	0.94444	0.95586	9	0.125	1	3	2	2
	ILP	0.485082741	0	0	13	0.11538	1.38462	3.4	2	5
	IM	0.99833442	1	0.96429	8	0.125	0.875	0	0	0
	ETM	0.998418906	0.88462	**0.96526**	9	0.125	1	3	2	2
16	α	0.285714286	1	**0.9**	14	0.09341	1.21429	3.167	13	5
	HM	0.999471858	1	**0.9**	8	0.125	0.875	0	0	0
	ILP	0.632302405	0	0	11	0.12727	1.27273	3.333	1	1
	IM	0.999471858	1	**0.9**	8	0.125	0.875	0	0	0
	ETM	**1**	0.77222	0.35	10	0.12222	1.1	4	0	1
19	α	0.796564669	0	0	10	0.13333	1.2	3	2	3
	HM	0.998594882	0.84848	**0.83983**	9	0.13889	1.1111	3	4	4
	ILP	**1**	**0.88333**	0.45778	9	0.13889	1.1111	3.5	1	1
	IM	**1**	**0.88333**	0.45778	9	0.13889	1.1111	4	0	1
	ETM	**1**	**0.88333**	0.45778	10	0.12222	1.1	3.333	1	1
29	α	0.491776479	0	0	8	0.26786	1.875	6	5	1
	HM	0.99682937	1	**0.66667**	7	0.14286	0.85714	0	0	0
	ILP	0.438372793	0	0	8	0.16071	1.125	3	2	0
	IM	**0.999582812**	1	0.4	8	0.14286	1	3	2	0
	ETM	0.99682937	1	**0.66667**	7	0.14286	0.85714	0	0	0

models usually have higher density [10]. According to these guidelines, the simplest models are those mined with ETM, HM and IM, α-algorithm, once again has the worst performance.

A final consideration concerns the possible relationship between complexity and quality measures. The evaluation does not permit any conclusion since there are models having a similar level of complexity and very different quality values, e.g. ILP and IM on log set 29 in Table 1, and other models with similar quality values and different complexity.

In summary, after an overall evaluation of all metrics, we can say that the most suitable mining algorithms in our context are IM and ETM. They result with the highest values of fitness and precision for each log set. Considering the average values IM is a bit better than ETM, and similar values can be observed for the generalization, in such case ETM is slightly better, then a new trace may be more readily accepted by models discovered by ETM than by IM. Also HM presents high values of fitness and precision for most of the log, but on those with high noise, e.g. Log 7, it underperforms. Since the noise in the event logs may increase as time goes, we preferred not to take into account an algorithm with such behavior. ILP and α-algorithm are least suitable because both underperform in all quality dimensions. With regard to the degree of simplicity, the algorithms are almost equivalent for the models corresponding to log without or with low noise, therefore the comparison was made on the remaining models. ILP and α-algorithm show significantly high complexity values, in some cases nearly twice those of other algorithms, so they remain consistent with poor performance. IM and ETM are comparable. They have similar values for most of the log set and present slightly different measures for those that are not similar. Models discovered by HM are on average a bit simpler than those of IM and ETM. We conclude that we preferred IM over ETM due to its performance.

Table 2. Aggregate values for quality dimensions.

		Min.	Max.	Avg.	SD
Fitness	α	0	1	0.836593796	0.284922192
	HM	0.45447	1	0.981982191	0.094753898
	ILP	0.438377	1	0.909793346	0.190947749
	IM	0.99375	1	**0.999559383**	**0.001182631**
	ETM	**0.99493**	1	0.999250868	0.001191822
Precision	α	0	1	0.774045	0.410313551
	HM	0	1	• 0.956853125	0.174626942
	ILP	0	1	0.7719325	0.381931605
	IM	**0.88333**	1	**0.988434375**	**0.026802914**
	ETM	0.77222	1	0.974649375	0.056454291
Generalization	α	0	0.9	0.127684688	0.240198833
	HM	0	0.95586	**0.35814125**	0.390181461
	ILP	0	0.49259	0.133032188	**0.179213299**
	IM	0	0.96429	0.267528125	0.316556286
	ETM	0	**0.98718**	0.32354	0.36362457

5   Conclusion and Future Work

In a competitive globalized market, manufacturing companies are forced to continuous improvements to advance. A relevant aspect is that manufacturing is characterized by quite complex production processes. In order to adjust such processes to new requirements a better understanding of the actual processes is needed. The concept of process mining provided appropriate techniques to achieve that purpose.

In this paper, we presented a benchmarking of five process mining algorithms to choose the most appropriate to the motivating case study. α-algorithm, HM,

ILP, IM ed ETM were applied. We then compared such mining algorithms using *fitness, precision* and *generalization* values and complexity metrics, for *simplicity*, of the discovered models. Models mined by HM, IM and ETM had high fitness, high precision and low complexity. At the end, the algorithm with the best comprehensive assessment is IM and therefore it is the most suitable for our purposes. Similar studies have already been performed while not in manufacturing. In [3] is presented a comprehensive experimental analysis on the quality of a broad range of mining algorithms: the study reveals that the HM provides the best outcomes, and this is consistent with the findings in our work if we exclude the IM and ETM which have not been taken into account in such study. The outcomes of our work are also validated by [7], where the comparison of mining algorithms, except α, shows that IM and ETM have the best results.

The results of this work have been used by the company for further analysis of the production process. This activity (analysis) revealed that only a small portion of non-standard traces depends on run-time errors of ASCCO. The remaining non-standard traces are due to incorrect managing on the production line of the procedures for fixing or replacing faulty components identified from testing, and of the implementation of some special, and infrequent, customizations. This awareness has driven the company to plan the reorganization of part of the production processes, in order to include such behaviors, and the consequent update of ASCCO for managing these changes.

This paper is part of a larger project whose aim is the use of process mining techniques to support the Business Process Evolution in production chain. The idea is to extend the current traceability system, ASCCO, in order to automatically extract logs, use Inductive Miner to discover the process model, and manage the evolution of such processes through version management approach.

Acknowledgments. We thank Nuova Simonelli and e-Lios for the fruitful collaboration in the project. In particular, we are indebted to Nuova Simonelli President Nando Ottavi for its support and Mauro Parrini who helped us in preparing and conducting this research.

References

1. Buijs, J., van Dongen, B., van der Aalst, W.: A genetic algorithm for discovering process trees. In: 2012 IEEE Congress on Evolutionary Computation (CEC), pp. 1–8. IEEE, June 2012
2. de Medeiros, A., Weijters, A., van der Aalst, W.M.: Genetic process mining: an experimental evaluation. Data Min. Knowl. Discov. **14**(2), 245–304 (2007)
3. De Weerdt, J., De Backer, M., Vanthienen, J., Baesens, B.: A multi-dimensional quality assessment of state-of-the-art process discovery algorithms using real-life event logs. Inf. Syst. **37**(7), 654–676 (2012)
4. Günther, C.W., Verbeek, E.: XES Standard Definition version 2.0 (2014)
5. van der Aalst, W., et al.: Process mining manifesto. In: Daniel, F., Barkaoui, K., Dustdar, S. (eds.) Business Process Management Workshops. LNBIP, vol. 99, pp. 169–194. Springer, Heidelberg (2012)

6. Leemans, S.J.J., Fahland, D., van der Aalst, W.M.P.: Discovering block-structured process models from event logs - a constructive approach. In: Colom, J.-M., Desel, J. (eds.) PETRI NETS 2013. LNCS, vol. 7927, pp. 311–329. Springer, Heidelberg (2013)

7. Leemans, S.J., Fahland, D., van der Aalst, W.M.: Discovering block-structured process models from event logs containing infrequent behaviour. In: Lohmann, N., Song, M., Wohed, P. (eds.) Business Process Management Workshops. LNBIP, vol. 171, pp. 66–78. Springer, Heidelberg (2014)

8. Lorenz, R., Mauser, S., Juhás, G., How to synthesize nets from languages: a survey. In: Proceedings of the Winter Simulation Conference (WSC) 2007, WSC 2007, pp. 637–647, Piscataway, NJ, USA. IEEE Press (2007)

9. Mendling, J.: Metrics for Process Models: Empirical Foundations of Verification, Error Prediction, and Guidelines for Correctness. LNBIP, vol. 6. Springer, Heidelberg (2008)

10. Mendling, J., Reijers, H.A., Cardoso, J.: What makes process models understandable? In: Alonso, G., Dadam, P., Rosemann, M. (eds.) BPM 2007. LNCS, vol. 4714, pp. 48–63. Springer, Heidelberg (2007)

11. OMG. Business Process Modeling Notation (BPMN)

12. Reijers, H., Mendling, J.: A study into the factors that influence the understandability of business process models. IEEE Trans. Syst. Man Cybern. Part A **41**(3), 449–462 (2011)

13. Rolón, E., Cardoso, J., García, F., Ruiz, F., Piattini, M.: Analysis and validation of control-flow complexity measures with BPMN process models. In: Halpin, T., Krogstie, J., Nurcan, S., Proper, E., Schmidt, R., Soffer, P., Ukor, R. (eds.) Enterprise, Business-Process and Information Systems Modeling. LNBIP, vol. 29, pp. 58–70. Springer, Heidelberg (2009)

14. van der Aalst, W.M.: Process Mining: Discovery, Conformance and Enhancement of Business Processes. Springer, Heidelberg (2011)

15. van der Aalst, W.M.: Processes, no knowledge without : process mining as a tool to find out what people and organizations really do. In: Fred, A., Filipe, J., Dietz, J., Aveiro, D., Liu, K. (eds.) Proceedings of the International Joint Conference on Knowledge Discovery, Knowledge Engineering and Knowledge Management (IC3K 2014), pp. 11–16, Rome (2014)

16. van der Aalst, W.M., van Hee, K.M., ter Hofstede, A.H., Sidorova, N., Verbeek, H., Voorhoeve, M., Wynn, M.: Soundness of workflow nets: classification, decidability, and analysis. Formal Aspects Comput. **23**(3), 333–363 (2011)

17. van der Aalst, W.M., Weijters, T., Maruster, L.: Workflow mining: discovering process models from event logs. IEEE Trans. Knowl. Data Eng. **16**(9), 1128–1142 (2004)

18. van der Werf, J.M.E., van Dongen, B.F., Hurkens, C.A., Serebrenik, A.: Process discovery using integer linear programming. Fundamenta Informaticae **94**(3–4), 387–412 (2009)

19. van Dongen, B.F., de Medeiros, A., Verbeek, H.M.W., Weijters, A., van der Aalst, W.M.: The ProM framework: a new era in process mining tool support. In: Ciardo, G., Darondeau, P. (eds.) Application and Theory of Petri Nets 2005. LNCS, vol. 3536, pp. 444–454. Springer, Heidelberg (2005)

20. Weijters, A., van der Aalst, W.M., de Medeiros, A.: Process Mining with the Heuristics Miner Algorithm (2006)

WISSE 2016

Software Vulnerability Life Cycles and the Age of Software Products: An Empirical Assertion with Operating System Products

Jukka Ruohonen, Sami Hyrynsalmi[✉], and Ville Leppänen

Department of Information Technology, University of Turku,
20014 Turun yliopisto, Finland
{juanruo,sthyry,ville.leppanen}@utu.fi

Abstract. This empirical paper examines whether the age of software products can explain the turnaround between the release of security advisories and the publication vulnerability information. Building on the theoretical rationale of vulnerability life cycle modeling, this assertion is examined with an empirical sample that covers operating system releases from Microsoft and two Linux vendors. Estimation is carried out with a linear regression model. The results indicate that the age of the observed Microsoft products does not affect the turnaround times, and only feeble statistical relationships are present for the examined Linux releases. With this negative result, the paper contributes to the vulnerability life cycle modeling research by presenting and rejecting one theoretically motivated and previously unexplored question. The rejection is also a positive result; there is no reason for users to fear that the turnaround times would significantly lengthen as operating system releases age.

Keywords: Security patching · Operating system · Negative result · Microsoft · Linux

1 Introduction

Vulnerability life cycle (VLC) modeling has been a popular methodology for understanding the longitudinal evolution of a vulnerability, from the initial birth at a version control system [18] through disclosure and patching [3,26] to the release of information to the public sphere, the availability of industrially developed of exploits, and the final loss of relevance [2]. Akin to software life cycle modeling [22], the primary interest in VLC modeling relates to the time lines between these and other theoretical stages, the most important ones of which are illustrated in Fig. 2. Different research questions emerge by shuffling the state diagram appropriately. For instance, in the worst case scenario, there are only three states: the birth, the discovery, and the development of an exploit;

The authors gratefully acknowledge Tekes – the Finnish Funding Agency for Innovation, DIGILE Oy, and the Cyber Trust research program for their support.

© Springer International Publishing Switzerland 2016
J. Krogstie et al. (Eds.): CAiSE 2016, LNBIP 249, pp. 207–218, 2016.
DOI: 10.1007/978-3-319-39564-7_20

Fig. 1. The principal vulnerability life cycle states (adopted from [2])

a zero-day vulnerability remains to be a zero-day vulnerability, never reaching the states of disclosure, remediation, publication, and, over the years or decades, the eventual lack of applicable computer systems.

In this paper, the empirical phenomenon of interest is located in the time delays that occur between the patching and publication states; the case that is marked with a ⋆ symbol in Fig. 1. Ideally, these delays should be small, given the overall optimum of short vulnerability life cycles. Because the birth, discovery, and disclosure have already occurred, the observed delays are also directly controllable by the associated software vendors and the non-profit institutions that are partially responsible for the systematic release of information to the public sphere. Given this general efficiency rationale, the paper examines an assertion that the time delays are associated with the age of operating system products at the time of security advisory releases.

This assertion can be motivated by a common-sense software engineering reasoning: old and aging code bases are difficult to maintain, which leads to expect that also the handling of vulnerabilities takes longer for older products. The operating system context adds some weight to this reasoning. The code bases are complex, containing large amounts of low-level code that often requires special expertise to maintain. Because the discovery of new vulnerabilities tends to slow down as operating systems age [22], and as maintenance is often a necessary evil for software vendors, there may be a temptation to allocate insufficient resources for maintenance, which may then cause delays in security patching. Also the software life cycles are long. In fact, in some cases the life cycles are so long that the still maintained code bases may attain a status of legacy code. Although security has not been the driving force, analogous reasoning largely applies to the so-called rapid releases, which have been an increasingly widespread strategy for many products but apparently without notable quality and security consequences [7,9,12]. While rapid releases have been adopted also for Linux distributions, there has been also a trend to the opposite direction, as manifested by the so-called long-term support (LTS) releases. Then, by hypothesis, also security patching should vary according to the support periods.

The overall research strategy is exploratory, of course. In other words, numerous different factors influence the length between VLC states, ranging from technical aspects to organizational factors and communication obstacles. Nevertheless, on one hand: if the assertion holds, release engineering strategies could benefit from a footnote that the support period lengths may also increase the turnaround times in the coordination of vulnerabilities. On the other hand: if the assertion is not passed for notable operating system product releases, there are neither reasons to reserve space for such footnotes nor to complicate empirical VLC models with unimportant explanatory variables.

2   The Assertion

Analytically, the interest relates to the difference

$$z_i = Time\ of\ advisory - Time\ of\ publication \qquad (1)$$
$$= \tau_1 - \tau_0, \quad given\ i\ and\ z_i \in (-\infty, \infty),$$

and where τ_1 refers to the date and time at which an operating system software vendor released a security advisory that covered the i:th vulnerability, which was publicized with a Common Vulnerabilities and Exposures (CVEs) identifier at τ_0. Note that z_i is only theoretically restricted to be finite. If a vendor never patches a vulnerability, the life cycle of the vulnerability approaches infinity.

The scalar z_i can be understood as a simple efficiency metric for security patching, and, more accurately, for the associated release of security advisories. In general, a large positive value implies that a long time was required for a vendor to patch a vulnerability and communicate the information to users. When $z_i < 0$, a vendor handled a vulnerability before it was publicized at the infrastructure provided by MITRE, Inc. and related non-profit institutions. All observed operating system vendors possess – either explicitly or via the commercial sponsors – authorities for CVE assignments, and, thus, these negative values are nothing special as such. For instance, Ubuntu released an advisory (USN-2628-1) for CVE-2015-4171 in 8th of June 2015, which was timestamped to the institutional databases two days later. Thus, an identifier was already available during the time of the advisory release, while the CVE publication was slightly delayed, possibly owning to additional processing and archiving work.

It should be also emphasized that a more traditional interest in empirical VLC modeling has related to the difference between τ_1 and the date at which information was first disclosed to a vendor or a third-party [3,27]. While such time lines are longer than the observed ones – disclosure must logically precede the publication of CVEs, the analytical meaning remains more or less similar (see Fig. 2). The reason to prefer the theoretical and conceptual state of publication, rather than the state of disclosure, relates to the well-known practical limitations imposed by the availability of robust data [14,18]. In particular, the date of disclosure is only seldom known in practice [23], and, hence, the attachment to the publication state is necessary to maintain a degree of theoretical

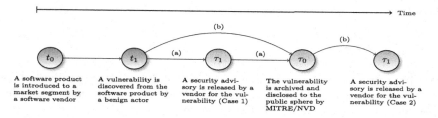

Fig. 2. A time line for security advisory releases (motivated by [6,11])

and conceptual rigor. In general, thus, this paper observes the later states in vulnerability life cycles (see Fig. 1). This observational focus is no less important than the length of vulnerability disclosure; systematically positive or negative but large values of z_i indicate that the coordination between operating system vendors, MITRE, and associated parties has been non-optimal.

Let $y_1, \ldots, y_n$ further denote a subset of time lines for which $z_i > 0$ for all i, that is, the cases that follow the route (b) in Fig. 2. Consider then that these positive turnaround times are linear functions of the *age*, A_i, of an operating system product at the time of patching. In other words,

$$y_i = \alpha + \beta A_i, \quad A_i = \tau_1 - t_0, \quad A_i \geq 0, \quad y_i > 0, \tag{2}$$

where α is a constant and β is a slope coefficient. When only fixed software life cycles and publicly disclosed vulnerabilities are observed, the value of A_i is always non-negative, meaning that security patching only applies to products that have been released. A case $A_i = 0$ implies that a vulnerability was patched already during a product's release date – during the very first day of the product's life cycle. In general, however, the values $A_1, \ldots, A_n$ should be relatively large due to the so-called honeymoon effect [7,8]. That is, new software releases tend to enjoy short grace periods before the first vulnerabilities are discovered.

Given the assumption of linearity, the sign of β is hypothesized to be positive: when the age of a product increases by one day, the mean length of the turnaround times, y_i, increase by β, all other things being equal. Thus, in general, aging operating system releases would be more difficult to patch. While the negative values from (1) have been also excluded in VLC modeling [26], in the present context it is relevant to augment the $\beta > 0$ assumption with a reverse formulation. That is, ψ can be asserted to be negative for an analogous relation

$$|x_i| = \alpha + \psi A_i, \quad x_i \leq 0, \tag{3}$$

given a subset $x_1, \ldots, x_n$ of observations for which $z_i \leq 0$. Because a modulus is used in (3), values $\psi < 0$ imply that aging products would tend to reduce the lead of vendors to the CVE-processing institutions; that is, the route (a) from τ_1 to τ_0 in Fig. 2 would reduce. These dual assumption constitute the *age assertion* of interest. Given that open source projects have been observed and argued to be slower in patching and vulnerability handling in general [23,24], it can be further expected that firing off the assertion is not universal among the contemporary population of operating systems products.

3   Evaluation

To evaluate the assertion, a dataset comprised of 46 operating system releases from three vendors is utilized by using a standard linear regression. While there is plenty of data (35,760 observations, to be precise), the data is not a representative sample from the contemporary operating system population. Thus, the specific term assertion carries a specific meaning: when the assertion is not passed for the products of the market leader, Microsoft, Inc., it can be safely concluded that the assertion does not sufficiently characterize the contemporary operating system population. The evaluation criterion itself is not statistical.

3.1   Data

The empirical sample covers operating system releases of Microsoft Windows, openSUSE, and Ubuntu Linux. The case selection satisfies the desirable data collection conditions: (a) open source software is included, and all observed products (a) have (and have had) a broad and loyal user base as well as (c) a large population of publicly disclosed vulnerabilities, which both allow to assume that (d) the products have been frequent targets of attacks and exploitation attempts [7]. In terms of operationalization, τ_1 in (1) and Fig. 2 is fixed to the corresponding security advisory release dates (see Table 1), while τ_0 is attached to the publication date at the National Vulnerability Database (NVD). Given the temporal resolution of days, it is plausible to assume (but not verify) that the released advisories have corresponded with the availability of patches from the vendors' download services. Finally, the age variable A_i in (2) is computed with respect to the release dates of the observed operating system products listed in Table 2.

Table 1. Data sources

	Institutions	Vendors / products		
	NVD	Microsoft	openSUSE	Ubuntu
Source(s)	[19]	[15, 16]	[20, 21, 25]	[4, 5]

Note that only openSUSE advisories are sampled, although the advisories released for the commercial SUSE often account also the openSUSE releases that are affected.

The dataset is generally in accordance with previous observations [13]. When the per-vendor frequency distributions of the differences in (1) are examined, it is clear that Microsoft has been faster than openSUSE and Ubuntu in fixing the specific vulnerabilities that have affected the observed Microsoft Windows operating system releases (see Fig. 3). A considerable amount of outliers is present, but mainly for the openSUSE and Ubuntu products. In general, much less dispersion is seen for the Microsoft products (see Fig. 4). In fact, Microsoft has patched as much as approximately 43 % of the observed vulnerabilities already during the same day when these were timestamped to NVD. All in all, these observations support the existing evidence that closed source vendors are faster than open source vendors [24]. As a prior-analysis expectation, the effects of β and ψ should thus be different for the Microsoft products.

Finally, it is important to emphasize that (a) all three vendors support parallel products, and, hence, a single CVE-referenced vulnerability typically affects multiple products (see Fig. 5). The effect is pronounced in the case of Microsoft

Table 2. The dataset

Windows				openSUSE				Ubuntu			
Prod	N	N_y	N_x	Prod	N	N_y	N_x	Prod	N	N_y	N_x
XP SP1	82	21	61	11.0	215	181	34	4.10	435	285	150
XP SP2	430	76	354	11.1	470	401	69	5.04	454	385	69
XP SP3	866	82	784	11.2	901	770	131	5.10	448	378	70
XP Prof. x64	260	53	207	11.3	1156	969	187	6.06 LTS	1476	1213	263
XP Prof. x64 SP2	922	89	833	11.4	670	510	160	6.10	473	398	75
Vista	276	36	240	12.3	1277	1143	134	7.04	468	394	74
Vista SP1	413	48	365	13.1	1242	1134	108	7.10	544	459	85
Vista SP2	1161	76	1085	13.2	557	498	59	8.04 LTS	1606	1186	420
Vista x64	276	36	240					8.10	710	580	130
Vista x64 SP1	416	48	368					9.04	667	503	164
Vista x64 SP2	1163	76	1087					9.10	746	553	193
7 i386	493	46	447					10.04 LTS	2373	1588	785
7 i386 SP1	953	47	906					10.10	883	589	294
7 x64	497	47	450					11.04	895	563	332
7 x64 SP1	966	48	918					11.10	1017	640	377
8 i386	702	19	683					12.04 LTS	2124	1321	803
8 x64	700	19	681					12.10	1029	652	377
								13.04	431	268	163
								13.10	464	329	135
								14.10	515	323	192
								14.04 LTS	938	558	380

Given the data collection in July 27, 2015, the column N reports the raw number of vulnerabilities that have affected a given product. The subsequent two symbols denote the number of vulnerabilities in the subsets of positive and non-positive values, respectively. The colored entries mark products that were still eligible for security patches at the time of data collection.

for which product variety has generally been larger within the observed product families. Moreover, there are (b) one-to-many references between advisories and CVEs, which leads to a notable operationalization problem. This issue is solved by using the largest per-product advisory timestamp (the latest day) for each referenced CVE. While also the reverse (the earliest dates) have been used [26], the present solution can be justified by maintaining that a given vulnerability was not entirely fixed and communicated to users until the last advisory released.

3.2   Control Variables

The same data sources are used for two control variables. The first, say S, denotes the *severity* of a vulnerability. The variable is based on the so-called base score in the Common Vulnerability Scoring System (CVSS). The scores range from zero to ten; the higher the value, the more severe the given vulnerability. The base

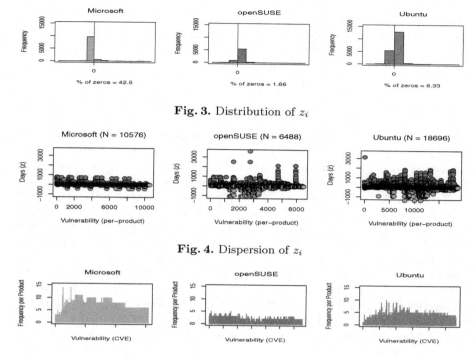

Fig. 3. Distribution of z_i

Fig. 4. Dispersion of z_i

Fig. 5. Vulnerabilities per product

score is a composite metric that is computed from two groups of metrics that account for the impact and exploitability aspects of vulnerabilities [1]. Existing research has used both the base scores [3] and the more fine-grained individual metrics [26]. The theoretical rationale is simple either way: it is expected that the time lines are shorter for more severe vulnerabilities. The empirical usefulness of all CVSS metrics has been questioned [1], however, and, consequently, S is included only as a control variable without further contemplations.

The other control variable, say *references*, R, is operationalized as the cumulative amount of per-release security advisory references that were made to the same CVE identifier. A comparable operationalization has been used previously to measure the quality of security patches [26]. As the construct validity of R as a measure of patch (or patching) quality is arguably rather limited, also this quantity enters as a statistical control variable. In the ideal case of simplicity, both S and R can be eliminated as empirically redundant.

3.3 Methods

The linear equation in (2) is estimated as it reads – as a regression model:

$$\mathcal{M}_1 : \; f(u_i) = \beta_0 + \beta_1 f(A_i) + \beta_2 f(A_i)^2 + \beta_3 f(S_i) + \beta_4 f(R_i) + \epsilon_i, \qquad (4)$$

where u_i refers either to y_i or $|x_i|$, $f(v) = \ln(v + 1)$, and ϵ_t is a residual term. The quadratic age term, $f(A_i)^2$, is included to account potential curvature. The function $f(v)$ is used to improve the assumption of normality [3]. Three smaller parsimonious models are sought with restrictions

$$\mathcal{M}_2 : \ \beta_2 = 0, \ \ \mathcal{M}_3 : \ \beta_1 = \beta_2 = 0, \ \ \text{and} \ \ \mathcal{M}_4 : \ \beta_1 = \beta_2 = \beta_4 = 0. \quad (5)$$

The model $\mathcal{M}_3$ assesses the actual age assertion by excluding both $f(A_i)$ and $f(A_i)^2$. In other words, the assertion implies that $\beta_1 \neq \beta_2 \neq 0$. While the single restriction $\beta_2 = 0$ can be evaluated with a t-test, all can be evaluated with the so-called Wald-tests [10], including the joint restrictions over the parameters. All models were estimated also with a so-called fixed effects strategy by including a set of dummy variables to control for the per-product heterogeneity. As none of the estimates changed notably, the results reported omit these effects, however.

Besides evaluating the assumption of normality with Q-Q plots, three diagnostic checks are computed to assess the overall statistical fits: (a) the so-called RESET test is used to account for potential non-linearity; (b) residual (auto)correlation (dependence between u_i and u_{i+1}) is evaluated with the Breusch-Godfrey test; and (c) heteroskedasticity (systematic dispersion in the residual terms) is checked with the Breusch-Pagan test (for details see, e.g., [10]). The rationale for the checks (b) and (c) relates to the sampling strategy that allows per-product "duplicate" vulnerabilities to enter into the estimation samples. Finally, estimation is carried out with R, using the *lmtest* package [29] for the three statistical tests. If required, the estimates are adjusted by using suitable covariance matrix estimators from the *sandwich* package [28]. The general performance is evaluated with adjusted R_a^2-values; higher values are better.

3.4   Sampling

The three vendor subsamples are analyzed as three separate, statistically independent cases. In general, however, the data in Table 2 cannot be directly estimated because the software life cycles vary across the observed products. To account for this variance, a vendor-specific sampling strategy is used on per-product basis in two steps. Given a vendor's all observed products, random samples (without replacement) are first picked for the vendor's each product. In the second step these random samples are merged into a per-vendor estimation sample, after which the sample split into y_i and $|x_i|$ observations is computed according to the $z_i > 0$ and $z_i \leq 0$ criteria, respectively.

This procedure ensures that estimation is balanced with respect to a vendor's varying per-release software life cycle lengths. The size of these per-product random samples is defined as the minimum per-product sample size in Table 2. For instance, 431 random vulnerabilities are sampled for each of the Ubuntu releases, given the minimum sample size of 431 observed vulnerabilities in Ubuntu 13.04. Since 431 random vulnerabilities are sampled also for 12.04 LTS, the estimation is not biased towards the longer age and, consequently, the larger amount of vulnerabilities in the long-term support releases. This random sampling procedure is repeated 100 times. The statistical results are recomputed in each iteration. Because the standard deviations are rather small across the iterations, arithmetic mean is used for summarizing the results.

3.5   Results

The regression analysis can be started from the diagnostic checks. To begin with, normal approximation is generally reasonable with the $f(v)$ transformation. By embedding normal Q-Q curves for the residuals from the two hundred regression models, the normality observation is illustrated in Fig. 6 for openSUSE. Thus, inference with statistical significance is generally justified. The other diagnostic checks indicate some problems, however. Only Microsoft passes all of the three formal tests; the models for openSUSE and Ubuntu indicate heteroskedasticity in the residual terms, and there appears to be also some (auto)correlation in the models for Ubuntu. To account for these issues, the results are recomputed with the Newey-West covariance matrix estimator [10, 17] for openSUSE and Ubuntu.

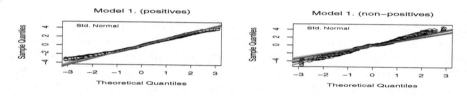

Fig. 6. Normal Q-Q plots for openSUSE ($\mathcal{M}_1$)

The regression results can be packed into the tight summary shown in Table 3. The panel (a) shows the mean p-values from the Wald-tests for both subsets. The conclusion is clear for Microsoft: the full model in (4) can be reduced all the way to $\mathcal{M}_4$ in (5). That is, the age assertion does not hold for Microsoft. The reduction, $\mathcal{M}_1 \mapsto \mathcal{M}_3$, cannot be done for Ubuntu and openSUSE with respect to the subsets of positive z_i values. As expected, the coefficients are positive for the $f(A_i)$ term in these subsets, as seen from the second column in the panel (b). However, the same does not hold in the $z \leq 0$ subsets; the reduction to $\mathcal{M}_3$ is applicable to all vendors according to the fourth column in the panel (a). Because the age assertion was specified in a dual fashion (see Sect. 2), openSUSE and Ubuntu pass the assertion only partially. It is also worth remarking that the coefficients for the severity variable attain their expected negative signs; severe vulnerabilities are processed slightly faster. Finally, the statistical performance is very limited; only approximately 10 % of the total variance is explained at best. Taken together, these observations suggest the age assertion cannot be used to characterize the contemporary operating system population.

Table 3. Regression results[1]

	(a) Wald-tests (mean p-values)						(b) Estimates (means, $\beta_2 = 0$)				
	$\mathcal{M}_1 \mapsto \mathcal{M}_2$		$\mathcal{M}_1 \mapsto \mathcal{M}_3$		$\mathcal{M}_1 \mapsto \mathcal{M}_4$		$\widehat{\beta}_0$	$\widehat{\beta}_1$	$\widehat{\beta}_3$	$\widehat{\beta}_4$	R_a^2
Subset	y	x	y	x	y	x	y	y	y	y	y
Microsoft	0.52	0.48	0.49	0.14	0.07	0.58	6.00	-0.06	-1.55	2.47	0.10
openSUSE[2]	0.30	0.36	0.00	0.24	0.00	0.00	3.00	0.18	-0.76	1.04	0.08
Ubuntu[2]	0.57	0.08	0.00	0.20	0.10	0.00	3.31	0.17	-0.61	0.25	0.04

[1] Colored entries refer to $p < 0.05$; due to lack of space, values 0.00 denote $p < 0.01$.
[2] Results are computed with the Newey-West estimator.

4   Discussion

This empirical paper investigated an assertion that the age of software products can be used to predict the time delays between security advisory releases and the publication of CVEs. The paper finds no systematic empirical evidence for such an assertion. Three conclusions can be drawn from the regression analysis of nearly fifty operating system releases. First, there is no notable statistical relationship between the age of Microsoft Windows releases and the turnaround times between Microsoft, Inc. and the institutional setup represented by MITRE, NVD, and associated parties. Second, only the handling of vulnerabilities that take the route (b) in Fig. 2 is mildly correlated with the age of openSUSE and Ubuntu releases, but otherwise the results are mixed. Last, all of the examined variables – age, severity, and amount of CVE-references – seem to be more or less irrelevant for predicting the turnaround times. Only about a ten percent of the total variation is explained by the three variables.

Thus, the observations constitute a negative result with respect to the theorized age assertion. By implication, it seems sensible to recommend that no particular attention is required in release engineering strategies for the concern that long support periods would systematically lengthen the delays between the patching and publication VLC states. In this sense the negative result is a positive result: there is no particular reason for users to fear that patching would take long for an old operating system release.

Although the results are generally in accordance with previous observations regarding the severity of vulnerabilities [26], the overall lack of explanatory power indicates that neither the statistical severity scoring deserves particular mentions in the strategies. Rather, something else largely explains the variation in the turnaround times. A plausible technical explanation may relate to the large amount of code that is shared particularly between successive operating system releases. That is, patching a vulnerability in a new release may often involve the same code that is present in an older release, which implies that the turnaround times should be rather similar for both releases.

Because the results are particularly clear for the observed Microsoft Windows releases, it seems reasonable to end with a remark about the much more fundamental assertion placed over the closed and open source continuum [23, 24]. Because Microsoft is generally fast at the coordination (and irrespectively of the three variables examined in this paper), a particularly worthwhile topic for further research is to map and examine the potential reasons that may hinder the efficiency at the open source front. As has been suspected [13], narrow time lines are explicitly targeted by Microsoft, but it is unclear why large open source vendors are unable to achieve the same level of efficiency. The reasons for this divergence are presumably economical and socio-technical rather than technical.

References

1. Allodi, L., Massacci, F.: Comparing vulnerability severity and exploits using case-control studies. ACM Trans. Inf. Syst. Secur. **17**(1), 1:1–1:20 (2014)
2. Arbaugh, W.A., Fithen, W.L., McHugh, J.: Window of vulnerability: a case study analysis. Computer **32**(12), 52–59 (2000)
3. Arora, A., Forman, C., Nandkumar, A., Telang, R.: Competition and patching of security vulnerabilities: an empirical analysis. Inf. Econ. Policy **22**(2), 164–177 (2010)
4. Canonical Ltd.: Releases (2015). https://wiki.ubuntu.com/Releases. July 2015
5. Canonical Ltd.: Ubuntu Security Notices (2015). http://www.ubuntu.com/usn/. March 2015
6. Cavusoglu, H., Cavusoglu, H., Raghunathan, R.: Efficiency of vulnerability disclosure mechanisms to disseminate vulnerability knowledge. IEEE Trans. Softw. Eng. **33**(3), 171–185 (2007)
7. Clark, S., Collis, M., Smith, J.M., Blaze, M.: Moving targets: security and rapid-release in Firefox. In: Proceedings of the 2014 ACM SIGSAC Conference on Computer and Communications Security (CCS 2014), pp. 1256–1266. ACM, Scottsdale (2014)
8. Clark, S., Frei, S., Blaze, M., Smith, J.: Familiarity breeds contempt: the honeymoon effect and the role of legacy code in zero-day vulnerabilities. In: Proceedings of the 26th Annual Computer Security Applications Conference (ASAC 2010), pp. 251–260. ACM, Austin, Texas (2010)
9. Khomh, F., Adams, B., Dhaliwal, T., Zou, Y.: Understanding the impact of rapid releases on software quality: the case of Firefox. Empir. Softw. Eng. **20**(2), 336–373 (2015)
10. Kleiber, C., Zeileis, A.: Applied Econometrics with R. Springer, Berlin (2010)
11. Li, P., Rao, R.: An examination of private intermediaries' roles in software vulnerability disclosure. Inf. Syst. Front. **9**(5), 531–539 (2007)
12. Mäntylä, M.V., Adams, B., Khomh, F., Engström, E., Petersen, K.: On rapid releases and software testing: a case study and a semi-systematic literature review. Empir. Softw. Eng. **20**(5), 1384–1425 (2014)
13. Marconato, G.V., Nicomette, V., Kaâniche, M.: Security-related vulnerability life cycle analysis. In: Proceedings of the 7th International Conference on Risk and Security of Internet and Systems (CRiSIS 2012), pp. 1–8. IEEE, Cork (2012)
14. Massacci, F., Nguyen, V.H.: Which is the right source for vulnerability studies? an empirical analysis on Mozilla Firefox. In: Proceedings of the 6th International Workshop on Security Measurements and Metrics (MetriSec 2010), pp. 4:1–4:8. ACM, Bolzano (2010)

15. Microsoft Inc.: Microsoft Security Bulletin Data (2015). http://www.microsoft.com/en-us/download/details.aspx?id=36982. July 2015
16. Microsoft Inc.: Windows Life Cycle Fact Sheet (2015). http://windows.microsoft.com/en-us/windows/lifecycle. July 2015
17. Newey, W.K., West, K.D.: A simple, positive-definite, heteroskedasticity and autocorrelation consistent covariance matrix. Econometrica **55**(3), 703–708 (1987)
18. Nguyen, V.H., Massacci, F.: The (un)reliability of NVD vulnerability versions data: an empirical experiment on Google chrome vulnerabilities. In: Proceedings of the 8th ACM SIGSAC Symposium on Information, Computer and Communications Security (ASIACCS 2013), pp. 493–498. ACM (2013)
19. NIST: NVD Data Feed and Product Integration (2015), National Institute of Standards and Technology (NIST), Annually Archived CVE Vulnerability Feeds: Security Related Software Flaws, NVD/CVE XML Feed with CVSS and CPE Mappings (Version 2.0). https://nvd.nist.gov/download.cfm. June 2015
20. Novell Inc. and others.: openSUSE: Lifetime (2015). https://en.opensuse.org/Lifetime. July 2015
21. Novell Inc. and others: openSUSE: Roadmap (2015). https://en.opensuse.org/openSUSE:Roadmap. July 2015
22. Ruohonen, J., Hyrynsalmi, S., Leppänen, V.: The sigmoidal growth of operating system security vulnerabilities: an empirical revisit. Comput. Secur. **55**, 1–20 (2015)
23. Schryen, G.: Is open source security a Myth? Commun. ACM **54**(5), 130–140 (2011)
24. Shahzad, M., Shafiq, M.Z., Liu, A.X.: A large scale exploratory analysis of software vulnerability life cycles. In: Proceedings of the 34th International Conference on Software Engineering (ICSE 2012), pp. 771–781. IEEE, Zurich (2012)
25. SUSE LLC: Published SUSE Linux Security Updates by CVE Number (2015). https://www.suse.com/security/cve/. June 2015
26. Temizkan, O., Kumar, R.L., Park, S., Subramaniam, C.: Patch release behaviors of software vendors in response to vulnerabilities: an empirical analysis. J. Manag. Inf. Syst. **28**(4), 305–337 (2012)
27. Vache, G.: Vulnerability analysis for a quantitative security evaluation. In: Proceedings of the 2009 3rd International Symposium on Empirical Software Engineering and Measurement (ESEM 2009), pp. 526–534. IEEE, Orlando (2009)
28. Zeileis, A.: Econometric computing with HC and HAC covariance matrix estimators. J. Stat. Softw. **11**(10), 1–17 (2004)
29. Zeileis, A., Hothorn, T.: Diagnostic checking in regression relationships. R News **2**(3), 7–10 (2002)

APPARATUS: Reasoning About Security Requirements in the Internet of Things

Orestis Mavropoulos[1]([⊠]), Haralambos Mouratidis[1], Andrew Fish[1],
Emmanouil Panaousis[1], and Christos Kalloniatis[1,2]

[1] School of Computing Engineering and Mathematics,
University of Brighton, Brighton, UK
{o.mavropoulos,h.mouratidis,andrew.fish,e.panaousis}@brighton.ac.uk
[2] Department of Cultural Technology and Communication,
University of the Aegean, Lesvos, Greece
chkallon@aegean.gr

Abstract. Internet of Things (IoT) can be seen as the main driver towards an era of ubiquitous computing. Taking into account the scale of IoT, the number of security issues that emerge are unprecedented, therefore the need for proposing new methodologies for elaborating about security in IoT systems is undoubtedly crucial and this is recognised by both academia and the industry alike. In this work we present APPARATUS, a conceptual model for reasoning about security in IoT systems through the lens of Security Requirements Engineering. APPARATUS is architecture-oriented and describes an IoT system as a cluster of nodes that share network connections. The information of the system is documented in a textual manner, using Javascript Notation Object (JSON) format, in order to elicit security requirements. To demonstrate its usage the security requirements of a temperature monitor system are identified and a first application of APPARATUS is exhibited.

Keywords: Internet of things · Security requirements engineering · IoT conceptual model · Information security

1 Introduction

One of the areas that attract attention from the research and industry worlds is Internet of Things (IoT). Weiser in 1991 [1], provides one of the most accurate yet simple vision of IoT by stating that the most profound technologies merge with the environment. Technology will be so evident that we will start perceiving it as a natural part of life. Indeed IoT along with cloud computing can turn the last statement into reality.

Despite IoT popularity a number of security challenges faced in these environments have already been revealed [2–5]. A prominent security concern, found in the surveys, are Denial of Service (DoS) attacks in embedded devices [6]. Such devices lack the necessary resources to withstand repeated requests

© Springer International Publishing Switzerland 2016
J. Krogstie et al. (Eds.): CAiSE 2016, LNBIP 249, pp. 219–230, 2016.
DOI: 10.1007/978-3-319-39564-7_21

from malicious attackers. Another commonly identified issue are Man-In-The-Middle (MITM) attacks [7], that take advantage of either weak encryption algorithms of embedded devices or weak authentication mechanisms among the systems [8]. Security specialists argue that the most effective way of ensuring security in systems is to incorporate security focused practices in the development cycle. As a practice, it ensures that the product will meet specific security standards, which in turn will ensure its robustness when it is actively deployed in real life scenarios. The practice of including secure practices in the development cycle is also advocated by the field of requirements engineering. Requirements engineering is applied along with the stakeholders early in the development cycle to identify security requirements [9]. To this end, our main concern in this paper is to propose a novel conceptual model that can be used by software designers in order to extract respective security requirements based on the system's architectural information, in addition to stakeholder needs.

To tackle the issue of requirements elicitation in IoT systems we propose APPARATUS. The speculation is, that if an IoT system is analysed in an abstract manner, the technical specifications of each scenario should not be relevant in security analysis. Moreover their core security requirements should be universal to any IoT system. APPARATUS is a conceptual model to enable reasoning about security in IoT using information from the architecture of the system. From that information, security requirements can be elicited. Security analysis in the architectural level offers both advantages and limitations. The architecture of a system offers information valuable for security analysis, such as types of network connections between node or their role in the network. On the other hand, certain aspects of the system are not expressed such as users or malicious attackers. To better identify the limitations, the concept of a "microworld" is introduced, where the security analysis is being conducted in a managed environment. To mitigate the limitations identified in the "microworld", APPARATUS will be integrated to other security requirements engineering methods. The reasoning behind adopting APPARATUS as a core model is that it can be integrated to other security frameworks. Therefore there is no need to introduce a new framework to the already many existing security requirements frameworks (e.g., [10–14]) that have been in active development for a number of years and offer a comprehensive and robust security analysis. Their expertise will be better utilized if APPARATUS acts as a "bridge" to other security requirements methods for IoT rather than it being developed as separate entity.

The paper is structured as follows: Sect. 2 describes the related work in the fields of IoT and Security Requirements Engineering. Section 3 presents the conceptual model of APPARATUS. Section 4 shows a security analysis of an IoT system using the APPARATUS security reasoning. Section 5 discusses future extensions of APPARATUS along with its limitations and also concludes this paper.

2   Related Work

Security requirements engineering has been used in a variety of systems and fields in order to analyse security during the development cycle. Although there are many surveys on identifying security issues in IoT [2–5], few attempts have been made to address them from a security requirements engineering point of view.

An attempt to provide a framework for security and privacy in IoT systems using requirements engineering was made by Alqassem [15]. He identifies the complexity of analysing security in IoT systems and he states that the key components in IoT are only two: RFID systems and sensor networks. To reason about security in IoT they propose the use of the $i*$ framework in order to undertake security analysis in future case studies. The paper does not consider other technologies and topologies that are being used in IoT. IoT is not restricted only to RFID systems, but uses any communication technology, such as Wi-Fi, NFC or Bluetooth. Moreover the architectural topologies are not restricted to networks solely comprised by sensors, but include any type of device.

IoT as a whole is composed by a multitude of devices. A large number of those devices are embedded devices. An informative paper from Gürgens describes a vision in applying security engineering to embedded systems [16]. He identifies a number of security challenges of embedded systems, that should be addressed in order to have a secure system. He reasons that specific security requirements tools should be designed, tailored to the needs of embedded systems. Another framework aiming to provide security in embedded IoT systems is proposed by Babar [17]. In his paper he classifies the types of attacks aimed at IoT systems. He proposes a basic three step security framework to elicit requirements in embedded systems. To accomplish that he identifies the building blocks of embedded systems in IoT. Tian designs a security framework specific to wireless sensor networks [18]. The framework proposes a system architecture, that is broken down into eight modules, with each module having specific functionality to mitigate security issues. To summarize, the presented works do not view IoT in a comprehensive manner, since they only aim to mitigate security issues in specific areas. Therefore, they cannot be used to offer a universal security analysis to any IoT scenario, but only aim to address specific instances of IoT systems.

Díaz identifies a number of issues and open challenges with the integration of IoT and Cloud computing [19]. Many functionalities of Internet of Things are only possible through the cloud infrastructure. Some scenarios may require the use of sensors as a service, while others may use cloud services for processing functionality. He states that IoT will function as the middle-ware that will transmit all its data to the cloud for processing. The paper shows that the current trend for IoT application development is based on Cloud computing.

Although outside the scope of requirements engineering, a framework for modeling and assessing security in IoT system is proposed by Ge [13]. The framework uses a graphical security model that evaluates the level of security using security metrics. The framework assesses security of IoT systems in a comprehensive manner and is not limited to specific IoT scenarios, such as embedded systems or RFID systems. A similar universal comprehensive approach in security of IoT is used in APPARATUS, in order to reason about security requirements in any IoT system, but from a requirements engineering point of view.

3   Presentation of APPARATUS Reasoning

APPARATUS is a conceptual model for reasoning about security in IoT systems. In the context of APPARATUS, security requirements are defined as *a restriction related to security issues, such as privacy, integrity and availability, which can influence the analysis and design of a multiagent system under development by restricting some alternative design solutions, by conflicting with some of the requirements of the system, or by refining some of the system s objectives*, an approach used by Secure Tropos concept of *security constrain* [12]. A similar definition of security requirements is given by Haley [14]. He defines them as *constraints on the systems functional requirements, rather than being themselves functional requirements*. The current version of Apparatus focuses on the proposed conceptual model, as shown in Fig. 1, through which designers can be assisted on capturing the necessary knowledge from the IoT system's architecture perspective in order to identify and extract security requirements. In order to achieve that, the information of the IoT system has to be presented in a specific format that will make the extraction of security requirements straightforward. The model does not aim to provide a detailed security analysis in any given IoT scenario. It provides the necessary information, for an IoT system to be secure in a "microworld", where users, malicious attackers and other communication with the world outside of the system are not part of the requirements elicitation. In order to provide a more detailed security analysis, APPARATUS will be integrated with other security requirements methods, such as Secure Tropos [11] and SQUARE [10]. Security analysis in IoT systems can be performed in a two step approach. APPARATUS will be used as the first step in the security analysis, where its security requirements are derived from the IoT architecture. The second step will be the usage of one of the aforementioned methods so as to facilitate a more complete security analysis of the system. The integration of APPARATUS to other methods will be part of future work and is out of the scope of this paper. The proposed conceptual model of APPARATUS is presented in Fig. 1 using an Entity-Relationship Diagram with crow's foot notation.

APPARATUS is an architecture-oriented model, where an IoT system is described as a cluster of IoT nodes connected to each other using network connections. Each IoT node has a set of properties that describe its functionality in the system. The properties include information such as the type of the device and its role within the system. There are two main concepts in Apparatus: the *IoT node* and the *network connection*.

Each of the main concepts has a set of properties that further describes the system. The properties of the *IoT node* are: (1) **identification**: gives an id to each of the stakeholders of the node. The stakeholders are four, *user, deployer, developer, manufacturer*; (2) **aspect**: declares whether the IoT node is a single node, or composed of sub nodes. (3) **layer**: the layer of the IoT architecture to which the node belongs; (4) **type**: what kind of device the node is; (5) **attribute**: the type of role or operation that the node performs for the network; (6) **input**: what is required in order for the node to perform its role or

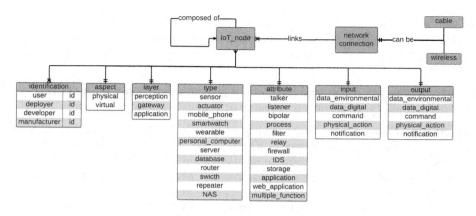

Fig. 1. Conceptual model of APPARATUS in entity-relationship diagram

operation; (7) **output**: the result of the node's operation or role. The IoT nodes are connected to each other using *network connections*. The type of connections can be two: (1) **Wireless**: signifying a connection using a wireless protocol and (2) **Cable**: signifying a connection using a wired medium.

Each node property can only hold a single value. If an IoT node that has more than one functionality, needs to be defined, it can be broken down into the same number of sub nodes as the functionalities we want to express. For example a laptop that acts both as processing server and as the system's database, will be composed of two sub nodes. One sub node that describes the server functionality and one sub node that describes the database functionality. These two sub nodes in return make the laptop IoT node. Identical nodes in an IoT system, such sensors and actuators can be grouped together and presented as a single node.

The properties of the IoT node are explained in detail: **Identification:** There are four types of stakeholders in an IoT network, *user* (user of the node), *deployer* (installer of the node), *developer* (producer of the software of the node), *manufacturer* (hardware producer of the node). In APPARATUS each of the stakeholders that is involved in an IoT system is assigned a unique ID. That ID is used to identify a stakeholder's role in an IoT node and takes an integer value.

Aspect: The property *aspect* can take one of two values. The node can either be a physical node, that declares the IoT node as a single node in the system, or as a virtual node, meaning that the node belongs to a set of virtual nodes that in turn compose a single physical node.

Layers: APPARATUS uses a three-layer architecture that consists of the Application Layer, Network Layer and the Perception Layer [20,21]. Other architectures provide more levels of abstractions. For example a SOA based approach identifies five layers, *application, service composition, service management, object abstraction, objects* [2]. Another approach identifies more layers, that are *application, middleware, coordination, backbone network, existed alone network, access layer, edge technology*[22]. The proposed architectures for Internet of Things have yet to fuse into a reference model [23], for that reason we chose the three-layer approach. It provides the necessary properties for reasoning about security, while allowing to be extended if more levels of abstraction are introduced into the reference model of IoT.

Type: Defines the device the IoT node represents. For example the type of an IoT node could be a sensor, an actuator or a mobile phone as shown in Fig. 1.

Attribute: Describes the functionality of a node in the system. Examples of a node's functionality are shown in Fig. 1. Some attributes are better suited to specific types of nodes. For example a *talker* node is a type of sensor, that only sends information to the network and does not perform any actions. A *listener* node is a type of actuator, that only performs actions and does not send any information from the environment. A *bipolar* is a node that is both a talker and a listener. When an IoT node is composed of virtual nodes, the attribute of their physical node is *multiple functions*.

Input & Output: Have the same set of values. As mentioned before the *input* signifies the required data for the node in order to produce the desired *output*. The value could be a loose term such as data, or a notification as shown presented in Fig. 1.

Network Connection: The construct *network connection* represents the type of the network link between nodes. The link can either be wireless, such as via Wi-Fi, Bluetooth and RFID, or using a cable, such as an Ethernet and a USB. From a high level security point of view, there is little difference if a technology such as Wi-Fi over Bluetooth is used. Since they both are wireless mediums, they share the same security requirements. The same applies to cable mediums. From a low level perspective what technology is used, has a pivotal role, since each one has specific vulnerabilities. That level of reasoning is not present in the current version of APPARATUS.

APPARATUS currently represents information in a textual format, since it will be used by machines for automated security analysis. An IoT system that has been described using APPARATUS, is formatted as a Javascript Notation Object (JSON) file. JSON format is an Open Standard used to transmit data objects consisting of attributevalue pairs. The "attribute" is immutable and corresponds to the names of the IoT node's properties. The "value" is mutable and corresponds to the values of the IoT node's properties. APPARATUS uses that formatting style in order to correlate the information of the IoT system with the necessary security requirements. Using JSON format the process of requirements elicitation can be automated, thus making the analysis of large IoT networks more efficient. That type of formatting is useful for establishing a more formal rule-based approach for correlating security requirements with properties of the IoT system. Using the textual notation of a JSON file, a visual notation will be incorporated into the next versions of APPARATUS in order to offer a human friendly approach.The skeleton template in JSON format is presented in Fig. 2.

```
{
  "IoT_system": [{
    "IoT_node_01": [{
      "identification": {
        "user": "",
        "deployer": "",
        "developer": "",
        "manufacturer": ""
      },
      "aspect": "",
      "type": "",
      "attribute": "",
      "input": "",
      "output": ""
    }, {
      "connection": {
        "connects_to": "node_name",
        "connection_type": ""
      }
    }]
  }]
}
```

Fig. 2. Skeleton JSON template

4 Example of Security Reasoning

In this section an application of the APPARATUS reasoning is presented using an IoT system implementation of a temperature monitoring application, that is hosted in a private in house network. The components of the network are the following: a (1) temperature sensor, a (2) router, a (3) server, that functions as a database and a data formatter for the database, and a (4) laptop. The temperature sensor gathers environmental data and sends them to the server through the router. The server formats the data and stores them in its database. The laptop then requests the information from the database. In Fig. 3 the layout of the system is shown.

Each of the devices, constitutes an IoT node in APPARATUS. For the sake of brevity the stakeholders of the system are two. The same "person" has installed and makes use of the devices. He acts as the *user* as well as the *deployer* and has been assigned the id: 01. Another "person" has produced all the devices along with their software, so he acts as both the *manufacturer* and the *developer* of the system with the id: 02. In Fig. 4, the temperature monitoring system is expressed in JSON format using APPARATUS reasoning.

Security Analysis: The security analysis is being conducted using the information presented in Fig. 4. During this part of the analysis the IoT system in part of a "microworld". As explained before, the "microworld" acts as partial view of the actual security dangers of the real life world.

The IoT nodes *sensor* and *laptop* are parts of the perception layer, as seen in lines 11 and 112 in Fig. 4. Devices in the perception layer allow physical access to their users. A security requirement resulting from that information, is that the nodes *sensor* and *laptop* need to be physically secure. Further analysis shows that both nodes communicate using wireless mediums (lines 19 and 119 in Fig. 4). Wireless mediums have limited range. Moreover all the nodes share

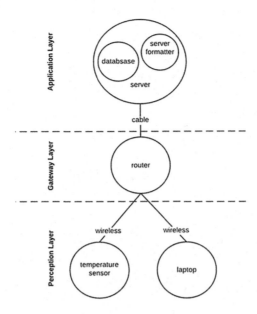

Fig. 3. Temperature monitoring application layout

the same user and developer. It can be deduced that all the nodes should be in close proximity to each other. Meaning that if an attacker has physical access to one, he probably has access to the other nodes of the system. The security requirement should be updated to include that all the nodes of the system need to be physically secure.

The IoT system uses wireless mediums (lines 19, 119 in Fig. 4). A requirement of wireless transmission is that access should only be allowed to authorised users and devices. All the nodes share the same manufacturer and developer (lines 7, 8, 28, 29, 48, 49, 68, 69, 88, 89, 108, 109 in Fig. 4). It can be assumed that some security mechanisms to prevent unauthorised access are in place. Those mechanisms should be taken into account when implementing the system.

The sensor node takes environmental data as an input (line 14 in Fig. 4). Environmental data are not controlled by the system, and a level of integrity must be ensured, in order to prevent Denial Of Service attacks or any other kind of tampering with the network. The security requirement is that environmental data cannot tamper with the system if they deviate from their expected behaviour.

One of the server's functions is to act as database (line 73 in Fig. 4). Databases take data as an input and store it a specific format. Two security requirements are elicited from that information. Firstly, database input must be subject to sanitation, to prevent SQL injection attempts or similar attacks. Secondly, the contents of the database should only be modified by authorised users and devices of the system.

The IoT nodes compose a network of devices. Chronological records of any activity that affects operations, procedures or events of the system must be

```
  1  {
  2      "IoT_system": [{
  3          "sensor": [{
  4              "identification": {
  5                  "user": "01",
  6                  "deployer": "01",
  7                  "developer": "02",
  8                  "manufacturer": "02"
  9              },
 10              "aspect": "physical",
 11              "layer": "perception",
 12              "type": "sensor",
 13              "attribute": "talker",
 14              "input": "data_environmental",
 15              "output": "data_digital"
 16          }, {
 17              "connection": {
 18                  "connects_to": "router",
 19                  "connection_type": "wireless"
 20              }
 21          }]
 22      },
 23      {
 24          "router": [{
 25              "identification": {
 26                  "user": "01",
 27                  "deployer": "01",
 28                  "developer": "02",
 29                  "manufacturer": "02"
 30              },
 31              "aspect": "physical",
 32              "layer": "gateway",
 33              "type": "sensor",
 34              "attribute": "relay",
 35              "input": "data_digital",
 36              "output": "data_digital"
 37          }, {
 38              "connection": {
 39                  "connects_to": "server",
 40                  "connection_type": "cable"
 41              }
 42          }]
 43      }, {
 44          "server": [{
 45              "identification": {
 46                  "user": "01",
 47                  "deployer": "01",
 48                  "developer": "02",
 49                  "manufacturer": "02"
 50              },
 51              "aspect": "physical",
 52              "layer": "application",
 53              "type": "server",
 54              "attribute": "multiple_function",
 55              "input": "data_digital",
 56              "output": "data_digital"
 57          }, {
 58              "connection": {
 59                  "connects_to": "router",
 60                  "connection_type": "cable"
 61              }
 62          }]
 63      }, {
 64          "database": [{
 65              "identification": {
 66                  "user": "01",
 67                  "deployer": "01",
 68                  "developer": "02",
 69                  "manufacturer": "02"
 70              },
 71              "aspect": "virtual",
 72              "layer": "application",
 73              "type": "database",
 74              "attribute": "storage",
 75              "input": "data_digital",
 76              "output": "data_digital"
 77          }, {
 78              "connection": {
 79                  "connects_to": "router",
 80                  "connection_type": "cable"
 81              }
 82          }]
 83      }, {
 84          "server_formatter": [{
 85              "identification": {
 86                  "user": "01",
 87                  "deployer": "01",
 88                  "developer": "02",
 89                  "manufacturer": "02"
 90              },
 91              "aspect": "virtual",
 92              "layer": "application",
 93              "type": "server",
 94              "attribute": "process",
 95              "input": "data_digital",
 96              "output": "data_digital"
 97          }, {
 98              "connection": {
 99                  "connects_to": "router",
100                  "connection_type": "cable"
101              }
102          }]
103      }, {
104          "laptop": [{
105              "identification": {
106                  "user": "01",
107                  "deployer": "01",
108                  "developer": "02",
109                  "manufacturer": "02"
110              },
111              "aspect": "physical",
112              "layer": "perception",
113              "type": "laptop",
114              "attribute": "listener",
115              "input": "data_digital",
116              "output": "notification"}, {
117              "connection": {
118                  "connects_to": "router",
119                  "connection_type": "wireless"
120              }
121          }]
122      },
123      ]
124  }
```

Fig. 4. Temperature monitoring system JSON format

kept. That functionality is a default security requirement of any IoT systems in APPARATUS.

The process of security requirements elicitation that was described above can be automated, by correlating security requirements with values in the IoT system. The identified security requirements compose a list, with each security requirement being a separate entry that correlates with IoT values shown in Fig. 1. An example of the automated security requirements elicitation specific to the temperature monitoring application is shown in Table 1.

Table 1. Security requirements elicited from IoT system properties

Security requirements	IoT system properties (lines)
Nodes should be physically protected	layer: perception (11, 112)
	connection: wireless (19, 119)
	user/deployer id:01 (all nodes)
	developer/manufacturer id:02 (all nodes)
System can only be used by authorised users and devices	connection: wireless (19, 119)
Environmental data should not tamper with the system	input: data_environmental (14)
Database data should only be modified by authorised users or devices	type: database (74)
Input of the database should subject to sanitation	type: database (74)
Nodes must keep chronological records of any activity that affects operations, procedures or events of the system	Default security requirement of IoT systems

5   Conclusion

This paper, starts by illustrating the importance of proposing a novel model to facilitate security analysis and reasoning for IoT. Security analysis should be use a generic approach while being able to be used along with specialized security methods when needed by the system. In that spirit, the proposed model should offer its capabilities to any IoT scenario without losing its properties, while offering enough flexibility for further extensions. In order to investigate security issues with the use of security requirements engineering, APPARATUS was presented. APPARATUS enables reasoning about security in IoT systems from a system architecture point of view. An IoT system is expressed as a cluster of IoT nodes, with each node having a set properties, that define its role within the system. The information of the system is conveyed in a textual manner, specifically using JSON format. Using APPARATUS, the security analysis of a temperature monitoring system was undertaken and described in this paper. Despite being novel and coherent, the current version of APPARATUS has a number of limitations. An IoT system is analysed from an architectural view and therefore cannot offer a comprehensive security analysis. To illustrate the limitations, the concept of "microworld" was introduced. The "microworld" facilitates security analysis by emulating a managed environment. Another limitation is the inability to express certain environments that have unknown variables, such as the Cloud or health applications. For example, in a Cloud system the internal architecture of the Cloud platform or its security configurations are not publicly known and as such cannot be expressed using APPARATUS.

In order to mitigate those limitations, our future work with APPARATUS aims to be able to adopt elements of other security requirements engineering methods by operating in an modular manner based on the different applications that are investigated. Furthermore, APPARATUS elicitation process will be automated by correlating security requirements with information extracted from the IoT system.

References

1. Weiser, M.: The computer for the 21st century. Sci. Am. **265**(3), 94–104 (1991)
2. Atzori, L., Iera, A., Morabito, G.: The internet of things: a survey. Comput. Netw. **54**(15), 2787–2805 (2010)
3. Al-Fuqaha, A., Guizani, M., Mohammadi, M., Aledhari, M., Ayyash, M.: Internet of things: a survey on enabling technologies, protocols, and applications. IEEE Commun. Surv. Tutorials **17**(4), 2347–2376 (2015)
4. Granjal, J., Monteiro, E., Silva, J.S.: Security for the internet of things: a survey of existing protocols and open research issues. IEEE Commun. Surv. Tutorials **17**(3), 1294–1312 (2015)
5. Jing, Q., Vasilakos, A.V., Wan, J., Lu, J., Qiu, D.: Security of the internet of things: perspectives and challenges. Wireless Netw. **20**(8), 2481–2501 (2014)
6. Suo, H., Wan, J., Zou, C., Liu, J.: Security in the internet of things: a review. In: 2012 International Conference on Computer Science and Electronics Engineering, (Hangzhou), pp. 648–651. Institute of Electrical & Electronics Engineers (IEEE) (2012)
7. Du, J., Chao, S.: A study of information security for M2M of IoT. In: 2010 3rd International Conference on Advanced Computer Theory and Engineering (ICACTE) (2010)
8. Liu, J., Xiao, Y., Chen, C.P.: Authentication and access control in the internet of things. In: 2012 32nd International Conference on Distributed Computing Systems Workshops, (Macau), pp. 588–592. Institute of Electrical & Electronics Engineers (IEEE) (2012)
9. Coles, E.S.: Analyzing and specifying security requirements in early stages of software development life cycle. J. Mobile Embed. Distrib. Syst. **7**(2), 87–94 (2015)
10. Mead, N.R., Stehney, T.: Security quality requirements engineering (square) methodology. ACM SIGSOFT Softw. Eng. Notes **30**(4), 1–7 (2005)
11. Giorgini, P., Mouratidis, H.: Secure tropos: a security-oriented extension of the tropos methodology. Int. J. Softw. Eng. Knowl. Eng. **17**(02), 285–309 (2011)
12. Mouratidis, H., Giorgini, P.: Secure tropos: a security-oriented extension of the tropos methodology. Int. J. Softw. Eng. Knowl. Eng. **17**, 285–309 (2007)
13. Ge, M., Kim, D.S.: A framework for modeling and assessing security of the internet of things. In: 2015 IEEE 21st International Conference on Parallel and Distributed Systems (ICPADS), (Melbourne, VIC), pp. 776–781. Institute of Electrical & Electronics Engineers (IEEE) (2015)

14. Haley, C., Laney, R., Moffett, J., Nuseibeh, B.: Security requirements engineering: a framework for representation and analysis. IEEE Trans. Softw. Eng. **34**(1), 133–153 (2008)
15. Alqassem, I.: Privacy and security requirements framework for the internet of things (IoT). In: Companion Proceedings of the 36th International Conference on Software Engineering - ICSE Companion 2014, pp. 739–741 (2014)
16. Gürgens, S., Rudolph, C., Maña, A., Nadjm-Tehrani, S.: Security engineering for embedded systems. In: Proceedings of the International Workshop on Security and Dependability for Resource Constrained Embedded Systems - S&D4RCES 2010 (2010)
17. Babar, S., Stango, A., Prasad, N., Sen, J., Prasad, R.: Proposed embedded security framework for internet of things (IoT). In: 2011 2nd International Conference on Wireless Communication, Vehicular Technology, Information Theory and Aerospace & Electronic Systems Technology (Wireless VITAE), pp. 1–5 (2011)
18. Tian, B., xian Yang, Y., Li, D., Li, Q., Xin, Y.: A security framework for wireless sensor networks. J. China Univ. Posts Telecommun. **17**(2), 118–122 (2010)
19. Díaz, M., Martín, C., Rubio, B.: State-of-the-art, challenges, and open issues in the integration of internet of things and cloud computing. J. Netw. Comput. Appl. 67, pp. 99–117 (2016)
20. Yang, Z., Yue, Y., Yang, Y., Peng, Y., Wang, X., Liu, W.: Study and application on the architecture and key technologies for IoT. In: 2011 International Conference on Multimedia Technology, (Hangzhou), pp. 747–751. Institute of Electrical & Electronics Engineers (IEEE) (2011)
21. Miao, W., Ting-lie, L., Fei-Yang, L., Ling, S., Hui-Ying, D.: Research on the architecture of internet of things (Chengdu), vol. 5, pp. 484–485. IEEE (2010)
22. Lu, T., Neng, W.: Future internet: the internet of things (Chengdu), vol. 5, p. 376. IEEE (2010)
23. Krco, S., Pokric, B., Carrez, F.: Designing IoT architecture(s): a European perspective. In: 2014 IEEE World Forum on Internet of Things (WF-IoT) (Seoul), pp. 79–84. Institute of Electrical & Electronics Engineers (IEEE) (2014)

Associating the Severity of Vulnerabilities with their Description

Dimitrios Toloudis, Georgios Spanos, and Lefteris Angelis$^{(\boxtimes)}$

Department of Informatics, Aristotle University of Thessaloniki,
Thessaloniki, Greece
`toloudisd@gmail.com, {gspanos,lef}@csd.auth.gr`

Abstract. Software vulnerabilities constitute a major problem for today's world, which relies more than ever to technological achievements. The characterization of vulnerabilities' severity is an issue of major importance in order to address them and extensively study their impact on information systems. That is why scoring systems have been developed for the ranking of vulnerabilities' severity. However, the severity scores are based on technical information and are calculated by combining experts' assessments. The motivation for the study conducted in this paper was the question of whether the severity of vulnerabilities is directly related to their description. Hence, the associations of severity scores and individual characteristics with vulnerability descriptions' terms were studied using Text Mining, Principal Components and correlation analysis techniques, applied to all vulnerabilities registered in the National Vulnerability Database. The results are promising for the determination of severity by the use of the description since significant correlations were found.

Keywords: Information security · Software vulnerability · Text mining · Statistical analysis

1 Introduction

It is well known that information is the most valid asset of the contemporary society. Due to the ever-increasing growth of technological achievements and the globalization of society, the need for collecting, storing and processing information has become extremely important. Within this scenery, the security of data and procedures in today's information systems holds a particularly significant role. Governments, industries as well as individuals pay great effort and invest a lot of assets to preserve the Confidentiality, Integrity and Availability (CIA triad) of information. Those three concepts constitute the main pillars of Information Security.

Information Security (InfoSec) has to deal with many primary or secondary problems but one of the most important may be considered the existence of software vulnerabilities. According to the Common Vulnerabilities and Exposures (CVE) reference system [1], *"An information security "vulnerability" is a mistake in software that can be directly used by a hacker to gain access to a system or network."* In other words, software vulnerability is a bug or a flaw in the code/design of a software program that can be exploited by an unauthorized user in order to intercept, alternate or

© Springer International Publishing Switzerland 2016
J. Krogstie et al. (Eds.): CAiSE 2016, LNBIP 249, pp. 231–242, 2016.
DOI: 10.1007/978-3-319-39564-7_22

interrupt information flow. Hence, the intruder can have access to sensitive information, misguide the user or even take control of an entire critical infrastructure.

Unfortunately, it is practically impossible for any development team to produce vulnerability-free software. Mistakes, big or small, may appear during the requirements gathering, in the design of the software, in the development/coding, even during the training of the final user. As software starts to be used, operators or experts find vulnerabilities that developers have to fix. But the number of the faults is enormous and the need for fast solutions is urgent. That is why, specific characteristics of vulnerabilities are measured and scores that represent their severity are computed. This way, IT security managers can prioritize them and deal initially with the vital and then with the relatively harmless ones.

The most widely used scoring system is the Common Vulnerability Scoring System (CVSS), version 2 [2] that constitutes the improvement of CVSS version 1 [3] and is used also from the National Vulnerability Database (NVD) [4]. A third version of CVSS with different scoring factors has been presented in December 2014 but since is not yet applied by NVD for all the vulnerabilities but only for the newest ones (after December 2015), it can not be examined in the present analysis. A relatively new scoring system, which uses alternative approach regarding the weighing of the vulnerability characteristics in comparison with CVSS, is the Weighted Impact Vulnerability Scoring System (WIVSS) [5] while an improvement of WIVSS has been published in [6]. Other known scoring systems constitute: the Vulnerability Rating Scoring System (VRSS) [7], the improvement of VRSS [8] and the PVL [9]. Furthermore, there are many vulnerability databases that gather data for all vulnerabilities or just for a specific category. The most famous and world widely used is the National Vulnerability Database (NVD), which holds a variety of data (score, dates, individual characteristics, description and more) for all kind of vulnerabilities.

The severity of the vulnerabilities is apparently an issue of major importance and their scoring is performed taking into account technical information coming from experts' characterizations. However the question that motivated the current research is whether the description of each vulnerability, which is registered in the database as text, is informative about the severity, i.e. whether the words used to describe the vulnerabilities are correlated with the overall severity scoring. Therefore, the purpose of this paper is to perform a text analysis of the vulnerability descriptions existing in the NVD -which was used as the data source for this research- and to extract useful relationships between the terms that were derived from the text mining and the characteristics/scores (the scores are provided from CVSS version 2 and the improvement of WIVSS) of vulnerabilities, using correlation analysis and principal component analysis.

The rest of this paper is organized as follows. Section 2 describes the related work, in Sect. 3, the database along with the vulnerability characteristics and scorings systems (CVSS, WIVSS) are described, while in Sect. 4 the results of the analysis are presented. Finally, Sect. 5 summarizes the conclusions.

2 Related Work

In order to characterize the severity of a vulnerability, experts have to evaluate and define its characteristics. This is a particularly time-consuming process, especially if someone takes into consideration the enormous number of new vulnerabilities and the great need for their immediate confrontation. That is why many scientists scrutinize the characteristics, the life cycle and the behavior of vulnerabilities, finding correlations between them and developing prediction models. In those researches, a variety of "tools" are being used, like statistical and data mining methods.

One of the above techniques is the Text Mining (TM), which can remove needless words and numbers and replace characters or terms so that finally can extract metadata into word-frequency-count Document-Term Matrices (DTM). This specific technique is constantly gaining ground among the scientific community by being increasingly used. Several studies, papers and books have been written for the use of TM and even more for researches in which the methodology was used.

Representative examples that use TM in biomedical research are the following: Theodosiou et al. [10] in 2007, presented a study about an alternative of gene functional annotation throw-out classification modeling and validation. For that purpose, they used TM in biomedical articles, excluding non-informative words and extracting useful metadata. Similar use of TM was made for another analysis of biomedical article datasets in 2008 [11] in which, Non-Linear Canonical Correlation Analysis (NLCCA) was used for exploring the correlation among the variables (words) of multiple representations of biomedical documents. Finally, Janasik et al. [12] published a paper in 2009, about the use of TM in qualitative research and the self-organizing map (SOM) method as well as the inference quality improvement that this implementation may achieve.

Regarding the Information Security field -which is also the research field of the present study- Hovsepyan et al. [13] transformed the source code of many programs into plain text, totally ignoring its complexity, its churn, its size or other characteristics. Thus, via the use of TM, they managed to predict vulnerabilities with fairly good results. Furthermore, in 2012, Liu et al. [14] achieved promising results on analysis and automatic classification of network vulnerabilities, applying TM in data, retrieved from a variety of online sources. Moreover, Nishanth et al. [15] used TM and data mining techniques in order to analyze and classify the risk levels of phishing attacks in financial firms. Using either MLP, PNN or DT, the achieved accuracy was above 80 %. Chen et al. [16] classified not only the risk levels of phishing attacks but also its impact to market value of the attacked firms, by using TM and data mining in phishing alerts and firms' financial data and they also distinguished variables with significant impact in the seriousness of the attacks. Finally, Wang et al. [17] conducted both quantitative and qualitative analysis in order to measure the financial impact of the information security incidents reported in firm financial reports. Initially they examined the influence of the amount of announcements on stock prices and then they correlated the impact with specific term that derived from the TM methodology. This way, they developed a model helpful in evaluation of disposed information of firms' incidents reports.

In this paper, we analyze the textual descriptions of vulnerabilities using TM techniques and associate the most important terms or groups of terms with the vulnerability characteristics and severity.

3   Database, Characteristics and Scoring Systems

For this study, logs of all vulnerabilities up to 5 Aug 2015 were retrieved from NVD [4]. The total number was higher than 70,000 (specifically 70,678) and they contained, among others, the values of vulnerability characteristics and a brief description for every one of them. It must be highlighted here, that the whole set of vulnerabilities that exist in NVD was used for this research, instead of an easier-to-manage sample, like vulnerabilities from one year or of those that affect specific software. This approach targeted in more accurate results and more general view.

For every vulnerability we can identify some characteristics that describe the way that a flaw can be exploited and the impact that may have to the affected systems. Their values are being determined by experts, either through their experience or by conducting specific measurements. Those characteristics are:

- **Access Vector**: defines the way a vulnerability can be exploited. The values that can take are: *Local*, *Adjacent Network* or *Network*.
- **Access Complexity**: defines how difficult is to exploit the vulnerability. The values that can take are: *High*, *Medium* or *Low*.
- **Authentication**: defines the level of user authentication levels needed for the exploitation of the vulnerability. The values that can take are: *Multiple*, *Single* or *None*.
- **Confidentiality Impact**: defines how much, the exploitation of vulnerability, can influence the confidentiality of the system. The values that can take are: *None*, *Partial* or *Complete*.
- **Integrity Impact**: defines how much, the exploitation of vulnerability, can influence the integrity of the system. The values that can take as above are: *None*, *Partial* or *Complete*.
- **Availability Impact**: defines how much, the exploitation of vulnerability, can influence the availability of the system: The possible values also are *None*, *Partial* or *Complete*.

The above characteristics are used for the computation of unified scoring systems that represent the severity of vulnerabilities. The most famous and widely used scoring system is the Common Vulnerability Scoring System (CVSS), which was originally developed by the National Infrastructure Advisory Council (NIAC) in 2004 [3]. In 2007, an improved version was released [2]. Nowadays, responsible for CVSS is the Forum of Incident Response and Security Teams (FIRST) [18] and the Common Vulnerability Scoring System-Special Interest Group (CVSS-SIG) [19].

Another scoring system, that improves CVSS in terms of diversity of values, is the Weighted Impact Vulnerability Scoring System (WIVSS). It was originally developed in 2013 by Spanos et al. [5], considering different weights for the Impact Metrics in contrast to CVSS, which considers the same weights for all Impact Metrics. In 2015, the second version of WIVSS was published [6], improving further the value diversity of the previous version. Both CVSS and WIVSS have the same scoring range (0.0–10.0) with scale step of 0.1. Detailed information regarding the computational formulas of the above scoring systems can be found in [6].

4   Correlation Analysis

The first step of the correlation analysis was to isolate the useful terms from the vulnerability descriptions. By the use of Text Mining numbers, commonly used words with no useful meaning and words like brands and software names were removed. Also, the remaining words were transformed in order to remove word endings, to convert upper to lower cases or to unify words with similar meaning. Finally, a Document Term Matrix (DTM) was created, containing the number of appearances for every term, in every vulnerability description. From that matrix, words with very low frequency of appearance were excluded and the result was a DTM with 33 words, which are shown in Fig. 1, sized according to their frequencies. Also, Table 1 contains the term frequencies (percentage form) in vulnerability descriptions.

Fig. 1. Word cloud of vulnerability description

The representation of Term Frequency - Inverse Document Frequency (TF-IDF) [20] has been selected for the representation of data in the DTM. TF-IDF is a numerical statistic that is used in text mining and reflects the importance of a word in a document, taking into consideration its general appearance frequency in a group of documents. It is widely used for the recognition and exclusion of useless terms, like stop words, for document categorization and summarization and also by search engines. As its name shows, TF-IDF is the combination of the Term Frequency statistic and the Inverse Document Frequency technique.

Additionally, the CVSS and WIVSS scores along with the characteristics of vulnerabilities were added to the previous matrix in order to conduct the correlation analysis. For the same reason, the vulnerability characteristics (Access Vector, Access

Table 1. The term frequencies

Term	Frequency	Term	Frequency	Term	Frequency
allow	95.43 %	*earlier*	13.57 %	*paramet*	22.87 %
arbitrari	52.63 %	*execut*	33.84 %	*remot*	77.52 %
attack	80.84 %	*file*	21.09 %	*script*	14.68 %
authent	11.60 %	*function*	10.18 %	*server*	13.62 %
buffer	10.68 %	*html*	13.13 %	*servic*	23.42 %
caus	21.90 %	*inform*	12.09 %	*unspecifi*	20.45 %
code	21.68 %	*inject*	22.08 %	*use*	11.19 %
command	13.54 %	*local*	12.97 %	*user*	22.55 %
craft	15.60 %	*multipl*	11.93 %	*vector*	19.43 %
crosssitscript	13.21 %	*obtain*	12.24 %	*vulner*	49.57 %
denial	21.04 %	*overflow*	11.20 %	*web*	19.01 %

Complexity, etc.) that are essentially ordinal variables in the sense that the order of their values reflects the vulnerability severity, were represented by numerical values, as shown in Table 2.

Table 2. Representation of values of the characteristics

Metric vector	Representation of values
Access Vector (AV)	1 = Local, 2 = Adjacent Network, 3 = Network
Access Complexity (AC)	1 = High, 2 = Medium, 3 = Low
Authentication (Auth)	1 = Multiple, 2 = Single, 3 = None
Confidentiality Impact (CI)	1 = None, 2 = Partial, 3 = Complete
Integrity Impact (II)	1 = None, 2 = Partial, 3 = Complete
Availability Impact (AI)	1 = None, 2 = Partial, 3 = Complete

Finally, correlation analysis was applied to the enhanced data matrix, using the non-parametric Spearman's rho correlation coefficient [21], which can be also used to test the correlation between ordinal and continuous variables. Spearman's correlation coefficient takes values in the interval $[-1, +1]$ and a value close to -1 or $+1$ respectively shows negative or positive monotonic correlation. All the correlation coefficients for all the pairs of variables formed as a combination of one variable-word/term and one variable-characteristic/score are shown in Table 3.

The analysis showed that the vast majority of correlations are statistically significant, as the significance (p-value) of the corresponding test is almost everywhere less than $a = 0.01$. However, the majority of them are very weak or weak (absolute value of Spearman's rho is less than 0.4). Note that rules-of- thumb characterize as "moderate" the correlation when the absolute value of Spearman's rho is in the interval [0.4, 0.6], "strong" for [0.6, 0.8] and very strong for [0.8, 1.0]. We decided to consider and comment only correlations with rho coefficient greater than 0.3 since we believe that even a weak or a moderate correlation can imply the existence of an informative word

Table 3. Spearman's rho correlation coefficients (terms vs characteristics and scores)

	AV	AC	Auth	CI	II	AI	CVSS	WIVSS
allow	-0.052	-0.056	-0.019	0.074	0.061	0.082	-0.048	-0.042
arbitrari	0.231	0.133	-0.057	0.016	0.218	0.013	0.174	0.235
attack	**0.301**	0.023	**-0.354**	0.093	0.123	0.11	0.15	0.086
authent	0.111	-0.003	**0.648**	0.085	0.079	0.059	-0.109	-0.078
buffer	-0.005	-0.042	-0.06	-0.139	-0.166	-0.086	0.237	0.236
caus	0.033	-0.073	-0.064	-0.212	-0.277	0.044	0.034	-0.199
code	0.128	0.031	-0.069	-0.135	-0.172	-0.108	**0.426**	**0.434**
com-mand	0.071	-0.188	0.005	0.201	0.163	0.226	0.218	0.206
craft	-0.115	0.21	-0.039	-0.098	-0.113	-0.061	0.084	0.058
crosssitescript	0.164	**0.422**	0.004	-0.128	**0.337**	-0.096	**-0.415**	**-0.344**
denial	0.039	-0.065	-0.062	-0.221	-0.284	0.047	0.038	-0.204
earlier	0.052	-0.054	-0.031	0.062	0.071	0.08	0	-0.005
execut	0.176	-0.093	-0.067	0.057	0.014	0.094	**0.537**	**0.538**
file	-0.067	-0.051	-0.041	0.072	-0.042	-0.004	0.003	0.051
function	-0.058	-0.031	-0.019	-0.049	-0.071	0	0.012	-0.015
html	0.161	**0.4**	0.005	-0.14	**0.304**	-0.108	**-0.396**	**-0.328**
inform	-0.161	0.057	-0.027	0.19	0.004	0.021	-0.114	-0.053
inject	0.218	0.197	0	0.099	**0.441**	0.131	-0.166	-0.13
local	**-0.701**	-0.112	-0.032	-0.129	-0.18	-0.156	-0.173	-0.054
multipl	0.105	0.082	-0.022	0.016	0.136	0.044	0	0.009
obtain	-0.185	0.044	-0.019	0.204	-0.01	0.017	-0.121	-0.051
overflow	0	-0.038	-0.06	-0.149	-0.173	-0.092	0.25	0.248
paramet	0.209	0.028	-0.064	0.223	**0.337**	0.199	0.008	0.03
remot	**0.526**	-0.007	0.032	0.166	0.199	0.182	0.084	0.013
script	0.143	**0.358**	-0.004	-0.099	**0.315**	-0.077	**-0.366**	-0.297
server	-0.142	0.03	0.018	0.028	-0.024	0.031	-0.014	-0.017
servic	0.037	-0.068	-0.041	-0.221	-0.288	0.026	0.041	-0.184
unspecifi	0.054	-0.005	0.142	-0.11	-0.088	-0.122	0.044	0.046
use	-0.039	-0.021	-0.018	-0.016	-0.047	-0.024	-0.008	0.002
user	**-0.489**	-0.095	**0.434**	-0.058	-0.094	-0.102	-0.259	-0.139
vector	0.071	-0.013	0.122	-0.102	-0.064	-0.107	0.042	0.055
vulner	0.216	0.129	0.035	0.02	0.202	0.013	0.022	0.063
web	0.189	**0.363**	-0.008	-0.099	0.235	-0.111	**-0.316**	-0.253

for the severity of vulnerabilities. All of them are of course statistically significant (p < 0.001) and are especially highlighted in Table 3.

We can identify positive correlation between Access Vector and the term "*attack*" (0.301), while negative correlation exists with the term "*user*" (−0.489). More important are the strong negative correlation (−0.701) between Access Vector and the term "*local*" and the positive correlation with the term "*remote*" (0. 526). These relationships are quite anticipated since Access Vector defines the way that a vulnerability can be exploited, i.e. locally or via network.

Moreover, notable positive correlations were found among Access Complexity and the terms "*crosssitescript*" (0.422), "*html*" (0.400), "*script*" (0.358) and "*web*" (0.363). These terms are related to the injection of scripts in web to exploit a vulnerability, so their relationship with less access complexity is reasonable.

Furthermore, according to the results of correlation analysis, Authentication has positive correlation with the term "*authent*" (0.648), which refers to what the metric measures. Also, Authentication is also correlated with the terms "*user*" (0.434) and "*attack*" (−0.354), positively and negatively respectively.

Continuing with the Impact metrics, there are not any notable correlations between the vulnerability description terms and the Confidentiality/Availability Impact but Integrity Impact seems to be positively correlated with five terms. These terms are: "*inject*" (0.441), "*crosssitscript*" (0.337), "*html*" (0.304), and "*script*" (0.315) and this is an indication that the injection of scripts in web is related to the defacement of websites. Finally the term "*paramet*" (0.337) is also correlated with the Integrity Impact.

Regarding the vulnerability scoring systems, they are correlated with all description terms quite similarly, although in some very weak correlations there is not even agreement in the sign. So, CVSS and WIVSS are positively correlated with the term "*code*" (0.426 and 0.434 respectively) and with the term "*execut*" (0.537 and 0.538). These correlations reflect that the execution of code to exploit vulnerabilities concerns more severe vulnerabilities. In contrary, the terms "*crosssitscript*" and "*html*" are negatively correlated with the two scoring systems (−0.415, −0.396 for CVSS and −0.344, −0.328 for WIVSS). Thus, these terms, which are related to the injection of scripts in the web (as mentioned above), are not correlated with severe vulnerabilities. Finally, CVSS is negatively correlated with the terms "*script*" (−0.366) and "*web*" (−0.316), which were found positively correlated with Access Complexity and Integrity Impact.

In order to consider the internal correlation structure of DTM with respect to characteristics and severity, the variables representing the terms of the description were analyzed by principle component analysis (PCA) with varimax rotation of the axes [22]. PCA produces uncorrelated linear combinations of the original variables. The new variables (or components) account for decreasing amounts of the total variation (i.e. the first component explains the maximum variance, and so on) and their estimations can be used for variable reduction and representation of the data points in lower dimensions. The components essentially form groupings of the participating variables with highly correlated variables within each group.

We tried several different PCA settings in order to find a good model and after excluding from the analysis the terms: {*craft, earlier, file, function, multipl, paramet, server, use, vulner*}, due to their low contribution to the model, we concluded in a model with 9 components which explains 83.08 % of the total variation. Each principal component extracted is highly correlated with a number of terms either positively or negatively. The nine components in descending order of importance (% of the variance they explain) together with the terms correlated with them are given in Table 4. The sign (+) or (−) following each term shows a positive or negative correlation.

Table 4. Results of PCA

Component number	Variance explained (%)	Terms correlated with the component
1	16.57	*crosssitscript*(+), *html*(+), *script*(+), *web*(+), *inject*(+)
2	12.13	*denial*(+), *caus*(+), *servic*(+)
3	10.04	*local*(−), *user*(−), *attack*(+), *remot*(+)
4	8.89	*buffer*(+), *overflow*(+)
5	8.31	*obtain*(+), *inform*(+)
6	7.92	*allow*(+), *arbitrary*(+), *execut*(+)
7	7.73	*vector*(+), *unspecifi*(+)
8	5.80	*command*(+), *code*(−)
9	5.69	*authent*(+)

Note that the model after the exclusion of 9 terms, explains the correlation structure of 24 terms.

It is interesting to see in Table 4 how the description terms are grouped in subsets according to their internal correlation. For example, the most important component in the dataset is Component #1 which explains 16.57 % of the total variability and is positively correlated with the terms {*crosssitscript, html, script, web, inject*} (these terms are "loaded" on the 1st component according to the standard PCA terminology). So PCA in our case is a way to "summarize" many terms together, essentially by finding new, latent variables that are correlated to subsets of them. The values of these new variables can be estimated and can be used for further analysis. We estimated these values by the Anderson-Rubin method, so new standardized (mean = 0 and standard deviation = 1) and uncorrelated among them variables were produced.

In Table 5 we provide the Spearman correlation coefficients between the components as formed and estimated from the correlation structure among description terms and the vulnerability characteristics and scores. Almost all correlations were found statistically significant (p < 0.01) but also most of them are very weak or weak. Notable correlations are between:

- Access Vector and the 3rd component (0.517), which represents the group of terms {*local, user, attack, remot*}. Note that the first two terms are loaded negatively on the component while the other two positively, so the anticipated interpretation is that higher values of the AV are correlated with the presence of *attack* and *remot* but with the absence of *local* and *user*.
- Authentication and the 9th component (0.349), which includes only one term, *authent*. The correlation between Authentication and *authent* was found also previously.
- CVSS and 1st component (−0.417), 3rd component (0.353) and 5th component (−0.352). As previously noticed, CVSS is correlated negatively with vulnerabilities related to injection of scripts in web and the 1st component concerns these vulnerabilities. Furthermore, the positive correlation with 3rd component depicts that

more severe vulnerabilities (according to CVSS) are those concerning remote attacks (terms: *remot* and *attack*) and not local users (terms: *local* and *user*). Moreover, the negative correlation with 5th component reflects that CVSS does not scores highly Confidentiality oriented vulnerabilities (terms *obtain* and *information*).

- WIVSS and 1st component (-0.429), 2nd component (-0.405) and 5th component (-0.334). Similar behavior with CVSS, regarding the correlations with 1st and 5th component (although, the negative correlation with 5th component seems somehow weird). Additionally, the negative correlation with 2nd component is reasonable since these terms (*denial*, *caus* and *servic*) are met in Availability oriented vulnerabilities and WIVSS considers Availability as the less severe factor in the CIA triad.

Table 5. Spearman's rho correlation coefficients (components vs characteristics and scores)

Component number	AV	AC	Auth	CI	II	AI	CVSS	WIVSS
1	-0.025	0.236	-0.050	-0.129	0.124	-0.057	**-0.417**	**-0.429**
2	-0.049	0.055	-0.101	-0.176	-0.128	-0.019	-0.264	**-0.405**
3	**0.517**	-0.068	-0.286	0.150	0.062	0.148	**0.353**	0.249
4	0.092	0.196	0.154	-0.108	0.033	-0.107	0.039	0.104
5	-0.147	0.024	-0.138	0.096	0.000	0.025	**-0.325**	**-0.334**
6	0.077	-0.030	-0.027	0.078	0.067	0.076	0.173	0.196
7	-0.060	-0.012	-0.042	-0.076	-0.044	-0.096	-0.088	-0.077
8	-0.039	-0.060	-0.020	0.048	0.180	0.179	-0.183	-0.262
9	0.296	-0.060	**0.349**	0.103	0.068	0.103	-0.185	-0.244

Overall, we can clearly see that the description terms either single or in groups appear to be correlated with the technical characteristics and the severity scores of vulnerabilities. Although the correlations are not strong, the findings are interesting in the sense that the descriptions contain certain terms or combinations of terms that are quite informative for several security aspects. In order to strengthen our previous results, we further conducted two simple linear least squares regression analyses: In both of them we considered as independent variables the 9 component scores found by PCA while as dependent variables we considered in the first model the CVSS score and in the second model the WIVSS score. The purpose was to see how a severity score, which in a sense summarizes the vulnerability characteristics (such as CVSS and WIVSS), is correlated with all the components together, which also are used for summarizing many terms. In both models all components were found significant ($p < 0.001$), while the r-square statistic for the CVSS model was 0.383 and for the WIVSS model was 0.361. That essentially means that by a simple linear model based on PCA components we can explain the 38 % of CVSS and the 36 % of WIVSS variation.

5 Conclusion

In this paper we considered and analyzed software vulnerabilities that constitute one of the most critical issues of computer security. Using a methodology with ever-increasing popularity and acceptance as the Text Mining, we transformed the vulnerability descriptions from text to numerical data and we obtained a data matrix, called Document Term Matrix, which we subsequently used in order to perform correlation analysis between the most frequently appeared terms of vulnerability descriptions and the vulnerability characteristics/scores. The results revealed that there are many worth-mentioning correlations among the above terms, either single or in groups, and the characteristics/scores. However, the nature of this dependence deserves further investigation. Although, simple linear models contribute in understanding a moderate amount of the severity, the fitting of more advanced, probably non-linear models seems to be necessary in order to express adequately the relation between severity and description terms.

The knowledge derived from the present work is useful for researchers in the field of Information Security, but also for IT security managers who can be aided in decision making, regarding the severity and the characteristics of a vulnerability by analyzing small descriptions that exist in vulnerability databases. Although automated severity characterization has its own risks, the diagnosis of severity by statistical tools can be useful aid for human decisions. In this paper we explored and showed that there are serious potentials in the utilization of the description in this regard.

The text analysis provided in the present paper, although was applied on the data of NVD (which is a technical database), the conclusions are generic and could help to the characterization of vulnerabilities by descriptions registered in other structured or non-structured data sources (journal articles, websites and blogs, etc.).

As future research, we plan to combine text mining and machine learning techniques in order to construct powerful diagnostic models, using training data from the wealthy NVD vulnerability source and having as ultimate goal the accurate and, if possible, automated assessment of the vulnerability severity and characteristics.

References

1. CVE – Terminology. https://cve.mitre.org/about/terminology.html
2. Mell, P., Scarfone, K., Romanosky, S.: A complete guide to the common vulnerability scoring system version 2.0 (2007). https://www.first.org/cvss/v2/guide
3. Schiffman, M., Cisco, C.I.A.G.: A complete guide to the common vulnerability scoring system (cvss) (2005). http://www.first.org/cvss/v1/guide
4. NVD – National Vulnerability Database. https://nvd.nist.gov/
5. Spanos, G., Sioziou, A., Angelis, L.: WIVSS: a new methodology for scoring information systems vulnerabilities. In: Proceedings of the 17th Panhellenic Conference on Informatics, pp. 83–90. ACM, New York (2013)
6. Spanos, G., Angelis, L.: Impact metrics of security vulnerabilities: analysis and weighing. Inf. Secur. J. Gobal Perspect. **24**(1–3), 57–71 (2015)

7. Liu, Q., Zhang, Y.: VRSS: a new system for rating and scoring vulnerabilities. Comput. Commun. **34**(3), 264–273 (2011)
8. Liu, Q., Zhang, Y., Kong, Y., Wu, Q.: Improving VRSS-based vulnerability prioritization using analytic hierarchy process. J. Syst. Softw. **85**(8), 1699–1708 (2012)
9. Wang, Y., Yang, Y.: PVL: a novel metric for single vulnerability rating and its application in IMS. J. Comput. Inf. Syst. **8**(2), 579–590 (2012)
10. Theodosiou, T., Angelis, L., Vakali, A., Thomopoulos, G.N.: Gene functional annotation by statistical analysis of biomedical articles. Int. J. Med. Inform. **76**, 601–613 (2007)
11. Theodosiou, T., Angelis, L., Vakali, A.: Non-linear correlation of content and metadata information extracted from biomedical article datasets. J. Biomed. Inform. **41**, 202–216 (2008)
12. Janasik, N., Honkela, T., Bruun, H.: Text mining in qualitative research: application of an unsupervised learning method. Organ. Res. Methods **12**, 436–460 (2009)
13. Hovsepyan, A., Scandariato, R., Joosen, W., Walden, J.: Software vulnerability prediction using text analysis techniques. In: 4th International Workshop on Security Measurements and Metrics, pp. 7–10. ACM, New York (2012)
14. Liu, C., Li, J., Chen, X.: Network vulnerability analysis using text mining. In: Pan, J.-S., Chen, S.-M., Nguyen, N.T. (eds.) ACIIDS 2012, Part II. LNCS, vol. 7197, pp. 274–283. Springer, Heidelberg (2012)
15. Nishanth, K., Ravi, V., Ankaiah, N., Bose, I.: Soft computing based imputation and hybrid data and text mining: the case of predicting the severity of phishing alerts. Expert Syst. Appl. **39**, 10583–10589 (2012)
16. Chen, X., Bose, I., Leung, A., Guo, C.: Assessing the severity of phishing attacks: a hybrid data mining approach. Decis. Support Syst. **50**, 662–672 (2011)
17. Wang, T.-W., Rees, J., Kannan, K.: Reading the disclosures with new eyes: bridging the gap between information security disclosures and incidents. In: 7th Workshop on the Economics of Information Security (WEIS), Hanover, NH (2008)
18. FIRST.org/FIRST - Improving security together. http://www.first.org
19. CVSS-SIG Team. https://www.first.org/cvss/v2/team
20. Rajaraman, A., Ullman, J.D.: Mining of Massive Datasets, vol. 1. Cambridge University Press, Cambridge (2012)
21. Sheskin, D.J.: Handbook of Parametric and Non-parametric Statistical Procedures. Chapman & Hall/CRC, Boca Raton (2004)
22. Bartholomew, D.J., Steele, F., Moustaki, I., Galbraith, J.I.: The Analysis and Interpretation of Multivariate Data for Social Scientists. Chapman & Hall/CRC, Boca Raton (2002)

Discovering Potential Interaction Violations among Requirements

Curtis Busby-Earle[1(✉)] and Robert B. France[2]

[1] The University of the West Indies, Mona, Jamaica
curtis.busbyearle@uwimona.edu.jm
[2] Colorado State University, Fort Collins, USA

Abstract. To fully embrace the challenge of developing more robust software, potential defects must be considered at the earliest stages of software development. Studies have shown that this reduces the time, cost and effort required to integrate corrective features into software during development. In this paper we describe a technique for uncovering potential software vulnerabilities through an analysis of software requirements and describe its use using small, motivating examples.

Keywords: Models · Requirements · Security · Path fixation

1 Introduction

Security requirements are seldom explicitly stated at the outset of a project [8]. Typical security considerations at the requirements development stage are: confidentiality of sensitive information [6]; potential system threats and exploits [8,14,15]; privacy and trust concerns [20,21]; and profiles of potential attackers [13,15]. Requirements engineers and security experts attempt to address security issues by using techniques such as misuse cases [14], abuse cases [15], UMLSec [13], the SQUARE method [10], KAOS [18] and security patterns [7]. Many of the current techniques, however, rely heavily on the expertise and subjective judgement of security professionals [1–4]. As an example of the subjectivity that comes into play when using these techniques, consider the use of misuse cases. A misuse case is a special kind of use case that is a description of behavior that should not occur in a system. Misuse cases are described alongside use cases. The development and analysis of misuse cases may proceed as follows:

1. Describe the services that the users want, regardless of any security considerations. Use cases are used for this purpose
2. Introduce the major misuse cases and mis-actors. Misuse cases are initiated by mis-actors.
3. Investigate the potential relations between misuse cases and use cases, and describe as use-case includes-relations. Many threats to a system can be realised by using the system's normal functionality.

R. B. France—Deceased February 15, 2015.

© Springer International Publishing Switzerland 2016
J. Krogstie et al. (Eds.): CAiSE 2016, LNBIP 249, pp. 243–253, 2016.
DOI: 10.1007/978-3-319-39564-7_23

4. Introduce new use cases that detect or prevent misuse cases.

Steps two and three are key to the process, but they are subjective and the results of their application are completely dependent upon a security expert's judgement. Although a requirements engineer has the task of specifying what an intended software system should do, a requirements engineer is not expected to be a security expert. Security is usually grouped with, and considered as, a non-functional requirement [18,19]. Non-functional requirements have traditionally only been considered in the later stages of software development, for example during architecture development [1,5] and coding [12].

In this paper we present a technique that provides a means by which the knowledge of domain experts including security experts can be captured, retained, used, refined and shared among requirements engineers and other software engineering practitioners, thus assisting them in their task of considering potential software defects at the earliest stages of software development. The expertise is captured in the form of dependencies between domain-specific terms that are included when writing requirements. The captured expertise is used in the technique to analyse functional requirements to uncover potential vulnerabilities. The technique does not replace human expertise, rather it exploits shareable knowledge and skill and augments available human know-how. The technique can be summarised as follows:

> Given a set of use case scenarios, each scenario is represented as a flow graph. Each scenario step is represented as a node in a graph and transitions from one scenario step to another as an edge. The analysis is performed by forming the transitive closure of the forest and identifying any interactions that violate stated security or other policies.

The proposed technique, called Loophole Analysis, addresses the problem of functional fixation in the context of requirements analysis. Functional fixation is the inability to see uses for something beyond what is presented [11]. In other words, it is the belief that something can only be used for its stated purpose. In the context of software systems we can and do use functionality provided by software in unintended ways.

For example, a Windows XP user with no administrator privileges can acquire them by creating a shortcut to IE6, enable the 'Run with different credentials' option, and open a shell as a local administrator. From a security standpoint, each step involved in accomplishing the task is allowed, but this particular usage leads to undesirable situations. Another example is provided by Linux, Android and other UNIX-based operating systems where automatic file completion is a very useful feature but, it also helps intruders to find target files more quickly [14]. Everyday objects, including software, may fulfill their stated goals and yet, may allow undesirable behaviour.

2   Background and Related Work

The loophole analysis seeks to identify interactions that are allowed but may result in undesirable situations when using software. The analysis is performed during the process of specifying requirements. Uncovering and mitigating potential vulnerabilities during requirements analysis, reduces the time, effort and cost of fixing these problems, when compared to addressing them later in the development process [10, 13]. Other approaches exist that attempt to address security during the early stages of development. A relatively current trend is the use of models [1, 2, 4]. Loophole Analysis seeks to identify use case scenario interactions that are allowed but may result in undesirable situations if the scenarios are implemented as specified.

The input to our technique is a requirements specification document consisting of a set of use case scenarios. The steps of the technique are,

1. Develop a domain meta-model to represent the vocabulary and key concepts of a problem domain
2. Develop a set of meta-use case scenarios from the domain model
3. Create a class model of the specific application/system to be built, using the domain meta-model developed during step 1
4. Create a set of application-specific use case scenarios using the meta-scenarios developed during step 2
5. Using unique identifiers for each use-case step described in all scenarios, create a flow graph that simulates transitions within the application being modeled
6. Apply the loophole analysis to the forest to identify any undocumented use case scenarios
7. Document any newly discovered scenarios and either expressly permit or prevent them. The newly discovered scenarios can be documented as misuse cases
8. Repeat, beginning at step 6, until no new scenarios are discovered

Steps one and two are project independent and can be completed by domain experts. Steps three to eight are project specific and are completed by requirements engineers. The use case scenarios that our technique supports describe a system from a user's perspective, and thus focus on user-system interactions. Specifically, a scenario is an ordered set of interactions between a system and a set of actors external to the system.

Scenarios are typically written in a natural language to facilitate understanding by as many stakeholders as is possible. A natural language however, does not readily lend itself to analysis and its use often leads to imprecise statements. For this reason, use case scenario templates are incorporated in our technique. The numbered steps and unique identification of each scenario enables the straightforward representation of each step as a node in a flow graph, and inter-scenario and intra-scenario step transitions as directed edges.

Although there are existing approaches and techniques that are based on security knowledge that is represented in various forms [3–5, 7, 10, 18], our approach seeks to improve a requirements document by revealing undocumented requirements, and attempting to make implicit security requirements explicit. In particular, implicit security requirements are attempted to be made explicit by a process that uses an Imposed Security Dependence (ISD) [17]. A domain model

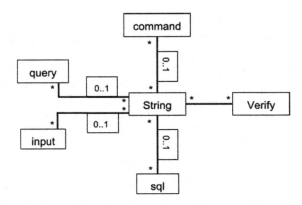

Fig. 1. Requirements terms domain model

captures domain and security expertise, and contains dependencies between domain-specific requirements terms (see Fig. 1).

For any two requirements terms (RT) α and β, we define an ISD as,

RT α has an ISD on RT β when the use of α in a requirement dictates the use of β in a separate requirement.

Two requirements therefore have an ISD relation when an ISD exists between requirements terms contained in each. In this paper we represent an ISD between two terms using the symbol $\not\vdash$ placed between them and the terms and symbol enclosed in parentheses. ISD relations have the following properties where t refers to a requirement term,

$$\neg(t1 \not\vdash t1), \tag{1}$$

$$(t1 \not\vdash t2) \not\Rightarrow (t2 \not\vdash t1), \tag{2}$$

$$(t1 \not\vdash t2) \ and \ (t2 \not\vdash t3) \Rightarrow (t1 \not\vdash t3) \tag{3}$$

Commonly used requirements terms and their imposed security dependencies are created by a requirements engineer/domain expert and a security expert. These experts use their knowledge and experience to create a domain model of requirements terms that is independent of any specific project. The model is then used to develop a table of ISDs. The domain specific ISD table is stored for subsequent use in individual, domain specific projects. Once such a table of terms and ISDs has been created, the knowledge and expertise of the domain and security experts will be captured and retained in the table. Through its use in various software development projects, the table and its content can be shared, refined and improved upon by other practitioners.

3   Discovering Undocumented Scenarios

To uncover the types of undesirable interactions previously discussed in Sect. 2 we use the notion of a path. A path is a sequence of use case scenario steps, where the sequence can cut across many use cases. Use case scenarios typically describe a system from a user's perspective, and thus focus on user-system interactions.

A scenario is an ordered set of interactions between partners, usually between a system and a set of actors external to the system. We define path fixation as the belief that the simple paths described in a specification document are the only ones that will exist in the implemented system. The discovery of paths that overturn such beliefs is the basis of our loophole analysis. Piessens defines a vulnerability as any aspect of a computer system that allows for breaches in its security policy [16]. In the context of requirements analysis, loopholes are paths that lead to violations in security or other policies that govern system behaviour.

3.1   Modeling a Domain

A plan has been formulated whereby a movie will be viewed at a movie theatre. The plan involves hiring a taxi from home to the train station, catch a train into the city, walk to the movie theatre and (hopefully) enjoy the movie, have a meal at a restaurant and then return home. All of the activities in the plan, except walking to the theatre, involve the utilisation of a service, for which payment is expected. In the plan, services include the taxi, train, viewing the movie and having a meal. Depending on the available technology, payment for the services could be made using cash or a card. The domain meta-model for the payment for the provision of a service, including the aforementioned services, can be represented as shown in Fig. 2.

The Account template depicted in Fig. 2 is optional, it may or may not be included in a class model derived from the domain model. Optional templates are denoted with a multiplicity written in the top left corner of the name compartment of the template box. Similarly, the associations between Customer and

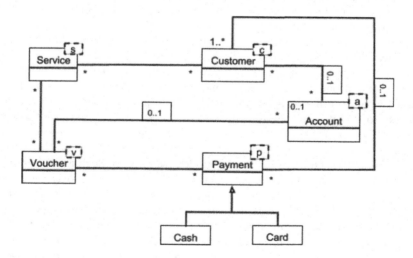

Fig. 2. Payment for service domain model

Payment, Customer and Account, and Account and Voucher may or may not exist in a particular system. These optional associations in the domain model are indicated by the enclosed association label 0..1. When included in a class model, an optional association's multiplicities may be specialised.

An application that can be developed within this domain may require a customer to enter some information and typically exchange data with other applications. The security considerations for such interactions can vary but fundamentally, the use of strings must be included in such considerations, where a string is a sequence of symbols/characters. There are different types of strings that are used when developing applications: command, input, sql, and query for example.

From a security standpoint, all strings must be verified when presented to an application to ensure that they conform to the application's expected data format. We therefore say that in this domain, the term string has an imposed security dependence on the term verify. Whenever a requirement specifies the use of a string, there must be another requirement that specifies how the string is to be verified. String verification remains one of the top sources of software vulnerabilities and programming flaws. We represent the ISD relationship among these terms as shown in Fig. 1.

The relationships among the terms that are captured in the model in Fig. 1 can then be stored in an ISD table and used during our analysis. In this model, the terms command, input, sql and query are used to clarify the type of string being used.

Using the templates in our domain model, we can now define payment systems for many (similar) types of services: taxi, train, movie theatre and restaurant. In this domain, a customer pays for a service and receives a voucher as evidence of payment. A voucher can therefore be a train or movie ticket, or a receipt from a taxi or restaurant. From the domain meta-model we can also develop meta-use case scenarios. The names of the templates taken from the domain meta-model become parameters in the meta-use case scenario. When a class model is developed from the domain meta-model, these parameters are substituted with the class names.

Using the domain meta-model and associated meta-use case scenarios, we can now model a particular system that provides a service that falls within the domain by creating a specialisation of the domain meta-model and providing arguments to the meta-use case scenarios. For example, a train ticketing service can be modeled as shown in Fig. 3. Service, Voucher and Customer have been specialised to Train, Ticket and Passenger respectively. Because the optional Account class has been included in this model, every account must be associated with at least one passenger; the multiplicity at the Passenger association end has thus been specialised from * in the domain meta-model to 1..* in the class model.

We can now utilise the meta-use case scenario to create a specific use case scenario for the train ticketing system. The names of the templates of the domain meta-model that were used to develop the meta-use case scenario are substituted with the names of the classes in the train ticketing model to create the use case for the train ticketing system.

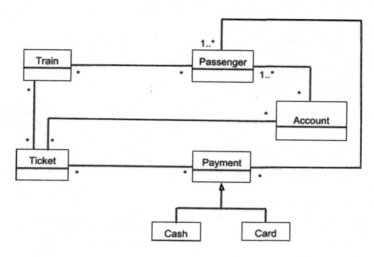

Fig. 3. Project specific model

3.2   Analysing the Model

From the use case scenario, we can now develop a flow graph that "simulates" the operation transitions within the particular system. Each step in the use case is represented as a node and transitioning from one step to the next is represented as a directed edge. To illustrate the types of undocumented scenarios we are looking for in our analysis we must include another use case scenario.

Consider another typical scenario where a customer wishes to debit her account associated with the train service. This account can be used to purchase tickets or pay for other affiliated services that may be available. The use case scenario for replenishing such an account and its flow graph are shown in Fig. 4. The steps involved in replenishing an account include the selection of a payment method i.e. cash or card, and therefore the steps involved in the replenish passenger account can be extended by those in the make payment scenario.

In this trivial example we note that it is therefore possible for a passenger, although intent on depositing money into her account could instead, pay for a ticket. In the flow graph this is depicted with a broken line from step 4 to step *4 where *4 represents step 4 from the Make Payment use case scenario. This is an unintended sequence of operations. In our system, this scenario must therefore be expressly prevented as the two operations should be discrete. This potential, unintended operation could have been possible because while modeling the system, we became fixated on the scenario steps (paths) for purchasing a ticket and replenishing an account.

Further, when processing a card as in step 2 of the main success scenario of the make payment use case, a passenger could be required to enter card information such as the name on the card, the card number and expiry date. These input strings should be verified when entered before being processed. The ISD table ensures that requirements are included in the application's specification

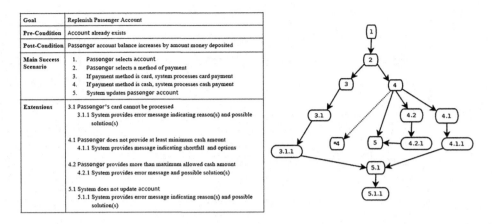

Goal	Replenish Passenger Account
Pre-Condition	Account already exists
Post-Condition	Passenger account balance increases by amount money deposited
Main Success Scenario	1. Passenger selects account 2. Passenger selects a method of payment 3. If payment method is card, system processes card payment 4. If payment method is cash, system processes cash payment 5. System updates passenger account

Extensions	3.1 Passenger's card cannot be processed
	    3.1.1 System provides error message indicating reason(s) and possible solution(s)
	
	4.1 Passenger does not provide at least minimum cash amount
	    4.1.1 System provides message indicating shortfall and options
	
	4.2 Passenger provides more than maximum allowed cash amount
	    4.2.1 System provides error message and possible solution(s)
	
	5.1 System does not update account
	    5.1.1 System provides error message indicating reason(s) and possible solution(s)

Fig. 4. Replenish account use case scenario and graph

document that address the verification procedures. This step attempts to make implicit security requirements, explicit and helps a requirements engineer create a more complete specification document.

3.3   The Loophole Algorithm

In Sect. 3.2 we developed a more complete set of requirements by making implicit requirements explicit and discovered an undocumented and unintended scenario. This was accomplished by incorporating ISD relationships among requirements terms to generate skeletal requirements and finding undocumented paths i.e. loopholes. In practice however, models and requirements are not so trivial.

The Loophole Algorithm is used to systematically and formally analyse a requirements specification for loopholes. We examine a set of requirements by choosing a relation R. Let N be the set of nodes that are in a forest representation of a requirements specification document, and R be a relation that maps a distinct node $n1 \in N$ to another distinct node $n2 \in N$ where $n2$ is directly reachable from $n1$.

We chose R with the following properties,

$$R : N \times N \tag{4}$$

$$\forall r : N \bullet (r, r) \notin R \tag{5}$$

$$\forall r, q : N \bullet (r, q) \in R \Rightarrow (q, r) \notin R \tag{6}$$

$$\forall r, q, s : N \bullet (r, q) \in R \land (q, s) \in R \Rightarrow (r, s) \in R \tag{7}$$

Because we are representing intended interactions in a system under development, intuitively, R is anti-reflexive, transitive (expressions 5 and 7) and must therefore also be anti-symmetric (expression 6). We want to identify undocumented paths in N using R. For this purpose, however, R is not sufficient as we have demonstrated that some of the possible paths are typically not explicitly included in a requirements document. These are the paths we are interested in. We therefore include the set of all reachable paths by finding the transitive closure of R.

From a security standpoint, a policy is described by the allowed interactions of the intended system's users and objects i.e. the members of N. To identify potential breaches, the discovery of undocumented paths can also identify potential vulnerabilities such as those described earlier (see the last paragraph in the Introduction).

The steps of the Loophole Analysis are as follows:

1. Represent the relation R as a binary matrix M.
2. Find the transitive closure of R, using the Floyd-Warshall algorithm [9]. Call this new relation R*.
3. Represent R* as a binary matrix M'.
4. Perform the bit-wise XOR of corresponding elements of M and M'. This will identify maplets created as a result of step 2 i.e. the indirect relationships that are not included in the original.
5. A maplet that exists in M' but not M represents an undocumented transition and the sequence of scenario steps that occur before and after it must be investigated.
6. A loophole (i.e. a vulnerability) exists when an undocumented scenario violates a stated policy.

4   Conclusion and Future Work

Although preliminary, we believe the results are promising. Loopholes are unknown, reachable paths that would exist if a system were to be developed in accordance with the specification document in the form prior to the loophole analysis. The analysis did not include nor require the motives, resources and skills of an attacker, or possible threats to the system to be postulated. Its foundation is based on the statement of policy and on path fixation. The algorithm includes completing the transitive closure on the forest, but other traversal methods such as a depth first search are being investigated.

We have been developing a tool to assist in the specification of requirements, and their analysis using the Loophole Algorithm. An engineer can: document a problem statement/description, permit stakeholders to enter user stories, enter data on concepts that are elicited from the user stories, create use cases and misuse cases using a Cockburn style template. The tool then takes this data and draws: a requirements model (we are in the process of allowing an engineer to include object constraint language (OCL) statements with the model), unified modeling language (UML) use case diagrams, UML sequence diagrams and a system operation simulation (flow graph). It is at this stage that the Loophole Analysis is performed and any undocumented scenarios are depicted in a flow graph, and misuse cases are generated by the tool that capture the undocumented scenarios. The engineer can then either accept these captured scenarios as valid, or leave them as misuse cases, and create new use cases that will serve as countermeasures.

We are in the process of conducting initial tests and implementing bug fixes. It will be tested both with documents that will provide empirical validation of its capabilities and in our software engineering courses during the forthcoming academic year 2016–2017 for its useability. We will then begin development that will include the ability to create domain meta-models and meta-use case scenarios. We are mindful that in the tool's continued development, consideration must be given to the issues involved in using informal use case descriptions, in particular the possibility of information loss and the introduction of errors.

References

1. Roudier, Y., Apvrille, L.: SysML-Sec-a model driven approach for designing safe and secure systems. In: International Special Session on Security and Privacy in Model Based Engineering: Proceedings of the 3rd International Conference on Model Driven Engineering and Software Development. MODELSWARD 2015, Angers, Loire Valley, France. IEEE Computer Society Press (2015)
2. Ivanova, M.G., Probst, C.W., Hansen, R.R., Kammüller, F.: Transforming graphical system models to graphical attack models. In: Mauw, S., et al. (eds.) GraMSec 2015. LNCS, vol. 9390, pp. 82–96. Springer, Heidelberg (2016). doi:10.1007/978-3-319-29968-6_6
3. Apvrille, L., Roudier, Y.: SysML-Sec attack graphs: compact representations for complex attacks. In: Mauw, S., et al. (eds.) GraMSec 2015. LNCS, vol. 9390, pp. 35–49. Springer, Heidelberg (2016). doi:10.1007/978-3-319-29968-6_3
4. Schilling, A., Werners, B.: Optimizing information systems security design based on existing security knowledge. In: Persson, A., Stirna, J. (eds.) CAiSE 2015 Workshops. LNBIP, vol. 215, pp. 447–458. Springer, Heidelberg (2015)
5. Gausemeier, J., Rammig, F.J., Schäfer, W., Sextro, W.: Case study. In: Gausemeier, J., Rammig, F.J., Schäfer, W., Sextro, W. (eds.) Dependability of Self-Optimizing Mechatronic Systems. LNME, vol. 2, pp. 175–192. Springer, Heidelberg (2014)
6. Landtsheer, D., Renaud, van Lamsweerde, A.: Reasoning about confidentiality at requirements engineering time. In: Proceedings of the 10th European Software Engineering Conference Held Jointly with 13th ACM SIGSOFT International Symposium on Foundations of Software Engineering. ESEC/FSE-13, Lisbon, Portugal. ACM (2005)
7. Hafiz, M., Adamczyk, P., Johnson, R.E.: Organizing security patterns. IEEE Softw. 24(4), 52–60 (2007). IEEE Computer Society Press
8. Stallings, W., Brown, L.: Computer Security: Principles and Practice, 2nd edn. Pearson Prentice Hall, Upper Saddle River (2012)
9. Cormen, T.H., Leiserson, C.E., Rivest, R.L., Stein, C.: Introduction to Algorithms, 3rd edn. MIT Press, Cambridge (2009)
10. Mead, N.R.: Identifying security requirements using the Security Quality Requirements Engineering (SQUARE) method. In: Mouratidis, H., Giorgini, P. (eds.) Integrating Security and Software Engineering: Advances and Future Vision, pp. 44–69. IGI Global, Hershey (2007)
11. Zatko, P.: Psychological security. In: Oram, A., Viega, J. (eds.) Beautiful Security: Leading Security Experts Explain How They Think, pp. 1–20. O'Reilly Media, California (2009)

12. Chung, L., Nixon, B.A., Yu, E., Mylopoulos, J.: Non-functional Requirements in Software Engineering. International Series in Software Engineering, vol. 5. Springer, Heidelberg (2000)

13. Jürjens, J.: UMLsec: extending UML for secure systems development. In: Jézéquel, J.-M., Hussmann, H., Cook, S. (eds.) UML 2002. LNCS, vol. 2460, pp. 412–425. Springer, Heidelberg (2002)

14. Sindre, G., Opdahl, A.: Eliciting security requirements by misuse cases. In: Proceedings of Technology of Object Oriented Languages and Systems. IEEE Computer Society (2000)

15. McDermott, J., Fox, C.: Using abuse case models for security requirements analysis. In: Proceedings of Computer Security Applications Conference. IEEE Computer Society (1999)

16. Piessens, F.: A Taxonomy (with Examples) of Cases of Software Vulnerabilities in Internet Software (CW346). Katholieke Universiteit Leuven, Belgium (2002)

17. Busby-Earle, C., Mugisa, E.K.: Metadata for boilerplate placement values for secure software development using derived requirements. In: Proceedings of the 13th IASTED International Conference on Software Engineering and Applications (SEA 2009). ACTA Press, Cambridge, Massachusetts (2009)

18. van Lamsweerde, A.: Requirements engineering in the year 00: a research perspective. In: Proceedings of the 22nd International Conference on Software Engineering. ICSE 2000, Limerick, Ireland. ACM (2000)

19. Devanbu, P.T., Stubblebine, S.: Software engineering for security: a roadmap. In: Proceedings of the Conference on the Future of Software Engineering. ICSE 2000, Limerick, Ireland. ACM (2000)

20. Wang, A.J.A.: Information security models and metrics. In: Proceedings of the 43rd Annual Southeast Regional Conference. ACM-SE 43, Kennesaw, Georgia. ACM (2005)

21. Liu, L., Yu, E., Mylopoulos, J.: Security and privacy requirements analysis within a social setting. In: Proceedings of the 11th IEEE International Conference on Requirements Engineering. RE 2003, Washington DC. IEEE Computer Society (2003)

Extending HARM to make Test Cases for Penetration Testing

Aparna Vegendla[✉], Thea Marie Søgaard, and Guttorm Sindre[✉]

Department of Computer and Information Science,
Norwegian University of Science and Technology (NTNU), Trondheim, Norway
{aparnav,guttors}@idi.ntnu.no

Abstract. **[Context and motivation]** Penetration testing is one key technique for discovering vulnerabilities, so that software can be made more secure. **[Question/problem]** Alignment between modeling techniques used earlier in a project and the development of penetration tests could enable a more systematic approach to such testing, and in some cases also enable creativity. **[Principal ideas/results]** This paper proposes an extension of HARM (Hacker Attack Representation Method) to achieve a systematic approach to penetration test development. **[Contributions]** The paper gives an outline of the approach, illustrated by an e-exam case study.

Keywords: Security · Penetration testing · Misuse cases · Socio-technical systems · e-exams

1 Introduction

The alignment of requirements and testing has been emphasized as an important problem in software development in general [1, 2] and also for security requirements in particular [3], where testing might then be a combination of penetration testing [4] and ethical hacking [5].

Penetration testing is often used for finding security vulnerabilities in software [6]. As observed by [4], it can be effective if combined with security-related findings from earlier lifecycle stages, but less effective if done completely ad hoc. Even with a systematic approach it is important to be aware that there may be other vulnerabilities remaining in addition to those the tests have uncovered [4].

Previously, our research group has been involved in the development of a method called HARM [7], with the purpose of representing hacker attacks in various ways. In the current paper, we explore how this method could be extended to provide a bridge between security requirements and testing. More precisely, our research question is **RQ1:** *How can HARM be extended to support the development of penetration test cases from security requirements?*

The rest of the paper is structured as follows: Sect. 2 provides background on HARM, illustrating the method with a running example related to the case study, as well as discussing related work. Section 3 discusses how HARM can be extended to include manual human attacks in addition to technical attacks, and to support the development of test cases. Section 4 then presents a case study where HARM is used to

© Springer International Publishing Switzerland 2016
J. Krogstie et al. (Eds.): CAiSE 2016, LNBIP 249, pp. 254–265, 2016.
DOI: 10.1007/978-3-319-39564-7_24

capture security requirements, analyze threats and suggest security test cases for a digital exam system. Section 5 concludes the paper and outlines some ideas for further work.

2   Background

2.1   Running Example: BYOD e-exams

Many universities are currently switching from traditional school exams using pen and paper to e-exams, in some cases performed at home (e.g., remote exams), in some cases in a controlled campus environment. For scalability and cost reduction, even the latter type will often require students to use their own laptops (BYOD, Bring Your Own Device), although this gives increased challenges with security [8]. Concentrating here on individual school exams with invigilators, it is typically necessary to ensure the rules/requirements related to cheating security as shown in Table 1.

Table 1. Some rules against cheating during controlled school exams

	Rule/requirement
R1	Only authenticated examinees shall be able to access and respond to exam questions
R2	It shall be possible to respond to exam questions only while seated at one's assigned place in a controlled venue
R3	Examinees are prohibited from communicating with each other or with outsiders during the exam
R4	Examinees are prohibited from using tools or resources other than those listed as being allowed for the specific exam
R5	Examinees are prohibited from peeking at and copying answers of other examinees

Since the focus here is on BYOD, it makes most sense to focus specifically on some key security requirements to prevent cheating via the laptop, such as:

SecR1. It shall be impossible to access other resources on the laptop than those specifically allowed for the exam.

SecR2. It shall be impossible to use the laptop for communication with co-examinees or outsiders during the exam.

A key approach to mitigate cheating with BYOD e-exams is the usage of so-called *lock-down browsers* [9]. By locking the screen in a way that cannot be escaped while connected to the exam server, this technology prevents examinees from starting up other programs, opening documents or accessing other web sites than the exam server. The e-exam application which delivers questions to the students and receives answers will typically be running on top a lockdown browser. By these measures, examinees should be prevented from accessing cheat material and getting illegitimate help from accomplices via their laptops − *if* the technology is a 100 % effective.

However, a number of attacks could circumvent lock-down browsers. One simple example: After starting up the lock-down browser, we may be unable to start up Skype to communicate with an accomplice. But what if we have Skype running *before* we start the lock-down browser? This is the outset of our running example. The problem of many hands can easily be envisioned here. The invigilators in the exam room − and the university administration, who give instructions for their conduct − might think that skyping via the laptops during the exams is made impossible by some component of the e-exam technology. The developers of the technology might have been thinking that Skype conversations is something that the invigilators should prevent. There could also be dispersion of responsibility between different technology providers. The developers of the e-exam application might believe that the lock-down browser pre-vents Skype conversations, while the developers of the lock-down browser consider this outside the scope of their tool, rather to be done by the e-exam application or monitoring software that the university should get from yet another vendor.

2.2   HARM (Hacker Attack Representation Method)

HARM [7] is a method for modeling threats and security attacks in combination with the system architecture, so as to better understand the potential attacks. In this section we summarize the method, so that the extensions that will be proposed later will be understandable. HARM combines several different specification formats to give a comprehensive view of the possible attacks. In the following, we will list these and illustrate them by means of our running example.

Attack Sequence Descriptions (ASD): These are simple natural language descrip-tions of the attack, forming a sequence of actions. An example ASD could be some-thing like *"(1) Start up a Skype call with an outside accomplice, and have it run in the background. (2) Enter the exam venue and begin the exam in the normal way. (3) Communicate questions to the accomplice and get answers back via Skype, using a hidden wireless earpiece. (4) Type the answers into the e-exam system and submit."*

Misuse Sequence Diagrams (MUSD): If preferring a more formal form of expression than the natural language ASD, a similar sequence can be described as a MUSD [10]. This is similar to a UML sequence diagram, but in addition to legitimate objects and message calls, it also contain attacking objects and message calls (having red boxes and red arrows). The diagram in Fig. 1 shows the cheating examinee setting up a Skype call with an accomplice before the start of the exam. Then the examinee starts up the lock-down browser and authenticates with an to get an access code to connect with the exam server. Via the Skype connection, the examinee communicates the questions to an accomplice, and the accomplice replies with answers. The dashed red ovals indicate vulnerabilities that are utilized to make the attack work, and their labels are explained to the right of the diagram.

Misuse Case Maps (MUCM): Like MUSD, MUCM [11] also show an attack sequence. The difference is that Misuse Case Maps put more focus on the relationship between the attack sequence and the architecture, showing each step in its architectural context [12], just like Use Case Maps show how legitimate functionality propagates through the architecture [13]. Figure 2 shows a MUCM for another one of the cheating threats investigated in our study, usage of disallowed material. The naïve approach of

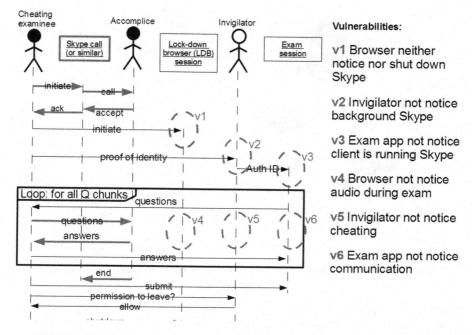

Fig. 1. MUSD for a cheat with pre-connected Skype call (Color figure online)

putting cheat files on the laptop's disk or memory sticks might fail if the lock-down browser prevents the opening of any files during the exam. A more sophisticated approach, as pointed out by Dawson [8], is to use a USB key injector containing the cheat notes. It behaves just like a keyboard, and would thus be unlikely to raise suspicion if there is automated monitoring - as students might be allowed to use external keyboards to their laptops for improved ergonomics of typing a lot of text quickly.

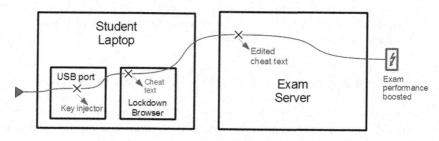

Fig. 2. MUCM for using a key injector with a cheat note

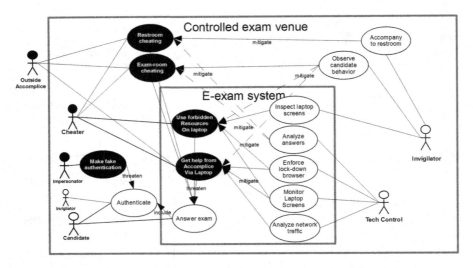

Fig. 3. Misuse case diagram including both electronic and traditional cheating

Misuse Case Diagrams (MUD): MUD extends UML use case diagrams to show how mis-users perform regular as well as irregular activities with the system. Figure 3 shows the MUD for cheating threats studied in our study. Compared to MUSD and MUCM, which show details of one particular type of attack, misuse case diagrams show a broader overview. In the particular diagram in Fig. 3, this overview is made extra broad by showing both the functions and threats particular to the e-exam application (inner system boundary) and cheating threats outside this (e.g., more traditional ways of cheating in the exam room).

Attack Trees (AT): These also show an overview of several threats. Unlike misuse case diagrams, which focus on relationships between threats and legitimate behavior, attack trees focus on the illegitimate behavior alone, breaking high level threats down to more detailed ones. The non-leaf nodes are decomposed into trees of conjunctive ("AND- branch") and disjunctive ("OR-branch") nodes. OR-nodes represent alternatives, while AND nodes represent sub goals where all must be fulfilled to achieve the goal. In Fig. 4, all branches are OR-branches, indicating various ways to perform the high level attack "Cheat during BYOD exams".

3   From Requirements to Penetration Test Cases via HARM

Whereas HARM as illustrated in the previous section has been described in earlier publications, the new contribution of this article is to propose a method to develop penetration test cases aided by HARM. Given some security requirements, like SecR1 and SecR2, there are actually two different approaches that can be used to develop a set of penetration tests:

- **Top down approach:** For each security requirement

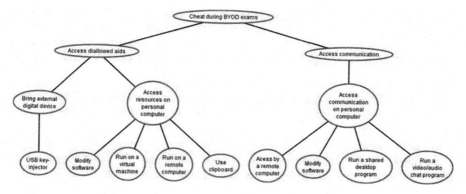

Fig. 4. Attack tree for using a key injector with a cheat note, from [14].

- Make an attack tree, starting with the top level node being a generic violation of that security requirement, then gradually breaking down towards concrete attacks. Brainstorming might be one possible technique to use in developing this tree.
- Make a misuse case diagram relating attacks to relevant legitimate use cases, including mitigations that are known to be in place. This can be used to eliminate from the attack tree those attacks that are not worth trying, or to adjust them to keep them worthwhile. For instance, if one attack is "Open document" with a cheat file during the exam, this should not be possible with the mitigating use case "Enforce lock-down browser" (cf. Fig. 3). So, to keep "Open document" it should have to be in an AND-relation with "Escape lock-down" in the attack tree.
- Make attack sequence descriptions explaining how the attack is going to be executed. If necessary, e.g., to understand a technically complicated attack which can be performed in several different ways, complement the simple textual description of the attack sequence with MUCM (if it is useful to see it in the architectural context) or MUSD (if it is useful to see how the cheat attack propagates via various objects and agents).
- This should be continued until there are attack sequences described for all the leaf nodes of the attack tree.
- **Bottom up approach:** For each security requirement
  - Start with finding some concrete ways of breaking them, and describe these as attack sequence diagrams, possibly also by MUCM and/or MUSD if this is helpful to understand possible attacks and different ways of doing things.
  - When you run out of ideas for concrete attacks, group the similar ones to make the higher level nodes and form the complete attack tree. Make the misuse case diagram to see relationship between attacks and possible countermeasures.
  - It could be a good idea here when the overall attack tree has been formed to work back down in a top down manner, to see if you get any new ideas for possible attacks after seeing the whole picture.

Whatever combination of top-down and bottom-up is chosen, the final step in the planning is to transform the attack sequence descriptions/misuse case maps/misuse sequence diagrams into penetration test scenarios, typically described in tabular form. With a situation similar to the e-exam case, tests would best be developed in two steps:

1. **lab tests**, with the purpose of finding out whether some attack is technically possible or not. Lab tests may investigate small partial attacks one at a time. Table 2 shows a lab penetration test scenario for the cheating via Skype example shown in Fig. 1.
2. **real world tests**, with the purpose of finding out whether attacks are likely to succeed in practice - which may hold bigger challenges than in the relaxed lab setting. Such a test scenario for the Skype example is shown in Table 3.

Since real world tests are more time consuming and expensive than lab tests, it is a good idea to describe the lab tests first. If it turns out that some type of attack was not even possible in the lab, it may be a waste of time to develop a real-life test for it, so resources should rather be spent on other attacks that were more likely of succeeding. (E.g., if we were not even able to have a Skype connection in the lab, there would be little point in trying in the exam-room with the additional challenge of invigilators, etc.). In the planning stage, the rightmost column of Table 2 (Result) would of course be left empty, to be filled in later, while here − to save space, we indicate at once the results that came out of our tests.

Table 2. Penetration test scenario for communicating via Skype

Lab penetration test scenario: *communicate via Skype*			
Step	Action	Success criterion	Result
1	Establish Skype connection between examinee's laptop and accomplice's PC	Connection established	OK
2	Start lock-down browser (SEB) on examinee's laptop	SEB running normally	OK
3	Examinee give info to accomplice	At least one works:	OK
3a	Speak	Accomplice hears	OK
3b	Visual (e.g., blink eyes)	Accomplice sees	OK
3c	Share screen	Accomplice sees	–
4	Accomplice give info to examinee	At least one works:	OK
4a	Speak	Examinee hears	OK
4b	Visual (e.g., blink eyes)	Examinee sees	–
4c	Share screen	Examinee sees	–

It can be noted that the penetration test in Table 2 only explores vulnerability v1 and v4 of the MUSD in Fig. 1, namely those related to the lock-down browser. The other vulnerabilities would be explored in the real-world test as described in Table 3.

Table 3. Test case for cheating during exam through assistance from outsider

Real-world penetration test scenario: *get help during exam via Skype*

Step	Action	Success criterion	Result
1	Establish Skype connection	Connection established	
2	Start lock-down browser (SEB)	SEB running normally	
3	Authenticate and access e-exam app	E-exam app starting normally	
4	Open exam question	Exam question appearing on screen	
5	Communicate question to accomplice (e.g., quietly speaking w/wireless hidden mic)	Accomplice receives question; No cheating is detected	
6	Receive hints from accomplice (e.g., through wireless earpiece) and type answer into e-exam app	Examinee receives and types info; No cheating is detected	
7	Repeat 4-6 until all questions answered, then submit	Exam answer submitted; No cheating detected	

In Table 3 the Result column is empty because none of the real-world tests have been performed yet. Whereas lab tests will tend to either succeed or fail, the real-world tests will more often have some probability of succeeding. For instance, it may depend on how far the penetration tester is seated from the nearest invigilator, how clever the tester is at speaking so quietly that it is inaudible to others yet comes through clear enough to the accomplice, how good the tester is at appearing calm in spite of cheating, how attentive the invigilator is, and what kind of other mitigations are in place in the exam room, such as monitoring software to discover suspicious communication from laptops, not matching the profile of the typical interaction between the lock-down browser and the e-exam server. Hence, while the lab test in Table 2 may only need to be run once to establish that skyping was actually possible in spite of the lock-down browser, the test in Table 3 would best be run several times, with different testers and invigilators, in rooms with different types of background noise, seated in different positions. This would enable to gather some statistics, like probability of getting caught, or mean time to failure (i.e., getting caught), to rank the attack relative to other attacks to determine which ones are most urgent to deal with.

4   Case-Study: Cheating-Related Exam Security

As part of a student project by the second author (supervised by the first and third author), a number of attacks were tested on a certain lock-down browser, namely Safe Exam Browser [15]. This browser was chosen because it is open source, and because the e-exam tool that our university is using, partly relies on that browser for security during the exams. It should be noted that the project did not try to cover the complete set of security related to e-exams. The following limitations were chosen:

- only look at threats *during* the exam, not before (e.g., getting premature access to exam questions) or after (e.g., manipulating answers after delivery, or manipulating grades).
- only look at *cheating* threats, not other kinds of security threats (e.g., like sabotage of the exam, denial of service). Although such other threats may also need to be handled, they are not threats that give a grade advantage and thus not classified as cheating.
- due to time and resource limitations, only lab tests were actually executed, while the real-world tests remained at the idea level.

Table 4 sums up results for all the different test cases that were tried in the project. Note that "Success" in the Result column means from the penetration tester's (i.e., attacker's) point of view. From the secure e-exam point of view, then, it is the rows with "Fail" that are the successful ones. So, it can be seen that SEB prevents well against attempts to circumvent it by running on a virtual machine when starting the lockdown browser (if this was not prevented against, the examinee could during the exam shift execution from the virtual to the real machine and then run any forbidden application). It also protects well against attempts to hide cheat text in the clipboard and then try to paste it once the exam has started, and as far as we could find, the examinee would not be able to share her desktop with an accomplice. As the table indicates, however, several other cheating options were available, potentially enabling a candidate with very little subject knowledge to get help from somebody much more clever, in the worst case getting an A where an F would have been the correct account of the examinee's competence. The results of the tests have been communicated to SEB developers, so these weaknesses may likely be mended in future versions of the software. It should also be noted − as pointed out in the previous section - that the success of the four lab attacks in Table 4 does not necessarily mean that the same attacks would be certain to succeed in a real-world exam situation, where there would be a combination of several tools involved, plus human invigilators to oversee the candidates. But some of the attacks do not require much visibly suspicious behavior by the examinee, so could be assumed hard to spot by invigilators.

5   Related Work

Dawson [8] presents five attacks against BYOD e-exams, whereof 4 were tried with various e-exam tools and found successful with at least one tool each. Some of the attacks tried out in our work are inspired by his proposals, especially the key injector attack and the Skype call attack. Dawson, however, does not present any modeling approach or other systematic approach to get from requirements to a test plan.

Cota et al. [16] proposed a framework, RACOON, which is a semi-automatic approach to configure accountability mechanisms (e.g. logging, auditing, monitoring) and reputation mechanisms on the P2P systems. The accountability mechanism helps to monitor cheating whereas the reputation mechanism helps to punish in case of cheating. The paper also discussed the approach to find cheating in the systems through game based simulations using game theory. Although the approach discussed in their paper useful to find cheating in digital exams, the details of penetration tests were not provided in the paper, which is the main consideration for our paper.

Table 4. Tests completed in the project [14] so far

Attack	Result	Description
Inject notes into exam software with USB key injector	Success	We saved a text on a rubber ducky USB and the string was injected into the web page open in SEB
Run SEB on a virtual machine	Fail	When initiating SEB, a pop-up window appears, stating that SEB has detected a virtual machine and will not work
Run SEB on a remote computer	Success	We managed to control SEB from a remote computer, while using SEB
Use clipboard to import notes into exam software	Fail	We were not able to right click or use CTRL + P to paste the clipboard content into SEB
Get assistance by being accessed from a remote computer	Success	We managed to control and access an SEB exam environment from a remote computer
Get assistance by sharing desktop	Fail	Neither Google Hangout nor Skype showed SEB with remote desktop, when it was initiated
Get assistance by communicating with audio/video	Success	Both examinee and assistant can hear each other and use their microphones. The assistant can also see the examinee on camera during a video conversation, but the examinees only sees the SEB environment

Wang et al. [17] present an approach to security testing based on threat models. Using UML sequence diagrams, there is some similarity with our approach (especially the misuse sequence diagrams), but the approach of Wang et al. is more formal, aiming to support automatic generation of test cases, while our approach aims to support brainstorming of test cases that will be performed manually. Other approaches aiming for partly automated generation of test cases from various types of models can be found in [18, 19], and a review of various model-based security testing techniques can be found in [20]. Agile security testing, proposed in [21], uses abuse stories or misuse cases as a starting point, thus having some resemblance with our approach, and in [22] it is further discussed how this can be fit into Scrum. These approaches have some similarities with ours in the initial part, having misuse cases as a possible starting point. Our approach however lacks the connection to agile/Scrum and does not make any assumption about the process, and instead proposes the choice of several different modeling representations, depending on what is found most fitting in the situation.

6 Conclusions and Further Work

This paper has proposed an approach to using models as a basis for brainstorming possible attacks and developing these into penetration tests. It must be admitted that the validation is so far limited, with only 8 lab tests executed so far. Future work in the investigation about e-exams would be to include a broader range of tests, including real-world. Indeed, real-world testing could also be applied to traditional pencil and paper exams, for instance to create a benchmark to establish if cheating is easier with e-exams than with traditional paper exams, which − although often intuitively assumed − need not be the case [23]. Since paper exams are not 100 % secure against cheating either, e-exams may be preferred even in spite of weaknesses, if they are found to have advantages in other respects [8, 24].

For the validation of the proposed method, future work could include experiments to investigate whether people come up with more or better penetration tests if using these modeling languages than if using other approaches (either completely ad hoc, some of those presented in related work, or other modeling approaches like for instance goal-oriented models). It would also be interesting to see if a top-down or bottom-up process to attack brainstorming is the most effective, as well as whether brainstorming is most effective in groups or individually.

References

1. Barmi, Z.A., Ebrahimi, A.H., Feldt, R.: Alignment of requirements specification and testing: a systematic mapping study. In: 2011 IEEE Fourth International Conference on Software Testing, Verification and Validation Workshops (ICSTW). IEEE (2011)
2. Unterkalmsteiner, M., Feldt, R., Gorschek, T.: A taxonomy for requirements engineering and software test alignment. ACM Trans. Soft. Eng. Method. (TOSEM) 23(2), 16 (2014)
3. Talukder, A.K., et al. Security-aware software development life cycle (SaSDLC) - processes and tools. In: IFIP International Conference on Wireless and Optical Communications Networks, WOCN 2009 (2009)
4. Arkin, B., Stender, S., McGraw, G.: Software penetration testing. IEEE Secur. Priv. 1, 84–87 (2005)
5. Palmer, C.C.: Ethical hacking. IBM Syst. J. 40(3), 769–780 (2001)
6. McDermott, J.P., Attack net penetration testing. In: Proceedings of the 2000 Workshop on New Security Paradigms, pp. 15–21. ACM: Ballycotton, County Cork, Ireland (2000)
7. Karpati, P., Opdahl, A., Sindre, G.: HARM: hacker attack representation method. In: Cordeiro, J., Virvou, M., Shishkov, B. (eds.) Software and Data Technologies, pp. 156–175. Springer, Heidelberg (2013)
8. Dawson, P., Five ways to hack and cheat with bring-your-own-device electronic examinations. Br. J. Educ. Technol. (2015). http://onlinelibrary.wiley.com/doi/10.1111/bjet.12246/epdf
9. Frankl, G., Schartner, P., Zebedin, G.: Secure online exams using students' devices. In: 2012 IEEE Global Engineering Education Conference (EDUCON). IEEE (2012)
10. Katta, V., Karpati, P., Opdahl, A.L., Raspotnig, C., Sindre, G.: Comparing two techniques for intrusion visualization. In: van Bommel, P., Hoppenbrouwers, S., Overbeek, S., Proper, E., Barjis, J. (eds.) PoEM 2010. LNBIP, vol. 68, pp. 1–15. Springer, Heidelberg (2010)

11. Karpati, P., Sindre, G., Opdahl, A.L.: Visualizing cyber attacks with misuse case maps. In: Wieringa, R., Persson, A. (eds.) REFSQ 2010. LNCS, vol. 6182, pp. 262–275. Springer, Heidelberg (2010)
12. Karpati, P., Opdahl, A.L., Sindre, G.: Investigating security threats in architectural context: Experimental evaluations of misuse case maps. J. Syst. Soft. **104**, 90–111 (2015)
13. Amyot, D., et al.: Generating scenarios from use case map specifications. QSIC **3**, 108–115 (2003)
14. Søgaard, T.M.: Cheating Threats in Digital BYOD Exams: A Preliminary Investigation. NTNU, Trondheim (2015)
15. Schneider, D.: Safe exam browser 2.0 how to (Install, Configure, Deploy and Use SEB 2.0) (2014). http://safeexambrowser.org/presentations/HowTo_SEB2.0.pdf
16. Cota, G.L., et al.: A framework for the design configuration of accountable selfish-resilient peer-to-peer systems. In: 2015 IEEE 34th Symposium on Reliable Distributed Systems (SRDS). IEEE (2015)
17. Wang, L., Wong, E., Xu, D.: A threat model driven approach for security testing. In: Proceedings of the Third International Workshop on Software Engineering for Secure Systems. IEEE Computer Society (2007)
18. Xu, D., et al.: Automated security test generation with formal threat models. IEEE Trans. Dependable Secure Comput. **9**(4), 526–540 (2012)
19. Marback, A., et al.: A threat model-based approach to security testing. Soft. Pract. Experience **43**(2), 241–258 (2013)
20. Schieferdecker, I., Grossmann, J., Schneider, M.: Model-based security testing (2012). arXiv preprint arXiv:1202.6118
21. Tappenden, A., et al.: Agile security testing of web-based systems via httpunit. In: Proceedings of the Agile Conference, 2005. IEEE (2005)
22. Erdogan, G., Meland, P.H., Mathieson, D.: Security testing in agile web application development - a case study using the EAST methodology. In: Sillitti, A., Martin, A., Wang, X., Whitworth, E. (eds.) XP 2010. LNBIP, vol. 48, pp. 14–27. Springer, Heidelberg (2010)
23. Sindre, G., Vegendla, A.: E-exams versus paper-based exams: a comparative analysis of security threats and countermeasures. In: Norwegian Information Security Conference (NISK 2015). Bibsys OJS: Ålesund (2015)
24. Sindre, G., Vegendla, A.: E-exams and exam process improvement. In: UDIT 2015. Bibsys OJS: Ålesund (2015)

File Type Identification for Digital Forensics

Konstantinos Karampidis[(✉)] and Giorgos Papadourakis

Department of Informatics Engineering, Technological Educational
Institute of Crete, Heraklion, Crete, Greece
karampidis@outlook.com, papadour@cs.teicrete.gr

Abstract. In modern world the use of digital devices for leisure or professional reasons (computers, tablets and smartphones etc.) is growing quickly. Nevertheless, criminals try to fool authorities and hide evidence in a computer or any other digital device, by changing the file type. File type detection is a very demanding task for a digital forensic examiner. In this paper a new methodology is proposed – in a digital forensics perspective- to identify altered file types with high accuracy by employing computational intelligence techniques. The proposed methodology is applied in the four most common types of files (jpg, png and gif). A three stage process involving feature extraction (Byte Frequency Distribution), feature selection (genetic algorithm) and classification (neural network) is proposed. Experimental results were conducted having files altered in a digital forensics perspective and the results are presented. The proposed model shows very high and exceptional accuracy in file type identification.

Keywords: Digital forensics · File type identification · Forensic examiner · Computational intelligence · Genetic algorithm

1 Introduction

Digital forensics is a relatively new field in Computer Science and focuses on the acquisition, preservation and analysis of digital evidence. Palmer [1] defined digital forensics as "the use of scientifically derived and proven methods toward the preservation, collection, validation, identification, analysis, interpretation, documentation, and presentation of digital evidence derived from digital sources for the purpose of facilitation or furthering the reconstruction of events found to be criminal, or helping to anticipate unauthorized actions shown to be disruptive to planned operations". Identification of the evidence is one of the most important and difficult stages during a forensic examination of the acquired data. File type detection methods can be categorized into three kinds: extension-based, magic bytes-based, and content-based methods [2]. Each of them has its own advantages and weaknesses, and none of them are comprehensive or infallible enough to satisfy all the requirements.

The original version of this chapter was revised.
An erratum to this chapter can be found at 10.1007/978-3-319-39564-7_26

© Springer International Publishing Switzerland 2016
J. Krogstie et al. (Eds.): CAiSE 2016, LNBIP 249, pp. 266–274, 2016.
DOI: 10.1007/978-3-319-39564-7_25

The fastest and easiest method of file type detection is the extension-based method. The main advantage of this method is the speed of file type detection. In the extension based method there is no need to open the file in order to determine the file type. Nevertheless, it has great vulnerability while it can be easily fooled by a simple extension renaming. As soon as a forensic program perceives such a deception, it will immediately highlight an extension mismatch.

The second method of file type detection is based on the magic bytes. Magic bytes are predefined signatures and they can be found on file's header. There are several thousand's file types for which magic bytes are defined and listed [3] and there are multiple lists of magic bytes that are not completely consistent. Checking the magic bytes of a file is indeed much slower method than just checking its extension since the file should be opened and its magic bytes should be read and compared with the predefined ones. One major drawback of this method is the lack of a predefined standard for the developers, so the magic bytes are not used in all file types. Moreover magic bytes only work on the binary files and predefined signatures differ in length for unlike file types. When a digital media with files of amended signature is attached, the forensic software will indicate the deception and suggest to the forensic analyst the true file type.

The third method of file type detection is the examination of file contents and the use of statistical modeling techniques to achieve detection. It is a new and promising research area and it is likely the only way to determine the bogus file types. McDaniel and Heydari [4, 5] were the first who actually suggested a way for content-based file type detection. They proposed three different algorithms for the content-based file type detection. The accuracy varied from 23 % to 96 % depending upon the algorithm used. Li et al. [6] made a few changes on McDaniel's and Heydari's method, in order to improve its accuracy. They proposed to compute a set of centroid models and use clustering to find a minimal set of centroids with good performance while the use of more pattern data is necessary. This approach resulted to 82 % accuracy (one centroid), 89.5 % accuracy (multi-centroid) and 93.8 % accuracy (more exemplar files). Dunham et al. [7] used neural networks for classification and achieved 91.3 % accuracy. Amirani et al. [8] used the Principal Component Analysis and unsupervised neural networks for the automatic feature extraction. The classifier they used was a neural network, achieving an accuracy of 98.33 % which was the best so far. Cao et al. [9] used Gram Frequency Distribution and vector space model with results of 90.34 % accuracy. Ahmed et al. [10] proposed two very interesting methods. Primary they used the cosine distance as a similarity metric when comparing the file content. Subsequent they decomposed the identification procedure into two steps. They used 2000 files of 10 file types as a dataset and achieved an accuracy of 90.19 %. Ahmed et al. [11] also proposed two new techniques to reduce the classification time. The first method was a feature selection technique and the K-nearest neighbor (KNN) classifier was used. The second method was the content sampling technique, which used a small portion of a file to obtain its byte-frequency distribution. Amirani et al. [12] then proposed an improved version of their first approach by using a Support Vector Machine classifier and finally succeeded in raising the accuracy of the method to 99.16 %. Finally, Evensen et al. [13] used an n-gram analysis with naïve Bayes classifier to a large dataset of 60000 files (6 file types) with very good results achieving 99.51 % topmost. The above papers refer to identification of whole files. Moreover, methods for identifying types of fragments are also proposed by scientists and both (whole files and fragments) are documented in detail [14].

The above methods showed poor to good results in file type identification, but the real problem during a forensic examination relies on the modification of file's signature and its extension at the same time. When this occurs the majority – if not all- of the forensic software cannot identify correctly the file type. In this paper a new methodology is proposed for file type identification using computational intelligence techniques in order to identify the correct file type if the file is altered, i.e. both file's extension and magic bytes are altered. The paper is organized as follows: In Sect. 2 the proposed methodology is described, then in Sect. 3 a large dataset is utilized and the experimental results are presented followed by conclusions.

2 Methodology of the Proposed Method

The proposed methodology uses computational intelligence techniques in order to identify the file type and to reveal the correct type if the file is altered. It is a three stage process involving feature extraction, feature selection and classification, as illustrated in Fig. 1. Initially all files from the dataset are loaded and the features are extracted. Afterwards, feature selection is accomplished using a genetic algorithm and finally a neural network performs the classification.

Byte Frequency Distribution (BFD) is used as a feature extraction method. In order to create the BFD, the number of occurrences of each byte value in an input file is counted and an array with elements from 0 to 255 is created. Then each element of the array is normalized by dividing with the maximum occurrence. The final result is a file containing 256 features for each instance. The next stage is feature selection, in order to decrease the number of features. Feature selection is the procedure of finding and selecting the minimum number of the most informative relevant features. As a search method a genetic algorithm was used. The idea of using a genetic algorithm, for feature extraction is not new [15–17] since they can provide candidate solutions. Each candidate solution (chromosome) is represented by a binary feature vector of dimension 256, where zero (0) indicates that the respective feature is not selected, and one (1) indicates that the feature is selected. The score of each candidate solution is evaluated by a fitness function. As a fitness function the Correlation based Feature Selection (CFS) [18] algorithm is utilized. This algorithm evaluates the candidate solutions from the genetic algorithm and choses those which include features highly associated to the file type category and low correlated with each other, by calculating each candidate's solution merit. Let S be a candidate solution consisting of k features. The merit of each candidate solution is calculated as shown in Eq. 1.

$$\text{Merits}_k = \frac{k\overline{r_{cf}}}{\sqrt{k + k(k-1)\overline{r_{ff}}}}, \tag{1}$$

where:

$\overline{r_{cf}}$ is the average value of all feature-classification correlations and
$\overline{r_{ff}}$ is the average value of all feature-feature correlations.

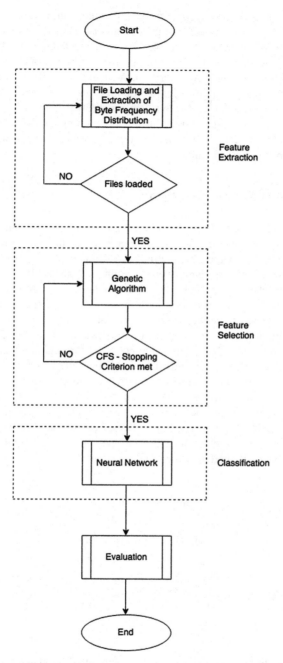

Fig. 1. Flowchart of the proposed method

CFS stops when five consecutive fully expanded candidate solutions show no improvement [18]. The utilization of the genetic algorithm as a search method and CFS as an evaluator led to the reduction of the 256 extracted features to 44.

The third and final stage is classification, performed with a one hidden layer neural network using the backpropagation algorithm. A neural network with one hidden layer was also used by Harris [19] in order to identify file types. Initially, the data are separated into a training set (70 %) and a test set (30 %). Furthermore, in order to estimate the accuracy of classification during the training phase a stratified 10 fold cross validation is used [20]. Subsequently, unseen instances from all categories are presented to the model for evaluation.

3   Experimental Setup and Results

Due to thousands of known file types, this research have focused only in images and portable documents, because of their significance to Digital Forensics. In particular, this research only included jpeg, png, gif (not animated) and pdf files. Furthermore, only whole files and not fragments were examined. Caltech 101 [21] was used as dataset. It is a dataset made by Caltech University and contains 9144 images in jpeg format from 101 categories. From this jpeg dataset, 5519 images were utilized. One third of these files were converted to png format and a similar number to gif format. The dataset was divided into a training set (70 %) and a test set (30 %). Additionally, 1840 pdf files were added, which were open access undergraduate theses found online from the library of the Technological Educational Institute of Crete [22]. The created dataset is uniformly distributed and its exact numbers are indicated in Table 1. In order to examine if the proposed methodology identifies the correct file type if the file is altered, one third of the testing pdf files (168) were replaced by image files and their extension and signature was changed to pdf. Three new test sets were created where the first contained 168 altered files of jpeg format, the second contained 168 files of png format and the third contained 168 files of gif format.

Table 1. The dataset

Dataset			
Total files		Training	Testing
jpeg	1840	1288	552
png	1840	1288	552
gif	1839	1287	552
pdf	1840	1288	552
Total	7359	5151	2208

A script written in MATLAB® [23] was implemented to create the BFD containing 256 features. Waikato Environment for Knowledge Analysis (Weka) [24], a popular machine learning software developed at the University of Waikato, New Zealand was used for all the experiments.

Weka uses Goldberg's Genetic Algorithm [25]. The population size was 256, the number of generations 100, crossover was set to 0.8 and mutation probability to 0.033. CFS was the fitness function, roulette wheel selection was used to probabilistically select individuals and the single-point crossover operator was selected. The use of CFS as a filter selection evaluator and the genetic algorithm as a search strategy resulted to the selection of 44 features (82.81 % reduction).

A multilayer neural network using the backpropagation algorithm was implemented as a classifier in Weka. The neural network consisted of one hidden layer with 3 nodes. The number of inputs was the 44 selected features and the number of outputs the four possible categories namely jpeg, png, gif and pdf. The learning rate was set to 0.3 and in order to avoid local minimum and to accelerate the learning process, the momentum parameter was set to 0.2. The training time (epochs) after experimentation was set to 500. When the training of the neural network was completed the three test sets described previously were evaluated and the results are shown in Tables 2, 3 and 4.

Table 2. Confusion matrix – identifying forged jpg images

Test set	Classified as			
Image type	jpg	pdf	png	gif
jpg	552	0	0	0
pdf	3	377	2	2
forged pdf (actual jpg)	168	0	0	0
png	0	3	548	1
gif	0	1	7	544

Table 2 shows the confusion matrix when the neural network tried to identify forged jpeg images (168). When the output of the neural network were compared to the testing dataset, the "misclassified" files were the altered jpg images. The accuracy of the proposed method to altered jpg images was 100 %.

Table 3. Confusion matrix – identifying forged png images

Test set	Classified as			
Image type	jpg	pdf	png	gif
jpg	552	0	0	0
pdf	3	377	2	2
forged pdf (actual png)	0	2	166	0
png	0	3	548	1
gif	0	1	7	544

Table 3 shows the confusion matrix when the neural network tried to identify forged png images (168) and 166 out of 168 images were detected. Two png images were wrongly identified as pdf files. In the two misclassified png images there were large areas of a specific color or small variations of a color. Small variations of a color can be found also on pdf files, which led to misclassification of the images. Therefore 2 out of 168 png altered files were not predicted correctly. The accuracy of the proposed method to altered png images was 98.81 %.

Table 4. Confusion matrix – identifying forged gif images

Test set	Classified as			
Image type	jpg	pdf	png	gif
jpg	552	0	0	0
pdf	3	377	2	2
forged pdf (actual gif)	0	0	0	168
png	0	3	548	1
gif	0	1	7	544

Table 4 shows the confusion matrix when the neural network tried to identify forged gif images (168). The "misclassified" files were the altered gif images, thus the accuracy of the proposed method in this case was 100 %. The accuracy results for the altered images (jpg, png, gif) of the proposed method are summarized in Table 5.

Table 5. Final confusion matrix of the proposed method

168 Forged images	Classified as			
Type	jpg	pdf	png	gif
jpg	168	0	0	0
png	0	2	166	0
gif	0	0	0	168

The above results showed that a very simple neural network achieved excellent results. In order to examine how well the proposed model identifies the other file types and not only the forged ones, the 168 forged pdf files were replaced by other normal ones (not forged pdf files). The same dataset was utilized and the same methodology was applied. The resulted confusion matrix and the detailed accuracy for every class (True Positive Rate, False Positive Rate, Precision and Recall) are shown on Tables 6 and 7.

Table 6. Confusion matrix of the classifier

	Classified as			
Actual file type	jpg	pdf	png	gif
jpg	552	0	0	0
pdf	3	545	2	2
png	0	3	548	1
gif	0	1	7	544

Table 7. Detailed accuracy by class

Class	True positive rate	False positive rate	Precision	Recall
jpg	1	0.002	0.995	1
pdf	0.987	0.002	0.993	0.987
png	0.993	0.005	0.984	0.993
gif	0.986	0.002	0.995	0.986

The results showed that the proposed model identified very well the other file types, as well as the forged ones.

4 Conclusions

In this paper a new methodology was proposed – in a digital forensics perspective- to identify altered file types with high accuracy by employing computational intelligence techniques. The proposed methodology was applied in the four most common types of files (jpg, png and gif). A three stage process involving feature extraction (BFD), feature selection (genetic algorithm) and classification (neural network) was proposed. Experimental results were conducted having files altered in a digital forensics perspective. The accuracy of the proposed method to altered jpg images and to gif images was 100 % and to altered png images was 98,81 %. Furthermore, the proposed methodology was also applied to the other file types with excellent results as well.

References

1. Palmer, G.: A road map for digital forensic research. In: Proceedings of the 2001 Digital Forensic Research Workshop (DFRWS 2004), pp. 1–42 (2001)
2. Meghanathan, N., Boumerdassi, S., Chaki, N., Nagamalai, D. (eds.): Recent Trends in Network Security and Applications. Springer, Heidelberg (2010)
3. Kessler, G.: File Signatures. http://www.garykessler.net/library/file_sigs.html
4. McDaniel, M.: Automatic File Type Detection Algorithm (2001)
5. McDaniel, M., Heydari, M.H.: Content based file type detection algorithms. In: 2003 Proceedings of the 36th Annual Hawaii International Conference System Sciences (2003)
6. Li, W.J., Wang, K., Stolfo, S.J., Herzog, B.: Fileprints: identifying file types by n-gram analysis. In: Proceedings from the 6th Annual IEEE Systems, Man, and Cybernetics Information Assurance Workshop SMC 2005, pp. 64–71 (2005)
7. Dunham, J., Sun, M., Tseng, J.: Classifying file type of stream ciphers in depth using neural networks. In: The 3rd ACS/IEEE International Conference on Computer Systems and Applications (2005)
8. Amirani, M.C., Toorani, M., Shirazi, A.A.B.: A new approach to content-based file type detection. In: Proceedings of the IEEE Symposium on Computers and Communications, pp. 1103–1108 (2008)

9. Cao, D., Luo, J., Yin, M., Yang, H.: Feature selection based file type identification algorithm. In: 2010 IEEE International Conference on Intelligent Computing and Intelligent Systems, pp. 58–62. IEEE (2010)

10. Ahmed, I., Lhee, K., Shin, H., Hong, M.: Content-based file-type identification using cosine similarity and a divide-and-conquer approach. IETE Tech. Rev. **27**, 465 (2010)

11. Ahmed, I., Lhee, K.-S., Shin, H.-J., Hong, M.-P.: Fast content-based file type identification. In: Peterson, G., Shenoi, S. (eds.) Advances in Digital Forensics VII. IFIP AICT, vol. 361, pp. 65–75. Springer, Heidelberg (2015)

12. Amirani, M.C., Toorani, M., Mihandoost, S.: Feature-based type identification of file fragments. Secur. Commun. Netw. **6**, 115–128 (2013)

13. Evensen, J.D., Lindahl, S., Goodwin, M.: File-Type Detection Using Naïve Bayes and n-gram Analysis (2014). http://ojs.bibsys.no/index.php/NISK/article/view/99

14. Karampidis, K., Papadourakis, G., Deligiannis, I.: File type identification – a literature review. In: Proceedings of 9th International Conference on New Horizons in Industry Business and Education, NHIBE 2015, p. 141, Skiathos, Greece (2015)

15. Vafaie, H., De Jong, K.: Genetic algorithms as a tool for feature selection in machine learning. In: International Conference on Tools with AI, pp. 200–203 (1992)

16. Zhuo, L., Zheng, J., Wang, F., Li, X., Ai, B., Qian, J.: A genetic algorithm based wrapper feature selection method for classification of hyper spectral data using support vector machine. Geogr. Res. **27**, 493–501 (2008)

17. Jourdan, L., Dhaenens, C., Talbi, E.: A genetic algorithm for feature selection in data-mining for genetics. In: Proceedings of the 4th Metaheuristics International Conference (2001)

18. Hall, M.: Correlation-based feature selection for machine learning (1999). http://www.cs.waikato.ac.nz/∼mhall/thesis.pdf

19. Harris, R.: Using artificial neural networks for forensic file type identification. Master's thesis, Purdue University (2007)

20. Kohavi, R.: A study of cross-validation and bootstrap for accuracy estimation and model selection. In: 14th International Joint Conference on Artificial Intelligence, pp. 1137–1143 (1995)

21. Fei-Fei, L., Fergus, R., Perona, P.: Learning generative visual models from few training examples: an incremental Bayesian approach tested on 101 object categories. In: Proceedings of Conference on Computer Vision and Pattern Recognition (CVPR), Workshop on Generative Model Based Vision 2004, p.178 (2004)

22. T.E.I of Crete: E-Thesis. http://nefeli.lib.teicrete.gr/search/

23. The MathWorks Inc.: MATLAB. http://www.mathworks.com/

24. Hall, M., Frank, E., Holmes, G., Pfahringer, B., Reutemann, P., Witten, I.H.: The WEKA data mining software. ACM SIGKDD Explor. Newsl. **11**, 10 (2009)

25. Goldberg, D.E.: Genetic Algorithms in Search, Optimization and Machine Learning. Addison-Wesley Publishing Company, Boston (1989)

Erratum to: File Type Identification for Digital Forensics

Konstantinos Karampidis[✉] and Giorgios Papadourakis

Department of Informatics Engineering,
Technological Educational Institute of Crete, Heraklion, Crete, Greece
karampidis@outlook.com, papadour@cs.teicrete.gr

Erratum to:
Chapter 25: J. Krogstie et al. (Eds.)
Advanced Information Systems Engineering Workshops
DOI: 10.1007/978-3-319-39564-7_25

The authorship of this chapter was incorrectly stated in the chapter and in the index. The names of the authors is reversed.

The authors are Mr. Konstantinos Karampidis and Mr. Giorgios Papadourakis, Department of Informatics Engineering, Technological Educational Institute of Crete, Heraklion, Crete, Greece.

The updated original online version for this chapter can be found at 10.1007/978-3-319-39564-7_25

© Springer International Publishing Switzerland 2016
J. Krogstie et al. (Eds.): CAiSE 2016, LNBIP 249, p. E1, 2016.
DOI: 10.1007/978-3-319-39564-7_26

Author Index

Achi, Abdelkader 78
Angelis, Lefteris 231

Baldoni, Roberto 143
Bettacchi, Alessandro 193
Bracone, Giuseppe 143
Buonanno, Daniele 143
Busby-Earle, Curtis 243

Cappiello, Cinzia 155
Caruso, Mario 143
Cattaneo, Giacomo 72
Cerocchi, Adriano 143

De Smedt, Johannes 169

España, Sergio 15

Farchi, Eitan 116
Fastnacht, Claas 29
Fish, Andrew 219
France, Robert B. 243

Grabis, Jānis 3, 52
Gripay, Yann 131

Hacklin, Fredrik 72
Hadar, Irit 109
Henkel, Martin 40
Hinkelmann, Knut 181
Hyrynsalmi, Sami 207

Janssens, Laurent 169

Kalloniatis, Christos 219
Kampars, Jānis 52
Karampidis, Konstantinos 266
Katz, Adi 93
Koç, Hasan 15, 29

Kritikos, Kyriakos 181
Kurjakovic, Sabrina 181

Lammel, Benjamin 181
Leotta, Francesco 143
Leppänen, Ville 207
Leva, Mariano 143
Lorenzoni, Gianni 65
Loucopoulos, Pericles 40

Mavropoulos, Orestis 219
Mecella, Massimo 143
Melià, Paco 155
Migiakis, Antonis 40
Mouratidis, Haralambos 219

Nesterenko, Dimitrijs 29

Ozgovde, Atay 131

Panaousis, Emmanouil 219
Papadourakis, Giorgios 266
Pinarer, Ozgun 131
Plebani, Pierluigi 155
Polzonetti, Alberto 193

Querzoni, Leonardo 143

Re, Barbara 193
Ruiz, Marcela 15
Ruohonen, Jukka 207

Salinesi, Camille 78
Sandkuhl, Kurt 3, 29
Servigne, Sylvie 131
Shmallo, Ronit 93
Sindre, Guttorm 254
Søgaard, Thea Marie 254
Sora, Daniele 143
Spanos, Georgios 231

Spichkova, Maria   116
Stirna, Janis   40
Stratigaki, Christina   40

Toloudis, Dimitrios   231

Unkelos-Shpigel, Naomi   122

van der Linden, Dirk   109
Vanthienen, Jan   169

Vegendla, Aparna   254
Viscusi, Gianluigi   78

Woitsch, Robert   181

Zamansky, Anna   103, 116
Zohar, Yoni   103
Zorgios, Yannis   40

Printed in the United States
By Bookmasters